CRIMIN

René Weis was born in 1953. He is Professor of English Literature at University College London and the author of numerous scholarly publications. He is also the author of *The Yellow Cross*, which was published by Viking in 2000. He lives in London.

CRIMINAL JUSTICE

The True Story of Edith Thompson

by

René J. A. Weis

PENGUIN BOOKS

PENGUIN BOOKS

Published by the Penguin Group
Penguin Books Ltd, 27 Wrights Lane, London W8 5TZ, England
Penguin Putnam Inc., 375 Hudson Street, New York, New York 10014, USA
Penguin Books Australia Ltd, Ringwood, Victoria, Australia
Penguin Books Canada Ltd, 10 Alcorn Avenue, Toronto, Ontario, Canada M4V 3B2
Penguin Books India (P) Ltd, 11 Community Centre,
Panchsheel Park, New Delhi – 110 017, India
Penguin Books (NZ) Ltd, Cnr Rosedale and Airborne Roads,
Albany, Auckland, New Zealand
Penguin Books (South Africa) (Pty) Ltd, 5 Watkins Street,
Denver Ext 4, Johannesburg 2094, South Africa

Penguin Books Ltd, Registered Offices: Harmondsworth, Middlesex, England

First published by Hamish Hamilton 1988
Published in Penguin Books 1990
Published with a new Preface in Penguin Books 2001

1

Copyright © René J. A. Weis, 1988, 2001
All rights reserved

The moral right of the author has been asserted

Printed in England by Clays Ltd, St Ives plc

To my students at University College London

Contents

Preface   ix
Acknowledgements   xli
List of Illustrations   xlv
Cast of Main Characters   xlvii

1   The Girl from Manor Park   1
2   The Darlingest Boy   39
3   One Little Hour   75
4   The Best Pal   173
5   The Trial   221
6   When Winter Came   275
    Postscript   313

    Sources   317
    Index   321

Preface

On a wet and windswept morning in November 1993 some eighty people gathered in a remote corner of Brookwood Cemetery near Woking in Surrey. We had come to pay our last respects to Edith Thompson, who had perished at the north London women's prison of Holloway on 9 January 1923. At first they had buried her inside the prison precinct. Then, forty-eight years later, during the night of 31 March 1971, her remains were exhumed. According to HM Prison Service, 'the coffin was found to be sound, and the body was completely covered by solidified lime and in an advanced state of decomposition. The remains were taken out and prepared by the attending doctors for reburial. They were then placed in an individual black casket.'[1]

The casket was transferred to Brookwood the following day and interred in a spot not far from the railway embankment which carries the express trains from London-Waterloo to Southampton. Present at that earlier ceremony in Brookwood on 1 April 1971 were the Regional Chaplain and the Cemetery Superintendent. The chaplain read the words of the burial service from *The Book of Common Prayer*, 'I am the resurrection and the life, saith the Lord . . .' These had been among the last words that Edith Thompson heard on earth as they carried her to the scaffold; if she heard anything at all in her semi-comatose state.

Edith Thompson henceforth shared a confined resting place, nine feet by four feet to be exact, with three other women, all of them

[1] Letter to the author from Mr J. Dickie of P1 Division of HM Prison Service, 30 January 1986.

convicted felons: the two 'baby farmers' Annie Walters and Amelia Sach (page 10), both hanged in 1903, and a Cypriot woman called Stillou Pantopiou Christofi, who was executed in 1954.

The grave in Brookwood was little more than a hole in the ground, and by the time that I first visited it in November 1984 the earth had sagged to form a shallow ditch. A peg in the ground with the number 224527 on it marked the plot where the hanged women lay in a grove of rhododendrons which flourished in this unconsecrated part of what had once been London's largest necropolis. Close to the peg, and buried among the decaying autumn leaves, I found a photograph. The elements had nearly washed off the celluloid, but I could still make out the head of a woman. It appeared to be a detail which had been enlarged from an original containing other figures. As I later discovered, it was an extract from the picture of Eastcote 1921 (see Inset). On the back, now barely legible, someone had written, 'Sleep on, beloved. Regrets. Her death was a legal formality. Edith Jessie Thompson, 25 December 1893 to 9 January 1923.' These words and dates now adorn her gravestone.

I walked back from Plot 117 to the lodge of Brookwood Cemetery, and sat down in front of the desk of D. J. T. Dally, the warden of Brookwood. We spoke about Edith Thompson, and he showed me the official entry in the register of the cemetery. The peg marking her place of burial had to remain identified, it seems, on specific Home Office instructions. Mr Dally knew the grave, he told me, and indeed he visited it from time to time. Not just, I learnt, to follow Home Office orders, but because he was, of all things, a native of Ilford, and born not far from where Edith and Percy Thompson had lived in the early 1920s. That the warden of Brookwood Cemetery hailed from close to Edith Thompson's home at 41 Kensington Gardens seemed, in retrospect, peculiarly fitting.

Shortly afterwards I acquired the grave jointly with my friend Mrs Audrey Russell from the Royal Courts of Justice, with a view to having it consecrated at some point in the future. Mrs Russell had interviewed Edith Thompson's sister Avis Graydon in the 1970s, and Avis had given her a necklace and an Edwardian tray-cloth which had once belonged to Edith. I remember hearing Avis Graydon's voice on tape for the first time. It was an unforgettable moment. Her quiet dignity constituted a moving tribute to her strength of character in adversity. It had done so on that day in December 1922 when she had impressed the court at the Old Bailey with the delivery of her evidence. Listening to Avis talk about her sister marked a personal turning point in my researches. If I had harboured the slightest doubt about the propriety of carrying on with this project, Avis Graydon's passionate belief in her sister's innocence, half a century later, confirmed my conviction that Edith's name must be cleared.

Avis Graydon was one of the main victims of the tragedy of 'Thompson and Bywaters'. She lost her boyfriend, her sister and her future. In the long years which followed she shared her parents' grief, and the word 'spinster' after her name on her death certificate starkly sums up her tragic story. Avis could never, she later claimed, have told a man whom she loved what had happened to her family, because it would have been too dreadful a thing to own up to. What she must have experienced during the final hours leading up inexorably to the violent and wilful extinction of her sister one can barely imagine.

Avis outlived the removal of her sister's remains to Brookwood by six years. The Home Office failed to notify her, as Edith Thompson's closest surviving kin, of the transfer and thus robbed Avis, a devout Roman Catholic, of the chance to visit her sister's place of burial. Even at that late stage it might have afforded Avis some comfort to mourn at Edith's grave in the leafy parklands of Brookwood, to stand there for herself and for her parents, and to know that at last her beloved sister no longer lay immured at Holloway. The verdant groves of the Surrey cemetery echo with the same sounds as Wanstead Park, where she and 'Edie' spent untroubled summer afternoons on their school's plant-learning trips. In those mellow, far-off days two bright little English girls playing with their peers in an ancient woodland could never have imagined what the wickedness of the world had set in store for them.

Avis's mother had yearned to have Edith's body returned to her. In a letter of March 1924 a prison visitor from Holloway had written to a Labour Party grandee, the Right Honourable Arthur Henderson, to say that she had 'been approached by the mother of poor Edith Thompson (whom I met under very sad circumstances) to find out whether anything could be done to get back the body of her child, or if at least she might be informed where she is buried'. What Henderson replied is not recorded, but the Home Office predictably wrote back to say that, in accordance with the law, Edith Thompson 'was buried and must remain buried within the precincts of the Prison'.

Throughout the proceedings of the winter months of 1922–3 the Home Office, the Prison Commission, and the judiciary had taken the view that Edith Thompson's life rated as little more than disposable waste. As Avis noted bitterly fifty years later:

> to think that these people, Christmas time, they hadn't, they hadn't got time to bother with her, with the, over the, the appeal. They just hadn't time to bother with her. It was Christmas time, let's get away and get away with it all.

The country's governing class and its intelligentsia cruelly failed this hard-working, high-achieving cockney family. T. S. Eliot's and Thomas Hardy's heartless responses to Edith Thompson's predicament are well documented (pages 291–2). Similarly Rebecca West, in *Reynolds*, 17 December 1922, wrote that Edith Thompson 'was, poor child, a shocking little piece of rubbish, and her mental furniture was meagre ... I am not asking for sympathy for Edith Thompson. She is a poor, flimsy, silly, mischievous little thing.' So much for the sisterly compassion of this proto-feminist intellectual, whom the same newspaper introduced as 'perhaps the most brilliant woman journalist of the day'. Had not Henry James, the great novelist whom West admired, memorably written, 'Never say you know the last word about any human heart'?

In a little over a year after her sister's death Avis read an article in *Thomson's Weekly News* by John Ellis, the man who had hanged Edith Thompson. It was called 'Secrets of My Life Revealed', and the sub-heading was 'How Edith Thompson Met Her Death on the Scaffold'. It was to this piece that Avis referred when she told Audrey Russell in 1973 that she had read that

> they said the morning of the execution there was a great struggle. She was kicking, and frantic, and fighting them all.

For Ellis the execution of Edith Thompson was a landmark event, primarily because it afforded him his first opportunity to travel by air. His flight on 8 January 1923 from Manchester to Croydon rated, he tells us, as a 'great experience'. The bonus was that 'some time later I was thrilled at learning that this same machine as I had flown in was smashed while on the journey back from London to Manchester'. Ellis was rather less coarse-grained when writing about Edith Thompson, and his detailed account of Edith's last twenty-four hours seems to be largely accurate, since it generally (but not in

every detail) tallies with the Governor's official report which is preserved in the Public Record Office in Kew. Here are Ellis's words
from the moment he stepped inside the condemned cell at 9 a.m. on 9
January 1923:

> Mrs Thompson was in a state of complete emotional collapse, and had
> absolutely lost all control of herself . . . Understanding my beckoning
> nod, the chaplain left Mrs Thompson's side, and the wardresses practi-
> cally lifted the sobbing woman to her feet, for she was totally unable to
> stand unaided.
>
> My own feelings defy description. The woman's cries and semi-
> demented body movements almost unnerved me, but I told myself that
> my only humane course was to work swiftly and cut Mrs Thompson's
> agony as short as possible. So pulling myself together I quickly pinioned
> her hands behind her back. By this time the poor woman's cries were
> being blotted out by the unconsciousness which now mercifully
> descended upon her and from which she never again emerged. She had
> sunk back into her chair . . . I called forward my two assistants and also
> the Pentonville warders. I instructed Phillips and Baxter to strap her skirts
> round her ankles and that they must carry Mrs Thompson to the scaffold
> with the help of the two warders. I then left the agonizing scene and
> hurried through to the scaffold.
>
> In a few moments I saw them coming bearing Mrs Thompson. She
> looked as if she were already dead . . . as soon as they reached the trap-
> doors I put the white cap on her head and face, and slipped the noose over
> all. It was a pitiable thing to see the woman being held up on her feet by
> four men. Her head had fallen forward on her breast, and she was utterly
> oblivious of all that was going on . . . I sprang to the lever. One flick of
> the wrist, and Mrs Thompson disappeared from view.

In the same piece Ellis also commented on Edith's striking weight
increase (page 304).

Twenty-five years later, during a long intervention on the death
penalty in the House of Commons, Sir Beverley Baxter, formerly an
editor of the *Daily Express*, stated that the faces of the two men who
came to see him after hanging Edith Thompson were 'not human. I
can assure you, Sir, they were like people out of another world. Edith
Thompson had disintegrated as a human creature on her way to the
gallows, and yet somehow they had to get her there' (*Hansard*, 14
April 1948).

Much has been written over the years regarding the allegation
that Edith Thompson disintegrated 'as a human creature' and the

further rumour that 'her insides fell out'. As I argue in this book, I believe that she may have been pregnant when she died, and her constipation and headaches, to which the Governor of Holloway referred in his report, may have been attributable to that. If so, she probably suffered a haemorrhage on the scaffold.

There is, however, another explanation, and one which is not exclusive of pregnancy. It is possible that Edith lost control of all bodily functions in those final moments of utter terror as the men grabbed her to carry her to her death. This may be hinted at by Ellis's claim that she 'lost all control of herself'. If so, then her alleged 'disintegrating as a human creature' and her 'insides falling out' would be a prudish euphemism. The spectacle of Edith Thompson's last moments inspires outrage even now, not least because it was grotesquely gendered: five men physically manhandling a young woman to kill her by law, with four other men and two women looking on. The alleged immorality of Edith's correspondence pales into insignificance when contrasted with such a scene.

Members of the Graydon family other than Avis could find no respite from their memories either. Thus a framed picture of Edith Thompson hung on the bedroom wall of one of her brothers for the rest of that family's life. The picture in question was one of two that Edith had given to Freddy Bywaters, and the one that carried her qualified stamp of approval (pages 66 and 104). This tragedy continued to affect the families of all those concerned down through the years. Every new generation needed to be told at some point what the past had held, who the unknown young woman in the photograph on the wall was, what the smart boy with the keen profile had done, why Percy Thompson could never grow old.

Whereas the upper executive and the establishment treated Edith Thompson as a mere cypher, many of those who came into close contact with her liked, and often loved, her. This was true particularly of the women staff at Holloway, who by all accounts did their utmost to make Edith Thompson's stay there more bearable; and prison regulations, regarding access to the condemned woman, notably the visitors' physical proximity to her, seem to have been repeatedly relaxed. The Governor of Holloway, Dr John Morton, was a decent man and, where Edith Thompson was concerned, he acted in the spirit rather than the letter of the law whenever he could, as, for example, when he tried to ignore the fact that Canon Palmer of Ilford was a Roman Catholic rather than an Anglican priest (pages 288–9). During the family's last visit to Holloway for the post-mortem on 9 January 1923, several staff at the prison were in tears, a fact that moved and comforted the stricken family.

I had long known that Mrs Lester, the Thompsons' sitting tenant, had taken Edith's side after the murder. But I had been unaware of an extended article and interview that she had contributed (probably assisted by a ghost writer) to a newspaper, and which throws new light on both the night of 3–4 October 1922 and the relationship of the doomed couple. It also touches on Edith's attachment to her material possessions, and in this regard it connects interestingly with the most striking new piece of information that has come my way since 1990.

In her piece Mrs Lester offers a passionate defence of the young woman at Holloway, whom she praises for her generosity, intelligence, hard work and elegance. Percy, on the other hand, she portrays as petty, morose and mean. She alleges moreover that Edith and Percy Thompson were asked to leave the Chamberses' home in Ilford because he was violent towards Edith:

> They came to [41] Kensington Gardens in a hurry, owing to a quarrel they had one night in the bedroom, when Thompson was knocking his wife about and his brother-in-law told them to go.

This was not the whole story, since the burgeoning dislike between Edith and Lily Chambers, Percy's sister, must have been a contributory factor (page 30). But the reference to bedroom rows at the Chamberses' has the distinct ring of authenticity, because the bedroom was the Thompsons' usual battleground. I had originally assumed, from the interview with Avis Graydon, that it was Kenneth Chambers's querulous temper that had caused the estrangement, although just before the reference to temper Avis described Chambers as 'a most charming man, most charming'. Here is what Avis said:

> Edie and Percy lived with Kenneth for some time, but he was so bad-tempered and he got on so badly with his family that they came and got this house in Kensington Gardens, and then the maid [Ethel Vernon] went to live with them; and then that maid came to our place to stay.

The placing of the first 'he' and Ethel Vernon's going to live with the Thompsons suggested to me, mistakenly it turns out, that the bad-tempered 'he' referred to Kenneth Chambers, when in fact it denoted Percy.

Mrs Lester asserts categorically that no one who knew Edith Thompson could imagine that she would attempt to murder her husband. The idea of Edith's 'powdering electric light globes to put into her husband's food is too stupid for words', she averred. Mrs Lester's implacable hostility towards Percy must have partly stemmed from his repeated attempts to evict her and her daughter, and shortly before his death he had intensified the pressure when the Lesters failed to move out by August 1922 as originally (it seems) agreed (page 151).

On the night of the murder Mrs Lester was woken up by her daughter Norah, with whom she shared a bed:

> 'Do you hear them, mother?' We thought it was the Thompsons coming in, and did not take a great deal of notice, because we were used to them arguing with each other at all hours of the night. But when my daughter drew my attention to the noise at the front door, I sat up in bed with a feeling of alarm. A moment later I nearly shrieked with fright when I heard heavy footsteps coming up the stairs, and someone came into my room with a lantern. It was a policeman, and his helmet could be seen in the comparative dark. 'What's the matter?' I said. 'Has somebody come in and left the front door open?' . . . 'No, it's all right, Ma'am,' he said. 'Will you come downstairs for a time? There is a young lady down there, and her husband has dropped dead in the street.'

Mrs Lester's account of that grim night at 41 Kensington Gardens makes for harrowing copy: the hysterical widow covered in her husband's blood, the police trying to help, the arrival on the scene of Percy's brother, then Edith's parents, more police (now wiser and suspicious after visiting the mortuary), and finally Edith Thompson's departure from her home, never to return there. It is Mrs Lester who advanced a mundane, but all too credible, reason for why Edith stayed with Percy:

> She told me, and I believed her, that she would not entertain any proposi-tion which meant her leaving 'The Retreat' and all it contained. It was her money with which the house had been bought, and most of the furniture had been bought by her from time to time. She prized it as all women will prize the home which has been laboriously got together, beyond every-

thing on earth. She told me from time to time that she would willingly have parted from her husband, but that nothing would induce her to leave the home which had taken so much trouble to get together.

The force of this was brought home to me only when I came across the inventory of Edith Thompson's house, and then I realized the full extent to which 41 Kensington Gardens had been Edith's rather than Percy's in almost every respect except the garden. It made me wonder yet again whether or not Edith would really have left Percy for Freddy if it meant surrendering her home.

There is a revealing moment during the interview with Avis Graydon when Mrs Russell puts it to Avis that Edith intended to elope with Freddy, and that they were planning to buy a flat together:

Avis: No, no – what was, what was going to happen to Percy?
Mrs Russell: Well, they were just going to run away and live together and leave Percy on his own.
Avis: No [laughing sadly]. Not my sister!
Mrs Russell: That's what she is talking about anyway in her letters.
Avis: Not my sister!

A very different interpretation was put on Edith's motives for not separating from Thompson by Percy's brother Richard. I allude to his articles in the press in this book, but they deserve to be discussed here alongside Mrs Lester's declarations; and they engendered a vehement public response from one of Edith's friends.

According to Richard Thompson, the black widow from Manor Park was hoping to lay her hands on her husband's estate so that she and Bywaters could enjoy the proceeds of murder without facing up to any of its consequences. The general tone of his pieces in *Lloyd's Sunday News* can be understood, perhaps, as the outpourings of a grief-stricken relative, but there is a measure of calculated malevolence about them as well, a desperate desire to ensure that the woman at Holloway should not escape the noose.

He paints a lurid picture of Edith Thompson as a Jezebel who drenched herself in perfume and bathed in water that was scented to the tune of one guinea's worth a throw. It was in the same luxuriant baths and bathroom that she composed her degenerate letters, he noted, and she dressed and undressed in the window, notwithstanding several complaints by neighbours about this.

As regards this alleged streak of exhibitionism, it is untrue that there were any recorded (that is, official) complaints about this. But it does seem to have been the case that Edith changed occasionally in the window, although how much of her could be glimpsed through the narrow slats of the venetian blinds in the upstairs bedroom at 41 Kensington Gardens is debatable. Two independent sources from the Thompsons' neighbourhood in Ilford also alleged that their menfolk had enthusiastically tried to catch furtive glimpses of Edith Thompson disrobing in her bedroom, and that her changing habits were known in the street. Perhaps; but these allegations were made after the notoriety of the murder, by which time everybody seemed eager to be thought to have known the protagonists. It is also just possible that Edith sometimes simply forgot to draw the curtains.

In his first piece, on 7 January 1923, Richard Thompson insinuated that Edith's income was not nearly large enough to allow her the kind of lifestyle that she led, particularly with regard to her gambling (as he called her occasional small flutter on the horses) and her finery. She must have, he intimated, supplemented her earnings from other sources, something to do with the men with whom she loved to surround herself. Although he later denied that he intended to imply this, he clearly meant that she was living off immoral earnings or prostitution: 'her trips to the West End – those escapades of which we know but a little', he hinted darkly.

To most fair-minded readers his articles on his sister-in-law constitute venomous diatribes. Thus, for example, he alleged that Edith took over the cooking at 41 Kensington Gardens systematically to poison her husband. He withheld the fact, of which he was well aware, that it was the rift between Percy and the Lesters which had caused Mrs Lester to stop cooking for the Thompsons.

What must have caused particular hurt to Edith's family was when he called the young woman sitting condemned to death a pervert: 'That Edith had a mind very far from pure I well knew. The extent of its vileness I only learnt when I saw letters addressed to her lover and never published; letters of an obscene kind that could have been written only by a moral pervert.'

This is doubly dishonest. Firstly, because he never saw any unpublished letters other than, perhaps, the ones that were not put in evidence in court; and, secondly, because like the Crown at the trial he intended to convey the impression that if only all the facts were known, then no one could have any doubt about the guilt of this vampish moral pariah. If Curtis-Bennett made one mistake in leading for the defence, it was his agreeing to the Crown's seemingly harmless wishes not to submit all the letters. The jury never knew why they were being withheld, or whether or not crucial and incriminating evidence might not be hidden in them. At the trial the Solicitor-General unscrupulously exploited this chink in the defence's armour.

To Richard Thompson Edith's alleged moral perversions chimed perfectly with her preference for 'a certain type of French novel, whose equivalent we do not allow to be published in this country; the type of novel which is concerned solely and nastily with sex'.

Finally, with bogus magnanimity, and in a malicious echo of one of Edith Thompson's letters from Holloway, he suggested that to let this extravagant sybarite live would be a worse punishment than hanging her.

Shocked by Richard Thompson's mendacity, a 'near-relative' of Edith Thompson's, her aunt Edith Walkinshaw, noted caustically towards the end of a newspaper article on her by then dead niece:

> In closing I would just like to thank Richard Halliday Thompson for his articles on Edith Thompson. I have seen several letters asking if his brother was anything like him.
>
> If only he can realize one iota of the sympathy extended to her from those who can read deeper than the surface, then, indeed, I am satisfied.

I had originally assumed that the 'near-relative' who wrote so movingly in Edith's defence in *Lloyd's Sunday News* was her aunt Lily Laxton (née Liles), who had accompanied the two Thompsons to the theatre on that fateful night of 3 October 1922. But although Lily and her husband undoubtedly visited Edith at Holloway, I now lean towards thinking that the author of the newspaper articles may have been Edith Walkinshaw, who was Edith's other aunt as well as her godmother; and she lived close enough to Holloway to visit her niece frequently.[2] When the writer of the articles refers to remembering

[2]Edith Walkinshaw was born Edith Florence Liles in 1871. She is the addressee of the newly discovered letter reproduced below. She was a year older than Edith's mother, while Edith's aunt Lily was only forty-two when her niece was on trial at the Old Bailey. Mrs Walkinshaw died on 27 August 1934, by which time she had moved from Lucerne Road (where Edith had known her) to 49 Grafton Street, Fitzroy Square, St Pancras, her last place of residence.

little Edith playing with her dolls in an imperious manner, she is perhaps referring to dolls that she as her godmother had given to the little girl as presents.

Richard Thompson's articles, and particularly their innuendoes about Edith Thompson as the natural creature of a *demi-monde* of vice, reduced a woman friend of Edith's to tears and caused her to launch into a detailed rebuttal of his charges in *Lloyd's Sunday News*. The newspaper described this young woman as Edith Thompson's 'life-long friend'. One by one she exposed Richard Thompson's charges as sham. The friend concluded her defence of Edith's reputation by sadly looking ahead into the future:

> It will be written of her that she was a woman without a heart; a murderess of vile and inconceivably wicked instincts. A creature whose passions were without bounds; whose duplicity was only matched by her lust.
>
> All that will be said of Edith Thompson, the bright-eyed, laughing child who romped through youth with me, the woman whom, in later years, I looked up to and admired as a natural leader, a true friend, with generous heart and tender impulses.

But Edith's friend would be proved wrong on her fear of how Edith Thompson would be reported by posterity. The vast literature on Bywaters and Thompson, from the 1920s to the present day, would be virtually unanimous in proclaiming her innocence.

When I first wrote *Criminal Justice* I had taken it for granted that the 'life-long friend' was Bessie of Reg and Bessie. But this is almost certainly wrong, because Bessie was Edith's senior by six years. It was only when I realized that Bessie's married name, given by Avis on tape, was *Akam* (and not Aitken, as I had originally written in *Criminal Justice*) that I could trace her. Bessie was born Maud Elizabeth Harriet Moore in Islington on 28 September 1887, and she was Jewish or half-Jewish. Even so she married Reginald Edward Akam in the Anglican faith in the parish church of Stoke Newington on 26 June 1913, when Edith Graydon was nineteen years old.

In *Criminal Justice* I wondered whether the friends whom Edith and Percy visited on Sunday 30 September 1922, the weekend before the murder, had been Reg and Bessie. Since we now know that Bessie had turned thirty-five two days earlier, the Thompsons may have gone there to celebrate her birthday. Did Edith issue a theatre invitation for Tuesday to the wealthy Akams? It is not impossible that the Akams joined them, but I believe that they would have been summoned if they had indeed been of that party hours before Percy Thompson's death.

It is almost inconceivable that the mysterious 'life-long friend' should not have been mentioned at some point in Edith's detailed, moment-by-moment correspondence between November 1921 and October 1922. There had all along been another candidate for the identity of the friend. I had originally considered her, and then had, for various reasons, decided that it could not be her after all. She was Edith's friend Lilian Vellender-Goodwin from Carlton & Prior.

Since the 'life-long friend' had been at school with Edith, I searched for Lilian (and for Bessie) in the Kensington Avenue Schools records, but I drew a blank. That may have been due to the fact that Jewish children such as Bessie and also Lily missed classes through Jewish holidays and therefore did not qualify for the 'perfect attendance' medals. The lists of medallists are the only major source of children's names in the schools' logbook.

It seemed too much of a coincidence that Edith should end up working in the same place as an old schoolmate, and the Vellenders were after all living in Islington by 1920. I had assumed that Lily's family came from either Islington or Stoke Newington, although I had noticed the name Goodwin in the 1922 Electoral Roll of Edith's home street, Shakespeare Crescent, and of Byron Avenue, Manor Park. But by then I had already concluded that Lily could not have been the 'friend' because, firstly, she was never mentioned in connection to the party that went to the Criterion Theatre in Piccadilly on 3 October 1922 and, secondly, and above all, because she did not refer to the theatre visit in court. For unlike Reg and Bessie Akam, Lily Vellender *did* testify at the Old Bailey, but she was not asked about the theatre. This may have been because she was examined by the prosecution who were only interested in Freddy's assignations with Edith in the days before the murder. Lily gave little away in her terse statement.

In the mid-1980s the Vellenders had eluded me because of a small, single-letter error. I had searched for, and recorded in this book, the name Vallender instead of Vellender. By so doing I perpetuated a mistake made by Filson Young in *Notable British Trials* (1923), the police and court records, and almost all other sources, and it was this misreading that prevented me from finding the Vellenders' marriage certificate. Even the clerk who drafted the said certificate wrote 'Vallender' at first and subsequently corrected it to Vellender.

In the end, though, I could not quite believe that the Vellenders, who seemed such solid London professionals, should have married somewhere abroad. In the summer of 2000 I therefore returned to the Family Records Centre, which had by then relocated from the Aldwych to spacious new premises in Islington. I now did what I should have done years ago, and checked through all the Goodwins. Whereas Vallender was a rare name, the Goodwins were many in number. Even so, it did not take long to discover that I had been coursing the wrong hare by a vowel.

Lilian Amy Florence Vellender was born Lilian Goodwin in Camberwell, south London. She was Jewish (the family had originally been called Goldswain), and she was Edith Thompson's junior by two years. Like Edith, Lily continued to be known at work by her maiden name. Lily converted to Catholicism when she married Norman Vellender, and after their marriage she and Norman settled in her mother's home at 66 Albion Grove (now Ripplevale Grove) beyond the Almeida theatre in Islington. The Vellenders' marriage was celebrated at the Church of the Blessed Sacrament in Islington on 7 August 1920; Lily was twenty-four and Norman twenty-seven. Edith and Percy Thompson would undoubtedly have attended their friends' wedding, and one of the staff from Carlton & Prior, John Dunford, acted as a witness.[3] The Vellenders' Catholicism may have been a contributory reason to Edith's eagerness to receive the ministrations of Canon Palmer during her last hours (page 289).

The 'life-long friend' met Edith Graydon at school for the first time when Edith was nine years old, and the friend later refers to having known Edith (who turned twenty-nine on Christmas Day 1922) for twenty years. She attended the Thompsons' wedding in Manor Park in 1916, and she knew Percy as well as his mother and family. She claims to have been present with Percy at the Thompsons' one day (presumably Richard Thompson's home in Ilford) when Edith was spotted with Bywaters in Wanstead Park, while Percy thought that she was at the theatre. Moreover, she knew about Bywaters, and she tells us how she once tried to warn Edith against carrying on with

[3] Pages 132 and 134 follow Edith's published letters in writing 'Dunsford', but on the Vellenders' marriage certificate 'Dunford' does not have a medial 's' and this is probably the correct version of the name.

Freddy. She recalls a visit in September 1922 to Edith's and Percy's home, and she remarks on how Edith seemed to be quite indulgent of Percy's grumpiness. She is also familiar with the appearance of the porch of Carlton & Prior's. But the most important clue of all perhaps is her casual defence of Edith's passion for hats (against Richard Thompson's charge of immoral extravagance) by noting that Edith sometimes changed her hats *twice* in one afternoon. It is probable that only someone who worked with Edith at Carlton & Prior and knew of her double duties as manageress and buyer, which required her to be smart at all times, could have known this.

Most of these details fit Lily Vellender, even though I could not find her father John Goodwin on the Electoral Roll of the official catchment area of the Kensington Avenue Schools for the period when Edith Graydon attended there. But then Lily's father abandoned his family when she was young, and Lily, her younger brother and her mother may have lived with her mother's family after the separation.

Lily and Norman visited Edith and Percy on Sunday 17 September 1922, and Edith was congratulated that day by Norman Vellender on her home-made chutney. Was it Lily who took the photographs of Edith and Percy which I originally dated at 3 September and attributed to Bessie? On at least one other occasion when Edith and Percy visited the Vellenders in *their* garden in Islington, a number of photographs were taken, and one of those shows Edith standing between Percy and Norman (see Inset).

Lily certainly knew about Edith's affair with Bywaters, and on Monday 25 September 1922 and again on the Friday before the murder she joined Freddy in Fuller's tea-room to keep him company until Edith was free.[4] Lily moreover dreamt one night in April 1922 that Percy was going to murder Edith because he had discovered that she had been out with 'a fair man' (page 102). Lily *related* her nightmare to Edith, and it may well be to this incident that the 'life-long friend' alluded in *Lloyd's Sunday News* of 7 January 1923, when she claimed to have tried to reason with Edith over Bywaters months earlier. Edith saw Lily every day except Sundays, and the Vellenders had been on holiday with the Thompsons on at least two recorded

[4] Bessie also knew about the affair, and she may have lied for Edith about a visit to the theatre with her on 30 March 1922, when in reality Edith was out on the town with Bywaters (pages 94–6). She also asked after Freddy on Sunday 21 May 1922 when she and Reg picked up Edith, Percy and Avis for a long spin in the car (page 120).

occasions, and probably more often. Lily is an intrinsically more likely candidate for a confidante than Bessie Akam.

Would Lily have fabricated her role in the outing to the theatre? I do not think so now any more than I did in 1988, when I assumed that the 'friend' was Bessie. But it *is* puzzling that she was not cross-examined about these crucial hours by Curtis-Bennett, and that neither Edith nor her aunt and uncle, the Laxtons, refer to Lily's presence then. The recollection of that evening by the 'life-long friend' is very precise (page 177), and she relates it twice in two separate articles. The fact that she remembers a remark in the foyer of the Criterion Theatre about the 'chill' that night and Percy's not wearing a coat authenticates her account further, since it was indeed cold on 3 October 1922.[5]

There is an additional piece of information extant about that same evening, and I may originally have underestimated its importance. In her plea for clemency to the Prime Minister, Avis Graydon insisted that a fortnight before 3 October she had been invited along to the theatre, and that she had planned to spend that night at her sister's in Ilford. She would therefore have accompanied the Thompsons on their way home from the station, which proved, according to Avis, that her sister could not possibly have set up an encounter with Bywaters in the Belgrave Road (page 271).

The outing of that night had indeed been initiated by the women's aunt Lily Laxton, and it is quite natural that the aunt should have invited Avis along, since the younger Graydon daughter, who was still without a male companion, frequently joined the others as a member of the party. I had originally set little store by Avis's cancelling at short notice, although the reason that she gave had always struck me as odd. She withdrew, she told Percy on the telephone, because she 'had already made arrangements to go out for mother'. If her mother had been sick this would have been perfectly intelligible, since Avis would have been needed to do her mother's shopping. But Mrs Graydon was fine. There was, I suspect, a reason much closer to Avis's heart for being at her mother's, and that is because the night of the theatre coincided with Freddy Bywaters's last night of shoreleave. Avis probably stayed at home to spend the evening with Freddy. I argued in 1988 that Edith's insistent invitation to Bywaters to 'do something tomorrow night', something that

[5] See page 173 and Filson Young (ed.), *Notable British Trials*, William Hodge & Co., Edinburgh, 1923, page 21 (evidence of police sergeant Walter Mew).

would make him forget even though it might hurt her, referred to his taking her sister out.

What happened was probably that Bywaters called Avis on Tuesday 3 October after lunching with Edith and arranged to go and see her in Manor Park; and that she then pulled out of the theatre. One of the terrible ironies of this story is that Freddy was gravitating back towards Avis, and both Avis and Edith knew this. If Freddy had not killed Percy Thompson that night, it is very likely from the way things were shaping up that he might have found his way back to Avis altogether during the course of his next visit. Instead, by the time his ship returned he was close to death at Pentonville.

It may be the case that Percy rang Edith after hearing from Avis that she was unable to join them, and that Edith then invited Lily to replace Avis; but it is more probable that she had already done so, since Bywaters must have told her over lunch at the latest about going out to East Ham that evening to see the Graydons. The fact that it was during the 'late afternoon' of 3 October that Avis dropped out only really leaves someone with whom Edith worked as a possible replacement. Lily Vellender fits this scenario better than anybody else from Edith's circle of friends and acquaintances.

We may never know the answer to these questions for certain. Lily, whom everybody had adored, the girl with the quick smile and the big heart, died almost destitute in a first-floor flat in Hove in December 1974. A removal firm cleared out all her belongings, including her correspondence. Among it there would almost certainly have been letters by Edith Thompson, whether or not Lily was the 'life-long friend' from *Lloyd's Sunday News*. Everything was destroyed, with the exception of a few snapshots, two of which are reproduced here (see Inset).

In order to understand what truly happened in this 1920s tragedy the full facts needed to be put before the reader, to allow Edith Thompson's innocence to speak for itself. A knowledge of the most intimate details of Edith's life was required to refute the allegations about her. The prosecution had turned her life before the murder into a simplistic, linear and purposeful narrative whose sole goal was murder. But human reality is so much more varied and complex, and I tried to convey some of that inconsequential chaos in my diaristic account of her life. By doing so I also hoped to be able to commemorate Edith Thompson more effectively, because I believed that my readers would empathize with the inner recesses of her life.

Such exposure may sometimes demean the subject under the spotlight, but no holds can be barred where a distortion of the truth cost a young woman her life. To establish the true facts it was necessary to talk about Edith Thompson's sexuality, her periods, her pregnancies and her weight. The hollow *pudeur* that precluded discussing these matters at the trial connived with dragging a healthy, innocent young woman to the gallows. This was forcefully recognized by James Douglas, a leading journalist of the day. He claimed, as a scoop in the *Sunday Express* of 21 January 1923, to have discovered that Edith Thompson's correspondence was in reality concerned with female sexuality and not murder; that many of the more sinister passages read out in court made sense only if they were interpreted as treating of terminations and abortifacients (or 'abortives' in the phrase of the time), and not of poisoning. Most people following the trial had suspected this all along, and by the time Douglas rode to Edith's rescue she was dead; instead of being her champion, he had cravenly betrayed her by not revealing a truth that might have saved her life.

In the course of writing this book in the 1980s I immersed myself more deeply in Edith Thompson's tragic and short existence than seemed at times bearable. She had been a living, breathing, human being with every right to her secrets. She gave much and was loved back by many. Like thousands of her contemporaries she was unhappily married, but her options for resolving this were fewer than they would be now. A passing glance at her immediate circle of acquaintances underlines the extent to which she was no different from others. Thus Dr Wallis, the GP who treated her as a little girl in Manor Park, became embroiled in a tragic love triangle (pages 83–4); her employer Herbert Carlton was a cheerful womanizer who in the end ran off with a girl from the shop-floor; and the Thompsons' friend, the wealthy Sidney Birnage, kept a mistress in a flat in London and tried to sell his married home behind his wife's back. He may well have wanted to step into Bywaters's shoes with the mistress of 41 Kensington Gardens (pages 114–15), and plenty of other men ('Mel' and 'Derry' among them) were only too eager to be seen with Edith.

Although these events happened nearly eighty years ago, Edith was not very different from the urban professionals of my generation. She had absorbed the same Shakespeare plays as my contemporaries and me, and at Holloway she was reading Dickens's *Our Mutual Friend*, which I had been urged to study in my first year at university. Her father's cry of incredulity, that something so outlandish as a trial for murder should happen to 'people like us', has echoed down the twentieth century. Writing about Edith Thompson, Professor Jane Miller of the University of London Institute of Education noted:

> If Edith and Freddy had been born fifty years later they would probably have stayed on at school until the age of sixteen, and, given their intelligence and their interests, the chances are good that they would have taken some A levels and proceeded to university, perhaps to read English. Yet their reading and their writing were disparaged as 'uneducated', undiscriminating, even though their brief schooling clearly 'took' in ways which must have had something to do with their confidence that they would get jobs after school and that the education they were getting would be useful in such jobs. (*School for Women*: Virago 1996, 187.)

Edith Thompson tried to bend reality to make her dreams come true. Like the rest of us she occasionally behaved foolishly and often selfishly, but she never acted in the spirit of wickedness that was imputed to her in court. She has sometimes been compared to Emma Bovary, the protagonist of Gustave Flaubert's famous novel *Madame Bovary* (1857). Emma had married in the hope of romantic love, but marriage failed to deliver happiness to her, and she therefore thought that she must have made a mistake. According to Flaubert, 'Et Emma cherchait à savoir ce que l'on entendait au juste dans la vie par les mots de *félicité*, de *passion* et d'*ivresse*, qui lui avaient paru si beaux dans les livres. (And Emma endeavoured to find out what exactly was meant in real life by the words *happiness*, *passion* and *total abandon* which had struck her as so beautiful in her books.)'

Edith Thompson dared to do just that with the consequences that we know.

The fact that people who had known Edith were still alive in the 1980s rendered a sense of her immediacy particularly acute then. Even at the time that I am writing this Preface, Edith Thompson's most famous surviving contemporary is thriving. It was a few days after Edith Thompson's death that the future King and Elizabeth of Glamis became officially engaged to be married.

At some point in the mid-1980s I visited Edith's and Percy's home in Ilford in the company of Mrs Audrey Russell. The Thompsons' garden was virtually identical to what it had been on 1 August 1921 when Percy struck Edith and Freddy Bywaters intervened (pages 54–5). It felt to us as if somehow the conversation of that day still hung heavily in the air. As we ascended the stairs towards the bedrooms, we both felt uneasy. When finally we stood in the ill-starred couple's room and looked up at the same ceiling and bow-window that Edith had gazed at in the early hours of the morning when she could not sleep, it seemed like a journey too far. All I could think of was how desperately she had wanted to come home to these very rooms from the nightmare of Holloway.

At 41 Kensington Gardens I thought that I had come as close as it was possible to be to this tragic tale. I was mistaken, because the most revealing window on this story was yet to open, and it was precisely to do with the house. It was in the early 1990s when a chance enquiry produced the auction catalogue for 41 Kensington Gardens which, I now learnt, was first sold with a ninety-nine-year lease on 25 March 1901, so that Edith's and Percy's lease ran to just over eighty years.

The catalogue preserves the Thompsons' rooms the way they were when Edith walked out of the house for the last time at noon on 4 October 1922. All that is missing are her and Percy's clothes, although a few of his personal belongings, such as his silver matchbox, silk handkerchiefs, and gent's leather suitcase were still in the house. What happened was that shortly after charging Edith Thompson and Freddy Bywaters with murder, the police sealed all the Thompsons' rooms in the house. At some point thereafter the Lesters were evicted, and on Thursday 27 September 1923 the house in Kensington Gardens was auctioned off.

In the catalogue's pages Edith's most precious possessions were itemized, those very things that Mrs Lester and others recalled her cherishing so much. Of all the intimate details of her most private life and thoughts that were exposed to the public gaze in and out of court, this inventory of her house and furnishings was the most poignant. I write 'her' rather than 'their' because almost everything in the house seems to have been chosen by her, and most of it she had paid for.

At the auction everything went, and people apparently were so desperate for mementoes from the property that they ripped the leaves off the privet hedge at the front of the house and tore twigs from the trees in the gardens.[6]

Some details about the furniture of Edith's house have long been known, of course, including the wicker couch and deck-chair in the garden. In the two most famous photographs of the doomed three-some, one with Edith pointing up, the other showing her sandwiched between the two men, the wicker settee is clearly visible; and Percy's right hand rests on the deck-chair in the last photograph of him and his wife.

Percy was a keen gardener and subscribed to gardening maga-zines, but that he boasted a blowlamp in his glasshouse in addition to a 'Green's mower' and an 18in. twin cylinder roller was an un-expected revelation in the catalogue; as was the fact that the Thompsons kept a dozen novels in the glasshouse. It turns out that hoards of novels were to be found in the bedrooms, as well as in the drawing-room, in its china cabinet, and in the hall where there were some sixty novels as well as a multi-volume *History of the Great War*.

At the time of the tragedy the couple occupied the drawing-room at the front of the house, the breakfast room (or morning room) at the back, the garden, the scullery with the outside lavatory, and the glasshouse (see the diagram, page 36). The hall, scullery, and per-haps the kitchen too, were covered by what the catalogue describes as 'black and white lino', that is, probably, a diamond-check pattern of black and white.

Upstairs they owned the large bow-window bedroom, which ran over the hall and drawing-room, and the small bedroom. This bed-room was briefly occupied by Freddy in 1921. It gave over the garden at the back, and it was adjacent to the bathroom, which must have been shared with the tenants. It was fitted with a bath, a WC, and a washhand basin. Its taps ran hot and cold water, probably from the boiler in the breakfast room. Edith occasionally used the bathroom for writing to Freddy or for escaping from Percy.

Two pieces of furniture from the master bedroom at 41 Kensington Gardens are prominently mentioned in Edith's letters. They were the ottoman at the foot of the Thompsons' bed and the broken mirror of Edith's dressing table.

[6]It has been reported that Edith's parents were present and bidding for some of their child's belongings, but that they could not afford them, because the prices were too high. I do not know what the source of that information is, and it may be anecdotal.

One night when Edith returned from an assignation with Freddy Bywaters, she found Percy reclining on the ottoman in one of his more melodramatic poses (page 124). At the auction someone paid £1.3s. for it. But an impressive £29, the equivalent of an above-average monthly middle-class salary, was fetched by the Thompsons' 'Inlaid Mahogany Bedroom Suite'. According to her father, the suite had originally been purchased by Edith from her own money. It comprised:

> [a] 4ft. dressing table with long oval-shaped bevelled swing mirror in centre, two trinket drawers over and one long and four small drawers under, and drop centre, [b] washstand with Sicilian marble top and back and chamber cupboard under, [c] 5ft. wardrobe with pair doors, each with long oval-shaped bevelled mirror, enclosing hanging presses and with two small drawers under, and [d] 2 cane-seat chairs.

It was the cheval glass mirror of the dressing table that Edith had inadvertently shattered in May 1922 while hanging new curtains with her mother (page 115). These were probably not the lace curtains that ran along the lower sash windows, but either the 'six pairs curtains' or the 'five pairs curtains' which were now selling at £1.6s. and £1.5s. respectively.

Edith may have liked mahogany, because her 4ft. 6in. bedstead consisted of inlaid mahogany as indeed did the chest of drawers and the mahogany furnishings of the drawing-room.[7] The bedroom also contained, among others, a cane easy-chair, a white enamelled wicker chair with cushion and at least two electric lights. The 'pink electric shade' had bead trimmings.

The master bedroom contained in addition a number of vases and china ornaments, at least five cushions, sheets, bolster, pillows, pillow cases, white quilt and a coloured eiderdown. Among the most affecting items in the catalogue was Edith's ten-piece, black and white '*service de toilette*', which was 'decorated with flowers and birds'.

There were no fireplaces in the upstairs bedrooms. Instead, both the front bedrooms were fitted with 'Register Stoves' and had Sicilian marble mantelpieces. One of the two large bedrooms had a built-in wardrobe cupboard. This would have been the Thompsons' room, and it probably ran past the outside wall towards the mantel-

[7] The chest of drawers contained the Thompsons' stationery, photographs and gloves: see *Notable British Trials*, page 35.

piece. That is certainly where the fitted wardobe (of a different vintage, of course) was in the 1980s.

In the small bedroom, which lay on the left of the landing from the master bedroom, was Percy's medicine chest, which is listed as a 'white enamelled medicine cupboard'. Avis had once retrieved tincture of opium from it (page 107). The furniture here was oak, and so was the 2ft. 6in. bedstead of the single bed 'with wire spring, wool mattress, feather pillow and bolster'. It was on this bed and in this room that Edith Thompson and Freddy Bywaters consummated their relationship for the first time on his nineteenth birthday on 27 June 1921.

The drawing-room floor downstairs was covered with linoleum on top of which sat a sheepskin rug and a 'bordered thick pile carpet' complete with 'circle designed centre'. Like the master bedroom above it, it was fitted with a 'Register Stove', and it had a tiled hearth and a marble mantelpiece. Percy Thompson had installed a gas fire in this room, and this is duly listed under Lot 87.[8] It also contained a mahogany drawing-room suite with silk upholstery, a mahogany sideboard, and a china cabinet which was 4ft. wide and stood 6ft. high, with a bow-front centre and a glass door.

Inside the cabinet Edith kept her finest china, consisting of a Limoges dessert service in dark blue and gold (perhaps a wedding present), and a number of other pieces, including a whole set of Goss china, which were little white and coloured china ornaments. It also contained, among others, three collections of novels, a number of Japanese prints (probably gifts from her sailor brothers), two small ebony elephants, cut tumblers and glasses, and 'a Moore & Moore pianoforte in black case', which may have been an elaborate porcelain ornament. As it happens, Edith had acquired a proper piano on hire-purchase, and this also stood in her drawing-room for a short time. It was repossessed soon after her arrest.

Here she also kept a black velvet cushion and three black satin ones. Two of these are clearly visible in the pictures of 10 July 1921, and pictures 25 and 26 show catalogue item 133, a 'black velvet cushion decorated one side with roses and bunch of grapes'.

One of the more remarkable items in the drawing-room was a 16in. bronzed figure on a black base of the poet John Milton. The blind author of *Paradise Lost* may have composed parts of his

[8] See *Notable British Trials*, page 30.

masterpiece while he was hiding in Bartholomew Close within a few yards of Edith's place of work in Aldersgate.

The Thompsons dined in the breakfast room. It was here that Edith entertained her family and friends for Sunday lunches and the occasional dinner party. The room, which had cork lino on the floor, opened into the garden through french windows with sun blinds, and it connected across the hall with the kitchen and scullery. It boasted a fireplace with tiled cheeks and tiled hearth, and above this ran an enamelled slate mantelpiece. There was an 'inter-oven stove with boiler back', which would have provided the hot water for the bathroom above it, china cupboards and a tall oak dresser. Above all, here stood the deal-top table against which Edith fell when Percy struck her on 1 August 1921. It had stained legs and one drawer, and it measured 4ft. 6in. × 2ft. 9in. The six chairs with imitation leather seats which are also listed would have comfortably fitted around it. But the saddest item in the room was a 'lady's folding work basket'. It had rested in Edith's lap on the same 1 August as she sat sewing in her garden and was unable to find a pin she needed.

The Thompsons' house was well appointed and full of beautiful things. By the time Edith and Percy were twenty-eight and thirty-two respectively, they were well off. Indeed they were almost prosperous, because the many acquisitions for the house did not come about at the cost of major material sacrifices. Edith regularly went out for City and West End lunches, *thés dansants* in the Waldorf, and theatres and concerts all over London. By the time of her arrest she had enjoyed a successful business career for at least twelve years. After reading *Criminal Justice* one of her contemporaries remarked to me, 'She didn't half have a good life, all those rich lunches and visits to the theatre.' The speaker was Mrs Myrtle Ellwood, née Aldridge. She was the owner of the photograph from which the print at the graveside had been taken, and I traced her not long after my first visit to Brookwood.

By the time I met her, Myrtle Ellwood was an octogenarian widow who lived alone in a small cottage at 86 Islingword Road in Brighton. She had earlier given a copy of one of her snapshots to the indefatigable Trevor Mallett, who at the time carried a lonely torch for Edith Thompson. It was Trevor who had placed it where I eventually found it. Few people know as much about this case as he does, and in his quiet and decent way Trevor Mallett has been a source of inspiration.

Myrtle Ellwood and I became fast friends. When *Criminal Justice* first appeared, she rang round the public libraries in Sussex to make sure that they all stocked it. She wanted to boost my sales, she told me. Myrtle and her sister had worked alongside Edith Thompson at Carlton & Prior's, first in the Barbican and later in Aldersgate. After one of the firm's outings Edith had even suggested that Myrtle and the other girls from the shop-floor should come and see her in Ilford.

Myrtle had carefully kept her photographs from the firm's day-trips to Horley and to Eastcote in 1921 and 1922 (a number of them are reproduced in the Inset). She never thought that they might be of interest to anyone other than herself.

But then in 1973 the BBC screened a lavish costume drama with Francesca Annis in the lead. It was called *A Pin to See the Peepshow*, after the famous novel by Tennyson Jesse which was based closely on the story of Edith Thompson and Freddy Bywaters. The BBC's production generated renewed interest in the case, and it prompted Myrtle Ellwood to write to the *Radio Times*. In her letter she expressed her sadness at the memory of those long-gone days echoed in her snapshots:

> You see, I worked at Carlton and Prior's and remember well the terrible shock it was at the time to us all. My snaps of Miss Graydon and Percy Thompson are happy ones, and my memories are, too.
>
> Looking at them, I wonder how many of the group are alive today . . . Many I know have followed poor Edith Thompson to Eternity.

Myrtle could not know that Edith Thompson's best friends from Carlton & Prior, Norman and Lily Vellender, had also retired to Brighton, where Norman died in 1969 at the age of seventy-six, pre-deceasing Lily by five years.

Lily Vellender died a year after the broadcasting of *A Pin to See the Peepshow*. Did she, like Avis, watch it? Such was the publicity for the BBC's production at the time that she could hardly avoid being aware of it, and she was lucid almost to the end. But a direct partici-pant from this 1920s tragedy was not only alive then, but lasted well beyond the original publication of this book in 1988. She was one of

Freddy Bywaters's sisters, and she lived not far from Myrtle Ellwood. It seems that she enjoyed a prosperous life after the terrible events of 1922–3, although, as with Avis Graydon, it is hard to imagine that a single day passed in those long subsequent years when she did not remember the fair-haired boy from her days in Westow Street.

One of Freddy's best childhood friends had been Bill West from Beechwood Gardens in Ilford, and Bill proved to be the most inspired source of information on his friend Freddy Bywaters. In the mid-1980s when we met he was in excellent health and regularly travelled from Gants Hill to the theatre in the Barbican. He was unaware of the fact that Avis Graydon, whom he had known in the 1910s, had for many years lived only four streets away from him.

Bill was blessed with an acute memory, and not only interpreted his wonderful photographs to me, but joined me in a visit to his old school. He was astonished by how little it had all changed, and he showed me where he and young Bywaters used to hang their coats on (probably) the same coat hooks. In front of the classrooms he pointed out the exact position of the table with the handbell. Bill remained proud of the fact that his friend Freddy had enjoyed the trust of the school to the point of becoming its bellman.

He then asked me whether we could drive past his own childhood home just across the Browning bridge. This we did. We sat in the car and looked up at the modest terraced villa in Chesterford Road before proceeding from there to Freddy Bywaters's house. As we turned the corner to head down towards 72 Rectory Road, Bill reminded me that it was at the intersection of the two roads before the bridge that he used to meet Freddy on the way to school. Bill West's composure and courtesy were those of a perfect Edwardian gentleman, but he was nearly overcome as we sat in silence outside Freddy's home. He had recognized it at once. 'It makes me very sad,' he remarked, and as we drove back towards his immaculate home he was subdued.

I last saw Bill West in the King George Hospital in Ilford. He had suffered a brain haemorrhage when he fell from a ladder while decorating his house. His daughter told me that at his bedside sat a library copy of *A Pin to See the Peepshow*. There seemed to be so much more for him and me to discuss, but I took comfort from the fact that I had enjoyed the privilege of his friendship at all, even if it was far too briefly. At Bill's funeral in the City of London cemetery I was mindful of the fact that Avis Graydon had come to this same place to mourn for her parents, and that both Percy and Richard Thompson rested not far from the chapel where we stood.

Since the publication of this book in 1988 I have received a substantial correspondence from members of the public. They desired to know whether an approach was being made to the Home Secretary, and they almost invariably expressed their indignation at the unjust treatment of Edith Thompson at the hands of a system that was pledged to protect the innocent.

Two people in particular made contact, and they profoundly influenced the direction this story was to take. They were Professor William Twining of the Faculty of Laws at University College London, my own university, and John Clarke of the Brookwood Cemetery Society, who has since also become a colleague at University College by joining its Institute of Child Health.

William Twining is a distinguished professor of jurisprudence and a world authority on Wigmorean analysis, a rigorous system of analysing forensic evidence named after its chief practitioner, the famous American jurist John Henry Wigmore. Unbeknown to me, William Twining had for years worked on the case of Thompson and Bywaters, and his extensive teaching notes on it were the foundation of a high-powered course at the Institute of Advanced Legal Studies in the University of London. Like me he was adamant that Edith Thompson was innocent, and that she had never been proved guilty by any acceptable legal standard of proof. His published analyses of some of the most incriminating material, such as the lines 'Darlint – do something tomorrow night will you? something to make you forget' and 'I'll risk and try if you will – we only have 3¾ years left darlingest', afford a classic deconstruction of the interpretation put on these sentences by the Crown in 1922. We decided to make common cause, and since the late 1980s William Twining and I have collaborated on the case of Edith Thompson.

John Clarke contacted me in the early 1990s. He was then a librarian in Sheffield, but a native of Surrey. He and the Brookwood Cemetery Society, which he chairs, became the driving force behind the move to erect a proper memorial to Edith Thompson. In the end a number of us shared the cost of the handsome granite slab which now covers Edith Thompson's final resting place.

*

Some seven or eight years earlier I had made the acquaintance of the Reverend Barry Arscott of St Barnabas in Manor Park, Edith Thompson's local church. Barry had taken me into the church where Edith Thompson was married in 1916, and he had allowed me to inspect the register in the vestry, which she had signed in that same place on 15 January 1916.

In 1993 Barry once more made himself available, this time as master of the proceedings. His sermon struck a chord in all our hearts. As we were gathered under a canopy of umbrellas, he spoke with solemn dignity about the young woman who had formerly been of his parish. Here are his words, from the 'Sermon at the Service for the Dedication of a Memorial Stone in memory of Edith Jessie Thompson, Saturday, 13 November 1993, 11 a.m. at Brookwood Cemetery':

Later on, we shall dedicate this stone in memory of Edith Jessie Thompson, seventy years after her death. Those who have worked hard to see that Edith's resting place does not go unmarked are to be congratulated.

Edith's tragic death and the circumstances are well known to us all and she will not be forgotten, but we place and dedicate this stone here today, first because it would have been what her family would have wanted and because *we* want to acknowledge and recognize Edith alongside all the departed; no one should be treated as though they never were; but secondly, we have this ceremony, I believe, because of the way in which she died, and the injustice of that should never be forgotten.

John Donne, the poet, said 'Every man's death diminishes me', and it is true that when someone we love dies, part of us dies too. But in the case of this particular death, we may well say Edith's death diminished humanity, and there are a number of lessons we need to learn and take heart from it.

First though I want to reinforce the Christian view about death; that it is not an end, that we go through death to eternal life, that all the departed remain in the loving hands of God. If that is your own particular belief, thank God for it and ask him to strengthen your faith and hope in eternal life. The God I believe in is a God who is present with us at all times, here and for ever. He is a God of love and forgiveness who holds us all in his heart. As our reading (Romans 8: 18, 28, 35, 37–9) suggested, nothing can separate

xxxvi

us from Him and His love, whoever we are, whatever we may have done.

We do not try to paint Edith as a saint; we know that, like all of us, she wasn't blameless. But it is not our place to judge. We leave whatever judging there may be to God who I have to say is much more loving and accepting and forgiving than we could ever be. It is reassuring to know that God knows us and understands our failings; He knows the truth about Edith. She is not beyond his love.

There are other lessons that need reinforcing. We believe that Edith was put to death unjustly. Her execution was just one of a number that have been proved to be unjust. It's a salutary reminder that it is not man's place to play God, and it's incumbent on all of us who believe capital punishment to be wrong, to make sure that those who may seek to re-introduce it fail to do so. In a sense, this ceremony today prevents the whole sordid issue from being swept under the carpet.

As we remember Edith today, we cannot forget all those other people who were caught up in this tragedy; Edith's parents and the rest of her family, especially Avis Graydon who kept faith with Edith right up to the end of her life; Percy Thompson and his family; Freddy Bywaters and his mother and family. They too all remain in God's loving embrace. We pray that they, along with Edith, know God's eternal peace and joy and mercy in the belief that nothing can separate them or us from Him and His love.

There then followed a prayer of dedication:

Eternal God and Father, from whose love neither death or life can separate us; we dedicate this stone in the name of the Father, Son, and Holy Spirit, to the memory of Edith Jessie Thompson; in Your mercy we ask You to bless her with Your love and pray that she, with all the departed, may know the peace and joy of eternal life in fellowship with You. We ask this in the name of Jesus Christ our Lord.

During the ceremony words spoken by William Twining came into my mind. We were driving to Ilford one day when, with reference to the Home Office's refusal in 1990 to reopen the case of Edith Thompson, William told me quietly, but firmly, 'We know that Edith was innocent, and so does everybody who has ever looked at this case. That in the end matters more than symbolic acts of restitution by the Home Office.'

But if Edith's innocence is so self-evident to anyone who has read and studied the evidence, then we need to go the extra distance and secure a full pardon, particularly now that the Criminal Cases Review Commission has been set up, with the aim precisely to investigate miscarriages of justice such as this one.

The last words in this new Preface should properly belong to Edith Thompson and her mother. I found two more letters after the paperback publication of *Criminal Justice* in 1990. The letter by Edith dates from Saturday 23 December 1922, two days before her twenty-ninth birthday at Christmas, and is addressed to her aunt Edith Walkinshaw, the mother of the Leonard Walkinshaw who is referred to in the letter and on page 267. The letter by Edith's mother needs no gloss.

Holloway Prison
December 23, 1922

Dear Auntie – It was good of you to send me in the book; it will help to pass a good many weary hours away, when my mind is more settled.

At present I can't think – I can't even feel. When I was told the result of the appeal yesterday [page 265], it seemed the end of everything.

In Life, Death seems too awful to contemplate, especially when Death is the punishment for something I have not done, did not know of, either at the time or previously.

I have been looking back over my life, & wondering what it has brought me – I once said 'Only ashes and dust and bitterness', and today it seems even less than this – if there can be less.

This last ordeal seems to be the ultimate end of that gradual drifting through Life, passing each event, each disappointment, so many of which I have encountered and met with a smiling face and an aching heart. [For these two paragraphs, see Inset.]

Auntie dear, I have learnt the lesson that it is not wise to meet and try to overcome all your trials alone – when the end comes, as it has to me, nobody understands.

If only I had been able to forfeit my pride, that pride that resents pity, and talk to someone, I can see now how different things might have been, but it's too late now to rake over ashes in the hope of finding some live coal.

When I first came into this world, and you stood to me as godmother, I am sure you never anticipated such an end as this for me. Do you know, people have told me from time to time that to be born on Christmas Day was unlucky, and my answer has always been, 'Superstition is only good for ignorant people', but now I am beginning to believe that they are right; it is unlucky.

However, what is to be will be. Somewhere I read 'The fate of every man hath he bound about his neck', and this, I suppose, I must accept as mine.

I'm glad I've talked to you for a little while. I feel better – it seems to lift me out of this abyss of depression into which I have fallen, and I know you will understand, not only what I have said, but all my thoughts that are not collected enough to put on paper.

Thank Leonard for me for his letter. It made me laugh, and it's good to laugh just for five minutes. I'll write to him another day. I can't now – but I know he will understand.

EDITH

Eighteen days later, after seeing her child's body at Holloway that morning, Edith's mother wrote a letter to the press:

My daughter looked so wonderful, so peaceful; her face was white with a look of quiet rest. It is the thought of the Hereafter into which our child, still beautiful, has passed, which fortifies us in these terrible moments. She cannot have suffered; her peaceful expression re-assured us as to her innocence and tranquil end.

René Weis
University College London, 2001

Acknowledgements

I owe much to the many who have listened to my endless enquiries and who have with unfailing courtesy tried to help. Audrey Russell in particular generously shared her memories of Avis Graydon with me and gave me free access to her invaluable recordings of Edith Thompson's sister. Bill West of Ilford warmly reminisced about his time with Freddy Bywaters in Manor Park with me. He did not live to see the publication of this book in which he took a great interest. He is much missed. Myrtle Ellwood (Aldridge) worked with Edith Thompson in Aldersgate. Her wonderful memory and her kindness have been an unfailing source of encouragement. Pat Dixon entertained me one winter afternoon with stories of Manor Park in the early part of this century, as did Kenneth and Ivy Langford who spent many years in Shakespeare Crescent next door to where the Graydons had lived. To them I am indebted for authenticating the descriptions of young Bywaters's and Edith Thompson's playgrounds. Tony Chapman of the Kensington Avenue Schools accommodated my several visits there and allowed me to consult the schools' Log-book. Barry Arscott of St Barnabas, Manor Park, showed me the church's marriage register. I also profited much from conversations with John Hart of the Redbridge Library Reference Division in Ilford and I must thank the staff at that library for their helpfulness. I am grateful to Trevor Mallett from Southend-on-Sea for imparting his truly encyclopaedic knowledge of the Thompson and Bywaters case to me.

I am grateful to Cramer Music for permission to quote the lyrics of 'One Little Hour' by Leslie Cooke and Evelyn Sharpe; to Fraser &

Dunlop Scripts for allowing me to quote from Ben Travers's farce *The Dippers*; and to the estate of T. S. Eliot for granting permission to reproduce a letter first published in the *Daily Mail* in 1923. Crown-copyright material in the Public Record Office is reproduced by permission of the Controller of Her Majesty's Stationery Office.

I was fortunate to meet in D. J. T. Dally, the warden of Brookwood cemetery, an Ilfordian and a sympathetic listener. Among the Metropolitan Police I am obliged to Bill Waddell for his assistance and to Chief Superintendent Robinson of the Ilford police station for allowing me to inspect the premises where Edith Thompson and Frederick Bywaters were first kept in custody. The governor of Pentonville, Mr B. A. Marchant, saw me, and Bill Mackay gave me a guided and most informative tour of the prison precincts and cemetery.

I am grateful to the Departmental Record Office at the Home Office and particularly to Miss Mary White for allowing me privileged access to the files on Thompson and Bywaters. Her kindness and concern were only equalled by Geoffrey Gower-Kerslake's, who patiently helped me elucidate cruces in the Home Office files and checked all quotations for me with great care. I must thank H. M. Coroner, City of London, Dr D. M. Paul, for granting me permission to consult the post-mortem report on Edith Thompson in the keeping of the Record Office, Guildhall, as well as the staff at the British Library in Colindale, at the Passmore Edwards Library in East Ham and several local libraries in London and Essex for running checks on Electoral Registers for me.

I am indebted to Bonny Hughes for her expert drawing of the inside of the Thompsons' house in Ilford. Rosemary Ashton in the Department of English at University College London read the first draft of this book. I have profited greatly from discussing it with her. Andrew Gibson of Royal Holloway and Bedford New College also commented on the manuscript and preserved me from many infelicities. Dan Jacobson of University College shared his incomparable knowledge of the English language with me and caused me to rethink several important points in the book. I wish to thank my colleagues in the Department of English at University College for their forbearance during the winter of this book. I am grateful particularly to Professor Karl Miller for providing a source of inspiration over a period of years. I am thankful to Julian Evans of Hamish Hamilton for his sound advice, humanity and understanding, and to Georgia

Garrett for all her editorial work. I owe much to Professor Ross Woodman of the University of Western Ontario.

In writing the new Preface to *Criminal Justice* in 2001, I incurred a number of additional debts.

I must thank the Brookwood Cemetery Society and its dedicated members for their tireless efforts on behalf of Edith Thompson. It is a particular pleasure to pay tribute to William Twining and John Clarke, both of University College London. Edith Thompson was the victim of bigotry, and in spite of her many talents she was ultimately excluded by class and gender from a fair treatment and from justice. It seems therefore entirely fitting that three of the people who have pleaded Edith's cause over the years should be associated with University College, which was founded in the nineteenth century with the specific mission to educate those who were traditionally excluded from higher education through creed, race and gender. I take pride in the fact that University College has stayed loyal to its radical, liberal ethos, and that arguing Edith Thompson's corner from within that great institution has seemed entirely natural.

I am grateful to Lynna White for her support, and to Bill Hill for sharing his own researches on Edith Thompson with me. There are several people who helped but who prefer to remain anonymous. I want them to know how much I appreciated their forbearance and trust. I hope that the revised Preface reflects their contributions fairly.

I received a substantial amount of mail in the years after 1988. Some of my correspondents added invaluably to my understanding of the case, and almost all of them protested Edith's innocence.

I must thank Marie-Hélène Ehrke, JP, for her careful scrutiny of the book. Bill Hamilton of A.M. Heath & Co. again stood by me, and so did my editor, Andrew Kidd of Penguin Books. It was a privilege to hear the Reverend Barry Arscott during the consecration ceremony at Brookwood in 1993, and I want to express my deep gratitude to him once more. Finally, I want to thank Jean for all her support and advice.

René Weis
University College London, 2001

List of Illustrations

1. Edith as a child. (© *The British Library*)
2. A school photo of Freddy Bywaters. (*Courtesy of William West*)
3. The Kensington Avenue Schools' football eleven in 1915. (*Courtesy of William West*)
4. Bywaters and Edith's brother Bill Graydon. (*Courtesy of William West*)
5. Percy Thompson in 1916. (*Courtesy of Illustrated London News*)
6. Edith Graydon and Percy in 1914. (*Courtesy of Associated Newspapers Press*)
7. Edith Thompson in 1918. (*Courtesy of Illustrated London News*)
8. Edith Thompson's wedding day. (*Courtesy of Associated Newspapers Press*)
9. Edith in an affectionate pose with a man.
10. Edith in a light summer dress on holiday. (© *The British Library*)
11. The showroom of Carlton & Prior in 1922. (*Courtesy of Myrtle Ellwood*)
12. Edith Thompson in one of the work rooms at Carlton & Prior. (*Courtesy of John Goodwin*)
13. Photograph taken shortly before the meeting between Edith Thompson and Freddy Bywaters. (*Courtesy of Associated Newspapers Press*)
14. Bywaters's ship *Morea*. (*Courtesy of the National Maritime Museum*)
15. An early 1920s view of Kingsway. (*Courtesy of Holborn Library, Camden*)
16. The inside of the Holborn Restaurant. (*Courtesy of Holborn Library, Camden*)
17. The bronze 'hear-no-evil' monkey.
18. Edith, Percy and Norman and Lily Vellender. (*Courtesy of John Goodwin*)
19. Freddy, Edith and Percy at Southsea in 1921. (© *The British Library*)

20. Eastcote in 1921. (*Courtesy of Myrtle Ellwood*)
21. Edith, Percy Thompson and Newenham Graydon in the garden of 41 Kensington Gardens. (*Courtesy of Associated Newspapers Press*)
22. Freddy Bywaters, Edith and Percy Thompson. (*Courtesy of Associated Newspapers Press*)
23. Freddy Bywaters, Percy and Edith Thompson. (*Courtesy of Popperfoto*)
24. Eastcote in 1922. (*Courtesy of Myrtle Ellwood*)
25. Edith at Eastcote in 1922. (*Courtesy of Myrtle Ellwood*)
26. Edith and Percy Thompson, with Lily Vellender, at Eastcote, 1922. (*Courtesy of Myrtle Ellwood*)
27. Edith in a three-legged race at Eastcote. (*Courtesy of Myrtle Ellwood*)
28. The last photo of Percy and Edith Thompson together.
29. Edith Thompson in her garden. (© *The British Library*)
30. The Thompsons' home the day after the murder.
31. Edith Thompson arriving at the Old Bailey on the first day of the trial.
32. Edith's father, her sister Avis, her brother Newenham and her mother photographed within a day or two of Edith's death sentence. (© *The British Library*)
33. Edith's parents reading telegrams of sympathy and support. (© *The British Library*)
34. Edith's longhand, showing an extract from her newly discovered letter.
35. The scene of the murder in 1987.

Cast of Main Characters

The Graydons and family

Edith Jessie Thompson (née Graydon)
Ethel J. Liles and William E. Graydon — Edith's parents
Avis Ethel — Edith's sister
Newenham, Bill and Harold — Edith's brothers
Edith Liles-Walkinshaw and Lily Liles-Laxton — Edith's aunts

The Thompsons and family

Percy Thompson
Richard Halliday — Percy's brother
Lily and Maggie — Percy's sisters
Kenneth Chambers — Lily Thompson's husband

The Bywaters family

Frederick Edward Francis Bywaters
Lilian — Freddy's mother
Lilian Bywaters-Willie — Freddy's elder sister
Florence — Freddy's younger sister
Frankie — Freddy's kid brother

Friends and acquaintances

in alphabetical order:
Reg and Bessie Akam, close friends of the Thompsons

Myrtle Aldridge, worked with Edith Thompson
The Birnages, Ilford friends of the Thompsons
Ida Burton, acquaintance of Edith Thompson's
Herbert Carlton, Edith Thompson's employer
Mr Derry, an acquaintance of Edith Thompson's
Rose Jacobs, worked at Carlton & Prior in the showroom
The Lesters, the Thompsons' tenants
H. McCollin Warren, Edith Thompson's dance instructor
The Mannings, friends of the Graydons
Mel, an acquaintance of Edith Thompson's
Molly, an Ilford girl
Miss E. Prior, junior partner in Carlton & Prior
Harry Renton, childhood friend of Edith Thompson's
Lily and Norman Vellender, close friends of the Thompsons
Ethel Vernon, friend of Edith Thompson's from St Ives
Dr Preston Wallis, the Graydons' doctor in Manor Park
Bill West, childhood friend of Freddy Bywaters

Others

in alphabetical order:

Sir John Anderson, Permanent Undersecretary of State, Home Office
Sir Ernley Blackwell, Legal Assistant Undersecretary of State, Home Office
Major W. Blake, governor of Pentonville
William C. Bridgeman, Home Secretary in Bonar Law's cabinet
Sir Henry Curtis-Bennett, leading the defence for Edith Thompson
Francis Hall, inspector of police
Sir Thomas Inskip, leading for the Crown
Dr J. H. Morton, governor of Holloway Prison
Rev. S. R. Glanvill Murray, senior chaplain at Holloway
Canon Palmer, Roman Catholic priest from Ilford
Sir Montague Shearman, trial judge at the Old Bailey
Sir Bernard Spilsbury, senior pathologist to the Home Office
F. A. S. Stern, Edith Thompson's solicitor
F. P. Wensley, senior Scotland Yard detective
Cecil Whiteley, leading the defence for Frederick Bywaters

1

The Girl from Manor Park

For William and Ethel Graydon the last weeks of Advent 1893 proved a time of anxious and excited anticipation. Their first baby was due any moment, and the signs were that it would come on Christmas day. 97 Norfolk Road, the little terraced house in Dalston where they lived, could barely contain the bustle of activity.

Ethel Graydon was born Ethel Jessie Liles of Sidney Villa, Stamford Hill, on 17 December 1872. Her father was police constable Alfred Cooper Liles. In those days he had been a strong man. Now, retired and diagnosed consumptive, he and his wife Deborah planned to retire permanently to the country after their daughter's marriage. But with the young couple's setting up home in Norfolk Road and the rapid announcement of Ethel's pregnancy in early April, the parents had remained at 16 Osterley Road from where, just over a year earlier, Ethel had left as a bride. Like all the Liles women, Ethel was tall and handsome, with a finely shaped, slightly oval face which in middle age would yield an impression of restrained and melancholic severity.

If she lacked the quite remarkable beauty of her elder sister Edith, her proud and lively carriage and her intelligent determination to move up in the world made her a much sought-after bride in the neighbourhood. This had not been lost on William Eustace Graydon, the wiry and dynamic young man from 16 Dalston Lane. He was born in 1867, the son of an engineer. At the age of twenty-five on his wedding day, he was well established as a clerk with the Imperial Tobacco Company. Among the things which had impressed Miss Liles about him, he was also a superb dancer.

*

On Monday 25 December, a mild and wet day, the baby arrived. It was a girl. They christened her Edith Jessie, after her aunt Edith and her mother's middle name 'Jessie'. In January she would be baptised at St John's, Mare Street. As the proud parents and happy relatives admired her sound and healthy looks, it was immediately apparent that she was a Liles girl. Little Edith or, as her parents soon called her, 'Edie', took her first tentative steps outside her home in the summer and winter of 1895. A photograph taken on her second birthday shows her as a bonny toddler, thickly wrapped in an Eskimo fur coat. A twinkle of mischief lingers in her dark and deep-set eyes as she archly poses for the camera. The faintly rounded cheeks, the high forehead and the inwardly arched eyebrows on either side of a slightly too wide nose were to stay with her throughout her life.

On 24 September 1895 Edith was presented with a little sister, Avis Ethel. If she was naturally jealous of this newcomer, she quickly overcame her unease. The 'rival' could be a source of pleasure, a helpless doll to be mothered. The relationship between the two sisters would follow this pattern through adolescence into adulthood, with the elder ever more confident and enterprising than her junior.

Life at No. 97 marked a happy period for the Graydons. With two healthy daughters, a stable income and intimate ties with the larger family circle, the prospects for the future were good. Furthermore, enough was left after the bills to be put aside for a mortgage. For some time now the young couple had planned on buying their own house; more space was needed and as the family was spreading north – Lily back to Stamford Hill and Edith to Highbury – Dalston was losing its residual appeal as the focal point for the clan. It was time to move on, the more so since Ethel Graydon was once again pregnant. The couple's sights were set on Manor Park, and particularly on the new houses which were springing up all over Poets' Estate, the string of streets embedded in the bulge formed by the High Street and Shakespeare Crescent, which arches north-east from the station at East Ham. Housing here was cheap, the area was rising. It was not quite Ilford, and it lacked a Town Hall. It was short on schools, but a brand new one was projected and intended to start functioning by the end of 1901.

In the spring or late summer of 1898 the Graydons and their two daughters moved to a new home, 231 Shakespeare Crescent. The parents would live here for forty years. Newenham ('Newnie') was born at No. 231 shortly after the move, followed two years later by William ('Billie') and, in the spring of 1902, by Harold ('Towser'), the youngest in the family. The three boys were all registered in West Ham as East Ham still had no Town Hall. For the children the traffic-free streets of Manor Park became their playground. The splendid resonance of the literary street names, Shakespeare Crescent, Byron Avenue, Sheridan Road and Hathaway Crescent defined the feel of the area, of which Shakespeare Crescent was the smart residential part. Today there is little to choose between the various streets in Manor Park. The uniformly grey and tawdry look of the immediate post-World War II period has never departed. The elaborate railings of cast-iron lace work which once adorned the Crescent were swallowed by the war effort and never replaced. Gone too are the laburnum trees which once blossomed here, huddled between sturdy planes and craning gaslights. The rolling music of the barrel organ and occasionally the organ grinder's monkey were familiar sounds and sights, as were the winkle man on Sunday afternoons and the muffin lady who travelled from door to door in the winter. The postman always called three times daily, and seven cream and jam slices bought at the baker's on top of Ruskin Avenue cost sixpence the lot. The rag lady came every day, as did the horse-drawn milk carts. Coal delivery was weekly. Everyone knew the names of the grocer, the tobacconist, the baker, the newspaper lady and the doctor.

231 Shakespeare Crescent was a terraced building with three bedrooms, cellar and loft. The main parlour opened on the Crescent and the Graydons' bedroom ran over it. The girls shared the room at the back, or else the middle room over the scullery. The view from either took in the sheds and gardens beyond the embankment, and the conservatories and outdoor lavatories of the drab backs of Chesterford Road some sixty yards off. One of the clinching factors in the Graydons' decision to purchase No. 231 may have been the prospect of a deep, if narrow, garden for their children to play in. They were not prosperous, but the little red-brick villa which they acquired was home, and it was comfortable.

Edith was now five years old and about to start kindergarten in Manor Park. It was at the meetings of the Sunday school at St Barnabas in Manor Park that she met 'Bessie', who would romp through childhood and school into adolescence with her. As the nineteenth century was closing, Britain and her empire had for two generations seemed untouchable. The new century, however, augured otherwise. In southern Africa the Boer War had ignited, but as yet had failed to make *The Times* headlines. The terrible conflagration which was to plunge Europe and Britain into a new age, in the troglodyte world of Flanders and Picardy, was fourteen years off in the future. In the meantime, the first year of the twentieth century presented Edith with a further brother, named William Eustace after his father.

The following year a momentous event for all the people of Manor Park took place. In the morning of Monday 26 August 1901 Miss Fanny Florence Ketcher, Head Teacher, entered the following sentence in LOG BOOK NO. 1, in neat handwriting: 'Today, the Kensington Avenue Schools are open for the purpose of admitting new children and arranging the stock and apparatus.' By Friday 30 August she recorded that '205 children have had their names entered on the books this week'. The newly completed school was the talk of the neighbourhood. Miss Ketcher was an inspired choice to head the schools. By the time Edith and her sister Avis attended at Kensington Avenue in 1905, Miss Ketcher commanded a staff of seventeen teachers and an estimated five hundred scholars. Along with her playmates from the kindergarten and Sunday school, little Edith witnessed the opening ceremony of the formidable looking building, whose twin bell-towers to this day lord it over an area without high-rise blocks of flats.

Edith Graydon was now an eight-year-old tomboy with a shock of auburn-red hair and a knack of getting her way. A contemporary described her as 'slight and reedy of figure, with supple body and pale dark-eyed face, and dark hair ... vivacious, quick-witted, and insinuating in manner'. It was at about this time that she ran into the mercurial Dr Preston Wallis whose surgery was conveniently sited at the intersection between the Crescent and Browning Road. Wallis was doing his visiting round when he encountered the friendly little Miss Graydon. As the family physician he greeted her cheerily, whereupon she started moaning about a tooth that had grown loose. He asked her to open up and without much ado pulled it out there and then in the middle of the road. His path and Edith's were to cross once more in twenty years' time, after he had moved from Manor Park to Lingfield in Surrey, in circumstances stranger than any fiction could supply.

Edith's brother Harold Albert was born late in the spring of 1902. The family was now complete: two girls and three boys. The youngest would be distinguished by his irrepressible appetite. His mother

4

affectionately called him 'Towser' because he 'ate like a dog'. Harold performed legendary feats on occasions like Christmas and New Year.

While Mrs Graydon was expecting Harold, a Mrs Lilian Bywaters and her somewhat younger husband Frederick Sam were preparing for the arrival of their second child at 72 Rectory Road, just round the corner from Shakespeare Crescent. The baby was born on 27 June 1902. They christened him Frederick Edward Francis, after the royalties of Europe and Great Britain, as was customary in their family. The boy was soon known at home by the names of 'Freddy' and 'Mick', and, at school, by his nickname 'Bido'. His elder sister Lilian had been born the year before. His younger sister Florence May ('Florrie') followed in 1904 and a much younger brother Frank William ('Frankie') in 1912. Unlike the Graydons, the Bywaters family had to struggle to make ends meet. The father was in employment, but the mother undertook part-time knitting and mending chores for the family to remain solvent. The smartly dressed and pert little Edith Graydon would not have cared even to notice the Bywaterses then. As it was, the Kensington Avenue Schools brought together her brothers and Freddy Bywaters as playfellows and schoolmates.

Edith Graydon was in her tenth year when she joined the Kensington Avenue Schools at Upper Infants level in 1903. On the day she left, 20 April 1909, she was aged fifteen years, three months and twenty-seven days. During this period, the school experienced its share of routine triumphs, human minidramas, excursions, inspections, festivals, vacations and visits from pompous officialdom. Because of its excellence it suffered from overcrowding, unlike its rivals on Monega Road and Essex Road. Worried by the risk of epidemics, the inspectors advised the Council to determine geographical boundaries for the school's catchment area. Infectious diseases such as measles and scarlet fever were not the Council's only worry: a memo of September 1905 recommends to the head the use of 'the Relieving Officer for relief in cases of children sent to School insufficiently fed'.

Prominent on the school's visiting agenda were the Tower of London and the Royal Mint, the National and Tate Galleries and Westminster Abbey. The scholars also paid regular visits to the public baths at East Ham and on fine days would occasionally be taken on naturalist expeditions to Wanstead Park. Edith Graydon was fond of these visits. She loved the outdoors and what could be more congenial than the infinite opportunities for romping about afforded by these thickly wooded and mysterious nooks and ponds. If ever the children were searching for a lost domain, they found it here in this thrilling, dark parkland redolent with echoes of the past and the sounds of herons and rooks in the surrounding elms and sycamores. The outings to Wanstead Park integrated fun and work in the best tradition. While there the children were taught to identify trees and to write short essays on them over their picnic. Edith proudly produced one of her several prize-winning essays in the park:

> I remember at school we used to have what was called a 'Reading Circle'. A Dickens book was chosen by our teacher, we read it at home, not at school, and then we each chose a character from the book and wrote a little essay on him or her, as the case might be. These essays we would all take to Wanstead Park on a Saturday afternoon: we would each read our own out loud, and then it was discussed in general.
>
> We usually took our tea to the park and made a little picnic party of it. I remember an essay I was highly commended on by the teacher. It was on 'Quilp'.

Her father's preferred essay was an imaginative little piece on a penknife which was duly honoured by the award of a school prize.

For the parents as for the scholars Shakespeare Day marked an unusual occasion. The school timetable for 23 April 1906 for example, when both Edith and Avis Graydon were present, stipulated that 'ordinary lessons have been suspended'. Instead the time was spent as follows:

11 am– 12 noon	Lessons on St George and 'Good old England'
2 pm – 3.30 pm	Lessons on Shakespeare and his works
3.30 – 4.15 pm	Long Play

Invariably Shakespeare Day produced recitations held at the weekend to which the parents were welcome. Edith appeared in two such recitative performances. Her first part was as a 'quaintly dignified little' Hippolyta in an excerpted school recitation from *A Midsummer Night's Dream*. Hippolyta's part in the play is important but curtailed. Replying to Theseus' rational and sceptical dismissal of the imaginative metamorphic power of love, she states:

> But all the story of the night told over,
> And all their minds transfigur'd so together,
> More witnesseth than fancy's images
> And grows to something of great constancy;
> But, howsoever, strange and admirable.

6

If any lines of Hippolyta's in the play deserve close attention for the purpose of a dramatic recitation, it is these. In Shakespeare's fiction and, in this case, in the life of the child-actress, 'fancy's images' extend a very real challenge to the comprehension of reason. Many years later, on Friday 17 March 1922, Edith Thompson wrote:

> We ourselves die & live in the books we read while we are reading them & then when we have finished, the books die and we live – or exist – just drag on thro years & years, until when? – who knows – I'm beginning to think no one does – no not even you & I, we are not the shapers of our destinies.

Little Edith Graydon may still have been in the Infants Department when she played Hippolyta. She must have been well into the elementary curriculum by the time she acted or recited the hugely demanding part of Portia in *The Merchant of Venice*. Her reportedly memorable delivery of the lines on the unstrained 'quality of mercy' left her with a life-long affection for the stage. Soon after leaving the school she was to be on the stage again. In fact Edith Graydon acted in amateur theatricals almost continuously from 1905 to 1913.

If Edith's progress at school was distinguished by sparks of imaginative composition and theatrical excellence, her academic record seems more varied. Thus on 6 March 1906 she is listed along with thirty-five of her contemporaries who all won medals in the calendar year 1905. Like several of her peers, she fails to make the Honours chart for the second-year class of 1906 (which shows her younger sister as a first-year medallist), nor is she mentioned 'for special consideration being away on account of epidemic'. That Edith may nevertheless have fallen a victim to the scarlet fever epidemic which caused serious concern during the latter half of 1906 is indicated by the fact that she didn't make the grade at all; for the Honours of 1907 she and Avis, in the company of fifteen other girls, appear as *second* years. The unusually high casualty rate among otherwise demonstrably able candidates points to the disruptive effect of illness rather than delinquency.

During her years at kindergarten and subsequently school, from 1900 to 1909, Edith's home life was comparatively untroubled. As the oldest child in the family she assisted her mother in the arduous task of looking after three little boys, the youngest of whom was still only a toddler when she reached puberty. She discharged her duties good-humouredly. The boys looked up to their big sister who of necessity had developed a way with children early on. Above all she was a popular schoolgirl with an attendant posse of female friends. Consequently 231 Shakespeare Crescent was frequently resorted to after school for a mug of tea, hot chocolate, or a bun. Her parents were known to be welcoming. Christmas, always a special treat, was even more so for Edith Graydon; and as her friends multiplied and she grew older her parents generously treated her to a yearly party. Snap-Dragon was one of her favourite games as were the endless contests of Hunt-the-Slipper and Blind Man's Buff. She excelled at charades and instructed the younger children in this favourite Christmas pastime.

Well before leaving school and starting work Edith Graydon had become an accomplished dancer. As improvised bands were springing up at virtually every street corner and swamping the big music-halls, the small pubs, and the tiny gazebos and bandstand kiosks of the metropolis, popular dancing at last caught up with the formal and widely practised Viennese dances, particularly the waltz. From their first year in the Crescent, and possibly before, Edith's father had known H. McCollin Warren of Hollington Road, West Ham. Warren and eventually his two sons ran a well advertised dance academy in the Assembly Rooms at 1 Holme Road. Mr Graydon helped out at the Academy till the two boys were of age; and it may have been Warren who secured a job as part-time instructor at the Cripplegate Institute for his friend Bill Graydon which in turn led to the post of occasional Master of Ceremonies at the Savoy in the Strand. Warren was certainly impressed by the eldest Graydon girl's remarkable and precocious facility and took her on. By the time she was sixteen, Edith was an indispensable help to her father at the Cripplegate; and Avis would join them before too long.

At about the same time as Edith transferred from Infants to Elementary school, a family called Thompson, in search of better living standards moved up from cramped quarters in the swampy and insalubrious dockland into Manor Park. There was a widowed mother, two teenage sons and two daughters. Twenty-five years earlier the parents had arrived in London when the father, a master mariner, found employment in the merchant navy. The precipitate arrival of four children in the 1890s kept the family's budget always tilting to the red, in spite of the father's quite reasonable salary. Then he was fatally injured on duty and left a family scarcely provided for by a widow's meagre pension. The mother bravely shouldered this new found responsibility. How she coped, whether by dint of washing and scouring floors, or cleaning in a local seamen's home, is impossible to establish. It must have been very hard, the more so since she was not of a sound constitution and would be an invalid before long.

Mrs. Thompson's eldest boy, Percy, stepped in as best he could. He was still at school when his father died and may have been one of the 200,000 British schoolchildren recorded in 1908 as working in odd jobs outside school hours. He was not academically inclined and would without regret leave school after reaching the compulsory minimum age of twelve. He was thirteen in 1903, in law old enough to embark on full-time adult employment. What he lacked in imagination, intellect and spirit, he supplied by a dogged determination to make a living and help his mother. Some time in 1904 he became employed with a shipping company in Bishopsgate. As another salary was now regularly flowing in, the mother could ease off. By 1907, after the eldest had been working for over a year, it was decided to move away from the river. Not long after the family's arrival at 87 Clements Road, Manor Park, the eldest son, now the head of the family, secured a new job as junior clerk with O. J. Parker & Co., shipping agents with offices also in Bishopsgate. Eventually the company moved their business premises to Peek House at 20 Eastcheap. From this it appears that Percy Thompson's adolescence in the London dockland and in East Ham was marked by a continuous struggle for subsistence. Unlike his father he had decided to make a dry living, but one nevertheless still connected with the sea.

In fact virtually all the characters in this story participate in the rhythms of the imperial trading routes from Tilbury to China, Japan and Australia. The Thompsons, the Graydons and the Bywaterses furnished the crews, sailors, pursers, stewards, writers and other non-commissioned personnel of the ocean giant companies like the Peninsular and Oriental (P & O), the White Star, Red Star, and Cunard Lines. While their men were at sea, the women were anxiously following the shipping news which every local paper carried. The land staff held the less glamorous desk jobs of junior and senior clerks. The sailors marvelled at their seeming lack of gumption; their unadventurous contentment with routine chores. Had they never heard of the *aurora borealis*, of the women who made themselves so cheekily available in every port, and of the immense longing which only the sea can feed? When Freddy Bywaters, a mere fifteen-year-old, sailed to India at the height of war in 1917 without parental consent, he acted true to his daring and reckless nature. Young Bywaters never considered that he might be in danger at sea; as a result by the time he was twenty he had been sailing all the oceans of the world for five years.

The first decade of the new century was drawing to a close. People wondered in mild surprise that the new century had come and failed to deliver either the millennium or Armageddon. There was a new king, it is true. But old, time-honoured customs, 'Victorian' as they came to be called now, were dying hard and reassured the country of its links with the traditions of the past.

When therefore two 'baby farmers'[1] were sentenced to death at the Central Criminal Court, the news did not create much of a stir. In judicial death Victorian men and women had generally been almost equal. The announcement that the executions would be a simultaneous double hanging and the first one ever at the now exclusively female prison of Holloway in Tufnell Park held however some special appeal. It was Henry A. Pierrepoint who hanged the two women, the middle-aged Annie Walters and the much younger Amelia Sach (twenty-nine) on the morning of Tuesday 3 February 1903. Sach was in an almost continuous swoon and had to be propped up on the scaffold by Pierrepoint. The prison governor and his deputy were very concerned by the state of the victims and particularly by the toll exacted on the wardresses who attended them and who came away crying from the gallows.

That same year Emily Swann was hanged at Leeds and, in August 1907, a red-haired woman in early middle age called Rhoda Willis/ Lascelles (alias Leslie James) spent an agonising death vigil in Cardiff prison. In a fit of despair she had suffocated a baby adopted for money whom she probably never intended to raise. After a respectable middle-class private education and two families by her husband and lover, Rhoda Willis had plummeted to the depths of the Cardiff slums, where she solicited till she was incapacitated by spirits. She bitterly repented of the baby's death and assumed full responsibility for her fate.

Rhoda Willis became the last woman hanged in Britain for a long time. Public sentiment was increasingly troubled by the cold-blooded judicial killing of women. Accordingly, between 1907 and 6 January 1923, successive Home Secretaries would pliantly be reprieving condemned female prisoners from the gallows. It is almost as if the killing of a woman had suddenly become un-English. It was the French

[1]'Baby farmers' were women who, for a sum of money, disposed of unwanted, and often illegitimate children by having them 'adopted' or by making them disappear.

THE GIRL FROM MANOR PARK

who shot Mata Hari and the enemy Germans who executed the field
nurse Edith Cavell. And during the war women had become an
essential asset to all the home work-forces; it was now they who
'manned' the factories.

After the war the story changed dramatically. In the 1920s
women became the nation's surplus commodity.

The big dramas of the world were not the immediate concern of the
schoolgirl from Manor Park and her peers. Little Daisy Gibson's
accident, caused by her reckless swinging round the support poles in
the school's shed, or Sibyl Lammas's misadventure in the playground
which left 'a deep cut in her forehead', circumscribed the limits of the
girls' experience. Naturally they were romantic, and naturally they
were discovering sex. In the adjacent boys' school in the same building
Edith Graydon had plenty of admirers, and there were several brief
childish romances. It is likely that Edith's mother explained the facts of
life to her daughter early on, because she was needed as an assistant
parent with her little brothers.

It was probably at about this time that Edith made the acquaintance
of young Harry Renton, who in his boyish way fell in love with her.
His letters to her were filled with adolescent ardour and Edith eagerly
shared their contents with Avis. When Avis asked her finally, 'Are you
going to marry Harry?', her sister archly replied: 'Well, I might.' But
Harry remained a 'boy' to her, even after suffering a crippling injury in
the trenches. Years later Edith Thompson would still see Harry, flirt
with him and find him his flat in Moscow Court, Kensington, and be
concerned about his war wound. In her hour of need Harry, who then
was still a bachelor, would stick by her.

The spring vacation of 1909 was Edith Graydon's first complete
break from mandatory school since she had attended the little
kindergarten in 1899. Now she would need to find work. It was not
long before the increasingly attractive and bright Graydon girl secured
employment as a junior clerk with a wholesale clothiers in the City. By
the end of the year, however, she had left and moved south of the river
into Southwark with a firm of cardboard manufacturers. Here she
would also spend a brief spell only. By the middle of 1910 she was
back in the City, this time as a book-keeper with Louis London,
'Wholesale Clothing Manufacturers' in Little Alie Street, southwest of
Aldgate station. Edith's best friend Bessie worked here and was

already head clerk of the office. She may originally have prevailed on Edith to join this unattractive but respectable firm; at least it meant dealing in fashion – much more the line of the fastidious Edith – rather than in cardboard. But even this new job did not assuage Edith's restlessness. She was looking elsewhere.

Late in 1911 she presented herself at Carlton & Prior, wholesale milliners with premises situated on the north side of Barbican, not far from Aldersgate station and in view of the Manchester Hotel at the corner of Long Lane. At her interview with Mr Herbert Carlton and his partner Miss Ellen Prior, Edith performed strikingly. They were impressed by her manner and by the ease with which this ordinary girl from Manor Park in moments of animation effortlessly shed background and accent. She would be a potential buyer and she clearly understood the workings of figures and knew about book-keeping. She was taken on for a probationary period. She stayed there for the rest of her life and rose swiftly in the firm.

By the time Edith had secured a position at Carlton & Prior she had met Percy Thompson and was active in the Stepney Elocution Class.

No one knows quite how Percy Thompson and Edith Graydon met. The five extant testimonies are at variance. The fact is that in the summer and winter of 1909 Edith was for the first time commuting regularly into the City from East Ham station. As for Percy Thompson, he needed to use the District Railway from East Ham to Mile End to connect with Bishopsgate. It is therefore likely that Edith and Percy first met on the platform of East Ham station on their way to work. Their relationship – even if it did not start there – was certainly cemented during the countless waits for trains and the third-class carriage rides through the desolate tangle of points, sheds and cinder of Bromley and Bow. Still not yet sixteen years old, Edith Graydon was amused and impressed by the attentions paid her by this smart-looking and good natured nineteen-year-old boy. He spoke to her in a reassuringly firm voice, he dressed well, and earned a reasonably good salary. Among their shared interests were the theatre, the music-hall and the Sunday League concerts. She mentioned dancing excitedly, but he demurred. Physical exertions such as dancing, swimming and football were not among his favoured activities. He enjoyed singing, as did Edith. Unlike her, however, Percy was blessed with a fine light voice and, if coaxed enough, would give impromptu performances of his favourite songs, particularly 'Maire, my Girl' by George Aitken or Emilie Clarke's 'Sincerity'.

It is to be doubted that he offered recitals to Edith on the Tube in and out of East Ham. But he did propose to chaperone her out to Stepney Green to share in the Thompsons' Thespian and other activities as members of the Elocution Class at Stepney. Edith was undeniably much taken with this solid earnest boy, while he was falling in love with the shapely, vivacious and nimble-witted Miss Graydon. As Christmas neared, the two decided that they ought to introduce each other to the respective parents. Percy particularly wished to do the proper thing, and Edith's birthday was to be the pretext. With Christmas just round the corner Edith asked her parents' permission to bring Percy Thompson round and introduce him. The parents readily concurred, though they voiced surprise and some anxiety in view of Edith's extreme youth.

On Christmas Eve, Friday 24 December 1909, Percy Thompson visited 231 Shakespeare Crescent for the first time. If the father had harboured any lingering anxieties over the propriety or wisdom of this budding relationship, they were dispelled by Percy's sound appearance and frank demeanour. He overcame his customary awkwardness and briskly explained to Mr Graydon, 'between men', that he was very fond of Edith and wished to be allowed 'to continue to pay her his addresses'. Because of Edith's age there could be no question of marriage, Mr Graydon gently remonstrated. But Percy was an honourable man. He had a sense of duty and had early learned to be responsible. He would not get his girl into trouble.

On Christmas Day, again at No. 231, Percy Thompson for the first time encountered the Christmas ritual of the Graydons. There were eight partakers of the dinner in all: Mr and Mrs Graydon, Edith aged sixteen, Percy nineteen, Avis fourteen, Newenham eleven, Billie eight, Harold six. Mr Graydon rose and said grace, then he toasted 'Mater', a tribute which drew tears every year from the usually unsentimental Mrs Graydon. This was followed by 'Happy Birthday' sung to Edith. The Christmas meal consisted of sardines on toast, followed by soup, the traditional poultry, Christmas pudding, nuts and wine. The welcome extended to him here, compounded by the buoyancy of the family and the cheery spiritedness of young Edith, formed a stark contrast to Percy's own home, presided over by an invalid mother who already was jealous of the girl from Shakespeare Crescent and had urged her son to let her go. But Percy was not a man to disown his mother. Although he would never tolerate malicious talk about his flashy sweetheart, not even from the mother, he remembered the hardship of the early days after his father's death when his mother coped wholly on her own to keep the children fed and clothed. As for his siblings, it appears that Percy enjoyed the company of his sisters Lilian and Margaret, but found the morose Richard difficult.

Percy Thompson pursued his courtship of Edith Graydon by visiting No. 231 every evening. The New Year for the young couple held only promise. 1910 was the year King Edward – the 'peacemaker' – died, and almost simultaneously Edith's grandfather passed away in Speen, where the grandparents had at last retired. It was the one blot on the calendar.

With her new boyfriend and his sister Lily as escort, Edith Graydon now discovered the amateur theatricals of the Stepney New Meeting House, a Congregationalist institution in Garden Street, Stepney Green. One can assume that it was Thompson and his sister's admirer, young Kenneth Chambers, who introduced her to the Elocution Class. In 1896 Chambers's father, the Reverend Charles Chambers, had taken on the ministry of Stepney Meeting House. He accomplished his arduous task as a minister with gargantuan energy and was soon embarked on the constituting of a troupe of amateur theatricals, the self-styled 'Stepney Elocution Class'. Recitals and performances got under way in about 1904. Then, as later, the repertoire consisted of adaptations of English classics. When Edith, Percy and his sister Lily joined late in 1909 two works were scheduled for rehearsal: *The Merchant of Venice* and Sheridan's *School for Scandal*. Edith must have warmed to the task of an adult recital performance of *The Merchant of Venice* and particularly to the prospect of herself in the role of Portia again. The big night, Saturday 9 April 1910, failed however to deliver stardom to its sanguine cast; the characters lacked life and were not imaginatively credible. Empathy and dramatic intelligence were conspicuously absent from the 'impersonations'. It was a chastened cast that took to the boards fourteen days later in *The School for Scandal*, this time to the accompaniment of vocal and instrumental music. This inventive move by the Reverend Chambers – who also directed and had himself adapted the play for recital – added further spark to the already finely honed performance of Percy's sister Lily as 'Lady Teazle' and Chambers's son Kenneth as 'Sir Peter Teazle'. They made a 'capital pair' and the recital was a great success, not least for its supporting cast.

Ten months later, on Saturday evening 4 February 1911, in front of 'a large and appreciative audience', the Stepney Elocution Class gave a costume rendition of *A Christmas Carol* in accordance 'with an original rendering' once again by the director of the class. The piano on this occasion was manned by a Mr Lewis Haskins and the cast of twenty-one included one Charles W. Stormont, Edith and Percy, Lily Thompson and Kenneth and Victor Chambers. 1911 may have been a particularly hectic year for, in the summer probably, the Elocutionists put on a dramatic recital of *A Midsummer Night's Dream*. Edith played her old part of Hippolyta, Percy was Starveling and C. W. Stormont was Snout. One surmises that the talented Lily Thompson would have played Titania to Chambers's Oberon and that the director himself would have cherished the role of Theseus. Charles Stormont remembered the productions with great fondness, and sixty years later took a dubious pride in the fame subsequently won by some members of the cast.

On occasions this jolly and carefree crowd of Thespians would adjourn to the Graydons' home for a little whist drive, singing at the piano, and supper. Mrs Graydon and Avis, with some help from Edith, would prepare mashed potatoes and a vegetable to accompany tinned pink salmon, costing all of sixpence, and a sweet. For the fifteen-year-old Avis these occasions were particularly memorable. She relished attending the performances at the Stepney Meeting House and thought her sister and her friends were awfully clever and brave. She was so shy that it would have been inconceivable for her to act on any stage. Meeting part of the cast at home therefore was a treat and a privilege. It also appealed to her romantic temper and she would look her best when her big sister's friends visited.

The following year, on Saturday 3 February 1912, the Elocution Class gave what an enthusiastic reviewer described as 'a highly creditable costume recital of "The Mysteries of Silas Marner"', which 'held the audience in rapt attention throughout'. The by now familiar figures were in attendance and the star parts in the adaption of George Eliot's masterpiece were probably taken by Lily Thompson and the flamboyant Chambers, while Edith and Percy would be in relatively minor roles.

Edith may have faintly resented Lily's undeniably superior theatrical talents; and she may have turned up her nose at the budding romance between Kenneth and Lily. In her nineteenth year now, she held a secure position at Carlton & Prior in the Barbican, with exciting prospects, including the tantalising thought of a trip to Paris. Her life was developing, and it was time to withdraw from this once heady, but now increasingly burdensome part of her experience with Percy in tow.

1913 brought Edith Graydon the incomparable reward of a trip to Paris in full recognition by Carlton & Prior of her exceptional taste in clothes and hat fashions. As Percy saw off his increasingly blossoming sweetheart at Victoria Station he may have wondered whether she would ever accept his pleas to become his wife. She was now earning more than her father and had overtaken her lover. She had furthermore attracted her employer's favour. Mr Herbert Carlton of Thorpe Bay, Westcliff, had always been a lady's man. With a shop full of girls, mostly in temporary apprentice work, and with his wife resigned to the spinsterish existence of minding the 'other' place in Hamlet Court Road in Westcliff, the Barbican establishment was a bachelor boys' paradise. The elegant Miss Graydon floated in like a gift: witty, astute, handsome, well spoken and never averse to a little flirtation. Her adeptness at accountancy quickly reconciled her to the 'dragon', the stern Miss Prior. As Carlton's junior partner with a large share in the business, Miss Prior could be depended on to police the morals of the firm. Though her left hand was missing and she wore a wooden one which was permanently gloved, Miss Prior would tie a parcel as neatly and as expeditiously as the next person. The girls dreaded her. They found a precarious revenge in the sure knowledge that although Miss Prior carefully chose her expensive underwear at Debenham & Freebody, no *man* was ever likely to see it. If Miss Prior harboured suspicions about Edith and Mr Carlton, she kept them to herself, of necessity indulgent of middle-aged male folly.

In preparation for her trip to Paris, Edith crammed her way through French primers and novels. Always an avid reader, she now positively sated herself as far as her acquaintance with the language would allow. She did not fail to notice the degree of 'licence' in such works as she read. Far from objecting to it, she relished their bolder portrayal of passion. Certainly her command of French grew to be quite competent. Her leaving and her homecoming filled 231 Shakespeare Crescent with justified pride. The girl from Manor Park was returned from the magical pleasure haunt of the Edwardian era, Paris. Almost overnight the young Miss Graydon found herself famous in her neighbourhood.

Late in 1913 or early in 1914 Edith was back in Paris to inspect the spring fashions and to buy for Carlton & Prior. As she strolled through the boulevards redolent still of the *Belle Époque*, the young 'Anglaise' with the lilting East London pronunciation of French would be no more than an object of passing curiosity. What in the end she made of Paris is not recorded. What is known is that her selection of French patterns and models aroused huge enthusiasm and warm congratulations again from Carlton & Prior. Percy and she now decided to go on holiday. Together with their friends Reg and Bessie they picked Ilfracombe. This was to be for June.

Even as they were planning their holiday the clouds of an all-out European war were gathering. The spark that ignited the conflagration was struck on 28 June 1914 when Gavrilo Princip assassinated the Habsburg heir to the throne. The four-year carnage would leave behind a radically redesigned European map and signal the terminal struggle of the imperial power balance on the Continent and overseas. The four weeks of June 1914 therefore emphatically belong to a world of the past. In this 'past' world Edith and Percy set off for Devon. The lovers were hardly ever separated, whether in Ilfracombe, or on day trips to Cardiff and Westward Ho. It was in Ilfracombe that Edith Graydon and Percy Thompson became lovers. It would now be that much harder for her to hold out against marriage to a man to whom she had given her virginity.

When the four of them returned home at the end of June, Freddy Bywaters was a few days short of his twelfth birthday. He had entered Kensington Avenue Infants school at the age of five. Another little boy who had just been enrolled at Kensington Avenue school was Bill West, friendly, affectionate, and shy. The two boys quickly became fast friends. Unity conferred strength, particularly against the boys of the rival Essex Road school in Sheridan Avenue. They were notoriously vicious and often tried to waylay the smarter Kensington Avenue scholars on the Browning bridge. Bill West was not a fighter, but nothing deterred Bywaters, slight though he was as a child. An eyewitness account of one such encounter in 1915 has survived through Pat Dixon, formerly a pupil at the rougher Essex Road school whose charges, unlike their rivals, had no caps and no badges. At the time of the incident Pat Dixon was about nine years old, while Bywaters and

Bill West were aged thirteen. The champion of the Essex Road boys was one Lawt, a bit slow, but 'a big fella'. Whether they waited for Freddy because of a chance remark during the weekend's football fixture out on Wanstead Flats, or whether Bywaters had unguardedly challenged the others to obstruct his way, the fact is that they blocked his passage at the corner of the Browning Road, just off the bridge. He would have to fight Lawt or be licked by the whole gang. Freddy agreed to fight. A human circle was formed and the two boys braced themselves for the encounter. Within seconds, Freddy, fast, tough and wiry, had 'chopped poor old Lawt to pieces', to the horror of the Essex Road scholars and the delight of the Kensington Avenuers who were beginning to catch up with the crowd at this point. In good if grudging sportmanship, the circle yielded a wholly untouched Freddy. Holding his head high, the hero of the day, he crossed over the bridge. A mortified Lawt, with his nose bleeding and 'bunged up', was in tears and vowed revenge as his mates supported him on the way to the school's washrooms. Recalling the incident seventy-two years later, Pat Dixon chuckled and commented about Bywaters 'I am certain his father must have shown him how to use his mits!' He remembered the smart-looking boy and his 'fair wavy hair' with affection and sorrow.

Freddy Bywaters's favourite novel was *Tom Brown's Schooldays*. A Tom Brownish mixture of childish mischief, high spirits and adult responses early on made up Freddy's characteristic identity. Notwithstanding an originally delicate constitution, he quickly built up strength and made friends easily, both at school and in the streets of Manor Park. He teamed up with Bill West, Bill and Harold Graydon and others. While in the Infants division Freddy was frequently visited between lessons by his mother who took him milk and cake and ensured that he wore his boots when it rained, though the family home at Rectory Road was not always idyllic. The father would rant and rage against the world in the children's presence. On one occasion he even fired a gun through the ceiling.

As he progressed from Infants to Elementary and was approaching his tenth birthday, Freddy was picking up well at school. It is wholly in character that his best essay should have been on the subject of 'Kindness to Dumb Animals'. His writing was now greatly improved. It is with the utmost pride that he wore the school colours, the Kensington Avenue ties and the fashionable Eton collar. Above all he was faithful to the school's motto of 'What I do, I do well'. If to his friends his increasingly daring exploits and athletic prowess made him into a 'born leader', the trust of his teachers in him is reflected not least in the caretaker delegating to him the prompt ringing of the school bell which marked the rounding up for the start of classes and also functioned indirectly as the area's alarm clock. If it were late dozens if not hundreds of commuters would miss their train from East Ham Station into the City.

Outside school Freddy Bywaters, Bill West and Bill Graydon gathered to cycle, swim and play football. By the time they were ten the boys all owned bikes and could cycle out to East Ham Central Park or to Valentine's Park in Ilford. Unlike young West and Bywaters, Bill Graydon was held rather more tightly in check. If the boys called at No. 231 at an awkward time for school – too early perhaps, with a view to a few pre-class pranks – Mrs Graydon would sternly put her foot down: 'I send my son to school when I see fit. Now run along boys.' On these rare occasions which never deterred the callers, Bill would later explain apologetically that it was 'one of those days, you know'. In general the parents were indulgent, and life in the Crescent under the circumstances shaped up ideally for the children, whether they were chestnut-hunting or cycling, swimming or playing Can-Copper. Open spaces were ever close by. Swimming in the East Ham baths was partly a curricular activity under the auspices of the school. On such occasions young Bywaters was dazzling. He would as easily plunge down from the highest diving board as others would from the side of the pool. The excitement of Valentine's Park was of a different order. The boys would assemble near the Browning bridge in the crisp hours of the early morning before 7a.m., and then cycle across to the park, where gossamer racks of mist were floating in still silence on the lake and even the summer water was chilly. They stripped to their trunks under the clock tower and went in.

Bill West's protestations about swimming in water *that* cold were never of much avail against his friend's willpower. During these blessed hours of solitary and unadulterated fun, 'Taffy' West, as Bido had nicknamed him, grew to admire the much more dynamic boy. More than seventy years on, he recalled those far-off days and noted sadly about Freddy Bywaters:

> He was a hero to me. I asked him about my homework and he'd treat me with scorn: 'You don't know *that*!' . . . I looked up to him, but he was so *kind* . . . what I thought of Freddy – it doesn't mean that he thought anything of me. My appreciation is the greater because I didn't have the qualities which he possessed. . . . He was such a force to me which I would say exists to this day.

As much as swimming, football was one of Freddy Bywaters's master passions. The boys, it appears, played for the school's honour as much as for their own eleven on Wanstead Flats. Every participant during these encounters dreamed of playing for West Ham one day. Freddy played a reputedly tough game, and a contemporary photo taken of the team in 1914–15 shows him proudly in the midst of his peers.

The boys did not always play on the Flats. Sometimes they would cross over Landser Road to the nearby Little Ilford Park or the Sports Grounds north of Church Road. The insalubrious River Roding flowed very close to the east of the houses here. Parents were not happy to let their children loose in this area, partly because of the river and partly through the proximity of Walton and Parkhurst Roads, infamous as the roughest and poorest in Manor Park. To the outside observer the children romping about in Little Ilford Park or the adjacent sportsground would have seemed indistinguishable. The children themselves were already uncannily attuned to fine social and geographical shadings. The Graydon boys never ventured here without parental consent. Freddy did so, and so did others who spent their childhood on the east side of the Browning bridge. One very particular little boy played here all his life. He had grown up in Walton Road. He was daring to a degree, like young Bywaters with whom he may well have exchanged courtesies, insults, marbles or footballs. Like Bywaters's, his name would soon hit the headlines. It would be in his death, for exceptional bravery, on 31 May 1916 during the Battle of Jutland, that John T. Cornwell – known to this day throughout East London by the name of 'Jacky Cornwell the boy VC' – at the age of sixteen became the country's youngest carrier of the Victoria Cross. His memory is today honoured in Manor Park by Jack Cornwell Street, which lies adjacent to his childhood home.

When young Bywaters left school at the early age of thirteen, after completing the curriculum, his father had already enlisted in the Royal Field Artillery and had been shipped to France. The year was 1916. Released from school in the spring, Freddy at once became employed as an office boy with the shipping firm of Charles Howard in Leadenhall Street. Within a few months, now aged fourteen, he transferred to a more challenging post with Van Hopplers, still in shipping and still in the City. During this period he kept in touch, though only erratically, with his old schoolfriends. He knew of Bill Graydon's elder sister's marriage and very occasionally ran into her in

Shakespeare Crescent. She didn't take any notice of the flashy young boy who three years before had bravely tried to attract her notice by offering her a sprig of flowers. She had then thought him very 'sweet' and had kindly foreborne to tease him about it in the company of adults. The incident had long since been forgotten, and it is to be doubted that she as much as recognised him on the crowded East Ham station platform when she was travelling to work either in her father's company, her sister's, or her husband's.

On 13 June 1917 Freddy was standing outside Baltic House in Leadenhall Street. He had just parted from an acquaintance and was heading for Mark Lane, unaware of the huge fleet of Gothas which had been steering its course inland and was about to disgorge its deadly load on the capital. Leadenhall Street took a direct hit. The blast instantly killed the friend whom Bywaters had left and floored the boy himself. Momentarily shell-shocked, he came round quickly. Wholly oblivious of his own safety, he started to run across Mansion Square and up to Aldersgate and Bartholomew Close. His sister 'Nellie' worked here. He found her safe and, after the raid was over, took her home to an anxious parent. Although Manor Park and Ilford were taking their share of Gotha and Zeppelin raids, they were never exposed to the fierce aerial punishment visited upon the City that afternoon. Even so the rumbling from the Northern European front was sometimes audible in London and rationing had come in early in 1917. By proxy the war was everywhere.

Freddy thought he ought to be in the thick of it. Jacky Cornwell was his hero and the sea was beckoning. Throughout the summer and autumn of 1917 he tried hard to join the merchant navy convoys. His first successful attempt at securing a position was thwarted by his mother, who blocked it by officially notifying the ship's purser of her intention to withhold parental consent, on the grounds that since 1 February 1917 Germany had been committed to 'unrestricted submarine warfare' against Britain. Stubborn as ever, Bywaters persisted. On 11 February 1918 he was taken on by the P & O, who for four days employed him in desk work at the Royal Albert Docks. On 15 February 1918, aged fifteen years and seven months, after signing a statement that he took up his duties as a writer in the full knowledge of the dangers to shipping at sea for a country at war, Freddy set sail. The ship was the P & O troop carrier *Nellore* bound for India. His mother was completely ignorant of his whereabouts.

The return journey took three months during which Freddy, for the first time in his life, encountered the wonders and dangers of the sea. Repeatedly the *Nellore* had to outmanoeuvre enemy craft and submarines. Unperturbed the boy writer and laundry steward carried out his duties and easily made friends with the troops. He told them about his father who landed in Salonika in 1915, survived the Somme in 1916 and, with the Royal Field Artillery, had moved through Egypt into Palestine. Freddy's assured gregariousness and his boyish delight at everything new, from cards to uninhibited men's talk and the sheer magic of exotic tales and places, easily recruited friends. These friends were real men! For the precocious writer of the P & O, the world would never be the same again.

One day in mid-May Freddy knocked on his mother's door in Rectory Road. The prodigal, tanned and fairer and fitter than ever, was home at last. For his prolonged absence parental forgiveness was promptly forthcoming, but if his mother hoped that he would now stick the rest of the war out at home, she was deluded: 'Surely you have had enough of it by this time' – 'Not a bit of it, Mum. I am going away again.' And so he did.

His father likewise could not be made to stay at home. He was gassed in France in 1918 and was sent to England to convalesce in a hospital. Restless, and against doctor's advice, he returned to France to witness the end. He developed a haemorrhage of the lungs on arrival and was forced back to England and again hospitalised. Freddy saw his father before leaving for China early in 1919. On 1 March Frederick Sam Bywaters died from a severe haemorrhage at Eggington Hall, Derby. His mother cabled the news to China to await Fred's arrival there. In his reply he comforted her and promised to the best of his ability to make up for the dead father. His own sorrow he nursed in private.

Home in the spring of 1919 he and his mother considered their next move, now that there was no resident breadwinner and Freddy's salary was not nearly adequate to feed and clothe the family. It was decided that the girls would do knitting and cleaning tasks up in the West End, while the mother was to set up shop as a 'costumier' in Upper Norwood, at 11 Westow Street, where there were modest shop premises. Property was considerably cheaper in Norwood than in Manor Park, as Mrs Bywaters knew from visiting relatives 'down south'. They would sell the house in Rectory Road. The profits accruing from that ought to defray the cost of buying the cottage in

Westow Street as well as a minimum stock of materials. The arrangement was to work remarkably well. In September 1919 the Bywaters family moved to Upper Norwood. For Freddy this seemed to signal the break with his boyhood past. All his friends were now working; Billie and Harold Graydon, like himself, had entered the merchant navy. So had Taffy West. The boys' leaves rarely coincided. Now that his family had moved south Freddy no longer had a base in East Ham. That he might miss the streets of his childhood and their inhabitants never struck him in the heady days of 1917 and 1918, the years of his first major voyages. In the end it was to be both sentiment and convenience that would bring him back here.

When Edith Graydon lost her virginity in Ilfracombe she did so in the knowledge that she was probably giving herself to her future husband. The abandon of the Ilfracombe days was rudely checked by the events of the summer. Already for Edith other considerations were troubling her. She was earning very well now at Carlton & Prior, and met increasingly sophisticated people, whom she charmed with her personality as much as with her ready knowledge of the latest French fashions. Partly as a consequence of this, she was getting profoundly restless. The inevitable confinement to the single partner in love was proving unusually difficult, and she was beginning to wonder about Percy's and her temperamental compatibility: he so stolid, broody, morose at times and unadventurous; she the exact opposite. Her love of dancing, her need for male and female company, her smartness and shrewdness, these could not forever be repressed or adjusted for Percy's sake. Further-more, once her initial curiosity about sex had been gratified, she was disappointed that it should have developed so quickly into a routine. Percy was not very imaginative, if at times ardent. He seemed not to tire of finding her body intriguing and exciting, which puzzled her. She, on the other hand, found male sexuality totally lacking in mystery. Her girlhood dreams, pure and impure, had been of a great love. This she had failed to discover. Though Percy was fascinated by Edith's physical appearance and grateful for her forbearance, he could not bring her out. This was no fault of his, and she did not resent him for it.

At 231 Shakespeare Crescent Edith and Percy would take over the front parlour for their courting, while the parents used the back room and the kitchen. Her mother would instruct Avis to 'go into the front room and say good evening to Mr Thompson. Don't stay. Come out here'. By 1915 this ritual may have been abandoned, but it is indicative of the decorum which then applied to respectable unmarried couples. Whenever it became quiet in the front room, Mrs Graydon would take it upon herself to 'pop in to see if everything was all right', just in case. If the mother guessed that Edith was sexually active she kept it to herself. She preferred not to know since, like her husband and her other daughter, she felt a slight disquiet about the prolonged courtship. Four years was usual in those days for young couples to prepare for the life-long commitment of marriage. This was Edith's and Percy's sixth year. The mother sensed her eldest daughter's reticence. Was Percy really the right man for her? Of course there was the war to consider and the sheer scale of the numbers of young men swallowed up in the mud massacres of France and Belgium. If this did not clinch the case for Percy's eligibility, it was a contributory factor. On 25 December 1915 Edith was twenty-two years old and became engaged to Percy Thompson. Notwithstanding the shadows cast by the war and Edith's unease about the whole business, the engagement created its own special aura. The big event was planned for 15 January 1916; in three weeks' time Edith Graydon would become Edith Thompson. Right now she slipped on the splendid five-stone diamond ring presented to his fiancée by Percy, while he admired the silver cigarette case and gold ring that she had given him. The young couple spent a happy as well as anxious Christmas together. Anxious they were, because it was almost certain that conscription would be introduced early in the New Year. The press had been agitating about the 650,000 'slackers' – of whom Percy was one – and claimed that they shamed their country and the brave men overseas. On Wednesday 5 January 1916 Asquith introduced the Government's Compulsory Service Bill in the Commons, which passed its first stage on the following day.

Saturday 15 January 1916: Throughout most of Friday night Mrs Graydon, her sisters, friends and relatives have been baking, cooking and cleaning. Upstairs the bride for the last time prepares to share a bedroom with her sister. Tomorrow she will become Mrs Edith Thompson. Before the two young women settle into bed, they hug each other tightly. For nineteen years they have shared every secret.

The inevitable morning dawns shortly after 8 a.m. Edith never liked chill January mornings, when the wan light of day seemed reluctant and joyless. There is just enough time for a quick dress rehearsal before the wedding guests arrive to express their good wishes. In small groups they proceed to St Barnabas on foot. Edith is to be driven there, led by her father, and accompanied by her mother and sister. The boys and, if he is home, the soldier brother, are waiting in St Barnabas, where the choir goes through an improvised review of their programme for the ceremony. The service is scheduled for noon.

Edith and Avis, as her only bridesmaid, are sitting on the bed in their room. The house is nearly empty. Edith is still pinning a huge bunch of artificial Parma violets on her sister when Mr Graydon comes up from the staircase and says to her: 'Come along, they are waiting for you.' The 'they' means the hired car. Edith panics and says: 'I, I can't go through with it, I don't want to go. . . .' Her father stares at her aghast for a second. Then, soothing her, he gently but firmly replies: 'Oh, you must . . . everybody is at the church waiting for you. . . .' Avis is concerned and impressed by her sister's manifest discomfort. She reaches out to press her hand and proceeds downstairs. Edith follows almost immediately. The moment she steps out of their little cottage, in full view of the neighbourhood, Edith unprompted straightens up. From the gathered crowd there are murmurs of approval of the sheer elegance of the bride. Dressed in some of the most stylish fabrics available in the West End in a war-time city, Edith looks truly a daughter of the house of Liles. All of her five foot seven and a quarter proudly erect, taller than her father on whose arm she is leaning, she smiles as she eases herself into the open car. As it slowly proceeds up through Rosebery Avenue Edith is transformed. She is suddenly excited about getting married. In the packed church, she is led to the altar by her father, who gives her away to Percy Thompson. Shortly after noon Edith has vowed to be Percy Thompson's wife for better or for worse and to obey him in everything. Then the couple and their witnesses adjourn to the sacristy to sign the parish register. The clerk is jittery and careless and mistakenly gives her address as 221 Shakespeare Crescent. For the last time in her life Edith signs herself officially with her maiden name 'Graydon'.

There has not been a bride quite as elegant as the Graydons' daughter in Manor Park in living memory. In her tiered, boat-necked dress with its fine embossed design, Edith Thompson cuts a splendid figure. From her hands a riot of roses tumbles down the front of her dress when she poses for a group photo next to her sister. As the crowd begins to thin and some repair to the local pubs, Edith and Percy, and Avis with Richard Thompson head the procession which winds its way back to No. 231, where some twenty invited guests crowd into the front parlour and the staircase. Champagne starts to flow, some of it provided by Mr Carlton who is at the breakfast, which consists of ample portions of beef, ham, vegetables and cake. After dinner drinks are served. Edith by now is much brighter, the soul of the party.

The atmosphere of this late January afternoon is caught perfectly in a vignette of Percy Thompson by an invited guest. Bessie is chatting with two friends in the party when up comes one of the Graydon boys and comments on Percy's teetotalism, on his wedding day no less. This produces a highly amused response from another friend in their little clique who was serving drinks earlier on. She tells them that as she passed Percy by, he stopped her and said laughing mischievously: 'Don't give it all away.' Then, leaning forward conspiratorially, he whispered: 'I'll have some whisky if you have got a coloured glass to put it in.' Hardly a duplicitous move – merely that Percy had promised Edith never to get drunk in her presence. At about 5 p.m. Edith disappears upstairs and changes into a cream blouse and a navy blue costume. A taxi comes, collects the newly wed couple and takes them to East Ham Station. From here they are to catch a through train to Westcliff and Southend-on-Sea. The honeymoon has started. While No. 231 continues to celebrate, Edith and Percy as man and wife are heading for the coast.

On Monday 17 January, in the company of Herbert Carlton, husband and wife commuted into Fenchurch Street from Westcliff. The only cloud on the horizon was Percy's imminent enlistment in the London Scottish. Even as Edith – who was to remain Miss Graydon at Carlton & Prior – resumed her duties in the Barbican, Percy was processing his papers for the regiment. Within ten days Thompson was 'voluntarily' enlisted, in the nick of time: conscription came in on 10 February 1916. He was twenty-six years old. A snapshot taken at the time shows an overweight and sheepish-looking Percy in the kilted uniform of his regiment. Thompson passed his medical at A1, and by the end of January 1916 was quartered in camp in Richmond Park. For some time he had been a steady smoker, and for the past four weeks he had been smoking up to fifty cigarettes a day. His professed intention 'never [to] go abroad' and to get his discharge seemed to be realised at the end of the month when he was hospitalised for suspected heart trouble. His wife, in the company occasionally of Avis, visited him three times a week and on Sundays. Every Tuesday she drew the 'wife's separation allowance' and took all of it to her mother-in-law. In late February Percy's regiment was shipped across to France, without him. As winter turned to spring and summer, Percy shuttled between hospital and camp. In July, at the time when the country adjusted to the stunning news of the carnage on the Somme, and while endless convoys of wounded jammed London's hospitals, Percy Thompson was honourably discharged as physically unfit for active military service. No heart condition as such was diagnosed. The young wife who collected a husband invalided out of the army in July 1916 was the happiest girl. She clung to him and leaned on his arm as once more they entered her parents' home to enjoy the 'interrupted honeymoon'. Edith Thompson would not be a war widow.

For nine more months, from the end of July 1916 to Easter 1917, Edith and Percy lived in at 231 Shakespeare Crescent. Conditions in the house were cramped and hardly private. The parents and the Thompsons needed a bedroom each. Avis probably settled for a put-you-up in the parental bedroom, while the boys crowded together in the third. The newly weds' attractive bedroom suite was purchased entirely out of the wife's money. She was the higher earner in the marriage. In their joint bank account at Barclays, 202 High Street North, they were saving hard towards the acquisition of their own home, a dream not to be realised for another four years. In the meantime they contributed to the running costs of No. 231 of course, and Edith helped with cooking and cleaning while Percy assisted with gardening. During this period Edith regularly wrote to her brother at the front and bravely coped with her panic-stricken husband during the Zeppelin raids. Whereas Edith and the Graydons stoically played whist at night while waiting for the raiders, Percy shook uncontrollably. On one occasion Edith was badly affected by 'flu and confined to bed when the Germans struck. She reputedly dragged herself out just to be with Thompson, knowing his fearful heart.

For Percy therefore a few months later to boast about his discharge in front of H. McCollin Warren – whose two sons had fought at Gallipoli – and relate how he had fooled the army's medical officers, was inconsiderate and offensive. Warren promptly called him a cad and a coward and pointed out that his wife's home had provided a gallant soldier. He was a disgrace. In his in-laws' dining room, Thompson felt sure of his ground and taunted Warren who immediately grappled with him. Mr Graydon indignantly stepped between them and demanded that they make their peace. They settled for a truce and Warren left.

The war dragged on into the new year 1917. Percy's health was causing concern, largely to himself. His addictive hypochondria prompted Dr Wallis to recommend a change of air. In April 1917 the Thompsons moved into furnished apartments at 25 Retreat Road, near the station in Westcliff. The landlords were Reg and Ruby Lockwood, with whom the Thompsons would live from Easter 1917 to September 1919. Edith was now no longer a suburban commuter. She might have been expected to be reluctant to move so far out from the metropolis. But the presence in Westcliff of Mr Carlton, and his company on the daily one-hour journey to and from London, smoothed the transition. Whereas previously Edith journeyed into work from No. 231 with her father and sister, followed half an hour later by her husband, she travelled now with Carlton and Percy. Once this novelty had worn off, she used the time and the comfort of a seating space to read.

Edith's and Percy's times in Westcliff were reasonably content by most accounts. As the train journey took her through East Ham it was easy for Edith to comply with her father's request to visit home at least one evening a week. It would be Fridays. This routine was never to be broken. Occasionally Edith would stay overnight with her parents, joined later in the evening by Percy. More frequently Edith would meet her parents for Friday dinner, and then on a late train they would all, including Avis, ride out to Westcliff to spend Saturday and Sunday at the sea or on Canvey Island in the nearby Thames estuary. As yet there was no work at Carlton & Prior on Saturday mornings. It is in this fashion that the people from Manor Park endured the tribulations of 1917 and 1918. In the summer of 1918 Newenham was miraculously still alive, as were his brothers Billie and Harold serving in the merchant navy. Then, on the eve of victory, Newenham came home. The parents and their daughters feverishly prepared for the occasion, which Edith was to remember as the happiest day of her life.

Newenham had toiled through the hell of the European front. It is from there that the previous autumn he had written to Avis to break the sad news of her lover's death. There was a party at No. 231 to

28

celebrate his return. 'Newnie' and the brave regiments of the Fifth Army were toasted and the piano accompanied popular classics like 'Tipperary' and the army's marching version of 'Auld Lang Syne': 'We're here because we're here because. . . .' Edith, who had a poor singing voice, chimed in. What she lacked in tone she made up for by a spirited performance, and while Mr Graydon said grace, Edith may have wished that God had provided her with such a man as her brother: quiet in his fortitude, solicitous for the 'widowed' sister, conscious of dreadful knowledge, gallant in accommodating himself to the innocence of Manor Park.

11 a.m., Monday 11 November 1918: Edith Thompson was six weeks short of her twenty-fifth birthday and up in London at Carlton & Prior. The booming sound of the maroons from Westminster ripped through the air, followed by the sonorous rolling of thousands of church bells all over the metropolis. The war was over. Like hundreds of thousands of Londoners, Edith and her workmates spontaneously burst into fits of happy laughter followed by frantic dancing in the streets. They joined the surge of the crowd thronging towards St Paul's, Westminster and Buckingham Palace. Now that Germany had surrendered, it appeared that the world could reassemble the pieces. In spite of her terrible losses, Britain would try to retain control over a loyal Empire and guarantee a prosperous mother country for her heroes. But the problems facing the country at home and abroad were immense and the official end of the war for Great Britain was fixed for 10 January 1920. The imminent prospect of universal male suffrage, the continuing stirrings of the suffragettes, the huge logistical problems posed by the demobilisation of four million men who needed to be reintegrated into jobs taken over by the stay-at-homes and by women, these social and economic issues needed to be tackled urgently. Furthermore, the country was visited twice in 1918 and in 1919 by an influenza epidemic, which left hundreds of thousands dead and which severely knocked morale. Under these testing circumstances Lloyd George's coalition, which swept to power in the 'Coupon Election', did remarkably well at least in generating enough wealth to spare the country the fate of violent revolution.

As the nation reverted to a superficially peaceful rhythm, Percy Thompson rediscovered a taste for living in London. There would be no more air raids, and the young couple, whose savings during the war had become considerable, expressed a desire to purchase a house. What better area than Ilford, the smartest of all the north-eastern suburbs, and very familiar to all parties concerned from their childhood? Furthermore Kenneth Chambers and his wife Lilian, Percy's sister, had moved there as a couple in 1915, and were resident at 65 Mansfield Road. Situated within five minutes' walking distance from Ilford station, with convenient connections every half hour into Liverpool Street, the Chamberses' home was spacious, and an invitation was issued to Edith and Percy to become paying guests there.

In September 1919, at about the same time as the Bywaters family moved from Manor Park to Upper Norwood, the Thompsons arrived at 65 Mansfield Road. Notwithstanding the superior mobility afforded them by living in suburbia, they were sad to leave Westcliff. There were other unforeseen disadvantages to the move. Neither Edith nor Percy was fully aware of the strains in the relationship between Lily and Kenneth. Furthermore the Chamberses' four-year-old son Graham was very demanding. He took a liking to Percy, but above all cherished the rare and less spontaneous attentions of his beautiful aunt Edith. The Chamberses' living-in maid was a young Cornish girl from St Ives, Ethel Vernon. She and Edith quickly discovered a bond in their shared dislike of Lily. It would not take very long for this initially muted antagonism to erupt into overt anxiety and downright hostility. To overcome her boredom at No. 65 as much as to get away in the evenings and on Saturdays, Edith took up tennis at the nearby Valentine's Park. She never learned to play properly, but warmed to the idea of engaging in such middle-class pursuits. The theatre more than ever fed her starved imagination. Now that the pressures of rationing were easing off rapidly, and as Edith's considerable wages were paid out weekly, the Thompsons became regular patrons of the West End theatres. Avis often accompanied them on these visits, after which they would carefully split the expenses equitably.

It was in the winter of 1919 that the Thompsons met Sidney J. Birnage and his wife. The Birnages lived at 74 Argyle Road, Ilford. Their garden backed on to that of the Chamberses. They were friendly neighbours and would converse over the fence which partitioned their two properties. Birnage worked for the Sun Life Insurance Company in Threadneedle Street. He and his wife met Edith and Percy over dinner at 65 Mansfield Road and took a liking to the smart couple who hoped to become adopted Ilfordians. Shortly after their first meeting, Percy Thompson called on the Birnages and asked Sidney to effect an insurance on his life. This was duly transacted. The amount grossed by the policy would be £250 payable on Percy's death or on the day of the policy's maturation at retirement.

The Birnages and the Thompsons remained on friendly terms after the latters' move to 41 Kensington Gardens. They exchanged regular visits and Mrs Birnage enlisted the Thompsons' and the Graydons' cooperation in staging and attending charitable events such as the garden fêtes at the Seamen's Orphanage in Wanstead. Not the least of her husband's achievements was to enrol Percy Thompson on the books of Sun Life, to work part-time on commission for the company.

Another acquaintance was renewed in this period to Edith's dismay. Seven roads up from the Chamberses, in the area where Edith and Percy were prospecting for their dream home, Richard Halliday Thompson, now married to Ethel Hull, had set up house at 49 Seymour Gardens. He had promised to keep an eye out for anything that might be going locally. It is quite possibly on a tip-off from him that the sale of 41 Kensington Gardens came to Edith's and Percy's notice, as he passed the road every morning on the way to work. Neither Percy nor Edith felt warmly towards Richard. She particularly disliked the idea of being swamped by her husband's family in Ilford. More than ever she therefore valued her parents' home at No. 231 and her beloved sister's company. From September 1919 to June 1920 Edith, and often her husband, would dine with the Graydons. Foremost among their topics of conversation were the excitements of the house hunting. But everything seemed to be going smoothly. Unlike so many of their contemporaries, Edith and Percy had no money worries, as Edith had again been promoted at Carlton & Prior.

The firm had recently moved from Barbican to much more spacious premises at 168 Aldersgate Street, on the same side as Aldersgate tube station, the Manchester Hotel and Postman's Park. The building faced east and was located on the southern corner of Manchester Avenue, directly opposite Fuller's teashop in Edmund Place. Immediately to the west of Carlton & Prior stretched Bartholomew Close which once provided shelter to the fugitive Milton. To the north and north-west lay Smithfield and Charterhouse, while to the east it faced the Barbican. The Cripplegate Institute, where Edith assisted her father in giving his weekly dance lessons, was situated nearby.

At the time of Edith's working in Aldersgate, Carlton & Prior was an undistinguished building, consisting of four operational levels. The nerve centre of the shop was the ground floor which consisted of the showroom and of administrative offices at the back. It was entered from the street through a glass door which opened onto a rising staircase. On its left, steps descended into the basement while on the right hand side were the hat racks and drawers of the showroom. Under the staircase and at the bottom end of the room Miss 'Tartar' Prior, Carlton and Edith as book-keeper had their offices. They also shared the only available typewriter. A contemporary cartoon and a print of G. F. Watt's pre-Raphaelite 'Hope' adorned the east wall. The selection of hats did not rank in the top five West End millinery shops, but Carlton & Prior prided themselves on their initiative and self-sufficiency. Not only did they boast buyers like Miss Graydon who could confidently be dispatched into the world of French fashion, but they employed remarkable contingents of well-paid work girls on two upstairs floors. The girls did all the cutting of the material, knitting and fitting, under the expert supervision of senior staff like Edith Graydon and Lily Vallender, a horsy, generous and amiable girl. Often Edith would excitedly chat with Lily in full view of the girls and, for their benefit, she would present herself in profile while touching her auburn hair, just to ensure that her bun was tied firmly. Really though she was showing off, as Myrtle Aldridge, who worked at Carlton & Prior with her sister at the time, well remembers. 'A woman's hair then was her glory', another contemporary of Edith's remarked with reference to this exhibitionist streak of hers. Few were taken in by her vanity, and several girls at the firm resented her for being the boss's favourite. Working conditions at Carlton and Prior were cost-effective without overly exploiting the staff. Edith loved it. For her it meant independence and attention – everything that her marriage was turning out not to be. But if she was brooding on the way events were shaping up, she managed to hide it well enough.

Then a house came up: 41 Kensington Gardens. It belonged to a Mr Hobday of 8 The Drive, Ilford. Hobday was keen to sell, because of protected tenants, the Lesters, who were becoming increasingly troublesome and proved impossible to evict. The house was double-fronted, with a horseshoe lawn at the front and an attractive garden at the back. Pear and apple trees proliferated here, where once the entire stretch, from Cranbrook Road down to Wanstead Park, had consti-tuted a huge orchard. No. 41 contained eight rooms. For this large Edwardian property Edith and Percy paid £250, the equivalent of ten times Edith's monthly salary, and thereby became outright owners of a substantial home; no one in their immediate family had ever lived in a comparable house. It needed some work done to it, but both Percy and Edith were very capable in this respect; and Mr Graydon would help.

It was in June 1920 that Percy signed the deeds which made 41 Kensington Gardens his. Edith contributed over half of the expense, but in keeping with contemporary custom, the house was legally entered in the husband's name. The time had come to leave 65 Mansfield Road. Things there had deteriorated steadily over the past few months. When Mr and Mrs Graydon went on holiday in May, Edith and Percy eagerly jumped at the opportunity of leaving the Chamberses and of moving into No. 231 for a fortnight. The 'rift with Lily', as Edith called it, had become unbridgeable.

In July 1920 the Thompsons moved into their Ilford home. In the meantime an event had taken place which, when viewed retrospectively, would prove momentous.

It was no more than a knock on a door one evening in January 1920. Freddy Bywaters was asking for his schoolfriend Billie Graydon. Whether he knew of Bill's leave from duty with the White Star Line, or whether he called out of nostalgia for the old times and haunts, or to procure lodgings at No. 231 near the docks is not materially relevant. Bywaters spent only an hour on his first visit. The conversation with Bill and his parents revolved around travels in the Far East and their former exploits at football and swimming. Freddy's ship, the P & O's *Plassy*, was getting ready at Tilbury. He was doing day duty on board during these January weeks of shore leave, hence his appearance in the Crescent which was only a twopenny fare away from the East India Docks.

The Graydons had last seen young Bywaters in the grim summer of 1916. He had then been a boy. Now, as a young man of seventeen and a half, he impressed them with his masculine looks and assured manner. He proved entertaining and was mature in outlook beyond his years. He was his own man entirely. During these three weeks of January Freddy Bywaters paid the Graydons some four visits in all. They welcomed him and he enjoyed their company. It was the sea that bound all of them together.

Before leaving he had become re-acquainted with the family: Bill and Harold, Newenham, the parents and the twenty-four year-old Avis. Bywaters was conscious of his attractiveness to women and instinctively picked up the signals emanating from the lively Miss Graydon. He knew how saddened she had been by the loss of her lover at Passchendaele. She was nicely turned out, he noticed approvingly, and thought that he might pay her rather more attention in the future. Right now he was due out for a long voyage. From the end of January and for three and a half months the *Plassy* with Bywaters on board would sail to China and Japan and back. It was mid-May therefore when Freddy once again appeared at 231 Shakespeare Crescent. This time he asked to be accommodated at the Graydons' as a paying lodger. The reason was that the *Plassy* had been moved to the East India docks in Tilbury for an eight-week reconditioning spell in which Bywaters was participating. No. 231 provided him with a convenient haven and freed him from the tedium of commuting to and from Upper Norwood. It also emancipated him from the overly solicitous attentions of his mother. If Freddy spent his first weekend home with his family in Westow Street and then moved with most of his effects to Manor Park, the date of his first meeting with Edith, as Mrs Thompson, would be Friday 24 May 1920.

As on every other Friday, on her way home to Westcliff or Mansfield Road, Edith stopped over at her parents'. On this day she arrived between 7.30 p.m. and 8 p.m., 'her arms full of flowers, a book, a newspaper, and the sides of her attaché case almost bursting with the purchases she had crammed into it'. As she entered and went through to the kitchen with her mother, Freddy Bywaters rose to be introduced to her. Edith, he realised, was handsomer than even the parents' wedding photographs suggested. For her part she was struck by the former adolescent's confident appearance: of medium height—five foot six and a half to her five foot seven and a quarter—muscular, broad-shouldered, tanned, with thick light brown wavy hair brushed back, and with dark eyes and eyebrows set in a square-jawed face.

After a few pleasantries had been exchanged, the women left the men to their devices and prepared supper. Percy would arrive at 8 p.m., after his customary late drink in Bishopsgate. He in turn was introduced to Bywaters. The two men, so different in temperament, at once hit it off. Percy was attracted to the youngster's blunt, bluff manner. As for Freddy's reaction to Percy, it appears to have matched Thompson's in warmth. He liked the older man's direct touch, his firm handshake, his connection, albeit at a desk, with matters seafaring. Before the Thompsons departed that night, Percy told Mr Graydon how much he had enjoyed Bywaters's company: 'I like him very much. He is a smart, interesting boy. A clean-looking fellow.'

Every Friday evening for the next seven weeks Freddy Bywaters would dine with the Graydons and the Thompsons. He occasionally lunched with Avis when he was up in the centre of town. No. 231 had virtually become his home during this transition period, although he regularly visited at 11 Westow Street. But Freddy was anxious to be off at sea, and early in July he secured a transfer to P & O's *Cap Polonia* at Southampton and promptly sailed for Bombay. After the *Cap Polonia*'s return to Southampton, Freddy was back for an hour at No. 231 in mid-October. A fortnight later he again dropped in briefly on the Graydons to tell them his latest news, learn of Edith's and Percy's house-buying progress, and promise a card from Bombay.

In the meantime the Thompsons had reluctantly agreed to their protected tenants' terms for the occupancy of the house: Edith and Percy would have the large front bedroom on the right of the house and the front drawing room under it, both with elegant bay windows. At the back they were to occupy the morning room on the left of the house with its access into the garden, along with the use of the scullery, kitchen and bathroom. Cellar and loft were also shared, and before long the Thompsons had secured the exclusive use of the small back bedroom over their morning room. This small bedroom at the end of the landing faced south-east and had a door which closed off the bottom end of the floor. As one left it, the bathroom was immediately on the left and the Lesters' bedroom opposite it on the right. Next along was the Thompsons' bedroom, also on the right. It opened directly on to the staircase and was adjacent to the third bedroom, facing back and occupied by the Lesters' twenty-eight year-old daughter Nora. It was largely on these ultra-respectable suburban premises that the future drama of human love and deceit was to be initiated.

As a protected tenant Mrs Fanny Maria Lester and her ailing husband paid a rent of merely 30 shillings (£1.50p) each month and half the rates and taxes. Even in 1920 that amount was wholly uncommercial and not realistic. The Thompsons almost at once gave the Lesters six months' notice to leave. In the end the tenants successfully deferred moving till the late summer of 1922, when Percy consulted his solicitors about forceful eviction. Till that time Mrs Lester ingratiated herself with Mrs Thompson, in particular by offering her services as a quasi-maid: on the gas stove in the scullery she would cook the porridge for everyone in the mornings, do the shopping, take the laundry down to Belgrave Road, and assist with the cleaning.

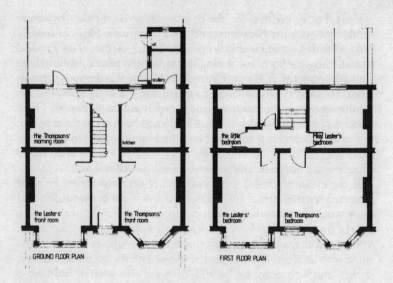

41 Kensington Gardens: 1922

The 'people from Manor Park', as Mrs Lester repeatedly referred to them, went with gusto at the task of giving No. 41 a face-lift. They christened it The Retreat, after the road where they had lived in West-cliff. The fence and the hedge which enclosed the front needed tending. The wooden cross-barred gate was oiled, the path was retiled and the rest of the semicircular drive was weeded. In the horseshoe which they made into a lawn, daffodils and red and yellow tulips as well as rose bushes were planted; and geraniums, Edith's favourite flowers, were everywhere. The same care went into tending the fruit trees and bushes in the back garden. At this Percy was accomplished. With his father-in-law in tandem, he could grow and mend anything.

The inside of the house gradually filled with the Thompsons' possessions. Their furniture and clothes were chosen with taste. Furthermore Edith owned a remarkable collection of Japanese and Chinese porcelain and exotic cushions, which her brothers Bill and Harold would bring her as presents from their trips in the Far East. She accorded a place of particular privilege to her array of trophies, accumulated from years of dancing competitions. As she looked at them with a tinge of regret, she had the consolation at least that here

36

she was in her own home; and her parents and sister, and occasionally the boys visited on Saturday evenings. On such occasions the family would sing Irish ballads round the piano, or the most recent music-hall hit. Edith usually prepared a small cold supper of salads and fruit jellies for these visits. To the external world the Thompsons were a reasonably happy and contented couple. They had every reason to be so: both were healthy and in full-time, well-paid employment. They owned their own home, could still afford frequent visits to the theatre, the music halls and the cinema; and they had even started to spend money on patronising the odd Masonic banquet, at Percy's request, to please his freemason friends. If Ladies' nights at the Masons bored Edith, we may be sure that she endured them with a measure of good humour. All seemed well – except for two details which do not fit into this picture of London suburban happiness.

2

The Darlingest Boy

On Friday 31 December 1920 a party, including the Thompsons, was gathering at 231 Shakespeare Crescent to see in the New Year. At some point one of the male guests inadvertently called Mrs Thompson by her first name. Her husband instantly took exception to this on the grounds of its impropriety. The guest apologised. A livid and humiliated Edith might well have put Thompson in his place had it not been for the occasion, and because she loathed the thought of a scene in her parents' home. While this was happening the *Malwa*, on the very last leg of her homebound journey from Bombay, was plying her way through the estuary towards Tilbury. As she was waiting in Tilbury in mid-stream, one of the *Malwa*'s writers, Bywaters, inexplicably jumped ship. The company's penalty for this was instant suspension, as he well knew. He rushed through the docks and made the last London train into Fenchurch. He finally reached No. 231 well after midnight, when the party was dwindling and the Thompsons had already returned to Ilford. The Graydons put him up for the night and renewed their offer of taking him in when he enquired about it.

The question that needs to be addressed pertains to Freddy's motive for jeopardising his job so recklessly. Was it to be with Avis, or simply his friends the Graydons; or was he missing Edith Thompson? The latter has always seemed more likely, in spite of the absence of corroborative evidence. In her massive correspondence with Bywaters Edith offers precise days and dates for their mutual declarations of love and subsequent sexual encounters. These postdate December 1920/January 1921 by at least six months. But it would appear nevertheless that they had already begun to trespass on the paths of

39

clandestine love as early as autumn 1920, if not even earlier. When the official police file on 'Thompson & Bywaters', MEPO 3/1582, was opened to the public on 1 January 1986, it was found to contain some material never published before, including six hitherto unknown telegram transcripts. The first two in particular are of crucial importance, because of their dates:

1. Bywaters. Stewards Dept., 22nd September, 1920 SS Malwa, Tilbury Dk
   'Chief away today cannot come'
   EDITH

2.   13 April, 1921
   F. Bywaters, 11 Westow St, Upper Norwood
   'Keep contents of mackintosh safe'
   PEIDI

Freddy certainly was in England on 22 September 1920 and he would shortly be sending Avis a birthday card for 24 September. As yet no declaration of love had passed between him and Edith Thompson (this would not happen for another nine months). So one suspects that their sudden intimacy took both of them by surprise. Early in the summer, while Freddy was sharing No. 231 with the Graydons, it had appeared that he and Avis were well matched. Whatever happened – whether Freddy summoned up all his courage one day and asked Edith rather than Avis for lunch and found to his amazement that she consented – no one will ever know. At this stage, 22 September 1920, the relationship could still be defused as a slightly improper flirt. No one needed to get hurt. For Christmas Edith sent Freddy an unsolicited card. He took this, as indeed it was, to be a signal of reciprocity. The very first casualty of 'Thompson & Bywaters' would be Freddy's job with the P & O on New Year's Eve of 1920.

The date of the second telegram is puzzling. The official log of the P & O shows that the *Orvieto* with Bywaters on board sailed from Tilbury to Brisbane via Fremantle, Adelaide, Melbourne and Sydney at 2.45 p.m. on 26 February 1921, and returned home at 6.12 p.m. on 4 June. Bywaters's re-employment by the P & O was largely thanks to the good offices of Percy Thompson, who had intervened on his behalf with the purser of the *Orvieto*. His record on the next six voyages would be unimpeachable: VG (very good) for both 'Ability' and 'Conduct'. The 26 February is demonstrably the date of departure. Moreover, Freddy had not stayed at 11 Westow Street at all during January and February. The only logical conclusion to draw is that the telegram was sent to Upper Norwood to be forwarded to Bywaters by his mother or sister. They were unaware of the identity concealed by the nickname Peidi, and the message, enigmatic though it is, seemed fairly innocuous. As yet Edith did not dare write a full letter to Bywaters directly, notwithstanding the earlier note and Christmas card. He was already in Australia when the telegram was posted, and would have received it whilst there. Edith Thompson was falling in love. So was Freddy Bywaters, but not with her only.

It was on this voyage, during the eight days of the *Orvieto*'s docking in Sydney that he renewed an Australian acquaintance which quickly turned into a romance. Edith was to take a poor view of the Australian girl, as she did also of Molly, a Manor Park girl, whom Bywaters had been courting prior to his family leaving the area. Edith Thompson, her sister, Molly and the Australian girl had all fallen for young Bywaters's charm. He relished it.

The *Orvieto* was well east of Suez on the way to Colombo when in London Clemence Dane's futuristic *A Bill of Divorcement* opened at the St Martin's Theatre. Set in 1932, after an imaginary change in the divorce law, it plots the tribulations of Margaret Fairfield, happily re-married at the beginning of the play after divorcing her lunatic first husband. His recovery from insanity and the return to his former wife claiming her and their daughter back confronts Margaret with a cruel dilemma: she has to choose between her new-found love and happiness and her duty and pity. Abandoning the second husband she tells him: 'For all this, I will always love *you*.' Although Clemence Dane essentially presents her audience with an open-ended fiction, balanced between liberal and orthodox views of marriage, bondage and duty, the play drew huge audiences and critical praise for its risqué, mature approach. Edith thought of herself very much as part of the *tout Londres* and avidly patronised the magical heartland of the London theatre. St Martin's in Leicester Square was a theatre she knew well, and the play in particular must have struck her as aptly timed to coincide with the budding of her romance with the young sailor.

The further relevance of *A Bill of Divorcement* is that it reflected the relaxing of the post-war austerity. It had been over a year since the official end of the war for Britain. The age of the endless Flapper parties, of bobs, shingle bobs, short skirts and open-shouldered dresses had dawned. The next five to six years are the 1920s of Lady Diana Cooper, David, Prince of Wales, Beverley Nichols, Evelyn Waugh and Nellie Melba, Stanley Holloway and Melville Gideon, and of Eric Liddell. The same years mark the age of the ruthless use of political power by press barons like Northcliffe, Beaverbrook and Rothermere, as well as the ascendancy in the political arena of judicial figures like Lord Birkenhead.

If on the one hand the flappers were agitating for full suffrage and shocking the nation by their loose morals, on the other hand the press, the *Daily Mail* in particular, quite unashamedly proposed the selective exportation of hundreds of thousands of British women to the under-stocked reaches of the Empire. The 'surplus woman' was perceived to be a liability; she would threaten marriages by her ready availability, and had already shown a willingness to supplant the men by taking their jobs during the war. Also she was bound to vote Labour! The *Daily Mail's* alternative was to turn her into a saleable commodity in the service of the Empire. The immense contribution made to the winning of the war by innumerable women in the factories at home, and serving in countless numbers in the field as VADs and with the Red Cross, was disregarded now. Ex-servicemen on return immediately repossessed the jobs held by women. Even this could not hide the country's plunge towards high male unemployment which, in 1921, had passed two million. Successive governments of the 1920s, beleaguered and bedevilled by social, economic and political disaster, would blame them on scapegoats. Among these, women were a favourite. It was as if the surplus woman had single-handedly created the surplus rather than the catastrophic casualty rate at the front.

In the same period that Lawrence's *Women in Love* was officially deemed morally threatening or dismissable as 'unfortunate', high praise was bestowed on Walter de la Mare's *Memoirs of a Midget* and the hugely successful *If Winter Comes* by A. S. M. Hutchinson. The latter is the tragi-comic tale of Mark Sabre, a man of honour who, after the war, sacrifices his reputation to protect the good name of a young pregnant woman and her dead lover. The novel articulated a mild protest at the speed with which the contemporary world was forgetting the crucified youth of only a few years before. In the words of one reviewer, the book was distinguished by its 'high ethical quality ... power and beauty' and was perhaps 'the year's most arresting achievement in fiction'. The verdict of posterity has been different, and Hutchinson's novel is seen as at best a period piece, on a level with the war novels by W. J. Locke and other popular writers of war fiction. The suspicion of the hero's adultery with a girl named Effie – who eventually commits suicide – haunts the second half of the novel. Little wonder that Edith found it interesting, even if she also sensed its imperfections, as 'none of the characters strike me as live men and women'.

Adultery, prejudice, bigamy, self-sacrifice and sexually obsessive passions inform two hugely successful plays which Edith Thompson saw at about this time: *The Garden of Allah*, adapted by Robert Hichens and Mary Anderson from Hichens's own novel of that name; and particularly E. Temple Thurston's *The Wandering Jew* at the New (now Albery) Theatre on St Martin's Lane. This latter ran from September 1920 to August 1921. Matheson Lang, one of Edith's favourite actors, took the lead as the Jew in his various incarnations. From his fated beginnings as the 'Accursed Man' – that is the legendary Jew who spat in Christ's face on his way to Calvary – the play traces the gradual conversion of the Jew through the first crusade, followed by thirteenth century Palermo and the Middle Ages in Spain, when he has become a healer and a Gladstonian converter of girls 'from harlotry'. It is for the sake of one such young woman that he dies a martyr.

Edith Thompson saw this play several times: its melodramatic, sentimental charge and outstanding cast were enough to warrant the expense. Money in any case was never made to stop with her, she once complained to Bywaters. From classical melodrama in the West End to vaudeville and pierrotic entertainment at the Ilford Hippodrome and the East Ham Palace, everything was on offer in the metropolis; and Edith Thompson spent money on it as freely as her more illustrious contemporaries.

While the weathermen were forecasting the hottest summer since records started, Edith and Percy decided to take their holidays on the Isle of Wight to overlap with their friends the Vallenders' stay there. They invited Avis to join them. It was now near the beginning of June, and the party placed their bookings in Shanklin with Osborne House, advertised as facing the pier on the Esplanade 'Near Chine; Board – Residence; Separate tables; Catering a Speciality. Terms Moderate. Apply Proprietress'. Electricity throughout the house and in every room was another selling point. The boarding terms would be about 73 shillings and 6 pence (£3.67p) a week.

Freddy Bywaters returned to Tilbury on Saturday 4 June 1921. He called on the Graydons at once. It so happened that the Thompsons were visiting. Bywaters casually expressed a wish to take a holiday. Thompson at once extended an invitation to him to join the party, since he knew that Avis was sweet on Bywaters and he, it seemed, on her. A foursome, he suggested, made better sense than a party of three. It is quite possible that Avis had already tactfully suggested to her brother-in-law that Freddy might like to come. But it is much more probable that Edith put it to Freddy to ask, and to Thompson to invite, under the pretext of Avis's manifest crush on young Bywaters. The invitation to Bywaters for Shanklin was accepted.

It was an animated party that met up at Victoria Station on Saturday 11 June and purchased their third-class return fares for the 11.35 a.m. train from Victoria to Shanklin. As there was enough time between connections at Portsmouth to explore the Southsea pier and water-front briefly, the quartet took a stroll down to the beach. Here in the early afternoon, Avis took a remarkably idyllic photograph of Edith, Percy and Freddy reclining on the pebbles. Edith is wearing a short voile dress, embroidered with an Oriental fern pattern. With her left leg crossed under her right she is leaning Thompson's way who faces the camera and squints slightly, as does his wife, because of the fierce sun. Freddy is curled up towards her, his face brushing against her right thigh. His eyes are closed – Edith's right hand holding a cigarette, rests in his hair. What is so extraordinary about the picture is its look of combined innocence and intimacy. The erotic charge of Bywaters's cheek pressing gently against Edith Thompson's thigh is unmistakable. That both Thompson and the photographer, Avis, missed it almost beggars belief, but then they were totally unsuspecting.

It was mid-afternoon when the Isle of Wight railway deposited the four Londoners at Shanklin station, from where a shuttle operated into the town centre and down to the Esplanade at the foot of the cliff. The Shanklin that welcomed the people from Manor Park and Ilford still boasted its Edwardian resort elegance. It was vastly more affluent than the present town, which breathes an air of living fossilisation. It offered a variety of vibrant day and night entertainments. Thus, on Monday of the week following the Thompsons' arrival here, the Playhouse featured Elsie Jarris in *The Merry Madcap* and the tenth episode of *The Son of Tarzan*. Then, at the same theatre, on Thursday and till Saturday Avery Hopwood's *Fair and Warmer*, the play 'that made the weather famous', would star May Alison. Furthermore, on

Sunday there would be a band concert in Rylstone Gardens conducted by Mr W. Adams who would also appear on Keats Green on Wednesday evening and again on Friday night, 17 June. If one adds to this the weekly Wednesday night dance on the lawn at the Marine Hotel and the nightly concert parties in the Town Hall on the High Street and in the Summer Theatre on the Esplanade, one can readily imagine the energy of Shanklin in 1921. The visitors were to sample all of these; and since they adored dancing and popular songs, they would patronise the Town Hall and Summer Theatre especially. Entertainments here included soprano artistes like Dorothy Grace, humorists and mimics like Winifred Fairie, comediennes and dancers such as Edith Price as well as revue numbers and 'light comedy songs'.

The cockney sestet were much taken with Osborne House. Its rooms were spacious and comfortable, and the two married couples' windows opened onto the front, affording an excellent view of the pier. Immediately to the north-east stood the fashionable Royal Spa Hotel, and next to it rose the column of the hydraulic lift to the top of the cliff on Keats Green. The famous Shanklin Chine lies to the south-west and connects with the Rylstone Pleasure Gardens. As the party were gathering for drinks on the verandah of Osborne House this Saturday evening, the air was warm and tangily scented from the surf. Had they come six weeks earlier, they would have smelt the blossoming of the garlic flowers wafting across from the nearby heights on the road to Ventnor.

The visitors' first two days were spent mostly relaxing in the sun on the shingly beach down from the hotel. Avis and Freddy braved the chilly waters with gusto, while Edith watched their nautical frolics with a measure of indulgence. Percy excused himself from swimming, 'on account of his weak heart'. In the evening, the men split and explored the pubs of Shanklin. Percy took his drink badly, but would not be left behind by Freddy and Norman. Thompson's return from his first night out with the boys, when he needed to be helped upstairs by Edith saying 'you better stay in bed', set the tone for several of these outings. Avis found it acutely embarrassing, as did her sister: it was never mentioned in public, but everyone knew that Percy could 'hardly stand'.

On Tuesday 14 June the London visitors decided to book a round the island charabanc tour for the following day. The fare for the eighty-seven mile round trip was a pound. That evening, Freddy and Edith were left on their own briefly at some point. They kissed for the first time. He held her so tight that her arms and wrists bruised, while she started running her fingers through his hair. For her he became the 'great lover', for him she was the formerly unobtainable girl from Manor Park whom he dreamed about as a little boy. It would be an easy day to remember. As she joined Percy in bed that night, Edith probably determined there and then that she and Freddy would not again be separated; she would lull Percy into a false sense of security through a show of wifely affection under which guise she would urge him to invite Bywaters back to 41 Kensington Gardens.

On Wednesday 15 June 1921 the party from London were having an early breakfast on the verandah. The light of the sun danced hard and scintillating on the sea as in a shimmering Seurat painting. It would be a hot day. Everyone dressed lightly. By 10.25 a.m. the charabanc was slowly steering through the Shanklin High Street towards its first stop on Ventnor Pier. Then it proceeded on to St Catherine's through a pine-scented and leafy tunnel road which cuts across St Catherine's point from the Undercliff. As the charabanc chugged along this matchless stretch of the route, its female passengers removed their hats and shook out their hair in the blissful cool reprieve. It appears that Edith Thompson forgot to put hers back on again, for she was to have a very sore, sun-burnt neck that night.

So far it had been very warm. Friday was announced as hotter still. It was to be the Thompsons' last full day here and, for different reasons, everyone in the party expressed regrets about it. It now emerged that Bywaters was unable to stay a second week. He was meant to, but had changed his mind. As the Vallenders were also leaving, Avis would be left on her own for another week of the holiday. Avis, who had hugely enjoyed having Freddy as her swimming pal, was saddened by Bywaters's premature departure. She would be hurt even more on her return to London. Reticent, kind and honest Avis Graydon never realised on the island that the seeds had been sown under her innocent eyes of an event that would radically alter the course of her life.

For their last night the Thompsons opted for the entertainment at the Summer Theatre. Edith wore her peach sports coat. The entertainment ran the gamut of the emotional scale, from wistful and schmaltzy to joyous and buoyant. Then a song with words by Leslie Cooke and music by Evelyn Sharpe made Edith sit up. She had always loved it. Now, on this night, it seemed to her to distil the essence of her relationship with young Bywaters. This remarkable and popular song was 'One Little Hour'. The pertinence of its simple lyrics to the participants in this story is immediately evident:

> One little hour of happiness divine
> One posy from the garden of your heart;
> One dream alone – that Heav'n had made you mine:
> And then to part!
> And then to part!
>
> One little hour of joy – a life's regret!
> A world of thorns for one elusive flow'r
> And after all to treasure dearly yet
> That little hour!
>
> One golden hour! for that eternal pain!
> Yet could you stand to-day where once you stood
> And ask me if for you I'd live again
> That little hour – I would.

The indulgent romanticism of the song and its lilting melancholic tune perfectly articulated Edith's sense of herself as a profoundly romantic and wounded heroine. If only she were given the chance to live the life of one of the glamorous women in the fiction which she read! Her existence could not possibly remain circumscribed by the routines of eating, sleeping, loving and living with Percy Thompson. For 'one little hour' of total abandon she could accept almost any penalty, even 'a world of thorns'. Quite how she viewed her love with Frederick Bywaters is suggested by these words addressed to him on Monday 2 October 1922:

Darlint, we've said we'll always be Pals havent we, shall we say we'll always be lovers – even tho' secret ones, or is it (this great big love) a thing we can't control – dare we say that – I think I will dare. Yes I will 'I'll always love you' – if you are dead – if you have left me even if you don't still love me, I always shall you.

Your love to me is new, it is something different, it is my life and if things should go badly with us, I shall always have this past year to look back upon and feel that 'Then I lived'. I never before and I never shall again.[1]

While the song was playing Freddy Bywaters looked glum and remained silent. They were on their own when Edith leaned forward

[1] Edith Thompson repeatedly uses the phrase 'darlint' which contracts 'darlingest'.

and asked 'What's the matter?' – 'You know what's the matter, I love you.' She reciprocated his declaration of love. In bed later she perhaps put it again to Percy how nice their break had been and how particularly jolly the idea of Freddy staying with them was. They needed the money, and he was ever such a pal to Avis and all of them.

On the return journey, it was decided that Freddy would stay in the 'little room' at 41 Kensington Gardens for a trial period of a week, free of charge. If he liked it, and if the Thompsons and the Lesters found it a workable arrangement, then he was to become a paying guest. The agreed terms were roughly 25 shillings (£1.25p) a week. For a month this would be a fairly modest rent of just over £5. But it seemed huge compared to the mere 30/– paid by the entire Lester family. Between them the Thompsons grossed nearly £50 a month. They hardly needed Freddy's meagre contribution, even if it were supplemented by food payments and shopping contributions. As far as he was concerned, quite apart from his infatuation with the mistress of the house, living in Ilford was far more convenient for the docks and the shipping offices in the City than Upper Norwood. Freddy now became landlocked. For nearly three months he expressed little desire to sail again, notwithstanding his excellent record on the last voyage which would have secured him a berth easily.

On Sunday, after spending the night at No. 41, he visited home and saw his family. They were delighted to see him, but disappointed about his decision to stay with the Thompsons. Mrs Bywaters cared little for her son's attachment to the 'uppity' folk from the Crescent, and particularly the snooty woman who had made good, Mrs Thompson. But Fred was not to be dissuaded. The room at the back of the first floor of the tiny, crookedly semi-detached cottage at the corner of Westow Street and Paddock Passage, was his for keeps. He would hold on to it as a base while sampling the splendours of the Thompsons' green and leafy suburban comforts. The contrast between the Victorian dereliction of Westow Street and the spacious gardens and villas of the Belgrave Road would have swayed others, even if there had not been a woman at the still point of these ever-closing concentric circles.

The following day, Monday 20 June, Freddy had agreed to collect Edith at 168 Aldersgate to go for lunch at the King's Hall in the Holborn Restaurant. As he headed up towards Carlton & Prior to meet her, he saw her affectionately chatting with Harry Renton outside. She hadn't seen Harry since leaving for the island. Poor faithful Harry Renton: Edith loved fooling around with him. Harry knew that she would never be his now, but her proximity and the sound of her laughter cheered his heart. So did her kindness to him after the war. Whether Edith hugged Harry and excused herself for having to rush, or whether it was merely a peck on the cheek, Freddy saw it and did not like it. He nearly made a scene over what Edith termed 'a trivial incident'. As yet though, little could disturb their idyll as they settled down for lunch in the Holborn Restaurant which would, from now on, be one of their favourite haunts. On Wednesday Freddy took Edith for a quick lunch in St Paul's Churchyard. She told him of her engagement for tea at the Waldorf that afternoon. He protested and attempted to dissuade her: was she going with Percy, or Harry or someone else such as Carlton, all of whom he now resented? She refused to yield and asked that he walk her back to the shop. He entered the showroom at Carlton & Prior for the very first time and was introduced to Carlton himself as the Thompsons' lodger. The men shook hands. They would not meet again till December 1922.

At about 2 p.m. Bywaters met his mother in St Paul's Churchyard. Every Wednesday she was up in the City to buy material. In the course of that afternoon Freddy rang City 6457, the Carlton & Prior number, to speak to Miss Graydon. He persisted in his, to her, unreasonable desire to stop her going to the Waldorf. She refused point-blank. Bywaters was miffed and angry. He returned to Westow Street for the night and left Edith to make an excuse to Percy for his unexplained absence. On Thursday the lovers did not communicate, and again he returned to Norwood in the night. Then, on Friday, they lunched together at the Holborn. It turned into an extended tête-à-tête. Suddenly Edith opened up to the young man fully and told him 'things that no one else knew'. Her longings and sense of entrapment with Percy all gushed out. Yesterday she had felt that her hold on Freddy was tenuous. She had nearly panicked and feared that she had missed a unique chance to pour out her suffering to the youth. Now he was back with her. He had to be told everything. There can be little doubt that Bywaters listened with a certain astonishment to all this; and mingled with it was pride in the fact that this older and attractive woman would single him out as lover and champion. He held her hands and promised to return to No. 41 that evening. Neither he nor she had forgotten that the following day Avis was due back from the island, while the Thompsons were on the Carlton & Prior annual outing in Eastcote. Freddy would meet Avis. Edith made him promise to be gentle with her, but clear. He would certainly impress on Avis the extent to which their relationship needed to remain circumscribed, at least for the time being.

For the all-day excursion to the Ship Inn at Eastcote, the rendezvous was at Carlton & Prior's. From here the party proceeded to Aldersgate and boarded the Metropolitan line to Uxbridge. This yearly event for the entire firm was organised by Herbert Carlton. Lily and Norman Vallender naturally took part in the outing. Carlton's own son Charlie also patronised these trips to Eastcote. Like his father he was a 'lady's man', and the prospect of the relaxed company of thirty-one nubile young women was irresistible. The weather could not be faulted, as the temperature was hitting the mid-nineties by noon. The particular attraction of the Ship Inn was its extensive grounds and its T-shaped Edwardian pavilion. It is to this that the party resorted for sandwiches and drinks before the afternoon games, of which Percy was a trusted and skilful organiser, but in which he did not participate otherwise.

In the meantime Avis was returning on her own from the Isle of Wight. Freddy was meeting her. On the Tube from Victoria to East Ham he broke to her the news that they could not be lovers for the time being. This 'understanding' did not wholly surprise Avis, but when Freddy left the island early, she had felt the pangs of loss already, and the last week had been desolate for her. The recent memory of their shared swims in the sea remained vivid, and her disappointment was proportionately greater.

Sunday came and with it the end of Freddy's 'probationary' period at 41 Kensington Gardens. As of Monday he would be a paying lodger. Did Percy Thompson know that that day was Freddy's nineteenth birthday?

Monday 27 June 1921: The Lesters are away this week. They are taking their annual holiday to interleave with the Thompsons' which ensures that each of the two resident households has the place to themselves for at least part of the time. Edith, unbeknown to her husband, arranged to take off Monday 27 June quite some time ago, possibly even before the Isle of Wight break. Whatever her reason for not going to town before Percy – as is her wont – she starts this hot summer day in the sun-flooded scullery by washing the accumulated dishes, cutlery and crockery from yesterday and this morning. Freddy is upstairs. She will take him his breakfast. It is his birthday after all, and she has bought him a present. As she climbs the staircase, she knows that the time has come. Freddy welcomes her and starts pressing her to undress. She resists, partly out of genuine modesty, and partly not to cheapen herself. An argument ensues, and she bursts into tears. 'Let me be a pal to you', he urges her on. 'Let me help you if I can.' She again tells him how unhappy she is and that she prefers suicide to living with Percy. She has never loved him and cannot possibly continue living in this dead relationship. Freddy is stroking her and holding her tight to comfort her. She promises him to put off suicide for five years. This will be their pact, and today is Day One of Year One of Thompson and Bywaters. She will in months to come interpret this with frightening literalism.

When Freddy's hands start wandering down her body they encounter no further resistance. He undresses her with a deft knowingness that startles her. Then he slips out of his pyjamas and they lie together and start making love. Edith and Freddy are surprised by the ease with which their inhibitions are shed. This 'naturalness' becomes so precious to her that many months later she will berate him for calling her his 'idol'. Edith does not reach orgasm this time, nor during any other of their encounters except the very last one. Nevertheless she fully enjoys this erotic experience. His strength, as he squeezes her arms, wrists and legs, leaves her again bruised. She will tease him about this. As he slides inside her she reassures him that she is safe. None of these early encounters leave her pregnant. The bearing of this on the credibility of her own monitoring of her menstrual cycle will emerge in due course. After their initial passion is spent, Freddy offers to rub Edith's back to take away 'that stiffness' from the Eastcote exertions. Feeling the movement of his hands on her body, now totally surrendered to him for any explorations he desires, she feels soothed and at peace.

Over the next few days more encounters between the lovers take place, and on the afternoon of Friday 1 July Edith and Freddy abscond. They see a film, *Romance*, at the Palace Theatre in Cambridge Circus, to celebrate the fact that it is three weeks to the day since they declared their love to each other in Shanklin. This adaptation of E. B. Sheldon's hugely successful play of 1913 about the tragic loves of an operatic diva commenced its exclusive London run on Monday 20 June. As in the stage version, so in the film, Doris Keane starred. Of particular interest was the Prologue, 'Lovers of the Ages', by Robb

Lawson of *Broken Blossoms* fame. The intention was to generate the right atmosphere for the setting of the film. An extended cast of well known players impersonated 'famous historical lovers', and Paula Ruby, attired in *Romance* costume, offered recitals from the operas in the play. It is nearly 6 p.m. as Mrs Thompson and young Bywaters leave the theatre. Mercifully this is the evening when Percy stays up late in the City for his Friday night drink.

The week starting Monday 4 July is one of the hottest ever recorded in England. Every day Edith rushes home early from work to be with her lover – Carlton has granted her request to work on a flexible schedule for the time being: she is now indispensable to the firm. These two weeks from 27 June to 10 July are the lovers' halcyon days. Short of a holiday together for just the two of them – one of Edith's favourite fantasies – the privacy afforded them by the empty house has been ideal for their mutual discovery of one another.

Sunday 10 July is the hottest July day since 1881. All of No. 231 is invited for Sunday dinner. Newenham will bring his camera – he loves photography and is renowned in the family for his skill and his ability to capture moods and expressions on celluloid. At dinner Edith is wearing one of her favourite summer dresses with three-quarter-length sleeves and an Oriental panel. Over it she has slipped a tunic blouse with a long sash trailing down in pleats.

The men are dressed in light suits and open collars. After lunch the party moves out of the morning room into the garden. It is oppressively sweltering here and everyone retires into the shade. The four pictures extant from the next ten minutes, from 1.40 p.m. to 1.50 p.m., tell a fascinating story.

In the first one Newenham catches Edith pointing at something at the top of the house, while Thompson and Bywaters stand on either side of her. The trio is facing north-east. The sun hits the backs of their heads. The photographer has moved into the middle of the garden. It is interesting to note that in the picture Bywaters, unlike Thompson, seems strained. Newenham's next direction is for the three of them to be seated and relax. Freddy picks up his novel and sits on the right of the wicker sofa. Percy sits on the left. He is holding a copy of the *Sunday Pictorial* and is gazing at its back page. Mrs Thompson is seated in the middle between the two men. The photographer specifically asks that no one look at the camera. Edith alone conveys a stilted impression as she fixes on a point at the bottom of the garden, with her hands folded in her lap. Her legs are exposed halfway up to her knees.

It is now Percy's turn to take a photograph and he yields his place and newspaper to Newenham. Freddy leans away from Edith rather more, while she remains stoically seated in suspended motion.

Then Freddy rises and takes the camera. Edith moves into his place, Thompson into hers, and Newenham stays put. He discards the paper and leans back against the cushions pretending to be asleep. This time Edith faces the camera, with her legs tightly closed, and her right arm propped up by a cushion. Of the four extant photographs, this one best highlights the mounting tensions between them. Thompson has defensively crossed his legs and arms, and stares straight into the camera. A look almost of defiance lingers in his eyes. There is no hint of a smile or of a gesture towards the camera. Edith studiously avoids catching Bywaters's eye and looks in the opposite direction from the camera. Is she concerned about giving Percy too much of a clue if he surprises her smiling at the camera? Or is she keen to avoid appearing too cosy in a family shot with Thompson and her brother?

The next two weeks of July pass uneventfully. The Lesters return, and day-time encounters between Freddy and Edith on the premises of No. 41 are now out of the question. On Wednesday 27 July, a month after they became lovers, Edith and Freddy travel out to Chorley-wood for the day, and on Saturday 30 July the lovers pay a day-long visit to Kew. The privacy afforded them by the Gardens impresses on both of them, and on her in particular, the impossible situation at No. 41. Percy remains in the dark, but he has noticed his wife's increasing reluctance to tolerate his company. His lodger and friend Bywaters acts strangely these days and shows no willingness to ship out. Percy feels his privacy invaded and is annoyed by Bywaters's dancing attendance on every one of his wife's whims. Percy has never thought of washing up as part of a man's duty; Freddy's willingness to hover about her to dry up and even to clear the dishes simply cannot be allowed to continue, nor must she go on acknowledging his help with an insolent gratefulness. He resolves to talk it over with her. It is only hours now to the first real confrontation between the husband and the lovers.

While Percy is bracing himself for a talk with his wife, the lovers are returning to Ilford equally resentful. A frosty dinner inevitably ends with Thompson asking his wife how she spent the day. He still does not imagine that she and Bywaters could have been out together. Within minutes a row is in full swing. The Lesters cannot help hearing it, as the Thompsons' voices are raised. Bywaters remains silent. Then he probably wanders off into the garden. The following day, Sunday, is spent in mutually watchful antagonism. Thompson knows nothing factual about Edith and Fred, but has been stung by his wife's defensiveness about their lodger. Another quarrel erupts as Edith refuses to pander to the proprietorial habits of her husband. Again Bywaters is present. Again he ignores it as far as he can. All three pass a miserable Sunday, made bearable only by a further truce. Percy's suspicions are pure conjecture so far, but not for much longer.

Monday 1 August: It is Bank Holiday Monday. Edith, Percy and Freddy are sitting out in the garden after dinner. The scene is similar to that of 10 July. Edith is reclining on the wicker sofa, sewing with a basket in her lap. Freddy is reading a book and Percy is either pottering about in the garden or reading the Sunday papers. It is about mid-afternoon, when Edith remarks that she needs a pin. The comment is not specifically addressed to her husband, though it is up to him, she intimates, to respond to her request. He ignores it, while Freddy rises with 'I will go and get you one'. During the time that he is inside the house rummaging in the drawers in the Thompsons' bedroom, Percy turns on his wife and starts berating her. Just as Bywaters re-emerges into the garden, he snaps, 'You like to have someone always tacked on to you to run all your little errands and obey all your little requests'. Edith remains stubbornly silent. She may look daggers, but speaks none for the moment. Freddy's reappearance temporarily halts Thompson's abuse. The atmosphere in the garden is taut, but all three are privately determined to exercise restraint, as Avis Graydon is due shortly for tea. As 4 p.m. approaches Edith rises, packs her sewing into the basket and with the men reluctantly in tow, moves through the French windows into the morning room. She starts laying out the silver tea service and then proceeds into the kitchen to prepare the tea. But Avis, very unusually, does not appear.

It is getting on for 4.30 p.m. There is no sign of the sister. Edith proposes that they wait for her. Freddy agrees. Thompson emphatically dissents and starts complaining. Bywaters gets up and steps outside into the garden. He can hear the voices inside. Much as he now despises Thompson, he does not wish to interfere; and Edith has asked him to keep a low profile, because she wants him to stay put at No. 41, to 'protect' her. Feeling poorly treated by his wife and now stood up by her sister, Percy begins to insult Edith, her family in general and her sister in particular. It is a rash and foolish thing to do, one moreover out of character with Thompson's usual behaviour. He had always been welcomed by the Graydons and was acutely conscious of their superior social standing. He may not have quite meant what he said. But Edith reacts sharply. She cannot allow her little sister to be insulted, particularly since she has taken her lover from her. Once stung into white anger, she gives as good as she gets. Avis has failed to turn up, the Lesters are away for the day. No holds are barred. She is screaming at Thompson when he hits her several times and, grabbing her, throws her across the room. As she stumbles, she knocks over a chair and falls against the table. It is this racket which leads Bywaters to charge into the room and to step literally between husband and wife. She is crying and screaming, and Thompson is hollering; he tells Bywaters to keep out of it and to get out. He doesn't budge and tells Percy to lay off. Edith stays dazed for a second and then bolts upstairs.

The two men do not fight, even though Bywaters physically impedes Thompson's movement towards his wife. Percy is cowed by Bywaters's smouldering but unmistakable anger as he interposes himself. This confrontation leaves Percy profoundly humiliated and hurt: he trusted Freddy and now he is proved a fool, though as yet he is ignorant of the adultery. As if to add insult to injury, while Thompson threatens Bywaters with throwing him out, the latter not only appears unperturbed, but tells him to leave Edith alone and not to knock her about any more; unless he wants to have to deal with him. Percy now demands that Freddy leave, which he shrugs off, agreeing to do so after talking to Edith. She in the meantime is upstairs, bruised and crying with anger and frustration. Freddy decides to go for a stroll. He needs a breath of fresh air. Edith probably watches him leave from the upstairs window.

At about 7 p.m. the Lesters return. Freddy is still out and shortly afterwards Edith leaves the house, followed before long by an angry Thompson. Where the three of them spend the next four hours is unclear, although a public house is the most likely venue for this conjugal crisis meeting. The scenario of the three of them sitting together and discussing separation, while Thompson suspects Bywaters merely to be a reckless meddler, is bizarre. To Percy's confident and comically magnanimous 'We will come to an agreement and have a separation', Edith caustically replies: 'You always tell me that when I mention the subject, and later, when it actually comes, you refuse to grant it me'; and again, 'Yes, I should like that, but you make a statement and then whine back to me and retract that statement; you have done that before.' Even as the three of them return to the house in the summer night, the day's events seem to each of them like a nightmare. Percy is shattered by the upheaval, Edith is sore from her bruises and Freddy now regrets telling Percy about how he should behave to his wife.

Tuesday morning, 2 August, 7.30 a.m.: Edith is assisting Mrs Lester with breakfast and prepares to take it upstairs to her husband. Asked whether he is unwell, she replies: 'He is all right, but will not have his meals in the same room as Freddy.' She is down pretty quickly, followed shortly by Freddy with whom she has breakfast in the morning room. The weather is unsettled which suits their sombre mood. When Edith leaves for work, Freddy returns to his room. By 9 a.m. Percy in turn has left for the station, followed shortly by Bywaters. When Edith returns from work in the evening, she shows Mrs Lester her arm. It is 'black from the shoulder to the elbow'. Mrs Lester: 'Oh my, what did that?', to which Edith replies, 'Percy did it last night. Freddy and he had a "bust up" and I went between them and he threw me across the room.' Edith is to remember this day as the first day when she had to face the prospect of Freddy's departure.

Wednesday and Thursday reinforce the futility of Bywaters's hanging on at No. 41. He will leave on Friday and return to Westow Street. Thursday night is the last one the lovers will spend under the same roof. It will be very difficult for them to keep a tryst in the house in the future, unless the Lesters are off the premises – which is unlikely since Mr Lester is ailing and will get worse.

Friday 5 August: Percy is still not dining or breakfasting in the same room as Bywaters. The lovers are on their own therefore in the morning room. Only Mrs Lester's presence in the kitchen prevents a tearful outburst from Edith, as she realises that Freddy will not be sleeping here again. When she walks out of the door he will go upstairs, pack his few belongings and leave No. 41 for good. In exactly a year to the day from now she will be writing to him from Carlton & Prior and recalling how 'the bestest pal a girl ever had' left her 'all by myself at 41 for good'.

Having said his goodbyes to Mrs Lester, Bywaters leaves the house. As Friday is the weekly visiting day at No. 231 he has undertaken to take Edith back to the Crescent from work. To avoid colliding with Thompson they will commute east from Fenchurch to Manor Park, and then walk across from Station Road to the Browning Road through Morris Avenue. At the bottom of the avenue, within shouting distance of the Graydons' home and a mere fifty yards from the

Avenue Hotel, Freddy and Edith kiss passionately. She is pleading with him to stay with her. Eventually they part and she notices that they are standing at the exact intersection of the Browning Road and Morris Avenue. She points this out to him and invites him to cherish the memory of this place as a milestone in their 'great' and suffering love: 'one of the treasured spots in our memory'.

This is the first night that the Thompsons spend without Bywaters at 41 Kensington Gardens. Before long 'high words' are exchanged in the bedroom. These arguments will continue throughout the week, usually in the privacy of the bedchamber – if one can call it privacy, since members of the Lester family on either side are only too eager to overhear. The overt cause of these rows is money. Edith resents her husband demanding Bywaters's departure from a house purchased primarily with her earnings and savings. In the meantime Freddy is explaining to his mother that he left Ilford because, as a result of Thompson's meanness, the husband and wife get on very badly. She advises him to keep out and tells him that Mrs Thompson can easily get a separation if she wishes.

For the next fortnight Edith Thompson and Freddy Bywaters meet regularly in the lunch hour and every Friday evening till 9 September. She is sleeping badly and is haunted by nightmares. From being an indifferent husband, the man next to her has in her mind become an ogre. On Thursday 11 August Edith returns to Bywaters a cache of letters sent him by the Australian girl. She extracted these from him as a proof of his affection. She may well have read them, for when asked later whether they were love letters, she replied that they were 'hardly' that. They were more like 'personal letters'. Her reason for getting rid of them is that she has nowhere to keep them except in her newly bought cash box at Carlton & Prior. This she wants to use for *her* letters only, just in case someone might find them – which would be too awful. She and Freddy meet again the following day, exactly a week after their passionate embrace at the corner of Morris Avenue. Then, on Friday 19 August Percy for good reason surmises that his wife and Bywaters have been together. Percy is catching on. He will never quite believe though that his wife and Bywaters have already committed adultery. But he does suspect now that they are romantically attached. In the evening he confronts her with it. She indignantly denies everything. The following morning, at about 8 a.m., Edith posts a short letter to Freddy from Ilford: 'Come & see me Monday lunch time, please darlint. He suspects. PEIDI.'

By Sunday Edith has recovered some of her balance. At last she is sleeping calmly again. On Monday Freddy meets her and does his best to reassure her. They will be more careful in the future, that's all. His buoyancy and confidence always buck her up, but she is aware of how restless he is becoming. He is eager now to get on a ship again. The rest of August marks a truce for the Thompsons. The first week after Bywaters's departure they barely spoke other than with raised voices at night. Now tempers are cooling and Percy's suspicions may even have the effect of restraining him. He knows that he cannot take his wife for granted any more. On 27 August Edith writes to Bywaters to mark their second 'anniversary' since 27 June. There will be many such moments for the lovers, in her imagination at least.

The lovers continue meeting intermittently, but they communicate regularly. On Monday 5 September Edith sends a telegram to 11 Westow Street that 'Peidi sends herself to other half no chance to write', and on Wednesday 7 September she again cables a message to 11 Westow Street: 'Yes I do know. PEIDI.' What the telegram refers to is unclear. It is, however, on this day that Freddy secures a position as writer on the P & O's *Morea*, a medium-sized passenger liner. Edith Thompson will become very fond of the *Morea*. Bywaters has landed the berth on the liner at very short notice and will have to be ready to sail on Friday.

For Edith the day of his departure, Friday 9 September, marks a watershed. There is no one now to turn to, unless she can write to him. She is a girl of immense imaginative ability. If she writes at length to Freddy, she can make him experience her life in London in the mind's eye, provided she offers the right kind of detail and sounds the correct note. Naturally such a correspondence will also act as a reminder of her existence and of her love for him.

The seventy letters and telegrams that have survived of her relationship with Bywaters are minor gems. Her range in them is impressive, her confidence startling. Some of her letters are wholly concerned with literary criticism of a sort, such as endings in fiction, the overlap between novels and life, and the presentation of character in the works of novelists such as Hichens, Chambers and Hutchinson. On other occasions she expands on her sexual revulsion from her husband and her longings for Freddy. She describes how she dreams about joining him in bed and making love; and then how he bolts downstairs to escape from her husband at the top of the landing. She records her periods to underline the intimacy of their relationship, and then pretends to be shocked when her lover takes her up on it. She offers contradictory and outrageous accounts of her miscarriage(s), and follows them with meticulous descriptions of visits to the theatre, cinema and music-hall. She discusses scores of people, real and fictional, mostly, but not always, forgiving rather than censuring. She can fight like a polecat when Bywaters is dismissive of her in his replies, and at the same time be as innocent as a schoolgirl before one of his escapades. She is at her best in the recording of the quotidian happenings in her life, involving her lover in the fêtes at the Seamen's Orphanage in Wanstead Park and the Eastcote outing, as well as the routines, trials and excitements at Carlton & Prior. Most of these letters have survived. Only for this first trip on the *Morea* have the records perished. In court Edith refused to admit that she had written to her lover then. He recalled it though and acknowledged that he had replied. So did she in a long letter written in the winter of 1921:

> I seem to be able to talk to you always & for ever, but you, I don't know, you don't seem the same as when you were away before [9 September to 29 October 1921], you did talk to me a lot that trip, but this time you don't seem to at all.

Freddy studiously kept all the letters that were sent him, particularly Edith Thompson's. Even he, popular with the ladies and used to their attentions, had not before been the recipient of such ardour and eloquence. The reason that suggests itself for their disappearance may be connected with the fact that he kept all his letters in a sailor's ditty box. It is possible that a new box was acquired for the second voyage of the *Morea* – the first trip was a great rush and happened very suddenly. The original lot may therefore well have been separated from the others, kept mostly on board ship and some at home. Where they are now no one knows. The police never set eyes on them, and have no record of them. They would have been eager to use them, as the prosecution was anxious to establish and prove an early date for the adultery, preferably to demonstrate conclusively that it had happened under the husband's hospitable roof. This early part of Edith Thompson's letters must have dealt with the summer events extensively, reflecting, interpreting, resuscitating, projecting and pleading. One day they may turn up, but though Freddy Bywaters knew where they were he took his secret with him.

On this warm Friday evening of September a downcast Mrs Thompson is replying to her parents' questions about young

Bywaters, Percy and herself. The huge coverage given in her daily paper to the return to England of Charlie Chaplin does little to raise her morale. Within the next few weeks, she will embark on the curious existence of living a double life: on the one hand that of the busy and competent businesswoman in the City of London; on the other hand the fantasy world of the cornered romantic heroine, keeping a home fire burning and in her mind following the young sailor plying the oceans of the world. She now closely reads the P & O shipping routes in the paper and knows his whereabouts at each step of the voyage. Every port of call is an address for a letter.

On Saturday 24 September Avis celebrates her twenty-sixth birthday. Last year Freddy sent greetings to her. This time he forgets and Avis is hurt. The autumn of 1921 remains one of the warmest on record. It is in early October that Edith sees D. W. Griffith's *Way Down East*, premièred in London at the Empire Theatre on Wednesday 7 September 1921. The lead is taken by Lillian Gish, supported by Richard Barthelmes as the devoted admirer, and a memorable performance by Lowell Sherman as the philandering villain who traps the innocent Anna Moore (Gish) into a mock marriage and abandons her when she is pregnant. For the three and a half months of its run at the Empire, the film plays to a packed house. In its riveting melodramatic finale and in its conclusion in a bitter-sweet white wedding, Edith Thompson feels herself uniquely addressed. Above all, however, one imagines her responding to Gish's rendering of wounded womanhood and the discovery, seemingly too late, of true love. In one of the letters presumed lost, Edith writes to Freddy at length about *Way Down East*, and how much she wishes he had shared the film with her.

Saturday 29 October 1921 is a dry and mild day. The *Morea* is docking at Tilbury. At 41 Kensington Gardens Edith is restless in anticipation. She prepares lunch for Percy and herself. Then, on some pretext or other, she excuses herself to go across to No. 231 on her own. Freddy has told her that he will be there. She can barely contain her excitement as she passes the corner of Morris Avenue and turns into the Crescent. The entire Graydon family is present when the lovers shake hands:

> that was all you and I could do, just imagine shaking hands, when we are all & everything to each other, two halves not yet united.

Their greetings of 'hallo Edie' and 'hallo Freddy' seem unexceptional to the family. But to the lovers their artifice is a betrayal. The afternoon passes in animated conversation. Parting at 5.30p.m. is hard. If only they could now just go off together on their own, instead of which she must return to 41 Kensington Gardens to cook for her husband, while Freddy stays behind in the Crescent. She cries on the way back – even he claims to have found their meeting trying and felt as if he 'wanted to die'.

With Bywaters back in England Edith predictably finds Sunday 'too awful to bear' and can only get through it by blunting her mind:

> my mind and thoughts I had to make frozen, I darent think, not about anything, I should have run away, I know I should, I felt quite sure.

The thought of Monday keeps her going. As soon as she arrives at 168 Aldersgate she is informed that a parcel is waiting for her. She knows who it is from and excitedly unwraps it. It contains Oriental silks and several sets of beads, one of which, the 'lilac one', she immediately fancies. All her friends at work gather to admire them – only Lily knows who sent them and what this might mean. They tease Edith about the present and ask to be left them in her will. There is also a letter from Bywaters telling her how dreadful he found Saturday, but she must cheer up: 'What I am saying [is] dont let this make you too miserable chère.' Edith spends her lunch hour replying to Bywaters and sends the letter by hand through Rose Jacobs, who assists in the showroom. She is dispatched to deliver the note to a gentleman matching a particular description, either across the road at Fuller's, or else in the porch of Aldersgate Station.

At 5 p.m. Edith finishes work, and five minutes later she is kissing and hugging her lover in frantic abandon. He is so taken aback by this enraptured reaction to his embrace that his bewilderment shows and amuses her. The lovers have about an hour and a half between leaving the shop and boarding the 6.45 p.m. to Ilford at Fenchurch Street. Now at last they can talk of their 'real' lives. She is very depressed and is, she claims, cheered only by the prospect of Thursday, when they will go out dancing together.

It rains all Monday night and all of Tuesday. The Thames floods. On Thursday 3 November the lovers take off for the day. Edith is wearing the silks which Freddy brought her. As a reminder of him she promises to wear them every day, like his lilac beads which are also much in evidence on her. It is cold and drizzling and groundfrost is forecast for the night. Where the lovers go, or whereabouts they make love, is impossible to establish. Nor can Percy's movements for this day and evening be accounted for. Perhaps he went to the theatre or attended a masonic evening. But what is not in question is the lovers' actual encounter and the husband's at last realising that his wife and former lodger are deeply involved.

From this day to Friday 20 January 1922 it is exactly seventy-nine days. These two dates are collocated here because they mark the inception and termination of Edith Thompson's first pregnancy, which fell eleven days short of three months. The question of her pregnancies is crucial to the letters, the trial and the stories which emerged in the direct aftermath of the events of 9 January 1923.

That on this day Edith dispenses with precautions, even though their meeting was planned well in advance, stretches credulity – as does the fact that Bywaters does not use a contraceptive. Nevertheless both he and she later acknowledge that they loved without protection. (It is for this reason that she will not allow Thompson to touch her for thirty-two days from 3 November.)

When she is finally back with Percy in their bedroom, he has startling news for her: he saw her and her sailor boy at the station. This inevitably leads to recriminations about Bywaters, and Thompson bursts out with 'he is no man or else he would ask my permission to take you out'. Edith makes a mental note of this to tell Freddy about it. Since Thompson has hinted that he will go to Carlton & Prior the following day, Edith sends Freddy a telegram warning him off: 'Don't come 168 wait Fenchurch.' The lovers meet at 5.15 p.m. at Fenchurch Street. Freddy soothes Edith's fears and rashly undertakes to visit 41 Kensington Gardens to put it to Thompson, as a friend, that he and his wife ought to separate.

Almost incredibly the following day, in the early afternoon of Saturday 5 November, Bywaters calls on the Thompsons. Mrs Lester lets him in. He stays for two hours and confronts Thompson. He tells him that he *is* a man, and that he does not require anyone's permission to take Mrs Thompson out: 'Why do you not come to an amicable agreement, either have a separation or you can get a divorce.' Edith is present during part of this meeting. Thompson hums and haws: 'Yes – No – I don't see it concerns you . . . Well, I have got her and will keep her.' In the end Bywaters extracts a promise from her husband that he will not 'knock' Edith about any more: 'You are making Edie's life a hell. You know she is not happy with you'. When he leaves, Thompson has agreed 'that he would not beat her' again. After he has gone Edith tells Mrs Lester that Freddy and her husband have made it up. 41 Kensington Gardens must feel a strange place after Bywaters's departure. Furthermore, the Thompsons know that Bywaters is proceeding straight to the Crescent, where they are due for dinner tonight. The Graydons by now know that Freddy and Percy are at odds, but remain ignorant of the true reason for their quarrel and of its seriousness.

Monday 7 November: On her way into work Edith stops in the Barbican and sends a telegram to Bywaters on the *Morea* to wait for her in Fenchurch at 5.15 p.m. She does not expect him in the lunch hour. Then, at some point during the day, something happens to her and the doctor is called. Most likely it is a prolonged faint. The doctor in attendance will charge 10 shillings and sixpence, and Edith, on receiving the bill on Saturday 4 March 1922, will be stunned by the amount. What renders this particular incident relevant is that Edith clearly sees a connection between it and the miscarriage of 20 January 1922. Whatever the details of the crisis, Freddy is given a full and graphic account of it that night, and she will expect him to remember it. In the country at large, this week is 'poppy week'. The lovers meet every day, as Thursday 10 November closes in all too quickly. Thursday is Bywaters's last full day in England for this year, and Edith is wearing his silks and beads. Whether they manage to spend the evening together or have to confine themselves to the two hours between 5 and 7 p.m. is not recorded. What is known is that they revert to their 'compact' repeatedly: a suicide agreement in five years' time, from their first kiss on the Isle of Wight, if they are not eternally united by then.

The day following their last meeting this year is Remembrance Day. It is also the day that the *Morea* sails for Bombay. At a quarter past two in the afternoon, while the vessel is floating down the estuary towards the open sea, Edith is sitting in her office in the City, brooding over the past few days. Did Freddy not for her sake jump ship and lose his job? Her husband would not have dared; and this moreover happened at the same time that Percy was rowing with a good man-friend of hers for calling her by her first name! Whereas Thompson out of fear had had himself discharged from the army, young Bywaters had sailed the ocean to India in a military convoy at the height of the German submarine offensive. It is not just Percy who cuts a poor figure compared to Freddy, but others also of Edith's admirers, such as the mysterious 'Mel'. He rings her twice at Carlton & Prior on this

Remembrance Day of 1921, but each time she is out. He is an Ilford man who works in the City, and attends dance lessons in the Cripplegate Institute. He knows all the protagonists involved here, including Bywaters and Avis. Before long he and Edith will have an interesting dinner together, and he will press her about Bywaters.

The sleeting, snowy weather continues. On Thursday 17 November 1921 a woman shops at Carlton & Prior who, Edith ruefully notes, lost her husbands 'not through the war: 2 were drowned and one committed suicide and some people I know cant lose one. How unfair everything is'. At least tonight she is seeing a variety show at the Ilford Hippodrome. This 'Pierrotic Extravaganza' is opened by two men with a 1921 hit, 'Feather Your Nest', a song which Edith adores. The costumes, scenic and lime-light effects, and individual performances impress the audience with their inventiveness. 'Land of Hope & Glory' is stirringly sung, and a skit called 'How to Make Love' contains the line which Edith Thompson remembers: '"Marriage is the inclination of a crazy man to board a lazy woman, for the rest of his natural life." Rather cutting I think, but there it came from a man.' The show concludes with the initiation of Jack Gallagher into the mysteries of the Suicide Club which 'provides much mirth'. As Edith walks home to her house with her husband, she is puzzled by the fact that she enjoyed the evening, particularly the dance numbers. Her suicide pact tonight seems almost as absurd as Gallagher's parody of it. She will shortly write to Bywaters: 'dont let us. I'd like to live'.

Friday 18 November is Derby Day, and Edith has money on the tipped favourite Front Line. It is 'that loose end sort of day' which precedes the weekend, and that means a full dose of Percy. She has not been asked out anywhere tonight, so she will have to make do with the weekly visit at No. 231. As she enters her parents' home, she finds Avis on her own. Her parents have gone to Highbury to attend to Mrs Liles, Edith's dying grandmother. She is laid up in the home of her daughter and son-in-law. Suffering from bronchitis syncope and unable to fend off the severe cold which came with the winter, Deborah Liles, aged eighty-one, is at death's door. She is asking after her nephews and nieces. Avis will call on her over the weekend. She cannot accompany her parents tonight because she spends the early part of Friday evening teaching ballroom dancing. During the lesson Mel has enquired about her sister and leaked the information to Avis that a friend of hers and Edith have been seen walking together. Avis tells her sister this tonight and that Mel has not revealed who the 'friend' was. Edith volunteers

no answer, and Avis does not press the point since, as her sister
suspects, she is sure to know that Bywaters is the man in question. It is
not hard to imagine Avis's feelings of hurt and betrayal.

Saturday 19 November 1921: Business at Carlton & Prior is picking
up rapidly, and the firm has decided to open from 9 to 12.30 on
Saturday mornings. Edith does not applaud the idea entirely –
Saturday 14 January 1922, when Bywaters is home, will now be a half
working-day – but it does reduce the amount of time she has to spend
in her husband's company; and it is going to earn her more money.
Percy, whose Saturday off this is, is not happy at the thought of his
wife monopolised by her work and grumbles: 'No home comfort
whatever, you'll have to stop at home, no other man's wife wants to
gad the town every day. They all find enough interest in their home.'
As soon as she arrives at work, she takes Freddy's picture out of her
desk for a daily, ritualised 'good morning' address. She keeps his
photograph in her 'WHERE IS IT' book. An 'irresistible feeling'
suddenly overcomes her to run her fingers through his hair. She loves
doing that, she confesses, 'it feels so lovely'. Most men, she reflects,
don't like it, even hate it, but he is vastly different from most men and,
unlike her husband, has a full head of very thick and curly hair. It is
nearly noon when she sits down and very quickly writes Bywaters a
few lines, before returning to Ilford. At about tea-time, Edith puts it to
Thompson that she needs a maid. He concurs but will not agree to
having Ethel Vernon: 'my people won't like it'. The 'people' are the
Chamberses of Mansfield Road, Ethel's former employers. In any
case, Percy tells Edith, he finds her 'fearfully strung up' and 'morbid'
these days. (Edith will eventually get her way, although when Ethel
arrives at Paddington from St Ives, on Wednesday 4 October 1922, her
prospective employer will have been dead for fourteen hours.)

Tonight Percy approaches his wife in bed. As he tries to touch her
she pulls away, determined to resist any sexual contact for a month
from 3 November. In the past she would eventually have surrendered
to her husband's desires, but not now. He starts to plead with her and
asks why she is no longer happy with him; they used to be happy. She
protests that she is not unhappy, merely indifferent. Secretly, however,
she wonders that she had once been content with her lot, 'before I
knew what real happiness could be like, before I loved you darlint'.
Pressed again, she tells him that she doesn't love him any more. He is
'astounded' and begs her to forgive and forget everything that he has
done or said in the past. Couldn't they 'start fresh and try and be happy

again and just [me and] him' so that when the anniversary of their wedding comes, on 15 January 1922, 'we shall be just as happy and contented as we were on that day 7 years ago'. Edith remains unmoved, but feels 'awful'. She promises, for the sake of peace, to do her share to make Percy happy and contented. This calms him down, while she resentfully tolerates his arms around her body.

On Monday there is more mail from Bywaters waiting for Edith at Carlton & Prior. She decides to take the lunch hour off and stay in to reply to the entire bulk of four, three from Tilbury and the one from Dover this morning. Two of the Tilbury letters came in a single long envelope, with a curiously distorted 'E' on it, 'to curb other people's curiosity'. Edith dislikes it and asks him to refrain from thus making a fool of both of them.

The letters are despondent and self-flagellating. Bywaters blames himself for leaving her in the lurch: 'I've run away and left you'; and he gratifies her self-esteem by fondly reminiscing about spots of time precious to them both. He liked *Maria*, a 'real live book', as did she. He mentions the three year appointed waiting period and she, replying, suggests that three months at a time is all she can contemplate. He asks her for a photograph, and she professes to be 'really sorry', for she never makes 'a good one darlint, not even a natural one, when I pose, and I don't know that I will have one taken, even to please you'. In the end she gives in. What troubles her is the way he once sneered at a photo sent him on the *Orvieto* by a lady, either Mólly or the Australian girl. Now that Edith fears that she has become 'fatter in the face' out of grief, the time is hardly right for a photograph. Freddy's enquiry about 'hair torture' meets with a concession — she will have her hair done. The cheeky greeting card which he enclosed makes her laugh, but she prefers not to receive another one like it, because such cards belie his true character. As for her desires, Freddy boldly advises her what to do when she wants him. Whatever this is, in her reply she concurs and jokingly offers even to bruise herself 'as you used and then take myself to Court for cruelty to myself'.

He enquires about books, and she explains that she is about to start Robert Service's *Trail of 98*, but cannot read it today, because Avis has rung and asked that she visit Highbury; and she is finding W. B. Maxwell's *The Guarded Flame* arduous: he writes, she claims, 'very strange books — some are very sensual — but in a learned kind of way. I cant explain any better than that.'

Next Freddy relates an incident about a 'lady and the mail bag', which caused him grievous indignation. It appears that the 'lady' is a native North African – the incident in question probably happened in Marseilles – and therefore Freddy describes her in terms of her colour: 'coffee and milk'. He blames her mistake on her race, and Edith protests firstly about the expression, and then about the dismissive attitude towards women revealed by Freddy's letter:

> coffee and milk coming from you to me – from you to anyone else – perhaps yes and after all is she any worse for being a native – anyway I dont know and I dont think you do and then you say 'If it had been one of the male sex'. Why 'it' darlint, I thought you were beginning to think just a little more of us than you used.

Bywaters goes on to promise Edith 'something at some future date, when both you and I are ready'. He means giving her a baby. He concludes by noting that for the last three hours he has 'been pushed to blazes'. This is one of his favourite expressions and she is tickled by it, as she can just imagine him saying it.

After work Edith leaves for Lucerne Road to visit Grandma Liles. She last saw the old lady in the summer, before her terminal illness left her emaciated and senile.

Two days later, on Wednesday 23 November, Mrs Liles dies. The Graydons, the Laxtons and the Walkinshaws go into mourning. The funeral is scheduled for Saturday. As the family gather in the shivering cold of a north London cemetery, a thick and icy fog is developing and threatens to engulf the metropolis. Trains and suburban traffic are affected by huge delays, as the points freeze together. What bothers Edith Thompson more than the pea-souper is the painful chilblain on the back of her heel, which her shoe cuts right in half. This does not prevent her, however, from visiting the theatre mid-week with tickets given her by Lily Laxton, now in mourning for her mother. The play is *Woman to Woman* at the Globe on Shaftesbury Avenue. It stars the American actress Wilette Kershaw, who performs with 'an immense amount of nervous intensity and skill'. Edith will in a few months' time see her again in the Hawaiian melodrama *The Bird of Paradise*. What distinguishes *Woman to Woman*, a sentimental Great War play, is the way it refuses morally to polarise adultery and legitimacy. Instead it places the emphasis on forgiveness growing from female intuition and maternal instinct. Edith professes to have loved it, 'as much as "Romance" altho the plot is not the same'.

On Thursday 1 December Edith is taking a country buyer to a business lunch at Cooks's in St Paul's Churchyard. They pass the Chapter House, and he eagerly turns to the elegant book-keeper from Carlton & Prior: 'Would you care for a glass of wine here, its quite a nice place.' – 'No thanks, really I'd rather not.' She had come here with Freddy in the summer before he went out on the *Morea* in September, and the places which they used to frequent are sacred to her: places like the Holborn, the Queen Anne Restaurant and the Strand, particularly 'those corner seats'. In the Chapter House they had spent a memorable evening one Friday, when she explained how her life could be happy, if she lived with 'only 2 people besides myself'. Today her answer to the same question about her happiness would be 'with only 2 people, 2 halves, one whole, darlint, just you & me, say "Yes, it's right," & it will be so'.

That night in bed Percy again trespasses on forbidden territory. He senses the extent to which his wife is withdrawn and alienated from him. But he has been trying hard recently to be more understanding of her and asks whether she is 'happier'. She coolly replies that she assumes that she is as happy as she'll ever be. He is not bothering her yet, but his next suggestion ruffles her composure. He thinks that they would both be happier if they 'had a baby'. Edith shies away with a panic-struck 'No, a thousand times No'. Even if she gives in to him, she will certainly not dispense with contraception – which is what he is asking of her. In any case she has good reason to believe that she is already pregnant by her lover. But she can't even bear the thought of Percy assuming that he is the father of a baby he did not engender. Percy is again begging her and questioning her, but she remains resolved. Finally she huddles up as close as she can against the wall, turning her back to him. He doesn't try to 'worry' her – the last time he did that was Saturday 19 November. But he does put his arms around her, and his hands touch her. What previously she accepted as the inevitable now disgusts her as 'horrid'. There is a residual undercurrent of guilt about her failing in her wifely duty – her parents seem so content by comparison that it nearly scares her. She cannot bring herself to confide in them the shame of her failed marriage.

Feeling 'very blue' on Friday morning, Edith writes to Bywaters telling him about the preceding night and gleefully, if also caustically, remarks that *he* wishes to learn to dance. *He* could then take her out to 'some nice ones'. Edith's comment on this is ' "Ain't we got fun", while you are away!' Again she notes that her periods have not yet returned and that she must be pregnant. At 5 p.m. she goes to the Waldorf for the *thé dansant* and dinner. As she leaves, it is very foggy, and all the trains are running late. She therefore hails a taxicab in the Aldwych and gets to 'Mother's at 10.20 pm'. Percy knows she is there, but will not come and collect her. This may be because she went dancing without him, or because of her reticence in bed yesterday. Her parents are clearly surprised at the husband's failure to come for his wife, in view of the lateness of the hour and the thick fog. Edith senses the parents' disapproval and feels humiliated. Another notch against Percy.

On Saturday Edith receives two letters in a single envelope, posted from Port Said. They sound apologetic and lack ardour. In her reply she crossly demands to know whether he still feels the same about her. If he does, then why are his letters so stiff and wooden? What she wants him to do is to engage not just in writing, but in talking, 'the real talking I was looking forward to'. She is always, she notes, *talking* to him; nor is it for her merely a chore. On the contrary, it is her all and everything and in a way recreates him for her as though he were present as a live interlocutor. What partly redeems his letters though is, she claims, his using the expression 'I do love 'em, etc'. It reminds her of the wonderful Shanklin days, which seem like days of innocence now.

On Sunday 4 December 1921 the Thompsons, the Graydons and the Walkinshaws have all gathered in Stamford Hill at 5 Rostrevor Avenue as guests of Auntie Lily and Uncle Jack. Uncle Jack, or John Ambrose Henry Laxton, is manager of the Furniture Record Publishers and works at 14 City Road, EC1. The little gabled villa, with its deep garden at the back, remains intact today, apart from the tawdry layer of stucco which it acquired in later years. It turns out to be a real family dinner, perhaps the first one since grandmother's death. Everyone enjoys the occasion, and the Walkinshaws invite the whole family to Highbury for a belated New Year's celebration on 7 January 1922, which coincides with Bywaters's return to Tilbury. Edith makes a despondent mental note of this while accepting the invitation.

It is on Monday of this week that his wife gives way to Percy in bed. Writing to Freddy in the morning, she moans: 'Peidi does want you now.' Moreover she is reading a very 'risqué' novel by Hichens of sexual and spiritual degeneracy, *Felix*. The book exudes a sickening aura of licence from its shallow presentation of adultery between an older drug-addicted society woman and a young aspiring writer. The intimations of carnal and perverted knowledge, associated with Parisian opium dens and the sorrows of addiction, give the work a veneer of both moral sobriety and aphrodisiacal suggestiveness. Edith notes that the book is 'weird – horrible and filthy – yet I am very interested'. She confesses that she feels let down by her lover – he won't 'talk' – and it is over a month since they made love. The self-imposed moratorium on married sex has expired. Last time, it is true, she abstained completely from her husband. But then Bywaters was still 'talking'.

On Tuesday evening Avis is visiting at 41 Kensington Gardens. Percy good-humouredly tells her that he has decided to learn to dance after all. Can she instruct him? Edith has refused, impatiently saying 'my days of dragging round beginners [are] over'. Avis does not mind and offers to give her brother-in-law his first dance lesson the following Tuesday.

On Thursday Edith is collecting her photos for Bywaters. Her own verdict is that they are awful and that she hopes that 'they are so rotten you'll send them all back'. On Friday she again patronises the Waldorf for the *thé dansant* in the Palm Court. Then she returns to the Crescent, and this time her husband dutifully collects her. In the wake of their seemingly re-established sex life, Percy is proving attentive, not to say uxorious.

Saturday 10 December: It is early morning in the kitchen at No. 41. Mrs Lester has prepared the porridge. During a brief moment of inattentiveness from her tenant, Edith furtively slips a drug into her bowl. It has a bitter taste, noticeable particularly in sugared porridge. As fate would have it, Percy takes the wrong bowl and eats the porridge, before she can intervene. This morning therefore poor Percy has porridge with abortifacient powder in it. He fails to comment on the taste. A similar accident will result in his drinking drugged tea by mistake, and on that occasion he will notice the taste and complain. At the trial the porridge and tea incidents achieved notoriety as corroborative proof of homicidal intent, when even then it was clear that abortion was the real issue at stake. It is an indictment of the skewed moral climate of the time that the woman in the dock did not dare admit in public that she had been trying to abort. The shame of that for herself and her family would have been too unbearable. It almost appeared preferable to be tried as a murderess.

By 9 a.m., at her desk in Carlton & Prior, Edith is chucklingly telling Freddy about her morning escapade. She wants 'bucking up' badly though. How can she reach out to him? She has today gone as far as to bruise her left wrist on either side with her right thumb and finger – just as Freddy had done but 'it doesn't do any good, it doesn't feel like you'. Anyway, tonight she is going out to dine with the gossipy Mel at the Café Marguerite on Oxford Street.

Over dinner Mel jumps the question of Bywaters on her and Edith reconstructs their conversation for Freddy's benefit:

Mel: Isn't your sister jealous of you?

Edith: My sister – why should she be?

Mel: It seems to me that you see more of her fiancé than she does herself.

Edith: How's that and what do you know about it anyway?

Mel: Well I saw you going down Ilford Hill the other evening and he was holding your arm – did you go to a dance together?

Edith: Oh shut up and talk about something else.

But Mel has her on the ropes. He will not let go. Repeatedly he reverts to Bywaters, prodding and trying to get it across to her that perhaps he is something of an unconventional chap himself. Edith does not really take offence at his suggestive conversation. She only notes that she 'had gone there to forget and instead of forgetting I was remembering all the time'.

Sunday night on 11 December brings about another sexual confrontation between Edith and Percy Thompson, the fourth one she records since Bywaters's departure for India. The husband can see no reason why, now that their sex life has returned at least to a certain intimacy, he cannot presume on his 'rights'. She quickly puts him right. A 'heated argument' ensues. The following dialogue is a partly reconstructed version from her reported speech as in the letter to Port Said of Saturday 10 to 12 December 1921:

Edith: Not now, please.

Percy: Why not?! Why are you different from what you used to be? Why have you changed since he left in August? Have you trans-ferred your affections from me to him?

Edith: No, for heaven's sake, shut up about Freddy. He has nothing to do with it. I just don't feel like it tonight. Can't you accept that?

Percy: You know perfectly well that we have not been right together since he left. You are my *wife* after all, if you know what that means.

Edith: Leave me alone; and leave Freddy out of this!

Percy: Has he written to you?

Edith: No!

Percy: That's another lie. . . . You are cunning the pair of you. You knew perfectly well that Saturday in October that he was coming back. *That's* why you went to the Crescent to see your mother about the curtains and to find out whether Bill was back. I assure you that this time when he gets home you two won't fool me. Every other man's wife does not hang out with all and sundry in town. If it isn't him, it's everybody else. And I KNOW he writes to you at Carlton & Prior's. Don't pretend that he doesn't. I'll put a stop to that, believe me.

At this Edith bites her lip and determines to get the doorman Jim, who delivers the post at Carlton & Prior, on her side, to keep her life-line of Bywaters's letters open. Perhaps for her peace of mind she allows herself to be possessed tonight. She decides to give in from now on anyway. Ought she to have lulled Thompson cynically into a false sense of security, she wonders, by letting him use her body like a prostitute's? That way he would never have suspected that anything was wrong.

It is still dark on Monday morning when Edith commutes into work. She eagerly expects to hear from Bywaters, at anchor in Bombay at this moment. But all she gets is a note of greetings and an apology for being unable to write to her. Her disappointment turns to anger, and she reverts to her lecture on talking rather than writing. I, she explains, also find it hard at times to write to you, particularly to write you a talking letter:

> but I just say to myself he's here with me, looking at me and listening to what I am saying and it seems to help darlint, couldn't you try and do this I feel awfully sad and lonely and think how much you would be cheering me up but perhaps you'll think I'm selfish about it all and I suppose I am, but remember when you are thinking badly or hardly of me your letters are the only thing I have in the world and darlint, I havent even all those.

For the next fortnight there will be no opportunity for Edith to talk to her lover or he to her, as Wednesday 14 December is the last day for Christmas mail posting. On the following Saturday Edith's mother is forty-nine years old. For the family at No. 231 December has retained its early magic, including, as it does, two birthdays, the parents' wedding anniversary and Christmas. Now more than ever the

72

Graydons can call themselves comparatively 'affluent'. The entire family is in full-time employment and doing better every day, no one more so than the eldest daughter. If the parents have noticed that the Thompsons' marriage is exhibiting signs of disharmony, they harbour not the slightest suspicion of the extent to which husband and wife are estranged. Mrs Graydon senses that Edith and Freddy like each other, but she still hopes that the youngster will eventually become engaged to Avis. It is shortly after her mother's birthday that Edith receives a note from Bywaters, addressed to her at 41 Kensington Gardens:

> Bombay
> 1st December 1921
>
> Dear Edie
>
> Do you remember last Xmas you wrote to me wishing me all the best. I never wrote you so this year I'm going to make sure of it. I want to wish you all that you can wish yourself. I know all those wishes of yours will run into a deuce of a lot of money. Such items as fur coats, cars and champagne, will be very prominent on the list – anyhow, good health and I hope you get it. Have a very real good time, the best that is possible. I shall be about 2 days this side of Suez. Never mind I will have a drink with you. Once more the very best at Xmas and always.
> > Yours very sincerely,
> > FREDDY

Its address, opening words, content and signature form part of a clumsy attempt to disguise their 'real' correspondence. Percy sees the note, as he was meant to, and will bring it up before long.

On Christmas Day Edith celebrates her twenty-eighth birthday. Percy and she are entertaining the family and various aunts and uncles. As a present she has been given a 22lb. turkey and 'many large boxes of chocolate'. The dinner party is a huge success, and even Percy is enjoying himself with some zest. Much has happened to Edith since her last birthday. Now she is an 'adulteress' who regularly cheats her husband. She has even wished him dead. She is almost certainly pregnant. As she casts her eyes about her – at the property and the comforts accumulated over the last two years; her own home in Ilford; her regular visits to dances and the theatre; her freedom from indigence of any kind – she knows that she will inevitably have to choose between these and her lover. The life inside her, she has already determined, must

73

not be born, because it would tie her down completely and irrevocably, and Percy would see the baby as a vindication of their marriage.

On Friday 30 December Edith acknowledges a woman friend's present for her birthday. In a largish hand she thanks 'M' for a camisole she has sent her, and then adds mysteriously, perhaps attributing to 'M' an ability to secure personal happiness that she lacks, 'I wish I were as clever as you.'

It is New Year's Eve. Like last year the Thompsons are again in the Crescent. Amidst all the revels Edith 'wondered if you were wondering the same as I. What will the New Year give to two halves – to you and I'. Her father used to 'call' at the Savoy on this evening. He may have done so earlier. He is now certainly present at the party, proud of his family and the quality of entertainment they can afford. Among the invited guests are all their close friends, including the grand Birnages. In the early hours of the morning of 1 January 1922 Mr and Mrs Thompson can be seen walking back the distance from Manor Park to Ilford. Later in the day they will be preparing a big New Year's dinner for the entire family from the Crescent.

This first day of January is the mildest in fifty years, and is taken to augur well for the year ahead. The evening passes quickly, and it is gone midnight when the guests depart. As this is the Thompsons' treat, Edith is clearing and washing up afterwards on her own. It is two o'clock in the morning by the time she joins her husband in bed. In a mere five hours she will be up to commute into work.

3

One Little Hour

On 2 January 1922 a whole mailbag sent from Marseilles is waiting for Edith at Carlton & Prior. She at once regrets 'slating him' during this trip for not being a better correspondent. She dispatches a note to this effect in which she further reassures him that his letters are safe in her keeping, and she destroys all letters sent her. His are no exception. The only one she has kept is the 'Dear Edith' letter. The fact is that Bywaters meant this letter to put Avis's mind at rest as much as Percy's about Edith and himself. He still cares about Avis and is already toying with the idea of breaking away from the wife. Bywaters now wonders in his latest letter whether or not he will be able to see Edith. She quickly replies that it must be up to him. Moreover Thompson, she tells him, knows that he is coming back on 7 January and will therefore watch her every step. To disarm his suspicions as far as she can she has 'surrendered to him unconditionally now'. To her husband's questions, after making love to her, as to whether she is happy now, she has lied and replied: 'Yes quite!'

If it secures her peace of mind she'll endure these marital abuses as long as necessary. In the meantime she derives strength, she tells him suggestively, from the certainty of loving a man on whom she can lean. She mentions that she had a New Year's card addressed to her from Osborne House, that she is enjoying R. W. Chambers's erotic novel *The Common Law*, that 'the man Lacosta in *Trail of 98*' by Robert B. Service 'was so vile I didn't think of him at all' and that she was relieved to hear that he didn't like photographs of himself any better than she of herself. She is sceptical about his relating a fortune teller's advice, setting the time for her elopement with him in around 'March'.

It used to be early in the New Year, Edith notes, not without sarcasm. She prefers to know the truth rather than be kept waiting in an 'expectant feeling of buoyancy for a myth'. Methodically she addresses issues raised in his letters point by point, including his interest in boxing. Like 'most women', she claims, she has always found it disgusting. For love of him she 'tried to look upon it as something strong and big' and to share his enthusiasm for the forthcoming encounter in the Albert Hall between Carpentier and Cook.

Bywaters arrives at Gravesend on Saturday, but Edith is in Highbury all day for a family occasion and cannot meet him. She must wait patiently until Monday.

Monday 9 January: When Edith Thompson crosses the threshold at Carlton & Prior a few minutes before 9 a.m., her only thought is of the imminent meeting with young Bywaters. As it happens, when her shift at the firm starts at 9 a.m., she has exactly one year left to live. Every second, minute, hour and week is now debited from a finite and formidably circumscribed total. At the moment Edith is very much alive, and at 4.45 p.m. she is in Bywaters's arms. He has brought her sweets, chocolates, Turkish Delight, and violets which she puts in her handbag. She then urgently tells him of her pregnancy and how she tried to stop it by a contraption, possibly with a sterilised wire: 'I cried all the time, but after it was done I felt easier, and after you have finished it for me I shall feel easier still.' It seems that Bywaters balks at the thought of assisting in this dangerous and very messy gynaecological venture. He derives little reassurance from her promising that 'the next real one I have perhaps I'll be able to keep for always'. His slowness to respond stings her into a furious outburst, of which she quickly repents. It is not only because of this that the evening fails to keep its promise. Freddy seems unable to generate the same ardour for their relationship as she; the 'palship of two halves', as she loves to see it, is supposed to consist of a mutuality that almost literally negates the separateness of two beings. As they part in Ilford at 7 p.m. after the ride in from Fenchurch, she is less than affectionate. At home, shortly before 9 p.m., while Percy is already upstairs, Edith puts the violets in water; she will be wearing them to work tomorrow, where she plans to keep them on her desk next to the 'hear-no-evil' monkey which Freddy had given her as a keepsake. After a restless night a subdued Edith Thompson is determined to sort things out with Freddy, who has already sent her a G.M.M.C. ['Good Morning Ma Chérie'] wire from the *Morea* in Tilbury. She writes him a quick note, stressing the sheer necessity of terminating this pregnancy. The note is passed to him in the lunch hour. They meet again in the evening and do so for the rest of the week.

Saturday 14 January 1922: Edith has taken this half-day off work and successfully dupes Percy about the afternoon, when she will go dancing with Freddy. Early in November she told Freddy that she had declined an invitation by him to a dance during the summer 'because I want to wait for that time – that *first dance* until it will be a real pleasure, *without* any pain'. Then, on 6 December, when Avis rehearsed the arrangements for a non-stop dance, Edith had to come to her rescue, because she could not bring herself to admit in front of Thompson that Freddy was to partner her. The morning of Saturday is entirely theirs. On her way into Liverpool Street Edith admires the way the night's heavy snowfall has shrouded even the grim commuter points of Stratford and the ugly belt of Victorian cottages at Bethnal Green in a mantle of silence. It is mild out of doors and still snowing. The snow is to continue unabated till Sunday morning, when, on Edith's and Percy's wedding anniversary, the metropolis and Essex and Kent will be a single white expanse.

They meet up in the City. Freddy has promised her the special thrills of a louche bar, 'a "low common place" for a woman to go'. Wherever this may be, the lovers enjoy a harmless morning there, drinking and eating sweets. The man in the 'confectioner's' thinks that Edith, who is busy buying while Freddy foots the bill, is 'terrible'. He is speaking in jest, prompted perhaps by Bywaters calling her 'fast'. As she warns jokingly, she really will be 'terrible' once he has 'a lot of money for me to spend'.

The somewhat furtive visit to the bar is followed by a snowball battle at which young Bywaters excels. This lovers' idyll of breaches of social decorum and romping about in the streets of the snowbound city sums up the morning of 14 January 1922 as Edith remembers it. In the early afternoon the lovers are heading for the dance at either the Waldorf, or the Shoreditch Town Hall. Dancing for Edith is a way of life. No sooner does she feel the pulse of a waltz, foxtrot, or Charleston than her feet itch and her legs move almost involuntarily. Her gracefulness on the dance floor has remained undiminished through the years. Although long ago she stopped teaching at the Cripplegate and at Warren's Academy, she still glides into every new dance variation with uncanny ease. What the sea is to Freddy, the dance floor is to her.

On Sunday 15 January 1922, it is six years since Edith walked as a bride out of No. 231. She is recollecting today what she felt then. Percy's clinging to the memory of their wedding anniversary like a drowning man does not make it easier for her. The fact that he still occasionally assumes that her contempt will yield to his bludgeoning has become her emotional safety-valve. It is easier to betray someone who mistreats you than a consistently kind and considerate man.

Thursday 19 January is Freddy's last night in England. Immediately after work, the lovers meet up and hurry to one of their favourite haunts. It is pitch dark already, and the slushy streets are lashed by sleet and gusts of rain. On their way Edith and Freddy pass the gloomy cathedral rearing its lit twin towers up against the elements. Safely sheltered at last, they have a 'real lovely' time, as she notes, quoting him. He reassures her that he loves only her, but admits that he still has 'something – something in connection with Australia'. She is puzzled, furious and jealous about this. Although she has read the Australian woman's letters and therefore knows that his involvement with her is not very deep, Edith realises the extent to which he will always consider himself free from bondage. As he is not due out to Australia, she can hold fire and preserve her composure. Why though, she wonders, has he chosen to tell her about a rival on this night of all others? The answer must be that she is pressing him to a point where he is not willing to go. There are other women in Bywaters's world. To bring Mrs Thompson back down to earth he attempts to expose her to the 'realities' of life. Perhaps for this reason she becomes frantic in the course of the evening to a degree that he cannot fathom:

> That feeling I had and still have about you going darlint I can't explain – not even to myself – first of all I feel that I shall want you & shall need you to lean on & you won't be there & then darlint – the 'drifting feeling' that I told you about before –. . . .

It is 11.30 p.m. when they part at Liverpool Street, and he is concerned about her getting home safely on such a dreadful night. In the jolting carriage, Edith is temporarily overwhelmed, as painful longings rise like lumps in her throat. In Ilford she is escorted home by a gentlemanly late visitor to the theatre, who travelled on the same train. Lying next to Percy, wound up by the intensity of the past few hours, she cannot sleep and is still awake when the alarm goes off.

Wearily she retraces her steps to the City on this dismal morning of Friday 20 January. She feels sickly, but attributes this to the drink and her sleepless night. A pulling, retching sensation tears away in her stomach. By 10.30 a.m. she is 'awfully ill' and for the next hour and a half she is fighting off 'terrible pains' which flood all over her. At about noon she faints. The showroom staff immediately gather about her and bring her round with smelling salts and a fortifying brandy. But Edith passes out again and then a third time. The doctor is summoned to the premises. He examines her briefly, tells them to loosen her dress and let her breathe more easily and to keep her warm with a hot water-bottle. They prop her up on a sofa and Lily looks after her. The doctor returns at 3.30 p.m., but finds her condition not improved. His diagnosis must be that this is female trouble, compounded by 'flu, particularly because the outbreak of influenza in London and in the country at large is this month reaching epidemic proportions. But the 'flu is to hit both the Thompsons shortly, so it can be discarded here.

Eventually the Carlton & Prior doorman runs Edith home to Ilford. She is lying flat in the big 'motor', while he negotiates his way east on the Whitechapel Road. She drags herself upstairs, undresses and lies down. For the next three hours she is fighting her own body. At about 7 p.m. she miscarries: 'something awful happened, darlint I dont know for certain what it was, but I can guess, can you, write & tell me'. The shock of her shredding pains, and this appalling mess of tissue and blood leave her numb. Mercifully her husband is not due back till much later tonight – and he will anyway call in first in the Crescent. By the time he arrives in Kensington Gardens she will have had time to dispose of part of the mess. She will explain to him that her periods are worse than ever, and that she must sleep on her own tonight. He is used to her prostrating indisposition, which regularly leaves her bed-bound for up to two days, swallowing aspirins by the dozen. Tonight, as Percy solicitously greets his wife, he notices how a hollow pallor has settled all over her. For once he will voluntarily use the little bedroom. This is the first time Edith has been pregnant. Hence her hesitation about the precise nature and detail of what happened:

> I've never had any experience in such matters and I never discuss them with members of my sex as so many girls do therefore I suppose I'm rather ignorant on such subjects . . .

The following day Edith feels 'a bit better, but not much'. The physiological stress of the miscarriage on her frame and the loss of blood leave her drained and prostrate all night. The risk of infection is high, but she remains unaffected. She is a strongly constituted woman who is only rarely sick. During the last two and a half months she has put on weight, which she attributes to her unhappiness. It is her sound health which pulls her through, though from now on she will be more often ailing; and a doctor is eventually going to warn her against pernicious anaemia. Edith spends most of Saturday in bed. Percy fusses and wants to call a doctor. He reminds her of their tickets for the Holborn Empire tonight. Painfully his wife rises, and dresses to go out. The thought of the doctor coming and telling her in Percy's presence that she has lost a baby is unbearable. In any case, she claims to be afraid that she would not be capable of withholding the truth, because 'someone else not you would have taken both the blame & pride for the thing they did not do'. She now admits to being 'a teeny bit disappointed'.

The evening of Saturday poses a number of questions. The most important one is whether twenty-four hours after a miscarriage, Edith Thompson could have 'really enjoyed myself, meeting heaps of people I knew & hadn't seen – some for 2 years'? The evening to which she alludes includes dinner and variety. The 'artistes' are a popular husband and wife team, 'Jack & Evelyn', whose comedy act is labelled 'Mixed Pickles' and is reputedly full of local and topical allusions. (They are friends of Mr Carlton's.) Tonight they improvise on the well known music-hall hit 'Three Little Words', a performance which Edith professes to have loved. Whether or not she really did enjoy herself, Freddy certainly appears to have believed what she told him. As he was implicated in the abortion (her letters do not say exactly how), he would be even more furious with her for going out this evening and will point out how dangerous it was in her condition to act this way.

On Sunday London is invaded by a very thick fog which by noon has shrouded whole parts of the city in complete darkness. The streaky grey pea-souper crawls in under doors and through the windowpanes. The metropolis is paralysed. At 8.30 p.m. Percy retires to bed. Edith stays up, seated in her armchair in front of the fire, thinking of Bywaters and of their uncertain future. At 10.30 p.m. she turns in, calling the evening 'an opportunity missed' on the path of their 'glorious adventure'. From this reference to J. Stuart Blackton's remarkable colour film, it appears that she saw *The Glorious Adventure* with Bywaters shortly before he left, at the Royal Opera House, Covent Garden. In this film, which was the first experimental picture to use colour, the action takes place during the Great Fire of

London. Lady Diana Cooper, once tipped to become Princess of Wales, stars as a distressed maiden who, after many romantic tribulations, is reunited with her lover. Before the year is out Lady Diana will have been interviewed, along with an illustrious contemporary, Dame Nellie Melba, about the young woman from Ilford lying in Holloway Prison.

On Monday Edith is back at Carlton & Prior. She replies at once to a note and letter from Freddy and relates to him the events of the weekend. At 5 p.m. she travels to East Ham Station where, so Freddy's note tells her, a parcel is waiting for her. It contains a present of books and a comb to wear in her hair. It is too early in the evening to head back to Ilford immediately, and she cannot very well drop in on her parents carrying a present from Bywaters. If she arrives home early, Thompson will guess that she is not working as late as she has claimed – in order to justify her catching the 6.45 p.m. from Fenchurch Street. As fate will have it though, Edith narrowly misses Mrs Bristow, her parents' next door neighbour at No. 229 and nearly bumps into Cossy, another neighbour, as she hurries up East Ham High Street to the Broadway.

On Wednesday 25 January Edith writes to Freddy thanking him for his telegram and telling him of the bitter cold weather in London. How she wishes he were here to hold her in the train! She asks for a slide for the back of her hair to match her new comb and enquires about his progress with R. W. Chambers's *The Common Law*. Could he remember to send her a long discussion of the book, particularly of the heroine's giving in? Bywaters had once said to Edith, on the same subject, 'But you would if I asked & wanted you to'. Between this sentence and the next paragraph Edith is rung by Avis to tell her that Mrs Graydon

> was taken ill last night with 'flu' & temperature 105 – the doctor is afraid of pneumonia – so I'm just going down to Manor Park. It is 12.30 now.

The next few evenings she spends looking after her mother. She remembers to send Bywaters the customary telegram for their 'birthday' on 27 January, and then prepares for a weekend of nursing the usually indomitable Mrs Graydon.

In the week starting Monday 6 February Percy is off work. He is nursing a bad cold, but nevertheless collects his wife at Carlton & Prior at 5 p.m. on Tuesday. She has no idea that he is coming for her and is out of the showroom when he enters and meets Miss Prior. As he apologises for being early, she assures him that he is not, since Carlton & Prior have 'not worked after 5 since last year'. It has been barely a fortnight since Edith's elaborate strategems to elude both her parents and Thompson on her return from East Ham Station. Percy enters her office and notices the bronze 'hear-no-evil' monkey on her desk. He does not comment on it, but merely remarks to his wife that according to Miss Prior, she has not been working after 5 p.m. She dismisses this as best she can, perhaps shrugging it off with a weary and obvious-sounding explanation.

At night Edith suggests to her husband that he move into the little room so that she will not be infected. 'No, you never catch my colds, I always catch yours,' is his rather peeved reply. So they spend the night together, he coughing, sneezing and retching, she enduring and cursing him. The night which follows, Wednesday 8 February, witnesses a further marital row 'over that same old subject'. The last thing she desires at the moment is sex, whether with Percy or anyone else. The nightmare memory of 20 January is still too vividly imprinted on her mind, and her sexuality now seems dangerous and burden-some. Percy has had a full day at home to brood. He remembers the monkey and the work hours, and that on both counts she lied to him. Percy's pressing her for sex, despite his poor health and depression, is not, one surmises, unconnected to his visit yesterday to Carlton & Prior. As soon as she refuses to surrender herself, he adduces Bywaters's name: it is all his fault that she has altered, he claims. She turns on him with a furious protest that, if he ever blames Bywaters again 'for any difference' in her, she will 'leave the house that minute and this is not an idle threat'. But he is undeterred and asks for Freddy's address. She scornfully gives it to him and he writes it in his notebook. Then he enquires about the Christmas greetings he sent her. Edith snaps back that she kept it, to which he replies:

Why, you never do keep letters from people.

Edith: I kept it for bravado, I knew you'd miss it and know I had kept it and one of these days ask me for it.

Percy: Have you anything belonging to him – anything mind you?

She knows that the question refers to the monkey and brazenly replies, 'I have nothing whatever belonging to him.' She recalls how much Bywaters detests lies. She had lied to him once and he had written 'It was a lie and Peidi I hate them.' Therefore in the letter that recounts this incident, she quickly reassures him that, when you think about it, what she told Percy was not really an untruth: the monkey after all belongs to *both* her and her lover. Even if it is a lie, she claims not to care: 'I'd tell heaps and heaps to help you.' Thompson continues his barrage of accusations, but she bites her lip and remains silent. Eventually the ill-fated couple go to sleep. At 2 a.m. Percy wakes, restless and suffering from the continued effects of the cold. His eyes look glassy and he needs water. He appeals to his wife for help, and she gets it for him, asking what the matter is. He tells her that an acquaintance of his in town gave him 'a prescription for a draught for insomnia'. He has taken it and it has made him sick. He indeed looks dreadful, and his wife is worried. At first she suspects that he is trying to frighten her, as he has repeatedly used his hypochondria to exercise emotional pressure, and will do so again before long. At the same time his fit, she will claim, offers her an opportunity, corroborated by the husband himself, to voice grave concern about his health. This is what she impresses on Freddy: what could be more natural than Thompson dying of an overdose from a drug which he was known liberally to indulge in and which had once before made him ill – as various witnesses could testify. Unfortunately she cannot find the prescription for it, as the chemist has kept it. Such silly and transparent plots on paper make little impression on the young sailor who spends this night on the *Morea*, deep in the Arabian Sea halfway to Bombay.

The next day the *Daily Sketch* reports developments in a news item which first caught Edith's attention in January when it appeared under the headline, 'Poisoned Curate', and referred to the impending inquest on the Reverend Horace George Bolding, found dead on 4 January. The story of Horace and Ada Bolding is as unsettling in some respects as that of Edith and Percy Thompson. It also is a tale of adultery and death, of lodgers and despairing spouses. In this case the adulterers are the younger woman, Mrs Ada Bolding, and the older Dr Preston Wallis – Edith's own former physician and neighbour in the Crescent. Wallis, who was a ship's surgeon, had made good partly by marrying the elder daughter of a head doctor at Guy's Hospital. Fifty years on Avis Graydon remembered her well, 'a perfect lady, tall, nearly six foot'. Then, shortly before the outbreak of war, Wallis employed a Mrs Ada Bolding, a twenty-eight-year-old nurse. Her husband was a young and ambitious curate who wished to read Theology at Oxford. What exactly happened in the surgery and the house in 1914 remains a mystery. The fact is that Mrs Wallis moved out and away from a husband who no longer loved her. It is possible that she left because she suspected the other woman of carrying on a relationship with him. A heart-rending letter from Mrs Wallis to the doctor for Christmas 1914 makes no mention of this, but tells him of her hurt at spending the first Christmas in eighteen years without him and asks why he has not even written to her.

In 1916 Ada Bolding, who lived with her husband in Manor Park, moved into the doctor's house. This happened at a time when Horace Bolding was up at Oxford where Wallis was now paying his fees. He and Mrs Bolding were now regularly seen driving through Shakespeare Crescent in the doctor's car. She had almost certainly become his mistress. Before long, the arrival of a baby was announced, and Wallis sold his house to the two Boldings, continuing to live in it himself as a paying guest and look after the surgery. That is how the Graydons knew the Boldings who also shopped at the same grocer's. In 1921 Bolding, aged thirty-nine, was appointed curate of Lingfield Parish Church. Dr Wallis moved with them as a lodger. On the night of 4 January 1922 the Rev. Horace Bolding died of hyoscine poisoning. He was known locally as 'happy, jovial' and 'a regular sport'. The inquest returned an open verdict, but the most probable conclusion is the one advanced by Avis Graydon and clearly the one popularly held: 'and whether he had seen things going on that shouldn't have been going on and didn't like it, I don't know, but he took poison. He killed himself'. The night he died his wife and her little boy were up in London. Both she and Wallis were cleared of suspicion of murder. The full irony of Edith Thompson's poring over this and forwarding the sensational newspaper cutting to Freddy would only emerge months later when the headlines of the same *Daily Sketch* for weeks on end were of 'Thompson and Bywaters'.

In the evening of Thursday Thompson's sister Maggie calls at 41 Kensington Gardens to see how Percy is recovering. Her brother treats her in lurid detail to an account of the previous night. The following day, Friday 10 February, Edith is lunching with Avis and tells her of Percy's sudden illness in the early hours of Thursday morning. She tries hard – she claims in the letter written to Bywaters after lunch – to appear truly agitated, 'as if it frightened & worried me as I thought perhaps it might be useful at some future time that I had told somebody'. In the same letter Edith hints how easy it would be to get rid of her husband: 'How about cigarettes?' – after all, Thompson had invalided himself out of military service by smoking. Or what of hyoscine poisoning? Might that not do the trick? These questions, silly as they may seem now, will sound ominous in a court of law. This night Edith Thompson has a dream:

> . . . I received a letter by hand by Avis & the envelope was addressed in Harry Renton's writing; only inside was a letter from you.
>
> It wasn't your writing darlint; it was a large round hand just like a schoolboy's. I read & read for a long time not recognising from whom it came until I came to the word Peidi & then I called out 'Why its from my own boy'. I dont know if I did really, but I did in the dream.
>
> Even now I cant determine in my own mind whether you sent the letters to him to send on to me, or whether he got hold of it somehow.

This anxiety dream articulates the extent to which Edith dreads the circuitous route their relationship is taking. It now actively involves her most intimate friends, Avis and Harry, in the primary tool of deceit: the clandestine correspondence.

Over the weekend Edith completes her reading of R. W. Chambers's *The Business of Life* which she will discuss with Freddy once he has read it. She finds it 'very like in detail [Chambers's] *The Common Law* but in the *one* question it is exactly opposite'. It also appeals to her more because 'it seemed to me more human in many ways'. The tawdry romance and marriage of the sullied buck James Deboro, landed aristocrat and New England *fainéant*, and the ravishingly lovely Jacqueline Nevers of the world of New York small commerce ends in a happy and married erotic encounter in bed. The flavour of it is gleaned from this short quotation of its last lines:

> His eyes closed. She lay there, in her frail Chinese robe, curled up beside him in the moonlight, her splendid hair framing a face as pale as the flower that had fallen from her half-closed hand. And at first she thought she was asleep.
>
> Then, in the moonlight, her eyes opened divinely, met his, lingered unafraid, and were slowly veiled again. Neither stirred until, at last, her arms stole up around his neck and her lips whispered his name as though it were a holy name, loved, honoured, and adored.

Here it seems is all the romance that Edith imagines she and Freddy could have if only they spent a few nights together. Instead, she has caught Thompson's cold and her joints ache. Percy, contrite, offers to spoil her. On Sunday he serves her breakfast in bed. She finds this amusing and vaguely contemptible. It has been a bad week, and a feeling of 'dont care, cant bother to fight' has left her dispirited. Edith's brother Bill is at anchor in Bombay at the same time as Freddy. The two boys, formerly team mates, now play football on opposite sides, the P & O's crew against the White Star line. They talk and shower together, which makes Edith wonder and worry whether they ever talk of her, or whether things happen in Bombay and other ports that she ought to know about. Looking at Freddy's picture she addresses it, 'talking' to him about her longings for a shared home with him. He would return then from a voyage, and she would throw herself into his arms; and they could embrace each other in total surrender 'for ever', which they cannot do in the public street or the crowded interior of a railway station.

In the meantime he has sent her a reassuring note to the effect that he has secured what is needed to solve their problems. She expresses delight at this: 'all I kept thinking of was your success – and my ultimate success I hope'. For now she wishes she could sleep out the time till his return since she can do nothing here yet, unless he sends her the drugs. Writing this on Monday 20 February, Edith also considers the prospects for their relationship, once they have committed the deed. What, she asks Freddy, is he going to think of her in a few years' time when they are together:

> Darlingest boy, this thing that I am going to do for both of us will it ever – at all, make any difference between us, darlint, do you understand what I mean. Will you ever think any less of me – not now, I know darlint – but later on – perhaps some years hence – do you think you will feel any different – because of this thing that I shall do.

If only she could make a 'clean – fresh start' with her lover, emancipated from lies and subterfuge! What is troubling her, the reason why she is hesitating, is not 'fear of any consequence of the action', but because he might despise her or take his love away from her. When one considers that the drug in question is quinine, and Bywaters will give it to her in the full knowledge that if administered, it cannot do any real harm, it becomes clear that the romance is drifting further and further from reality.

This week is the week in which a summons is issued by the Director of Public Prosecutions to Horatio Bottomley MP, on charges of embezzlement; and, on Saturday, when Edith is commuting into the City to work, Landru dies in a public street in Versailles on the guillotine scaffold. She has no time for such horrors. Although she is now toying with the idea of inflicting violent death and professes having considered its consequences, she does not ever associate her fantasies with the reality of it. Her thoughts this morning are of the mail, the boy who on this day leaves Bombay, and the uncomfortable suspense of waiting for her period which is overdue. Above all, tonight she will be seeing the music-hall troupe 'The Co-Optimists' at the Palace Theatre in Cambridge Circus. She has 'heard them raved about' and is full of expectation.

The show is subtitled 'A Midsummer Night's Scream'. The star performers are Stanley Holloway, the composers Melville Gideon and Laddie Cliff, David Burnaby and 'everybody's favourite', Phyllis Monkman. The evening's entertainment is divided between songs and burlesques. The songs include Melville Gideon's mock ballad of the tropics 'Amapoo', Gilbert Child's 'Roast Beef of old England', Laddie Cliff's negro-minstrelsy and dancing numbers, and songs like 'The Success of Dance', and a rendering of John Ireland's 'Sea Fever'. Stanley Holloway, 'rollicking baritone' and master of Cockney monologues, excels in ballads and parodies, notably of McNeile's successful Wyndham play *Bulldog Drummond*. For popular entertainment the Co-Optimists are as good as any. But Edith is 'awfully disappointed in them', and does not relish their sunny outlook on life. She is not in any case feeling too good. A pulling sensation is invading her.

On Sunday 26 February she is prostrate in bed. Her period has come, and she seems back to normal. But the pains and bleeding, she surmises, are worse than they used to be before 20 January. She has retired to the little room and will spend the next couple of nights there: the 'only effect I feel of anything is a languid lazy sort of feeling – no energy – just pale & limp'. For good measure her cold returns. In spite of both afflictions she is determined to go into Carlton & Prior tomorrow, otherwise she'll miss Freddy's letters – and they would be bound to forward her mail to 41 Kensington Gardens.

Monday is another 'birthday' and Edith Thompson hurriedly writes a note to Bywaters to say how sorely tempted she was to buy herself a birthday present from him: 'You know all & everything I wish you darlingest & myself . . .' she starts, and then alludes to the birthday present she has in mind: 'they looked so lovely everywhere you go you see them now. . . .' Her sole comfort, she professes, is in his letters. He expresses concern for her, saying that he 'felt' that she had been ill; and he again blames her for foolishly jeopardising her health by not staying

87

put in bed. He remains unimpressed by her visit to dinner and to the Holborn Empire on 21 January. Moreover he wishes that she had acknowledged his cable of 24 January, while he in turn undertakes to remember to address all her queries in future: 'I must let you know of all those things that you ask me & I have forgotten.' He gloomily hints that he may be losing her love. She will hasten to reassure him on that.

Shrove Tuesday is mild and wet. Princess Mary's wedding on this day is almost a public holiday – the Kensington Avenue schools have even closed. Not feeling well, Edith commutes home early. To keep her company she buys W. J. Locke's *The Red Planet*, which she finds disappointing: 'it is a war story and I'm not very keen'. Freddy has read it and recommended it to her, but under the mistaken impression that it was *The Rough Road*, another Great War yarn by Locke. As if things weren't bad enough Mrs Graydon takes another turn for the worse, and Edith will spend Ash Wednesday and Thursday looking after her.

On Saturday she receives the doctor's bill for the call on 7 November at Carlton & Prior. The charge of 10 shillings and sixpence (52½p) rattles her, and she immediately considers the likely cost of 20 January which is bound to be much higher still. In the afternoon Edith calls in at Percy's office in Bishopsgate. For the next three hours she pores over his account books and sorts them out for him. She has been doing this for ten years. At 5 p.m. the Thompsons meet up with the parents and Avis, and together they travel south to visit the Mannings for dinner and a whist drive. The Mannings are close friends and will share the Graydons' joys and sorrows up to the outbreak of World War II. Their acquaintance dates back to the time when Mr Graydon taught Tom and Ginny Manning and Ginny's sister Beatty to dance. In the course of the evening Beatty asks Percy whether he and Edith can make the following Saturday for dinner at their place. Percy is happy to agree to the invitation. Back in the Crescent Edith mentions the subject of the proposed visit, and Thompson does not dissent. By Tuesday, however, he assures her that 'he wasn't't going': he will not, he now lectures her, let her make arrangements to go anywhere 'without first consulting him, and obtaining his consent'. If she is angered by his contrary behaviour, she coldly controls herself and, the following morning, sends Beatty a politely apologetic card cancelling their Saturday dinner arrangement. The reason for Percy's change of mind will emerge later.

On Tuesday 7 March Avis is due at the Thompsons' for tea and dinner. She is early and the Lesters let her in. She joins them in their sitting room. Mr Lester is there and unwell. Premature senility has overtaken the invalid. While Avis and Mrs Lester are 'toasting some Sally Luns in front of their fire', he suddenly remarks:

> I don't know who the lady of the house is, but she is a very beautiful woman, and such a good woman to her husband.

Edith is immensely tickled by this and, naughtily, asks Bywaters whether she ought to feel 'honoured or otherwise'.

The weather is filthy this evening, and on her way into work on Wednesday morning Edith encounters the elements at their most fearful, as gales of up to 108 miles an hour are pelting travellers and lashing into the train's windows. All cross-Channel traffic is cancelled which worries her, for it means that the mail might be delayed. She is intrigued by the *Daily Sketch* cover on this day, showing Freda Kempton, a dancer found dead in her Paddington flat in mysterious circumstances. The police suspect cocaine poisoning and the use also of cyanide of potassium. She cuts out the relevant paragraphs to forward them to Bywaters, along with more detailed notes from Friday's (10 March) edition of the *Daily Sketch*, headed 'Dancing Girl's Mystery Death. Story of Dope, Drugged Drink, Night Club & Chinese Café'. Edith's comment, in a 2300-word-long letter, written between Friday 10 March and Monday 13 1922, is that the 'Kempton cutting may be interesting if it's to be the same method'. This particular letter, Exhibit 20 in court, characteristically veers from a day-to-day account of her London life to a series of dark hints about getting rid of her husband. These are in turn laced with a series of disconcerting references to the study of fictional characters in Hichens's novel *The Slave*:

> I didn't know what to make of that girl – yes I think she is possible – perhaps and apart from being happy with her body – he was quite happy seeing her with those jewels. They were two similar natures – what pleased him – pleased her – not English at all, either of them.

After further disquisitions on the 'rigmarole' in the novel and complaining about the fact that Bywaters does not properly address her many questions, she reverts to the 'business' in hand: 'what about Dr Wallis's case . . . you said it was interesting but you didn't discuss it with me'. She promises to get a furnished flat in the meantime, while they wait for an unfurnished one to turn up, then turns her attention to fiction once again: 'Yes, I can imagine her real – but Aubrey – I could shake him – no go – no initiative of his own. . . .'

Another news item in Wednesday's paper is to bear on Edith's fate in a curious but all too credible manner: a man called Ronald True is charged with the murder of Olive Young, a young prostitute. His trial and sentence, and the Home Secretary's decision to reprieve, will be directly instrumental in the tightening of the law on 'excusable' homicide in the second half of 1922. For Mrs Thompson today the most frustrating piece of domestic news is her husband's announcement that next week his firm is moving from Bishopsgate to new offices in Peek House at No. 20 Eastcheap. Percy will therefore start using Fenchurch Street instead of Liverpool Street. So much for her trysts with Freddy in Fenchurch Street, she notes caustically. She might, she hopes, nevertheless just snatch an hour with Freddy in Fenchurch Street on the Saturday of his return. This reminds her of his saying, 'Never run away, face things and argue and beat everybody.' She claims to be miffed by this, and he should know: when has she ever bolted? He'll have to kiss all that hurt away! Doesn't he know that she only lives for the day when they will be united forever, 'for "one little hour" – our kind of hour, not the song kind'. And in that 'hour' there will be enough time for her to soothe his anger by ruffling his hair 'lots of times until you have to melt – and smile at me – then you'll take me in both your arms and hold me so tight I can't breathe, and kiss me all over until I have to say "Stop, stop at once"'.

The following morning, Friday 10 March, a note from him awaits her. He is due back early, a mere week from today. He asks whether he can meet her at Carlton & Prior after 5.30 p.m. or, if not, at Fenchurch Street. She replies that, depending on how busy they are, she cannot undertake to be at work after 5.30 p.m. If he wires that he can meet her, she would prefer Fenchurch. In the lunch hour she boards a 25 bus to Victoria Station to buy Toblerone to send with the tissue paper she bought for him. But her shop is out of stock, and she returns via Holborn Station, where she alights to settle the piano account in Southampton Row. On her way back near the Holborn Restaurant, she runs into Mr Derry, an 'acquaintance' from the White Horse pub opposite Ilford railway station. Derry, whom Edith characterises as 'the little man', knows her well enough to press her for lunch in the Holborn. She excuses herself at first, but then consents to going into the hotel's buffet with him, where she consumes a Guinness with port in it, followed by two more ports and a pound of French almonds. Derry does not offer her chocolates – he knows 'from previous experience' that Mrs Thompson doesn't like chocolates.

Whether this is said ironically or whether it alludes to a particular incident at the White Horse is immaterial. What is significant is that little Derry, Mel and others evidently feel perfectly at ease in courting the smart Edith Thompson. She is a girl full of game, and she talks little of her husband, who is in any case not the young man whom she is seeing, and seen with, in the City. Her lively company and many interests make for great conversation and generate an erotic charge to which the men keenly respond. She in turn enjoys their admiration and desire.

She arrives back at work feeling heady, as she has drunk on an empty stomach. At 3 p.m. she receives a call from her brother Bill to tell her that he is back from Bombay and that he looks forward to seeing her tonight in the Crescent. When she finally meets Bill, she anxiously expects him to communicate something about Freddy and Bombay – if only the result of the football match that they played. But Bill, whose face looks thin from the rigours of the voyage, never mentions a word about either, which makes her wonder again how much he knows and whether her lover and he have had a disagreement.

On the same day, in Whitehall, an ambitious civil servant is promoted. His name is Sir John Anderson. He is appointed Permanent Undersecretary of State for the Home Department to replace Sir Edward Troup, himself a colleague of the former legal adviser to the Home Office, Sir Ernley Blackwell. Troup and particularly Blackwell brought Casement to the scaffold, and Blackwell's and Anderson's paths will eventually cross those of Thompson and Bywaters.

On Saturday the Thompsons were meant to have had dinner with Beatty Davies, had Percy not changed his mind and refused to go. With the whole afternoon ahead of her and with the weather at its most clement for weeks, Edith heads for Ilford

> and had a general clean up everywhere. The sun was shining in the windows beautifully – it was a typically English spring day and I did so want to be in the park with you darlint.

Thompson finally returns home at 5.30 p.m. Edith is no fool, but she cannot be bothered even to wish to monitor his movements. He almost certainly is 'seeing' another lady, about whom Edith and Avis will later tease him.

On Sunday the Thompsons dine with Bessie and Reg, and on Monday Edith completes her long letter to Bywaters, urging him once again to bring her whatever is required:

I'd like to see you at the top – feel that I'd helped you there – perhaps darlint in my heart right deep down I don't want to stop in a hat shop always – if things are different.

On Tuesday she is again writing, this time an apologetic note for claiming on Monday to have sent two parcels, when really she only sent one: 'Je suis faché darlint', she says and 'consumed with impatience'. Only two more full days to go, and then he will be holding her in his arms. Furthermore the planned non-stop for Thursday is cancelled, because Reggie has gone to Derbyshire and Avis's partner is sick with the 'flu. Edith is pleased with this development, because she would hate to be worn out on Friday when seeing Freddy.

On the cover of her paper today there is a picture of the widow of the former London County Council chairman Sir Edward White. Alice, Lady White, has been murdered in the Spencer Hotel in Portman Street. The killer has been apprehended almost immediately. He is a young dim-witted laundry boy called Henry Jacobi. By next Monday evening he will be charged, and on Tuesday will appear at Marylebone police court. Jacobi's paths and Edith Thompson's do not intersect directly, but the same spider's web will close around them and the same officials will participate in its weaving.

It is a cold and cloudy Friday when Edith and Freddy embrace each other in Fenchurch Street in the evening of 17 March. He tells her of her present which he cannot give her now, because she is returning to Ilford. He will send the pearls and Oriental cloth to Carlton & Prior tomorrow and with it the quinine, at that time readily available and commonly used by sailors as a febrifuge. Edith has two brothers in the merchant navy and several acquaintances who regularly go east to India and China. She knows as well as Freddy that it is virtually impossible to kill anyone with an overdose of quinine, quite apart from the fact that the tonic cannot easily be administered. Out of curiosity she will taste the quinine shortly after Bywaters's departure to render a credible account of its taste in tea.

On this first Friday home, young Bywaters accompanies Edith to Ilford. The lovers meet again on Saturday for lunch. Edith is keen for Freddy to get on with Chambers's *The Business of Life* which they will be discussing in lengthy epistles at the end of April and early in May.

On this night the Thompsons, the Graydons and Avis are guests at Mrs Birnage's party, and on Sunday there is still more socialising, when the Thompsons are invited to dinner in Stamford Hill. As Freddy is home for a fortnight only, the lovers meet regularly at lunchtime, for tea at Fuller's and on her way home – although they have to be more circumspect now that the husband is also using Fenchurch Street. On either Monday or Tuesday Edith receives her big present, which includes a box of Turkish Delight. It is delicious. She selects a piece to keep and send to him in a fortnight's time, specially 'tendered' by giving it 'fresh water with salt in every morning'. In her note thanking him, she feels down and out, like 'a desert' dried up by her life with Percy. Only her books, she feels, keep her afloat.

> arent books a consolation and a solace? We ourselves die and live in the books we read . . .

Time passes, and while Freddy visits the Crescent a couple of times, it is not till the Monday of the second week of his leave that the lovers get together for an extended tryst. It happens to be a 27th and therefore a 'birthday'. Edith takes the afternoon off and probably goes shopping with Freddy. On Tuesday she forwards a number of books that she feels are 'worth reading' to Bywaters. It is on this day that Freddy is asked by Edith to hand over, for the second time, the Australian girl's letters. She wishes to keep them till after his return from Australia – which is where the *Morea*'s summer schedule is to take her. Edith has not forgotten the reference to the other woman in January.

While she is writing him the note about her 'doubt about Australia', an organ passes outside Carlton & Prior, playing 'Margie', one of their favourite songs. For the moment Bywaters obliges and surrenders the correspondence, thinking her petty and jealous. Edith's reply to this charge is to assert that the releasing of the letters into her custody is a love test; and since Freddy passed so graciously, she loves him 'more and more every time I thought about it'. The letters, she hastens to assure him, are safe with her. She seals up the envelope, puts them away and claims not to have looked at them

> except at a small slip of paper I found in one of the small pockets. I did read that – and then put it with the others – did you know it was there darlint – it was about a chase – a paperchase I think and a request not to be wakened early.

Whatever the hint which she is giving Bywaters here refers to – and there is a possible sexual innuendo in the 'paperchase' and the desire not to be wakened early – the main point is that the letters must have been fairly restrained and struck Edith Thompson as such. Strange as it may seem in retrospect, these letters were not produced in court, nor have they surfaced since. On Wednesday, before leaving Edith in Ilford that night, Bywaters slips her a hurt letter about her 'doubt'. She slides it into her underwear and will sleep on it, as no opportunity avails itself for her to read it. Just before kissing her goodbye, Freddy asks that she try not to think of him. That way their parting will be easier for her. She pretends to try, but expresses the hope that he will not do likewise!

Thursday 30 March: This is Freddy's last day of shore leave. Edith rises at 5.45 a.m. to read his letter. Outside it is wet and very cold. Hail and sleet showers are forecast. Undaunted, Edith decides on her dress for tonight. While Percy is still sleeping upstairs, his wife sorts out her pearls, earrings, bracelets, undergarments and perfumes, mentally rehearsing her bit about the theatre; for a visit to the theatre is her excuse for being out this evening. The night will be exciting and she is thrilled at the thought of giving Freddy a big present, a gold watch. That the theatre subterfuge involves somebody else is virtually certain. A third party is required as an alibi, and Thompson's oblique references to Reg and Bessie on Saturday 1 April point to the likely identity of this party. It is conceivable that Edith and Bywaters stay at Bessie's; Edith having told Percy that she is accompanying her girlfriend to the theatre because Reg is away. She can then have acquired a programme from Bessie to attest her veracity. Reg is away in Derbyshire for the entire week and is not due back till after Sunday.

While she prepares to leave home, Bywaters parts from his family in Upper Norwood under a cloud. There have been continual disagreements during his shore leave between Freddy and his mother. Their topic of rowing is now always Mrs Thompson. A brief meeting between the two women arranged by Edith to discuss a hat which she sent to Mrs Bywaters and which the latter found unsuitable, left them with a pronounced dislike for each other; Mrs Bywaters now decidedly resents the stuck-up woman from Manor Park for her assumed nice manners and her intentions on her son. The row between son and mother smoulders on. Before long it will explode and temporarily create a rift in the family. No reference is made to this subject at lunch as the lovers consider their plans for the evening. It is nearly April, yet outside it feels like the depth of winter, as snowflakes repeatedly whirl about. In the afternoon, while Edith is at work, Bywaters encounters his sister. He totally ignores her, since earlier, she had sided with his mother. It is this which strikes the spark needed to ignite the stored resentments. Edith only learns of this incident after his departure.

What exactly happens and where the lovers go after 5.15 p.m. remains speculation. Two facts can be established, however, which in themselves articulate the story as much as is required. One, the lovers have drinks somewhere. Two, they share a passionate sexual encounter. This is how Edith Thompson describes what happened:

> Darlint you're not and never will be satisfied with half and I don't ever want to give half – all every ounce of me that lives to you . . . you say you're sorry for some things that happened. Yes! I suppose I am in a way but darlint, I feel I don't do enough. I want to show you how large my love is and when it is something you want and you do want it just at that moment don't you – I want to give it you – I want to stifle all my own feelings for you.
>
> Darlingest boy you said to me 'Say no, Peidi, say No' on Thursday didn't you – but *at that very moment* you didn't wish me to say 'No' did you? You felt you wanted all me in exchange for all you. I knew this – felt this – and wouldn't say 'No' for that very reason.
>
> Half an hour afterwards or perhaps ten minutes afterwards you'd really have wanted me to say 'No' but not at that especial moment.
>
> Darlint, I feel that I never want to withhold anything from you – if you really want it and one of these days youre going to teach me to give all and everything quite voluntarily aren't you? Please darlint.

This encounter clearly takes place indoors in view particularly of the Arctic conditions prevailing on the day. Freddy's begging her to stop the consummation from running its course may reflect his fear of launching another pregnancy. It also indicates the extent to which she is an active sexual partner, not quite as passive as the 'little girl' pose – which occasionally she likes to strike – would lead one to believe. Her inability to achieve a climax, 'to give all and everything voluntarily', worries him and she rushes to assure him that with his guidance she will reach orgasm. The lovers probably wait for Bessie to return before setting out on the walk back to 41 Kensington Gardens, which may account for the lateness of the hour, when they are wandering through the streets of Ilford. It is shortly before midnight when the idea of checking into a hotel appears to have occurred to them. They do not seriously consider it though, and content themselves with noting that there is nowhere in Ilford for quick overnight encounters. If there had been, Edith reflects:

> before we had arrived at the Hotel, I should have thought about things and so would you and I can hear you say just when we reach the door 'Peidi, you're going home' pour moi – just this once darlint & I should have gone.

In this striking bow in the direction of respectability, Edith acknowledges the limits imposed upon her by her sex, class and character.

Freddy leaves her at the corner of Kensington Gardens. As he strolls back he carries strapped to his wrist the splendid new watch that she has given him as a present, to add to the three books that she had earlier bought him as reading matter: Hichens's *Felix*, and the novels *The Shulamite* and *The Woman Deborah* by Claude and Alice Askew. It is a quarter past midnight when Edith Thompson lets herself into the house. Arriving upstairs, she finds Percy out. She is getting into bed when she hears a car draw up outside. Minutes later Percy enters the bedroom, 'looking . . . with that injured air of mystery on his face'. He bends down to kiss her and she withdraws, but not quickly enough for him to miss the smell of alcohol wafting on her breath: 'Phew – drink', he notes laconically and with disgust. While he is undressing to join her in bed, he tells her that he took the 11.55 from Liverpool Street and then a taxi from the station. Percy is holding a theatre programme but, to his wife's surprise, neither tells her what he has been to see, nor does he enquire what she saw or how her evening went. All he does is voice mild surprise at her presence in the house, when he didn't meet her on the train. Edith is disconcerted, the more so since she knows that there is no 11.55 p.m. train from Liverpool Street to Ilford. Percy must have been on the 11.30 p.m. He may therefore have noticed something if indeed he has spent the last half hour walking the streets between the station and Kensington Gardens. Edith foolishly imputes to Percy a stupidity he lacks. Her belief that Thompson failed to notice that she had theatre tickets on Bywaters's last night on shore in January and again tonight is mistaken. Percy knows only too well, as she is to find out on Saturday. Now, at 1 a.m. on Friday, even Percy cannot bear the thought of another row.

Meanwhile Bywaters is walking up Gipsy Hill in Norwood. His mother is waiting up for him. After all her son is due to sail to Bombay tomorrow; and she will *not* stand by while he grossly insults his sister by ignoring her. This is so unlike him that it must be attributable to the pernicious influence of that older woman. Within seconds of his arrival voices are raised, and then a fully-fledged row flares up in the tiny house in Westow Street. Freddy's kid brother and younger sister Florrie are of course on the premises and overhear every word. Florrie, who is eighteen, fully realises what the fight downstairs is all about. She takes offence at Fred's bullying and his demanding that the mother retract her abuse of Edith Thompson. When Mrs Bywaters furiously reminds him of his duties to his sisters, he snaps back: 'My sisters! They only want me for what they can get out of me.' This hits home. Florence May Bywaters angrily recalls later in writing to him that all he has ever brought her is 'some powder', which he will be welcome to retrieve. He owes her 3 shillings and sixpence for the laundry anyway, collars included. As it is Florrie who takes her brother's dirty linen to the local laundry every Monday, she doubly resents the charge that she is sponging off him.

Eventually Freddy retires to bed in his room at the back of the house. His mother, determined to have her way, sits down and writes him a letter which she will pass to him later in the morning. He will reply to it in kind.

Early on Friday morning, while Edith is commuting into the City, Freddy heads for Tilbury. As soon as he gets there he cables her a telegram: 'G.M.M.C. always stop – don't worry.' She knows he is due to set sail for Tilbury at about 2 p.m. and begins to wonder what he feels like: is he 'hopeful & not too downhearted', and what exactly does it mean to him when the ship begins to move and he realises that 'you'll not [be] on England or anybody connected with you & England for two whole months'. These are her thoughts, as she sits brooding in Aldersgate in the early afternoon. Outside it is snowing again.

After work Edith heads for Liverpool Street, where she has tea in the buffet and reads the paper. It is 8.15 p.m. when she finally arrives in the Crescent on her weekly visit. The place is buoyant. Almost as soon as Edith is inside, her mother offers her a cigarette. The following dialogue then takes place:

Edith: Where did you get these? They look posh.

Mother: Never mind, I had them given me.

Edith: Well I don't suppose you bought them – where did you get them?

Mother: Fred Bywaters gave them to me.

Edith: Has he been down here?

Dad: Yes, he's been 3 or 4 times.

Edith: Oh, I [am] sorry I missed him. Next time he comes remember me to him & say if he lets me know when he's coming to 231 I'll come too.

Dad: He's sailed now, went out today. By the way, have you had a row with him?

Edith: Have I, no, the last time we met we were pals.

Dad: Has Percy had a row with him then?

Edith: Yes – he did.

Dad: And is it over yet? I thought it was when Percy came back to say goodbye just before Xmas.

Edith: No, its not over and not likely to be – but still I'm sorry I didn't see Freddy. I should like to have done very much.

Dad: Yes, I'[m] sure you would & I'm sure he would like to see you.

Mother: What do you think of the fags?

Edith: Not much, they are scented & I don't care for such posh ones.

At this Mrs Graydon professes to be quite indignant and says, 'If they'd been given to you you'd like them,' to which her daughter, smiling, replies, 'Would I?' It is not long after this that Percy enters. Mrs Graydon offers him a cigarette. He looks at it and says, 'Ambre! Oh they are doped cigarettes' –

Mother: What do you mean by doped?

Percy: The tobacco is grown on opium fields.

Listening to this, Edith feels herself chuckling deep inside and wishes Freddy were there to share the 'joke' with her. The thought of poor Mrs Graydon unwittingly smoking doped cigarettes may not be an egregiously funny prank, but it is entirely in keeping with the boy's sense of humour. Freddy's guilelessness is evident in Mrs Graydon's innocent remark to Avis that 'by the way he [Fred] spoke . . . he must have seen Edie'. She is only now puzzled by this since Edith has let it be known that she would have loved to see Freddy. No more is said about it, and the Thompsons eventually set off home through a cold winter night. The snow still shrouds the streets in white, and further showers are expected during the night and for tomorrow, the day of the Oxford and Cambridge boat race.

On Saturday 1 April 1922, Bywaters is writing an angry letter to his mother:

> I am writing to you though at the cost of my dignity, to remind you of the foul, unjust and spiteful allegations you made against one, whom you do not know.

The letter continues in this outraged vein ('I ask you, I tell you, and warn you . . .'), but mellows towards the end:

> Mum, do please try and realise that I am not Frankie [Bywaters's little brother].

> If you do want to answer Mum, please think about what you say or do.

>> Your ever affectionate Son
>> F.E.F.

Edith Thompson's comment on reading these last two paragraphs in a copy of the letter is that 'this is more like the boy I know – not like the shell'. His mother receives the letter when allegedly she is already suffering a 'nervous breakdown together with blood-poisoning'. The contents and tone of her son's epistle do little to raise her spirits. Her son's folly, in turning against her for the sake of that woman deeply enmeshed in a marital crisis, pains her deeply; naturally her love of him is not separated from jealousy of Mrs Thompson.

On Saturday afternoon Edith and Avis go on a shopping spree in Ilford. Freddy is foremost in Avis's mind and dominates the sisters' conversation. Edith notes that Avis seems to be quite friendly with Freddy whom she has seen almost every morning at the station. Wouldn't it be much cheaper in fares, Avis wonders, if he were again to stay with them in East Ham? Then they would see more of him, and that would be nice. But perhaps money is no problem for him: he is wearing – she tells Edith – a diamond ring on his engagement finger in spite of the fact that ships' writers do not 'make more than £5 per trip'. Avis is wrong on this – Bywaters makes nearly that much in a week.

In reply to Edith's disingenuous question as to whether Bywaters is engaged, her sister replies: 'Probably. He was always knocking about with some girl or other before he knew me, and now he doesn't see me and he probably does the same.' A somewhat chastened Edith is further humiliated when she learns that her sister and her lover have met up for a drink at Avis's prompting; she can see nothing wrong in going round to Freddy's, presumably at the P & O offices, for a drink since they are 'pals . . . if nothing else'. During their shopping in a grey and snowbound Ilford on a spring afternoon, Avis continues talking of Freddy, confiding in her sister just how much she feels for the young sailor and that, perhaps, if he is allowed to sow his wild oats, he might eventually return to her. Her intuition is not far wrong.

The sisters return to No. 41 for tea and Avis innocently remarks that 'the last time I came Bess & Reg were here'. Percy at once makes some veiled reference to Bessie which puts Edith on her guard. After her sister's early departure at 7.30 p.m., to 'keep an appointment', she asks her husband to explain further his remarks about Reg and Bessie:

A remark you passed at tea-time about Bess, what do you mean by it I want to know.
Percy: You want to know do you − well you shant, you can just imagine how much I know & how much I don't & I hope you'll feel uncomfortable about it.

This remark immediately triggers a huge row between the Thompsons. Edith loses her temper and lets Percy have a mouthful, regretting it as soon as it is out. Her final outburst is 'Go to Hell!' Thompson retaliates by calling her the 'vilest tempered girl living' and adds with pointed sarcasm: 'you used not to be, but you're under a very good tutor now, it seems'. This clinches it, and she rushes upstairs. She retires to bed early, hating the man downstairs and angry with herself for giving way. Why was she foolish enough to enquire after Reg and Bess when Percy must have been bluffing? He clearly sensed that something was wrong on Thursday and that the other couple were vaguely connected with it. But does he really know any more than that? Edith's cold comfort today is that Cambridge has won the race and earned her 5 shillings. Most men, including Freddy, support Oxford, she surmises, but 'I'm Cambridge'.

The Thompsons' Sunday is a dreary affair, distinguished solely by 'banging doors & sour silent faces' which, Edith fears, will turn her prematurely grey. Their visit that evening for dinner in the Crescent fails to reconcile them to each other. During their discussion of the rates in Ilford, Thompson insists that he will not pay up. Avis suggests that 'If you don't pay they'll take you to prison', to which he replies: 'No they won't, I'll see to that.'

Avis: Well, they'll take your wife.
Percy: A good thing too.

His wife certainly hears it and so do the Graydons. Nevertheless they have no intimation of quite how bad things are between their daughter and son-in-law.

On Monday, while Edith Thompson pores over a letter from Bywaters, a solicitor and retired Army major, Herbert Rowse Armstrong of Hay-on-Wye, goes on trial in Hereford for suspected arsenic poisoning. The defence is spearheaded by the renowned Sir Henry Curtis-Bennett. The presiding judge is a justice called Darling, affectionately known as the 'wit of the bench' for his recurrent remarks in court, distastefully intended to amuse his compeers in the judiciary. Mr Justice Darling will surface again in this narrative on the occasion of one of his 'jokes'.

Tuesday 4 April: It is snowing 'in thick lumps', and London is silenced by a mantle of snow. At Carlton & Prior trade is virtually at a standstill as the streets become inaccessible to vehicles and Aldersgate is almost deserted. Edith wishes Browning could now be·in this cold-locked England, to witness what today's April is really like:

What poet was it who wrote 'Oh to be in England now Spring is here?' I wish he were alive & feeling miserable as I, on this nice English Spring Day.

Just before continuing her writing to Freddy again, Edith attends to a lady customer whom she has not met in five years. In this period the customer has married, had two children, and suffered the death of one child and her husband. Edith Graydon on the other hand, according to this lady, is not looking any older and is certainly unchanged. If the lady were to guess that the elegant Miss Graydon actually envies her her dead husband, she might be more cautious about complimenting her on her looks. We may safely assume that at Carlton & Prior Miss Graydon never lets on about her loathing of Percy.

The following day she is feeling poorly and arrives for work at 11 a.m. Several consecutive fainting fits leave her momentarily incapacitated, and she professes to Bywaters that she is worried about a new pregnancy, started within the past three weeks. After telling him this news, she rushes to the GPO to post her letter. On the way back, she meets Harry Renton. They decide to lunch together at the Manchester. Edith can only spare one hour at the most, as she did not get in this morning till late. She always enjoys the gentle Harry's company, and the only interference today with her pleasure is that 'a wretched man sat near me who absolutely reeked of scent'. The smell is 'beastly', and repels her particularly because the user is male rather than female. Their conversation concerns Harry's flat in Moscow Court; Harry has been advised to move out of the metropolis, else his shoulder wound might bring on consumption. Does she know of anyone who might want to buy it? he asks Edith. What a perfect lovers' nest it would be, she remarks to herself.

At dinner this evening the Thompsons are entertaining Avis. She leaves for home at 11.30 p.m. and Percy offers to walk her to the tram. Edith wants to accompany them, but Thompson emphatically forbids it. He will try and quiz Avis about Bessie and Edith, and on whether or not they went to the theatre together. Edith suspects that Thompson will enquire about Freddy, and whether Avis saw him. Whatever her sister replies, she will keep silent to Edith about Percy's queries, and Edith will not dare ask.

Thursday reminds Edith of Freddy's last day of shore leave, exactly a week ago. The difference between the experience of the two days throws into stark relief her present isolation and misery. At Carlton & Prior during the day she can cope and has Lily to confide in. But at night the depression worsens and is compounded by her starting a fever, with her teeth aching and her head and neck stiffening. Inwardly she cries, as all night she tries her utmost to hold on to the thought of Freddy. But like an insubstantial vision he continuously evades her and gradually recedes from her altogether. Her tears, real or imaginary, plead with him, but to no avail. It is 5 a.m. on Friday when she feels herself drifting into sleep and faintly hears the clock strike the hour. At the same time, over at 66 Albion Grove, Barnsbury, Lily Vallender also experiences the visitations of a nightmare. Her earlier conversation with Edith clearly left an impression on her. She guesses that her friend is struggling with moral chaos. The end can only be disastrous. In Lily's dream the Birnages come to Carlton & Prior to warn Miss Graydon that her husband is going to murder her, as he found out that she spent a night away from home with 'a fair man'. This suggests that Lily knows that her friend Edith and the attractive Fred went out and made love a week ago. She will relate her dream to Edith, not without apprehension.

On Friday Edith is badly wound up from a restless night. Her feeling of exhaustion is aggravated by a chance meeting with Freddy's sister, who ignores her but not before giving her a contemptuous glare. It makes Edith feel that 'the whole world was up against me and it wasn't really much good living'. The only thing for it is to put it all on paper in a letter. Accordingly, on Saturday, she launches into a mammoth 3000-word letter which she completes on Monday. Then she returns to Ilford to prepare dinner for her father and Percy. It is Palm Sunday weekend. The two men have agreed to cut some glass for the frames of Percy's glasshouse. While they are engaged in this, Percy runs a sliver into a finger. Mr Graydon promptly removes the splinter and the matter ends there. It is not so much as mentioned when later, in the afternoon Avis and her mother join the rest of the family at 41 Kensington Gardens for tea. For Edith this is a busy afternoon. Little can she have guessed that the glass splinter – of which she probably knows nothing – will assume the importance of a sinister landmark in the imagination of her brother-in-law. The real coda to the splinter incident is that in the middle of the following week Percy complains to Mrs Graydon about his finger being sore from the sliver. Mrs Graydon prepares a bowl of hot boracic water and invites him to steep the finger in it. Shortly after, the remainder of the glass splinter, a tiny particle, appears. Eight months later Richard Halliday Thompson will publicly interpret this entirely innocuous incident as evidence of a cumulative plot to administer poison and broken glass. In his version, it will be Mrs Thompson, Percy's invalid mother, who allegedly treated the infected finger:

> He came several times to his mother complaining of the pain, for which he could get no relief.
> My mother poulticed it, and it only healed when a long, thin sliver of glass worked out.

It is still unsettlingly cold when Edith commutes into work on the Monday of Easter week. On the platform in Ilford she meets Molly, Freddy's former flame; and she observes with a certain relish that Molly's 'face and lips are rouged terribly and thick black lines [are] pencilled under her eyes – and her face is fearfully thin fallen in under the cheek bones'. Premature ageing from working in the West End will be the allotted fate for some, Edith suggests, because they are not able to cope with the stress. Molly's crestfallen looks are not Edith Thompson's only reason for feeling good today. When she arrives at

Carlton & Prior she finds a long letter from Freddy waiting for her. This letter, his first communication since the Gibraltar telegram of Tuesday 4 April, is accompanied by a copy of his letter to his mother already quoted, and by the letter which his mother originally sent him. Freddy's letter replies primarily to Edith's of last Tuesday, when she told him of her return from their Thursday night out, Avis's visit and her subsequent comments on Bywaters, Reg and Bessie and the 'doped' cigarettes. He furthermore responds to the note she slipped him after they parted, and of course he also refers to their lovemaking on that last night of shore leave. He is 'sorry' for 'some things that happened', probably their sexual encounter. In his earlier letter he has already told her about the row with his mother and sister. Now he does not touch on this topic. Instead he compliments her on the watch which is keeping good time and tells her that he plans to wear it always. She eagerly replies that he might keep it on in his sleep, just as she now wears something of his, day and night: can he guess what it is? He enquires further whether she marked the passage on photos in *Felix* because of the two pictures of her which he now owns. As it happens, he likes her photos, although she professes to hate them, 'especially that one that I look so fat in'. She tells him that he may keep the other one, which he will – it is reproduced on the cover of this book. While Edith relishes Freddy's letter, she probably blushes to the roots of her hair when she reads Mrs Bywaters's note to Fred, telling him bluntly that 'that woman' simply is 'no good'. How, Edith groans, dare Mrs Bywaters take it upon herself to judge her – she, Edith, would never presume to judge anyone. In spite of her anger and frustration Edith is shocked by the severity of Freddy's reply: 'I ask you, I tell you, and warn you, not to interfere in any manner or form, with me or my private affairs.' In moments of self-doubt as now, she always reaches back to her respectable upbringing, which unreservedly forbids this tone of voice to a parent.

Before completing the letter and posting it, Edith adds a note starting, 'Don't keep this piece.' It relates how she tried to poison Percy's tea by putting quinine into it. He, she alleges, commented to his mother on the tea tasting bitter, 'as if something had been put into it'. He also is said to have told 'his people' that 'he fought and fought with himself to keep consciousness' and said: 'I'll never die, except naturally – I'm like a cat with nine lives.' Too bad about the taste, Edith remarks; she'll just have to resort to light bulbs again: 'I'm going to try the glass again occasionally – when it is safe. I've got an electric light globe this time.'

That this piece of fantasy could ever be construed as part of a premeditated murder plot defies belief. Bywaters knew it was fiction and that she had herself tasted the quinine in the tea to be able to give an accurate account of Percy's complaint. In court the jury were told that 'the passage is full of crime'. Yes, as long as it is understood that 'crime' means 'imaginary crime'. It is never easy to separate fact and fiction in Edith Thompson's extensive and intense correspondence, and though outside evidence is available to help distinguish one from the other, the more intimately acquainted the reader becomes with the correspondence, the more complex its rash interweaving of fact and fiction is bound to appear. In most of our lives such a blurring is not uncommon. It is not always harmless. But it is seldom the matter of life and death into which it developed here.

When Bywaters was cross-examined on the tea tasting bitter to Thompson, the prosecution asked him: 'To whom did it taste bitter?' and he replied: 'Mrs Thompson'. The unlikelihood of this being true when measured solely against the written evidence – which specifically used 'he' – provided the prosecution with much needed ammunition to implicate the wife. That Freddy knew that she was lying to tie him to her more closely, and that she was a highly strung neurotic woman who wished to be transported out of Ilford suburbia to romance and abandon – such a truth could not easily be articulated in the public atmosphere of the Old Bailey. Above all, facing each other across the well of the court, the lovers bravely guarded their ultimate secret: that all along they knew each other's weaknesses and loved in spite of them.

It is getting on for 7 p.m. when Edith finally leaves Carlton & Prior. The shop has been very busy all day as Easter is imminent, and continues in its hectic pre-holiday rhythm till 11 p.m. Thursday 13 April, when Carlton & Prior closes. In anticipation of the break Edith dashes off a quick letter to Freddy on Wednesday to tell him that the four days ahead would seem like four hours in his company, whereas Percy will make them into four years. If only Freddy could now hold her tightly, instead of her having only his picture to 'live on'.

Easter 1922: The four days of Easter do not, as feared by Edith, turn into a prolonged nightmare. Instead the Thompsons and the Graydons enjoy the break to the utmost. At 1 p.m. on Maundy Thursday Edith,

Lily and several other friends from Carlton & Prior go to the Waldorf for lunch. They stay for the *thé dansant*, even though Edith only manages a single foxtrot, she claims, because her heart is not in it. They leave to meet up with Avis at 6.30 p.m. for a late shopping raid in the West End. After buying Avis 'a costume', the women split up and the two sisters return home to Ilford, where Avis spends the night.

Good Friday 1922, 9.30 a.m., 41 Kensington Gardens: spring cleaning gets under way. This 'good old fashioned English housewife's occupation', as Edith Thompson calls it, takes up all of her day. Her husband and her lodgers are not much in evidence as she sweeps through the premises with doors and windows wide open. Then, shortly before 6 p.m., she goes to wash and dress before accompanying her husband over to the Crescent. After dinner Mr Graydon treats them all to a Sunday League Concert at the East Ham Palace. The rest of the evening is spent together, and Edith and her husband are put up for the night at No. 231.

The next night, Saturday night at the Ilford Hippodrome, is on Edith. The show includes Tom Edwards, a minor music hall star and former Adeler & Sutton pierrot, who appears with a girl in a nurse's uniform singing 'He makes me all fussed up'. Freddy may have introduced the Graydon girls to this song, or he may teasingly have tried it on Avis, perhaps on the island. Avis certainly remarks on the connection between the song and Bywaters to her sister, who recognises the allusion. Edwards continues his act with his famous ventriloquial 'Nursing the Baby' skit and with several virtuoso patter numbers. If the delights of Tom Edwards and others contribute to the enjoyment of the show for Edith, the presence of Freddy's ex-girlfriend Molly in the row behind, sitting with another girl and a boy, annoys her. Her conversation, according to Mrs Thompson, sounds very affected. Is she just putting it on to humiliate her, Edith wonders? She certainly thinks it might be and likes to make sure that Freddy knows.

The two women share the big bed whenever Avis is up overnight and invariably have a cup of tea together in bed in the mornings. As this is Easter Sunday, and as Edith has done the spring cleaning, Percy is spoiling her and her sister by waiting on them. The Graydon parents are expected for dinner, and Avis and her sister are kept busy most of the day, cooking, baking and washing up. The only notable piece of news is a nugatory argument about the price of Cuticura. Avis claims that when she bought it – for a friend – it cost tenpence halfpenny. Her mother disagrees because she got some for Fred Bywaters, and it came to a shilling, with which Edith concurs. Percy's somewhat wistful contribution to this discussion is to remark that 'you all in turn seem to have bought it for him'.

Easter Monday is of course a holiday. In the morning, while Edith is resting in front of the fire, Avis is assisting Percy in 'knocking apart a grand piano case' in the garden. Thompson suddenly hits his finger and asks Avis, 'Will you go up to my room, to my medicine chest, and get me a bottle of New Skin?' The cabinet is in fact located in the little room which Percy calls 'mine', because he is sleeping there while Avis is staying. As she opens it, she sees a large half-pint bottle of tincture of opium, then freely available. She comes down with the New Skin and approaches her sister in the morning room: 'There is a bottle of opium in Percy's medicine chest. Nip up and get it.' Edith obliges while her sister puts New Skin on Percy's finger. After she has returned the New Skin to the cabinet, she asks Edith:

Have you taken that bottle of opium as I asked you?

Edith: Yes.

Avis: Where is it?

Edith: On the side there – on the sideboard.

Avis: I will do away with this, so there can be no more trouble.

Avis takes the bottle to the scullery and pours its contents down the sink. The bottle itself she throws into the fire in the back room where her sister is seated. Avis's reference to 'trouble' and her strong reaction to finding a bottle of opium seem to imply that she and Edith may well have talked in bed this weekend of marriage problems and that the wife has attributed them to either her husband's drink or use of drugs or both. It is interesting to compare this incident with Edith's own inventive account of it to Bywaters a few days later:

Bye the way – what is 'Aromatic tincture of opium' – Avis drew my attention to a bottle of this sealed in the medicine chest in your room.

I took possession of it and when he missed it and asked me for it – I refused to give it him – he refuses to tell me where he got it and for what reason he wants it – so I shall keep it till I hear from you.

I used the 'light bulb' three times but the third time – he found a piece – so I've given it up – until you come home.

This passage neatly illustrates the cross-plotting of fact and fiction in the correspondence.[1] The thought of Percy discovering a piece of a light bulb in his porridge or dinner is almost comic, were it not for the consequences. Edith must have been puzzled by the opium tincture in Percy's cabinet, and she will of course have wondered whether he intended to use it and how. It may have been a draught of opium tincture which brought on the fit during the night of 8 February when she noticed that his eyes looked 'glassy' and that he appeared genuinely sick – and *that* Edith *did* tell Avis about, 'as if it frightened and worried me as I thought perhaps it might be useful at some future time'. In the evening the people from Manor Park and the Birnages, with whom they have had tea, see another show at the Hippodrome.

During the night Edith dreams a dream of sex, guilt and fear. Freddy has taken her out, and they have returned together to No. 41. He insists on coming in, and they make love:

> Eventually you and I slept in your little bed – in the morning I woke early and went into the big room and found Harold [Edith's youngest brother] was sleeping with him – you were unbolting the front door in your pyjamas to get out quickly when he came down the stairs, so you went into Mrs Lester's room. She didn't like it a bit and you thought you had better make a clean breast of it and came up to him and told him what had happened – there was a fight – I don't remember how it went – in [sic] Dad and Mother were there with him and they had been discussing things and wouldn't let me stop there I don't know what became of me or you.

The dream imagery is fuelled by Edith's sharing a bed this weekend with Avis, and her desire to spend the night with young Bywaters can be detected perhaps in the wife's yielding her place in the marriage bed to the youngest brother, a contemporary of Freddy's. Harold's presence in the dream and his imaginary sharing of Thompson's bed underlines the extent to which Edith feels her marriage to be unnatural, a feeling expressed in her unconscious mind in a homosexual counterpoint to Bywaters and herself: the young sailor and Mrs Thompson on the one hand, and the young man almost exactly Fred's age and Percy Thompson on the other. Edith is haunted by the memory of her last evening with Freddy, when they so desperately wished to spend the night together and could not. As in the dream, they made love that night; but they could not retire to the privacy of a

---

[1]That neither used glass or poison is clear from Spilsbury's autopsy report (quoted p.215).

bedroom afterwards, as once they did when he was staying at No. 41. The pleasure of the dream is marred by the nightmare visions of a jealous husband, suspicious lodger and upright parents who would be expected to side with marriage against adultery.

On Tuesday 18 April, her first day back at work, Edith receives a mysterious parcel, 'a large gold foil egg filled with chocolate about 2lbs by the weight'. It has been posted anonymously in EC2 and appears to originate from the same source as the parcel sent her for Christmas. Edith suspects that the sender is one of her admirers, perhaps Mel or Derry. It is about this time that Edith completes Hichens's *The Fruitful Vine*, 'a very very interesting book' which, she surmises, in some of its details could 'lead to hours and hours of discussion'. She will be sending Freddy the book along with *Bella Donna* on Thursday. They will go through it together in their correspondence character by character, paragraph by paragraph, and particularly 'the one act'. A full summary of the plot, and of the moral issues posed by *The Fruitful Vine* is offered later and measured against Mrs Thompson's striking essay on the book in a letter of Friday 18 August.

On Thursday Edith receives a doctor's bill at 168. She happens to be at the door when it arrives and therefore takes it in herself. It is one of the finest days so far this year, and she is anticipating a chance to nip out into the open and breathe the vernal air. It may help to release the irritation that is building up inside her. Much as she welcomes it, premenstrual tension always leaves her exhausted and frustrated, like her periods themselves.

At 11.30 a.m. the following day, Friday, Mr Carlton hands Edith Freddy's letter, pretending to mistake it for one of her brother's. The letter does not propel her into an enthusiastic response, particularly because she feels offended by his question: 'the last time we met, we were *pals*, weren't we chère?' Why does he have to ask the obvious, unless he is beginning to harbour further doubts after all? Her reaction, as ever, is to resort to a long letter. On Saturday evening, in return for the Easter Monday tea, the Thompsons attend a 'very posh' dinner party at the Birnages: 'full course dinner and she cooked everything herself – I think she is awfully clever'. She enjoys it, but on Sunday is prostrate with a painful face-ache. Whether this is an inflammatory illness caught from her lover – as she wonders – or the result of severe migraine accompanying her period is not material, although the latter seems more probable. Throughout the day she is swallowing aspirin, twenty-four in all in six doses of four, before trying to sleep on 'a pillow of thermagene'. Her period is imminent but refuses to come.

Feeling better, but faint and despondent, Edith commutes into the City, in the hope of finding a letter from Suez waiting for her. But she is disappointed in this. Adding a brief account of her experiences of the weekend to Freddy's epistle, she disconsolately mails it on her way to Fenchurch Street. Her period has arrived. She anxiously notes that the bleeding is unusually light and that she is not 'ill as I should have been, altho' I was a little – but not as usual'. If this is repeated next month, she will want him to advise her on what action to take. It will be under a week before his return to London: 'I still have the herbs', she assures him. No reference will be made to these abortion-inducing herbs at the trial, even though the letter in question will be used in evidence.

For the next few days Edith is fighting off fainting fits as she gets in and out of bed. Her discomfort is compounded by the weather switching to cold again. By Thursday she has a sore throat and her voice is going. On Friday the youth Henry Jacobi is sentenced to death at the Old Bailey. The jury strongly recommends him to mercy. Later in the evening Avis visits her sister who has been too unwell to pay her weekly call in the Crescent and gone straight home to Ilford. The Thompsons, Avis learns, have abandoned the idea of a summer holiday in Llandudno, because it will be 'too expensive'. Instead they have opted for Bournemouth, for a fortnight from 8 July. Would Avis like to join them, Percy asks. Both the sisters are surprised by his question, and when Avis asks, 'well, what about Edie? what does she say?' he replies, 'I'm asking you. It doesn't matter about her. I'm asking you.' Recalling the incident in these words fifty years on, Avis Graydon suspected that her sister and brother-in-law 'might have had a bust up and he thought, you know, that if I came there I might have a dampening feeling on her, and she would respond a bit more. You see, I knew so little of their married life'. More than half a century separates the sisters' remarkably concurring reactions to Percy's invitation: 'The suggestion was nothing to do with me . . . I'm glad – because if things are still the same and we do go – a third party helps to make you forget.'

On Saturday, voiceless apart from a 'very high up squeak' which amuses everyone, Edith is writing to Bywaters about her suspected pregnancy and commends him for his behaviour towards a girl whom he has met – on shore presumably – and liked, because she 'doesn't swear'. Well then, she wonders, what of her own swearing? She does, after all, occasionally use words like 'damn' and a few stronger words sometimes – or 'don't these words constitute swearing as you hear it?' Then she turns to the fiction which he discussed, particularly *Felix*. Bywaters has professed to be disappointed in the ending, when the young man abandons his older drug-addicted mistress Valeria Ismey in a carriage on Victoria Station, bound for Paris, to attend instead to his very sick mother. Bywaters 'expected him to do a lot for Valeria' and he did not. Edith disagrees and claims that Felix, whose life passion is reading the novels of Balzac, never had it in him to be a pillar for anyone – witness his encounter with Ismey and Victoria:

> 'Let me pass please. I am her husband'. It was Mr Ismey who spoke – clearly, with a sort of cold defiance and pride. Felix looked round and saw a tall figure getting into the carriage. Under the ray of the lamp he met the eyes whose deep melancholy had once made him wonder. He did not wonder now. Mrs Ismey saw her husband. She shrank back in the corner of the seat, pressed her head against the cushions, opened her white lips and cursed him.
>
> 'Thank God, you are here!', Felix whispered.
>
> 'Help me!'.
>
> But Mr Ismey took him by the arm.
>
> 'Go away', he said, with a sort of pitiful sternness. 'Go away. This is no matter for a boy. You can do nothing here'.

Felix is even by Hichens's standards overly injected with heavy erotic innuendos and its language is remarkably candid. If the lovers appear to be at cross purposes in this literary critical exercise, the reason is that Bywaters repeatedly attempts to advance the interpretation of character that he feels is expected of him, a point over which his mistress will forcefully remonstrate with him when he reads *The Fruitful Vine*. In the same letter to her he notes that the quinine which he gave her was enough to kill an elephant – why then is Thompson still about, he seems to ask. Her reply to this is that it tastes bitter and that she prefers Freddy not to reproach her with it. She leaves the letter at that.

On Monday 1 May 1922 Edith Thompson has a riveting letter from her lover, which makes her cry, because among others he professes to be despondent at her lack of progress with glass and powder. She admits that her helplessness is putting her to shame, but undertakes to love him even more for it later, when they are happily living united.

Then he asks her about a character in *The Shulamite*, a novel by Alice and Claude Askew, which, along with *The Woman Deborah* she demanded he read for 'discussion' across the ocean.

As a novel *The Shulamite* suffers from an oversimplified, melodramatic plot. At the same time it abounds with impressive caricatures, atmosphere and unadulterated racism. The story is set in the South African veldt after the Boer war. A young and handsome English gold prospector, Robert Waring, joins the farm of the old Boer Simeon Krillet who is married to a beautiful and darkly passionate childwife, Deborah. She is the shulamite. Her parents had traded her for securities to the vicious old man who whips himself into a sensual frenzy through ritualised readings of the Canticles. The girl is profoundly repelled by her lascivious and abusive father-husband and turns to Waring in despair. He undertakes to protect her and confides this to his diary, which the old man promptly discovers in Waring's temporary absence and construes as evidence of adultery. He decides on a spectacular execution of the faithless wife, by tying her to a tree to shoot her the moment her alleged lover appears in view on his return from his errand. But Krillet is betrayed by one of the 'kaffir' girls whom he abuses nightly and Waring shoots him. The plot thickens when Waring departs for England, failing to make love to Deborah because of his commitment to his fiancée, Joan. He marries Joan, thereby provoking the shulamite into blackmailing him for murdering old Krillet. The story ends unhappily and leaves behind a sense of pain and loss, of misplaced pride and failure of recognition. After his wife's and child's death, Waring returns to claim the shulamite, who in the meantime has heroically battled against the vile and huge 'tantes', sisters and relatives of Simeon, bent on exacting at least one execution, if not two, from the old man's death; and hoping, in the process, to retrieve his fabled pot of gold. The shulamite's self-sacrifice saves Waring from the gallows and leaves her, stern and impoverished, seeing him vanish on the horizon:

> Deborah Krillet stood on the stoep of the lonely farm, shading her eyes from the sun-glow, watching a speck on the plain, a moving speck. Soon it would pass out of sight and become lost in the unknown.

What intrigues Edith in the novel, apart from its sentimentality, is its gripping portrayal of passion and the geographical movement of the plot, since like Deborah, she loves a man who protects her and is always travelling in far distant lands. Above all, Edith's attitude towards her marriage – the enforced physical intimacy with an unloved partner – finds a voice, if a hugely exaggerated one, in Deborah's merciless oration to Waring over her husband's coffin:

'I believe,' she went on slowly, 'that you were sent here that all should happen as it has. He was hard, and cruel, and old; it was not fair he should live and I should die; also – you are not a woman, so will not understand –. but his kindness was worse than his whip.' She trembled a little and the firm mouth quivered.

'My dear,' – Robert Waring forgot the English girl Joan, forgot everything in the world except the woman facing him, this child-woman with her fierce virtue that refused love except to love, – 'don't think of the past; forget it all, forget it.' His voice shook as he spoke; she was such a revelation of woman.

'Can I' – she looked at him steadily – 'forget that he bought me like a chattel and treated me like a toy, loved me because I pleased his eye? There are some sins against herself a woman never forgets, and the love of such a man as Simeon Krillet is one. Days of shame and nights of hell. Do you realise that he plucked my youth from me with coarse fingers? Oh, God, how I have suffered! and because I was his wife I had to smile and seem content. I have been through all this, endured it silently, and yet you wonder that I have the nerve to dress the man for his grave. If only you knew how he has crushed my soul! You were sorry for my bruised flesh, and I thought then how little a man understands a woman.' She stopped speaking and brushed away the first tear he had seen her shed.

Commenting on this passage, Edith adds two interesting qualifications. Firstly, that 'the feeling of repugnance' engendered by such a relationship not only extends to the partner but produces a commensurate self-loathing. The victim of such forced sexuality turns against herself for her inability to defeat the prostitution of her entire being. Secondly, the male and female joint authors (as she surmises) are necessarily at odds in scenes like this one, mutually checking each other. If anything, Edith appears to be saying, the horrors of the scenes with Krillet are understated. Few people would compare Percy Thompson to the execrable Simeon Krillet, and even Edith Thompson refrains from directly suggesting that. Even so, in their imaginative projections of their 'real' world, the two lovers are losing their grip on the necessary perspective required by sanity. In the same breath, Mrs Thompson discusses her regretted failure to kill her husband, a novel of near-adultery and murder, and the fact that the stationers are out of paper and that she therefore has to write part of her letter on unattractive notepaper.

*

Spring has come at last and temperatures rise throughout this week. On Thursday 4 May the Thompsons along with the Birnages go to see the troupe known as 'Les Rouges et Noirs' at the Queen's Theatre on Shaftesbury Avenue. All the members of the cast are ex-soldiers from the First Army who started as a *succès d'estime*, but quickly established themselves in vaudeville. They specialise in male and female impersonations which Edith for one enjoys hugely – 'these were splendid – very clever and very funny – I did laugh such a lot – it was really dancing through the hours' – and are best known for their original songs and individual performers. Perhaps the visit to the theatre follows on from the agreement between Percy and Sidney on Thompson's acting for a commission as an agent for the Sun Life Insurance Co. The Birnages are friendly with all the Thompsons and the Graydons; and Sidney enjoys Mrs Thompson's company particularly. He is something of a maverick and, like others, senses that Percy's wife is restless. If catastrophe had not overtaken the protagonists of this story, there might well have been further complications between Edith and some of her male admirers.

Friday 5 May is a perfect summer day. On her arrival at Carlton & Prior this morning Edith learns that Miss Prior's brother-in-law has suddenly died and 'that she needs someone to go up West to buy mourning clothes'. As Miss Graydon is Miss Prior's 'stamp' and has excellent taste, she is asked to oblige, which she does readily. The prospect of expensive West End shops is irresistible. Also Edith wishes to complete some of her own purchases for her summer wear. In the end she buys Miss Prior a dark costume, a silk frock and a cloth frock, a jumper, shoes, stockings and gloves. For herself she gets a cream gaberdine and pleated skirt, to wear with a sports coat. She is mightily pleased with her own shopping and the dress for Miss Prior, who is herself most appreciative. When Edith suggests that they match the clothes to one of their several widows' hats on the premises, everyone superstitiously shies away from the idea. Doesn't she know that it brings bad luck? Edith gaily dismisses their fears, dresses in black and promptly tries on all the widows' hats in the shop, reflecting that if this spells ill luck for everyone else, it might just do the reverse for her. Teasingly she tells Freddy that her workmates 'all think terrible things are going to happen to me now'.

At lunchtime Sidney Birnage calls for Edith to take her out to lunch again. She leaves him at 2p.m., no doubt faintly intrigued by his interest in her and determined not to encourage it too far. When therefore she is advising with Lily on the new designs downstairs at about 4p.m. and is told that a gentleman – who turns out to be Birnage – is expecting her upstairs in the showroom to go for tea, she is distinctly unenthusiastic. She takes him to Fuller's and plays it cool. It would not do for her to jeopardise their friendship with the Birnages because of the husband's overly zealous attentions. Reading the paper this morning and particularly the *Daily Sketch*'s feature on 'Battle of Calves & Ankles', Edith notices with mild dismay that Parisian designers are promoting a return to the longer fashion. She will of course follow suit, but Freddy is not going to like it: he prefers her in short skirts, open-necked blouses and tight-fitting sweaters.

The weekend is forecast to be very warm. After a cheery morning at work Edith rushes back to Ilford for lunch and then to wait for her mother who will assist her in hanging some clean curtains in the house. The curtains in the Thompsons' bedroom in particular need changing. To get into the large bay window Mrs Graydon and Edith try to move the dressing table further towards the centre of the room by pushing it. A careless gesture suffices to dislocate the large cheval-glass from its pivot and to smash the mirror into 'a thousand pieces'. Edith notes that 'This is supposed to mean bad luck for 7 years – I am wondering if it's for us (you and I) or her. What do you think?' For two days running now she has defiantly sneered at omens, superstitions and fate. Why not? She thinks of herself as a sensible and rational girl, gifted with an eye for fashions and accounting, and earning the largest salary in her set. Undeterred, Edith enjoys the weekend relaxing in the garden in Ilford.

Monday 8 May 1922 is the hottest day of the year so far. At Carlton & Prior Bywaters's mail is waiting for Edith Thompson. She has no opportunity to read it alone. In the lunch hour she therefore hurries down to St Paul's to board a bus to Hyde Park Corner. She occupies a back seat on the open top and then abandons herself to the delights of the letter, light clothes, sun and the London cityscape. Freddy is telling her about 'a boy and a girl and a chocolate incident' which makes him smile and think 'a lot'. She wants to know why, suspecting that it is connected with her love of sweets. On her return to Carlton & Prior or perhaps even on a bench in Hyde Park, Edith writes a reply and tells him of her liking for Montelimar as well as Turkish Delight. Freddy does not care for Waring in *The Shulamite*, which pleases her, because she fears that he might identify with the vagrant lover. Deborah catches both their imaginations for being 'primitive' and 'natural'.

Edith therefore 'admires' her, even though she cannot 'love' her. Fred enquires 'whether Avis liked the books or not', a question to which Edith does not know the answer, even though she assures him that Avis could not muster the intellectual acumen to practise literary criticism. If she is slightly annoyed by his enquiry after the sister, she controls it well. Freddy's dislike of the buckish Desboro in Chambers's *The Business of Life* puzzles her, and she proposes to argue with him about it at the appropriate time. The sooner Freddy reads *The Fruitful Vine*, the better for both of them. Edith posts her reply to Bywaters on her way to Ilford, while he is halfway across the Arabian Sea.

On Tuesday 9 May Edith purchases Hichens's *Bella Donna* and immediately finds it engrossing. A further claim on her attention is the *Daily Sketch*'s announcement under 'Test for Derby Horses Today' that Scamp will be out 'for the first time this season'. Freddy has recommended her to back him for the Derby, and she puts 5 shillings each way and gets odds of 20 to 1. Tomorrow he will fail badly at a mile and the *Daily Sketch* will call him a 'non-stayer'. As it is, Edith has already lost the 30 shillings she made from another horse called Paragon in the 'City & Sub'.

Shortly before arriving at Liverpool Street on Wednesday morning, Edith has reached the middle of Chapter 7 of *Bella Donna*, the exact moment when Dr Isaacson, the medical Jewish sleuth of the novel, alights on the following passage in a textbook on poisons:

> It must be ever remembered that digitalin is a cumulative poison, and that the same dose, harmless if taken once, yet frequently repeated becomes deadly.

Is this any use, Edith asks Freddy, meaning for the killing of her husband? She might be talking casually about an insecticide, for all the matter-of-factness of her question. Then she turns to his letter received in the morning and immediately remonstrates with him for his comment on the Co-Optimist song which exalts the virtue of being only 'practically true' to a partner. If that is how he feels, she prefers not to have him at all. He enquires whether or not she has heard anything so far from his mother or sister – an apology to Mrs Thompson has been demanded – and whether Edith is still there waiting for him. She vehemently protests her loyalty and berates him for even doubting her and asking questions when he means to state facts. She feels contrite for accusing him of being a bully: 'I'm not bullying you, I'm deciding for you chère' is Freddy's reply, and she readily concurs. He should do all the deciding for her. That way she has a shoulder to lean on. Then, in characteristic fashion, Edith turns to the fiction: 'Now I'll talk a bit about the books.' The books in question are *Beyond the Shadow* and *The Way of These Women* respectively. What particularly puzzles Edith about the former is that it is 'hardly a possible story'. (The mind boggles at the thought that the other novels she read were deemed by her to be life-enhancing by virtue of their perceived realism.) With reference to the cast-off heroine Marian, and her few moments of happiness in *Beyond the Shadow*, Edith slightly misquotes Tennyson's lines from *In Memoriam*, that 'It is better to have loved and lost/ Than never to have loved at all.' Her most interesting instructions to Bywaters on reading certain works of fiction come with regard to R. W. Chambers:

> I agree with you about Chambers endings darlint but the endings are not the story. The end is written to please nine out of ten people who read his books. . . . Forget the ends, lose yourself in the characters and the story and, in your own mind make your own end. Its lovely to do that darlint – try it. . . .

Then she goes to lunch in St Paul's churchyard. On the way she happens to bump into Mrs Bywaters, carrying a large bunch of red roses, in the company of 'that tall man' whom both she and Freddy have noticed before. Unable to ignore her, Edith leans over the roses with 'Let me smell, How are you?' and passes on quickly. No sooner is she back at 168 than she adds a coda to her letter of the morning: 'Supposing I were to meet your mother in the street darlint, what should I do? What would you want me to do? Answer this, please, particularly.' One or two days after, she confesses that the question is disingenuous, as it supposes something to take place which has already happened. In Edith Thompson's letters the boundaries between fact and fiction are constantly shifting.

On Thursday the British climate exacts revenge on the early summer birds. Overnight the temperature drops dramatically from the 90s Fahrenheit to the 80s to 52: 'What a country to live in', notes Edith. At lunchtime she squeezes in ten minutes to talk to Freddy, telling him how dull, depressed and 'cold in the body inside' she feels. But a bit of excitement is generated in the afternoon by George Carpentier's visit under police escort to Pagets, the sports shop over the road from 168. George Carpentier is the charismatic French boxer whom Jack Dempsey defeated not long ago with a knock-out punch. Tonight at the Olympia is a different affair. Carpentier's opponent is Kid Lewis, who goes down in the 150th second exactly, during an 'incident'. Young Paget, speaking to the women of No. 168 with the authority of a man who has met the champ himself, notes that the fight 'was a frost and very unfair'. The press generally concurred, because Carpentier seemed to strike the decisive blow a fraction of a second *after* the two boxers were made to break by the referee. Lewis was therefore caught off guard. Edith loathes boxing but Freddy loves it, so she dutifully reports these details to him.

The biting cold of Thursday is relenting and Friday is milder and cloudy. Edith takes her tussore 'to be made up' and also has a new navy costume made at the same time. She is complimented at the tailor's on the quality of the tussore which pleases her no end, as she prides herself on never buying cheaply or badly. The long coat which accompanies the costume will not meet with Bywaters's approval, but she pleads her case by noting that the cream skirt was bought to please him, the coat her.

From Friday's *Daily Sketch* Edith cuts out a feature headed 'Holiday – Then Death Pact. Passionate Farewell Letters in Seaside Drama. Woman's Sacrifice'. The correspondence of the lovers in question, George William Hibbert, aged thirty-eight and Maud, twenty-three, the much younger wife of his younger brother, leaves an impression of tender affection and bottomless despair. The double suicide attempt in a gas-filled room in Brighton ends with the man dead and the wife unconscious. Edith immediately identifies with the couple. She fails to comment on the extent to which their situations differ: the Brighton lovers were reportedly so distressed by their treachery to the husband and brother that they preferred death to destroying him.

On Sunday 14 May the Thompsons are entertaining Bill for tea. They are sitting out in the garden and he raises the topic of opium; if he knew where to plant poppy, he says, he would get some. The conversation becomes animated, since the issue of opium is a very hot one. The only word in fact which Edith 'deletes' in all her correspondence is this word. The law may not have been solely to blame: sexual reticence is also a factor here, if somewhat contingently, because of the known links between sexual fulfilment and opium consumption. Edith professes to want to change to a different topic, but fails to do so since Percy is conspicuously interested in keeping it going. Later in the day the Thompsons learn that Mr Lester has died. The Lesters at once draw the blinds on their side of the house, both at the front and at the back. The Thompsons briefly consider going into mourning on their side too, but then decide otherwise. Their practical assistance will be much more welcome than the mere gesture of darkening the house. Edith in fact will prove indispensable to the two Lesters with arrangements for the funeral, clothes, hats and even bills. But such practical matters and the immediate involvement with the Lesters' death wholly fail to distract her from her grand passion. She has a letter to Freddy to finish, and there is possibly more mail waiting for her at 168.

Her sanguine expectations are fulfilled on Monday. Freddy complains about his 'ancle' – which, as she points out, is spelt with a 'k': 'it looks so funy with a "c"'. The football damages it repeatedly. Why bother playing then, she asks. If he nurses it carefully it will be back to normal by the time he gets home, and then he will be able to teach her to play tennis after all. She warms to the prospect of their visit to Tunbridge Wells suggested by him. She has been there once only and adored it. But what, she remonstrates with him, is she to make of his silly questions about her love for him: 'and you are mine Peidi, arent you? I shall always try to keep you'. Why does he doubt her love for him? When they meet this time she wants him not just to say 'how are you "chère"' – which is surely 'prosaic' – but to kiss her and hold her wherever they meet and whoever may see them. Her insistence on this reflects her increasing fears about underlying hesitations in his letters to her, as though the more he is withdrawing from her the more he urges her to keep faith.

Walking near St Paul's churchyard on Wednesday in the company of Harry Renton, Edith catches a glimpse of Mrs Bywaters and 'purposely' keeps behind. The following day, with a mere week to go now till Freddy's return, she sends a parcel for him to await his arrival in Plymouth. In it are Hichens's *Bella Donna* and *The Fruitful Vine* which he is instructed to read in that order, the former whilst on shore, the latter after they are again parted. Also enclosed are a small parcel of tissues and a bar of Toblerone to be eaten on Thursday 25 May, his first day home, at the same time that she will be eating the twin piece of Toblerone to be with him in her imagination. The temporary buoyancy of Edith's mood stems partly from her anticipation of Freddy's imminent return, and partly from the fact that Miss Prior is due to leave for Paris on Friday 19 May. She'll be gone for at least a week. Her absence will be felt in the shop like a cloud lifting. For good measure, the unseasonable weather is yielding to warm summery winds. The next three weeks will witness soaring and record temperatures for London, easily matching the heatwave of 1921.

As if to mark the occasion of Miss Prior's departure, on Saturday 20 May Mr Carlton runs his favourite buyer home in 'a red posh car', no less attractive in her eyes for being borrowed from a friend of his. If Miss Prior knew of it, Edith muses, she might want to sack her. But she will not tell, and neither will Carlton. Home in Ilford Edith completes her shopping for Sunday's dinner party, when she is entertaining her family. In the evening her brother Billie takes his sweetheart Miss Ashley to meet his parents at No. 231. 'What about that then', Edith asks, and what ought she to make of Bill's remark that Miss Ashley is 'very mean'? She may be joking. At the same time as the Graydons are given a chance to form an opinion of their own about Billie's girl, a P & O liner bound for Bombay, the *Egypt*, collides off the French coast with a French vessel, the *Seine* en route to le Havre. The *Egypt* has sailed from Tilbury on Friday and goes down quickly with ninety-five people left on board. The first news bulletins of this latest maritime disaster merely report the sinking of a P & O liner. For a moment it must have seemed that it could be any P & O vessel, including the *Morea*.

Sunday 21 May: At 41 Kensington Gardens Edith is cooking a chicken. It is, remarkably, her first attempt at poultry. While she is preparing the stuffing, the bread sauce and the rest of the meal, including the gooseberry pie, she is thinking of her lover and wishing it was him she was cooking for. At about 2.30 p.m., while the Thompsons and their guests are relaxing in the garden, Reg and Bessie appear unexpectedly with the car. The weather is glorious and the Thompsons and Avis eagerly accept the invitation to go for a long ride into the country. In the course of the afternoon Bessie asks after Freddy and breaks the news of the shipwreck without giving the name of the vessel at first. How far their ride on this day takes them cannot be determined. But it is pushing 9.30 p.m. when the party finally arrives back at base in Kensington Gardens. The light is fading, and the windless evening air floats like balm over the streets off the Belgrave Road.

After a warm night, temperatures on Monday morning steadily climb. By noon they have reached 88 degrees Fahrenheit in the shade and London is reported to be 'in shirt sleeves everywhere'. Edith receives a long letter from Freddy at Carlton & Prior, but cannot read it for sheer pressure of work. Miss Prior's absence in Paris leaves her with 'tons to do'. She has to choose between reading his letters or letting him have a few lines of greeting at Plymouth. She decides to write and tells Bywaters that she will see him on Friday; only four more days to go. She teases him about his suspected dislike of her appearance today. She is wearing her foulard frock because of the heat. When he takes her out she will obligingly wear her black frock with the white beads again that he likes. If her money lasts, she promises, she might even buy another frock just for him to take her out to dinner in. Finally, should she take Wednesday 31 May off? It will be Derby Day, and they can either go there or keep a tryst elsewhere, just the two of them. Could he think about it?

Tuesday 23 May marks the opening of the Chelsea Flower Show. The heat is overwhelming, at one point hitting 127°F in the sun in Greater London. Business is less hectic and Edith can indulge in the luxury of reading and replying to her lover's letter. His comments on Molly please her, although she is quick to dissociate herself from their more censorious import; after giving Freddy a damning picture of poor Molly all tarted up and putting on airs, she retreats so as not to seem mean-minded. Bywaters informs her of his schedule for the next trip, which will take him to Australia, and he expresses regret for his lack of conversation with her on 'books and things'. She gladly notes his penance and claims to be resigned to her lot of loving an undemonstrative man. Finally, if he feels, as he claims, like being confined in a shell, shouldn't he remember that hers 'is a real live cage with a keeper as well . . . to whom I have to account every day, every hour, every minute really'.

About her 'new' novel, *Bella Donna*, she remarks that he 'may learn something from it to help us' and then she quotes ominously from Chapter 15 of the book: 'The fate of every man have we bound about his neck.' This pronouncement is inscribed on the lintel of the entrance of Mahmoud Baroudi's private apartments which are pervaded by an aura of luxurious, floating sensuality. Edith is intrigued by the spurious wisdom of the sentence and asks about it:

> Have we darlint? have we the fate of one – or we two halves. I dont know – I darent think . . . its like making sand pies at the sea-side . . . they always topple over.

Having written this, and after adding that she is full of excitement about his imminent return home, she signs off and rushes out to post it.

The heatwave continues unabated. The night of Wednesday 24 May is one of the hottest on record. At 5 a.m. on Thursday morning the air ignites and a tremendous thunderstorm explodes over London. For nearly two hours the metropolis presents the spectacle of a growling and impenetrable curtain of sheeted waters. By the time commuter traffic gets under way, it is warm again, but all the signs are that another downpour is likely. Edith is safely entrenched at Carlton & Prior when it breaks with 'almost tropical intensity'. Hailstones as large as walnuts and torrential rains flush shoppers out of the London shopping precincts. What a day for the lovers to keep their appointed communion, through the simultaneous eating of a bar of Toblerone chocolate.

Friday 26 May has come at last. In the evening the lovers meet at Fenchurch Street station. He is home for two weeks exactly, before a long cruise of more than three months to Australia. The last Monday in May marks the conviction and sentencing at the Old Bailey of Horatio Bottomley, and on Wednesday 31 May, Derby Day, which the lovers have allotted themselves for an all-day tryst, Major H. R. Armstrong is hanged in Gloucester Gaol at 8 a.m. When he dies Edith is still getting ready in Ilford. There can be little doubt that she and Bywaters make love this day and that she reassures him about it, by claiming to be pregnant again anyway.

The glorious weather holds and the Whitsun weekend promises to be perfect. But the lovers are separated for its duration. It is not surprising therefore that on the Tuesday after the Bank Holiday, Edith breaks from work at her earliest opportunity to be with Freddy at Fenchurch Street. They take off for part of the evening. When quizzed about her absence later on her return home, Edith tells Percy that she saw Mr Carlton off to Westcliff at Fenchurch, and that she there met and conversed with a mutual acquaintance of theirs called Booth. However, not only will Booth deny to Percy that any encounter took place between him and Edith, but it appears that another friend of Thompson's saw the wife and a fair-haired young man together at the station.

While the people from Manor Park and Ilford thus pursue their ordinary and extraordinary lives on this sunny evening, in the corridors of Whitehall a last ditch attempt is made to save a young life. A deputation of two jurors and several MPs have unsuccessfully tried all day to meet with the Home Secretary and the King. The life in question is Henry Jacobi's, now starting his last night at Pentonville.

The jury had strongly recommended the slow-witted boy to mercy. This plea for mitigation has been ignored. The only official that the party are finally given leave to see is Sir Ernley Blackwell. He turns them away. During the day Jacobi is confirmed in the chapel at Pentonville by the Bishop of Stepney, who will later extend his charity to Edith Thompson and Freddy Bywaters. The hangman, Ellis, the country's most experienced executioner, is rumoured to have expressed disgust at the thought of hanging the feeble-minded boy. But the following morning, at 8.55, after a warm June night, he enters the death cell at Pentonville and supports the shaking boy on to the scaffold before kicking the lever. When Edith enters Carlton & Prior on Wednesday 7 June Henry Julius Jacobi is already dead. At 12.34 pm in the London Central Telegraph Office, she sends a wire to the *Morea*, Tilbury Docks, telling Freddy that she will not go to 231 tonight: 'Have already said not going 231 see you and talk six'. Dressed in her black frock with the pearl beads, Edith flies into her lover's arms in Fenchurch Street. Unbeknown to them they are spotted by a Miss M'Donald, who lives near the Graydons in the Crescent. She is friends with Edith and Avis, and knows Freddy. Tomorrow she will tell Avis, who is to reproach her sister for being out with Bywaters while she, Avis, was deeply saddened by his departure. Edith's half-hearted attempt at denial will be at once exposed by a detailed description of her frock. Shamefacedly she will admit to the younger sister that she met Freddy, but will wriggle out of this corner by explaining that Freddy saw her to Katz's, her hairdressers near Broad Street. She now has a fringed bob cut – the heat of the past weeks and the trends in fashion have finally persuaded Edith to opt for short hair – which suits her well. In the meantime Percy has made his way to No. 231. His wife is not there and he is alarmed to learn from the family that Bywaters is 'taking a pal out' tonight. Thompson does not let on in front of the Graydons quite how badly he feels about that – they in any case do not harbour any suspicion about the identity of the 'pal' and even Percy cannot be sure. She will have to come clean tonight. He now also knows that Freddy is due to leave Friday. If his wife means to see Bywaters on Thursday night, he will put his foot down.

Thursday 8 June is a hot summer day. Mrs Edith Thompson has been instructed by her husband to return home without fail shortly after Carlton & Prior close and that he will be there to meet her. She has agreed to this without so much as batting an eyelid. But, for the first time perhaps, Edith has openly disobeyed Percy, fully aware of the fact that she will tonight have to outface and outscream him. This time she *will* do as she likes, whether he objects or not. At some point during the day she pens a note to her lover. She will slip it to him in due course, after they have talked about its content: a second abortion. Assuming this pregnancy to be a genuine one – and some doubts must attach to such a proposition – it will not proceed beyond eighty days; by Saturday 17 June she will have terminated it. Tonight her lover is taking her out to dinner and they can talk. Perhaps they also make love. She tells him that she is expecting and wishes to abort. Would he please desist from pleading with her to keep it? He agrees not to be sorry, nor to be angry with her. In her note she intimates the same confusion:

> I want to leave every little thing to you darlingest boy, I know you will decide and do what is best for two halves, only I should like to know all your thoughts & plans darlint, just to help me bear up & live, no exist thro. this life, until it is time for us to be joined together. . . . It is fearfully hard to decide, thats why I want you to pour moi & whatever you say or do I shall accept without fear or doubt or question, & think all the time, even if it seems wrong to me, that you know it will, at some indefinite period be, best for us.

The tone and also the content of this note recall the earlier one of Saturday 7 January 1922 when Edith described her attempt at aborting and hoped that Freddy would complete it for her. Then she had begged him not to 'be cross about it' and held out the prospect of keeping 'the next real one' perhaps 'for always'. What concerns her primarily about the unborn life within her is the physical and sentimental traumas that it brings with it. That abortion ought to pose moral dilemmas does not appear to worry either of the lovers much.

Freddy eventually takes her home to Ilford. It is pushing midnight. When she reaches her bedroom, Percy is reclining melodramatically on the ottoman at the foot of the bed. Presumably he is clutching his chest as he tells her that he is dying and wants to because of her; his heart is giving way and he'll suffer a heart attack. She has been at this juncture before, and she has just come from a passionate valedictory encounter with her young lover. Hardened and repelled by six years of Thompson's hypochondriacal antics, Edith retaliates with hysterical laughter. Her failure to respond to his threats propels Percy into a rage, and storming about he loudly berates her for making his life a hell. She snaps back that he ought to agree to a separation and that that would take care of his problems; she would be gone like a shot. Percy replies that he knows that that is what she wants, but that he will not give her a divorce, because it would make things 'far too easy' for both her and especially Bywaters. Thompson is now bitterly lashing out at her: the fact that on Thursday 30 March they were out together – yes! he knows! – and her seeing Bywaters on Tuesday at Fenchurch, he knows all about that too. Both she and Bywaters are liars and he is making her worse. Furthermore he, Percy, will put a stop to Freddy's correspondence coming for her at 168: 'It's useless for you to deny he writes to you – because I know he does.' Doesn't Edith remember, Percy asks more gently now, how she had told him that she had written to Bywaters asking him not to see her 'this time'? She remains implacably silent on this point, but will remark to Freddy that this promise had referred specifically to his last stay in England, not this one. The unhappy husband is fighting a losing battle, as he now begins to realise. While he is pondering this and hurting as only the rejected and humiliated in love can, she lies awake next to him, shaken, angry, and terrified in case the boy's letters fall into the husband's hands. This is a practical proposition, and she will handle it accordingly. It is unimaginable though that she does not feel the horror of the conjugal split, the pity of dividing up her lovely possessions, and the shame of becoming a divorcée, when her parents and grandparents had been such proud and upright people.

On Friday 9 June at 1.49 p.m. Bywaters sails in the *Morea* for Australia. He will be gone for fifteen weeks, till Saturday 23 September. His four previous voyages have never taken more than eight weeks at a time. Edith will spend the whole summer without him and compensate for her enforced celibacy by writing him some twenty-four letters of varying length. More than ever in these conversation pieces she 'talks' to him and intimately involves him in her life. Because 27 June is looming near, she gets off to a propitious start; it is both Freddy's birthday, and it marks the first anniversary of their romance's blossoming. Moreover it is almost a year to the day that they left for the Isle of Wight where so much happened that they would forever cherish. It is this doubling up of memories and of recreating his presence that endows these letters with their very remarkable sense of a life-enhancing imagination engaged in retracing its own past from moment to moment. Few people can ever have been as assiduously devoted to the momentary life as Edith Thompson.

Panic-stricken by her husband's threat to discontinue her mail at Carlton & Prior, she invents a pretext to leave the premises shortly after clocking in, and from the City, at 9.35 a.m., she sends a cable: 'To – Bywaters, Steamer Morea, Tilbury Docks / Send everything Fisher care G.P.O. call Monday'. From now on till two days before Freddy's return in September, all of his mail will go to the GPO in King Edward Street. When the Thompsons meet on this evening at 231 Shakespeare Crescent, they have buried the hatchet, but only temporarily. Perhaps it is Avis's remark about Miss M'Donald seeing Edith and Freddy on Wednesday evening which, on the way home to Ilford, makes tempers flare up again. By the time they have reached No. 41 Edith has determined that she cannot possibly spend the night with her husband. She will sleep in the little room instead. Percy won't have any of it. When she makes a move to cross the landing from the marital bedroom past the Lesters' to the small back room, he obstructs her. A scuffle ensues and Percy forces his way past the wife into the room and on to the bed. Rather than returning to the large bedroom Edith takes refuge in the strategically located bathroom. It locks from the inside and it allows her to monitor Percy's movements in the room next door and across the landing. When, half an hour later, Percy goes downstairs, she at once darts into the little room and locks the door behind her. Settled at last for the night in the same room where just under a year ago she and Freddy made love for the first time, she more than ever yearns to be free.

Over breakfast on Saturday the air at 41 Kensington Gardens is heavy with reproach. Thompson tells his wife that he is 'going to break' her in somehow and that she has always had too much her own way. Is he not a model husband? In any case he wants the bedroom to be cleaned out on *Thursdays* in future (this is presumably intended as a punishment for her faithless behaviour on several Thursday evenings). He is going to be master, and she will be his mistress alone, 'not half a dozen mens'. She takes all this in, mostly in silence, as she usually does, to avoid a direct confrontation. Whether or not she has notice of her father's intention to visit in the evening and stay over for the night, the fact is that on Saturday night Mr Graydon asks her to put him up. She suggests that he share the big bed with Percy, but he emphatically rejects this proposition: 'so sooner than make another fuss – I gave in'. The presence of Mr Graydon at 41 this evening raises an interesting problem, since it coincides with what has become her most famous fantasy-crossing from reality into fiction and back. According to her letter of Monday and Tuesday, 12 and 13 June, an enraged Thompson has told her father and everyone else at 231 Shakespeare Crescent that Freddy and she have been seeing each other. Allegedly her father is outraged that Bywaters should come between husband and wife and has promised to talk to his wayward daughter: 'what a scandal if it should get in the papers'. All this information Edith claims to have gathered from Avis whom she alleges to have warned that she would fight back against any imputations levelled against her: after all she didn't go whining to her 'people' when Thompson misbehaved. In the end her father, Edith notes, says nothing to her when he comes to stay on Saturday night.

Whatever really happens this weekend, Bywaters appears not to credit Mrs Thompson's version of events. Replying to her from Port Said, he invites her to talk to her father about him. He suspects that Edith is lying because, unbeknown to her, at a time when she said her father was very antagonistic to the adulterous interloper, Mr Graydon had, exceptionally, written Bywaters a letter. The letter, dated 13 June 1922, relates to the progress of the Graydons' youngest son, Harold. He is temporarily established at the Elito Café at 85 Ackland Street, St Kilda, Melbourne, and is free from 1 p.m. to 6 p.m. Hence, Mr Graydon notes, he should easily be able to collect his bag from the *Morea* when she docks at Melbourne on 10, 11 and 12 August. Can Fred kindly drop Harold a line to that effect from Fremantle? The letter concludes with the customary good wishes, a neutral 'Well, I dont think I've much more news to tell you' and is signed 'W. E. Graydon'. Receiving this simultaneously with Edith's letter, Bywaters may well wonder what, if anything, really has taken place. He may also find it hard to imagine that Avis can with equanimity comment on him carrying on with her married sister as Edith reports when, in the same letter, Edith describes her as badly upset by Freddy's departure. Moreover, when Avis is examined in court on this point by Curtis-Bennett – whom she has presumably alerted to the importance of this passage in her sister's letters – she will vehemently deny that anything like her father's indignant outburst has happened, or that Thompson descended on No. 231 in any manner, let alone as reported. It seems in retrospect to be the case that her father's presence at Kensington Gardens over the weekend confronted Edith with childhood fears about being a bad girl.

On Monday morning Edith composes a long letter to Bywaters and then takes it to the GPO. When she asks to collect Miss P. Fisher's mail, the man at the counter refuses to release it unless she can prove that she is Miss Fisher. Edith thinks this 'a devil of a mess', but never one to let circumstances defeat her she eventually decides to have some personal cards printed. Later in the day, when she finds herself in the basement of Carlton & Prior with Rose Jacobs, she asks her: 'Would you mind writing a letter for me and address it to Miss Fisher c/o Carlton & Prior, 168 Aldersgate Street.' Rose is the showroom factotum and closely monitors the adulterous steps of Miss Graydon. For her the intrigue thickens considerably as she sits down and at Edith's dictation writes: 'Dear Miss Fisher, I beg to call your attention to our next Committee Meeting which will be held on Friday . . . and your presence will be required. Yours truly, R. James.' Miss Graydon seals the note in an envelope and keeps it on her. It will provide proof, if needed, that she is indeed Miss Fisher.

On Tuesday morning Edith successfully collects Miss Fisher's mail from the GPO. It includes the watch which she gave Freddy as a present. It is running ten minutes fast, he claims – meaning 'slow', as she points out. She takes it back to have it mended and promises to forward it to Sydney in due course. He also encloses a cheque for her to cash and put money on the Hunt Cup for both of them. His enquiry about their winnings from the Oaks race at Epsom on 2 June meets with a disappointing answer: the money has not been paid out, and there is little hope now that it will be. Oddly, she notes, he completely forgets to mention the letter she slipped him on Thursday about the pregnancy. Could he please address himself to that? He will, but in such a way as to leave her shaking with rage.

In the evening Edith and Percy pay one of their rare visits to the Thompsons at 49 Seymour Gardens. Edith is in a good mood, because her new costume has been delivered and looks splendid. But even the light of an English summer evening cannot dispel the gloom and doom of Richard Halliday Thompson. Edith soon feels crotchety. For two hours she is treated to the Thompsons indulging their ailments. It is, as she remarks mischievously, 'exhilerating especially when you feel blue'. Then Percy pointedly asks why his nephew Graham never visits at No. 41. Edith snappily interrupts: 'Why do you ask for him to come round when you know he's not allowed to.' Immediately the entire Thompson clan gang up on her. They assure her that it is inconceivable that either Kenneth or Lily would forbid Graham to speak to her. She retorts that she can believe that about the boy's father, but will not be duped into believing the same about the mother – the row between the two women is still smouldering, more than two years on from the Thompsons' departure from 65 Mansfield Road. Percy is hurt by his wife's unashamed disowning of his sister. When they depart, they are both bad-tempered again. Edith particularly resents the Thompsons' intrusive presence, because on this night it is exactly a year since Freddy first kissed her on the Isle of Wight. In her mind she is holding him in her arms before going to sleep. This week, indeed this month of June, is full of memories which crowd her mind and almost challenge her sense of the present.

Commuting into work on Wednesday 14 June Edith is taken ill. She really must see a doctor, she decides: 'I don't like doing these silly things in public places.' If she is indeed pregnant, she must have aborted between 14 June and Saturday 17 June, because by the time she visits the surgery on Saturday she has lost 'an awful lot of blood'. In the office she hears that the mother of one of their boys at Carlton & Prior has died of ptomaine poisoning from a tin of salmon, after only a three-day illness. How does one catch it? she wants to know. She feels 'very blue . . . an inactive sort of drifting feeling'. Soon he will be at the other end of the world. If he were here now they could spend time together so easily: Carlton & Prior have just decided to stop work at 5 p.m., because business is slowing down during the summer.

In the lunch hour Edith enters the bank just down from Carlton & Prior to cash his cheque. She is asked whether she is Mrs Bywaters:

Edith: No.

Clerk: Did you endorse the back?

Edith: No.

Clerk: Just write your name on this paper please.

She obliges and is then asked whether she holds any authority from F. Bywaters to cash the cheque. She produces his letter and they pay out. But she could have done without the aggravation. After telling him of this she seals the envelope and then suddenly recalls the racing results of the Ascot and particularly the Royal Hunt Cup run on this day and hastily scribbles them on the blank sealed envelope with a brief 'accountant's' warning about their increasing losses at horse racing. She then puts the blank envelope into a new one, addresses it and posts it to Marseilles.

Thursday morning is cloudy and distinctly cool. Edith is at her desk writing three short paragraphs to her lover. 'This time last year' . . . that recurrent phrase. This is the Isle of Wight week in the Thompson and Bywaters calendar. She will be writing to him every day. A year ago she won the sweepstake for the Gold Cup. This year she has lost a pound. Freddy is getting into Marseilles tonight. How she wishes she were out there with him. After work she goes west to purchase a new frock for the Eastcote outing on Saturday 24 June. The frock she buys comes from the same shop which she visited once before and where she saw a splendid 'White & Jade Frock'. She enquires after it now. They still have it and get it for her: 'it was lovely & so was the price – 12 guineas so it had to stay in the shop'. This economic detail, nugatory in itself, has a distinct bearing on allegations levelled against Mrs Thompson later by her brother-in-law: particularly that her tastes were so extravagant and insatiably self-indulgent that she could only afford to gratify them with the help of immoral earnings.

Looking into another shop-window and about to move on, Edith notices that Freddy's sister and her fiancé Fallowfield-Cooper are standing next to her, also scrutinising the window. They must, she concludes, be trousseau-hunting. They probably are, although in the end Florence May Bywaters will not become married till 1925, over two years after the tragedy.

Friday 16 June, 5 p.m.: recalling perhaps the glorious weather a year ago outside Osborne House, Edith wishes she could 'see into the future'. Then, she hopes, she can make up to her lover for all the unhappiness that she has already caused him:

There are 2 halves in this world who want nothing on earth but to be joined together and circumstances persistently keep them apart.

It is the anniversary of his first declaration of love, that last Friday in Shanklin. They had looked forward to a return to London, where they would become lovers and live together. Instead he now is at anchor off Marseilles bound for the Antipodes, while she is preparing to return to the Crescent and Percy Thompson.

On Saturday Edith pays her visit to the doctor at last. The verbal exchange which takes place, and is reproduced in Edith's next letter to Bywaters, is almost certainly authentic, but not very informative about the true circumstances of her 'pregnancy' and 'abortion'. The doctor starts by asking her 'lots of questions' and then suggests that he examine her. She refuses and he asks: 'are you ençeinte?', to which her reply is 'No, I think not.' She explains the symptoms to him though – early morning faints for example – and he concludes that she suffers from 'chronic anaemia' which might trigger 'pernicious anaemia', if she is not careful. 'What exactly is "pernicious anaemia"?', she asks, and he informs her that 'all your blood every drop turns to water'. It is not common among the young, he stresses, but frequently occurs in older people. It only affects younger people as a rule 'when they have had an accident and lost a lot of blood; have you had one?' Caught out by this well directed question, Edith hesitates and then says 'No – because it wasn't really an accident and I didn't want to tell him everything – he might have wanted to see my husband.' To cure her serious anaemia the doctor prescribes burgundy wine with every meal – '4 glasses a day' – and also medicine and pills to induce her periods to return. From these fragments of dialogue it appears that the doctor suspects either an abortion or a miscarriage, particularly since his patient is singularly reticent. What this account confirms is that if Edith Thompson aborted a second time, it was not in a backstreet parlour, but on her own.

Mr Graydon again visits on Saturday evening, and he stays the night for the second time in two weeks on a weekend night. The warm Sunday passes without further incident. Monday comes: 'Its Monday now darlint, that day you came up and took me to lunch at the Kings Hall do you remember?', writes Edith as soon as she gets into Carlton & Prior, continuing the letter she was writing on Thursday and Friday. Everything is very quiet at work, and Mr Carlton is on holiday till Thursday, when he will organise the outing to Eastcote. Edith moans to Freddy about her forthcoming holiday in Bournemouth, so unlike what she hoped for: swimming with Freddy in Cornwall and learning to play tennis properly. Finally, just before attending to a customer, perhaps, or some business, she wonders whether he might meet Harold (as indeed he will, according to Mr Graydon's earlier note). If so, could he 'knock a bit of sense into him' for her sake? The Graydons are concerned by Harold's letters and particularly by the fact that he has written to Doris Grafton, a local girl, for her to come out and join him to get married: 'he is sending over her passage money'. Edith's comment is that, because there is 'a lot more of rot like that – darlint I'm sure he's not normal sometimes'.

On Tuesday morning Edith is back at her desk giving more details of the weekend, particularly her visit to the doctor's. Then she hurries to the GPO for the Marseilles mail. What she finds there nearly leaves her dumb. He has merely dropped her a note informing her of his putting off a more extended letter from Port Said. This is the second postponement and she is getting agitated and is hurt by the casual tone of his 'Don't be too disappointed' and 'try to be brave'. In her own indignant and recriminatory words:

> You can't possibly know what it feels like to want and wait each day – every little hour – for something – something that means 'life' to you and then not to get it. . . . You force me to conclude that the life you lead away from England is all absorbing that you haven't got time nor inclination to remember England or anything England holds.

Her outrage is understandable, but for Bywaters she is becoming uncomfortably dependent. Her ardour, compounded by the multiple complications that will follow on from an elopement or a divorce suit, have further strengthened Bywaters's resolve to put an end to their affair. He does not wish to hurt her, but he wants her to calm down and settle back into normality. At the same time his thoughts are already returning to Avis. They did see each other during his last leave and he rediscovered her charm and the worth of her simple integrity. Edith fires off her missive to Bywaters at once. Her spirits are bolstered somewhat by one of the firm's buyers, Dunsford, offering her a lift in the car on the following day, Wednesday, to cheer the return to London of the Prince of Wales, after his eight-month voyage in the Far East. Dunsford proposes to hoist her up onto the roof of the car to give her a prime view of the procession. Edith enthusiastically agrees to go. Home at No. 41 Edith tells Percy of Wednesday's expedition to the 'West'. He professes to be 'terribly shocked': how will she get on the car roof? She retorts that the plan is for her 'to climb up by a rope ladder at the side of the motor'. This wholly absurd answer still soothes the husband's jealousy at the thought of any man feeling his wife's waist, let alone grabbing her and lifting her up.

Wednesday 21 June is warm and summery. All of London eagerly awaits the arrival at 3.30 p.m. in Paddington from Plymouth of the Prince of Wales. In the early afternoon a group of men and women from Carlton & Prior crowd into Dunsford's car to drive up to Marble Arch or Piccadilly. The royal cortège arrives as scheduled. It passes through Sussex Gardens and Cambridge Terrace, then over into Edgware Road. It crosses Oxford Street at Marble Arch, then bears down Eastern Drive and turns left into Piccadilly before reaching St James Street and the Mall. The procession arrives at the palace between 4.15 and 4.30 p.m. and the Prince, reunited at last with his family, acknowledges the massive show of loyal affection from his subjects. Edith sees 'everything beautifully it was rather fun'. Can she guess that in just over three months from now her name will be known to almost all the people thronging these streets. The same papers that she reads will give exclusive coverage of *her* life story, and she will become infamous as part of 'Thompson & Bywaters'. Even her Prince will read about her.

On Thursday Edith sends an apology to Bywaters for her intemperate outburst on Tuesday. If only she had been more patient and not posted the letter at once, she would have had an opportunity to tear it up, or at least explain it. Business this morning is slack, and Mr Carlton is up to plan the Eastcote outing in concert with his senior staff. The royal return is the subject of lively discussions. But the nation's celebratory mood on this day is dampened by the assassination at the hands of the IRA of Field-Marshal Sir Henry Wilson. The funeral is fixed for Monday 26 June.

The weekend is approaching. Edith quickly drops Freddy a line to remind him of the fact that it is a year, 'by the *day* not the date', since he took her to lunch at the Holborn. She remembers that she still has his watch. As he has so far failed to acknowledge her queries about it, she has decided not to forward it. She will retain it till he returns in September. Tonight is the Wanstead Garden fête and this, as well as Eastcote, should help her to overcome the tedium of the weekend. She will tell him all about both events on Monday.

It is cool on Friday evening and there is some cloud. The garden party and fête in aid of the Seamen's Orphanage at Wanstead is one of the big local occasions, when everyone gathers in a spirit of fun to raise money. The Thompsons patronise this particular happening, because of their families' traditional links with the sea, and now particularly through the Birnages' prominent participation in the organising of it. The stately orphanage with its extensive gardens still stands in its walled enclosure on Hermon Hill, as the Wanstead Hospital. The grounds have shrunk from the pressure of new building, but the old fairground area is easily recognised still. Here is how Edith described the evening:

It was rather fun on Thursday [Friday] at the Garden Party – They had swings & roundabouts & Flip Flaps cocoa nut shies Aunt Sallies – Hoopla and all that sort of things I went in for them all & on them all & shocked a lot of people I think. I didnt care tho' & going home Mr Birnage said he'd like some fried Fish and potatoes – I'd got rather a posh frock on – wth. georgette & trd. with rows & rows of jade ribbon velvet & my white fur & a large wht. hat, but all that didnt deter me from going into a fried fish shop in Snaresbrook and buying the fish & chips.

Getting it home was the worst part – it absolutely smelt the bus out: I didn't mind – it was rather fun: only I wished you had been with me: I think 2 halves together would have enjoyed themselves – better than 1 half by herself.

Saturday 24 June is a mild and dry day. The Eastcote excursion provides Edith with her first chance to show off her new frock of 'pale mauve voile embroidered in grey on the bodice & on the skirt & a sash of darker mauve ribbon'. The sash and the fashionable 'organdie' frock were clearly remembered by Myrtle Aldridge, who took part in the outing. Sixty-three years later, she described Edith's dress:

I remember the colouring . . . that mauve, a light lilac-coloured dress, organdie I think it was, organdie with white embroideries, sort of stitching and white coat and hat, white shoes . . . and a darker mauve sash . . . oh yes I remember that . . . she was very smart, she loved clothes, she knew how to dress.

After lunch the games consist of popular pastimes and are indulged in to the full. In Edith's own account of it:

Darlint, your own pal is getting quite a sport.

On Saturday I was first in the Egg & Spoon race & first in the 100 yards Flat race & 3rd in the 50 yards Flat race.

Everybody tells me Im like a racehorse – can get up speed only on a long distance & my reply was 'that if a thoroughbred did those things then I felt flattered.'

Then I was M.C. for the Lancers we stood up 10 Sets had some boys in from an adjoining cricket field. I sat on the top of the piano & made a megaphone of my hands & just yelled – nothing else – Mr Carlton said all that shouting was worth 2 long drinks afterwards so I had 2 double brandies & Sodas with him.

We had a very good day indeed: In fact I think I enjoyed the actual outing better than last year – until we got to Lpool St. coming home & then *he* started to make a fuss – says I take too much notice of Dunsford & he does of me & created quite a scene. I am really sick of this sort of thing – he gets jealous & sulks if I speak to any man now.

The following Monday marks a wet beginning of the Wimbledon fortnight on the magnificent new Centre Court. A stark contrast to the excitement of the tennis is provided by the sombre scene of the funeral procession of Sir Henry Wilson on its way to a ceremony at St Paul's. Shortly before 1 p.m. Edith rushes to the GPO and sends a message to Bywaters on the *Morea* via Eastern Radio: 'M H R 27 6 21 PEIDI'. But he may not receive these anniversary greetings in time, since the *Morea* is already out of radio range from Aden and not yet near enough to Bombay. She will send more greetings in another telegram tomorrow.

Tuesday 27 June 1922: Freddy Bywaters is twenty years old today. A fortnight ago, anticipating that they would be separated on this day, Edith sanguinely forecast that on his birthday he would be thinking of 'a girl whose best pal you are in England'. She in turn will be focussing her whole being on him 'all day every little minute'. The first thing she does after checking in this morning at Carlton & Prior is to pen him a frantic birthday note, for it is *his* birthday *and* 'the birthday of the Palship of 2 halves'. They became lovers a year ago. The memory of it resuscitates her flagging spirits. She posts the note at once, and receives his greetings at the same time. Later in the day she again sits down and addresses him once more:

> Darlingest own Pal, I love you heaps & heaps more than yesterday and such a lot less than I shall tomorrow.

The last days of June are uneventful ones for Edith Thompson. Her only break is Miss Prior's departure for her holidays on Wednesday. This means more work, as Miss Graydon customarily assumes the junior partner's mantle in her absence. At the same time it grants Edith and her employer the freedom of each other's unrestricted company; and the role of deputy manageress also means extra free days and early checking-out from work. The elation of Wednesday is dampened by an encounter in the lunch hour with Freddy's mother in the City, who cuts her dead after Edith goes up to her, bows, smiles and says: 'How do you do?'

On Thursday afternoon Edith enters the GPO to collect the Port Said mail. The petty little man who earlier fussed over whether or not she could prove her identity as Miss Fisher is on duty. He refuses to surrender Bywaters's Port Said letter, though he lets her have his registered envelope addressed to Miss Fisher. This contains a present of garters. The clerk informs Miss Fisher that, if she has a London address, she is not entitled to receive mail at the GPO. Miss Fisher denies living in London, but fails to convince him. Impatient with herself and not willing further to attempt to 'overcome (or try to) his bad temper', she gives up and will leave the letter till Monday, when she succeeds in retrieving it. She has waited twenty-four days for it and after reading the letter, she feels that it has hardly been worth the wait. He is preparing her for breaking off the relationship. He will continue, he says, writing to her 'because it will help', but at the same time he suggests that he will not write 'from some ports – because I want to help you'. It is a deeply troubled Edith Thompson who at 4 p.m. leaves Carlton & Prior to return home.

Tuesday 4 July is a cool, cloudy and eventually wet day. On the platform at Ilford station Edith meets Mr Derry and Molly talking and laughing together. As she passes them, she bows and says good morning. But her outward indifference is a mask. All day long she will wonder what the two of them may have exchanged by way of gossip about her. Her letter to Bywaters, the first one since Tuesday night of last week, will help her forget any envious thoughts; and at 11.30 a.m. she is having a drink with Mr Carlton. The atmosphere at Carlton & Prior is warm and relaxed: morning drinks, 4 p.m. departures from work, whole and half days off, and plenty of company. On Tuesday evening Carlton offers his buyer Thursday off, as she has been invited (by an unknown party) to the Henley Regatta. At first Edith refuses the offer of a day at Henley. Now she accepts. Percy is not invited. But on Thursday 6 July gales reach up to sixty m.p.h. and the whole country is flooded by pouring rains. The party which gathers for lunch at Phyllis Court, 'at the invitation of an MP, Mr Stanley Baldwin', looks over a grim prospect of leaden skies and a slate-coloured river. It rains all afternoon and a miserable Edith Thompson arrives home at a quarter to seven.

The following day, on her way into Liverpool Street, she again runs into Derry who teasingly addresses her with 'So you know that young lady I was talking to the other morning':

Edith: No, I don't know her.

Derry: But she knows you & all about you.

Edith: Oh, probably: lots of people know me & about me that I'd rather not know.

Derry: I believe you're jealous.

This uneasy banter amuses Edith, she reasons with herself. Certainly the thought of her being jealous of Molly for talking to Derry is ridiculous: 'Some men have such a high opinion of themselves and their charms that I'm afraid I cant climb up to them.' She feels frustrated though that she is none the wiser after talking to Derry about what passed between Molly and him.

On Saturday 8 July the rains are abating, but the gales continue. At Wimbledon a delayed ladies' final is won by Suzanne Lenglen, who overwhelms Molla Mallory of the USA: 6–2, 6–0. For Edith Thompson this day marks the return of her period for the first time since 23 April. Then she had an unusually light bleeding which had left her in little doubt about a second pregnancy. This time she does not feel faint, but aches all over. Even if she had been on duty, she could not have gone in to work. In the evening she sees the doctor who advised her on 17 June. He is pleased, because his medications have worked. If they were prescribed with a view to reactivating her menstrual cycle, they have certainly proved successful over a period of three weeks, the time it would take to build up and strengthen the body's blood-supply with vitamin C and iron tablets.

On Monday 10 July the Australian Gerald Patterson becomes the men's Wimbledon champion. Early this week Edith is writing to Bywaters again. As yet, she complains, she has not had Freddy's *promised* letter from Aden. Shortly before noon Avis enters the premises of Carlton & Prior and finds her sister and Mr Carlton enjoying a brandy. He invites her to share their drink which she does, feeling 'very flattered'. As soon as Avis is gone, Edith completes her letter to Fred. She has decided not to wait for the Aden post, but to send this one off in the lunch hour to make sure it gets to Fremantle in time. There is a sudden, poignant urgency about her concluding lines. She remembers him telling her that he wanted to 'help' her by not writing to her as often as he used to, and by not seeing her on his return to London. She almost panics now at the suggestion and starts to plead with him as best she knows:

> I wonder what 'my only pal' is doing now & how he is feeling – when I try & contrast my feelings of going away this year to those of going away last year – I really wonder if Im living in the same world – I suppose I am – but its not the same world to me darlint – that world last year didnt contain a pal – just one only, to whom I need not wear a mask – but this year does – altho he is still so very far away that I go on wearing that mask to everyone I meet – every day – I wonder if there ever will be a time when I shall appear as I really am – only you see me as I really am – the 'pretence me' is my

ordinary every day wearing apparel the 'real' me is only visible for such a very short time when you're in London. Darlingest Boy – I can't bear to think of you being in England and not seeing me – must we be so very strict & stern – cant you imagine what your only pal – (no, not pal – Im talking to you darlint as the girl that loves you, Im talking to my veriest own lover not as & to a pal) will feel like knowing youre in London, & expecting to see you at every turn & really knowing deep down in her heart that she wont. Must you be so cruel darlint? See me once – for one whole day together for all that time & I wont mind if I dont see you any more the whole time you are in London I cant bear it if you go away without seeing me again – nearly 4 more months after September – that makes it January 1923 its too long to wait Darlint – too much to ask of any human being – especially is it too much to ask of you and I – we're not ordinary human beings – we're apart – different – we've never known pleasure – real pleasure I mean in anothers company – until we knew each other – weve had so few pleasures – & so many rebuffs – every one that is added now makes it harder.

Am I selfish? No I dont think its a selfish feeling cos its for both of us – Im fighting for our rights to break down that reserve that youre going to build up against yourself & between

PEIDI

On Thursday 13 July Edith collects Freddy's letter from Aden at the GPO. It is very late coming, and she is puzzled by his despondent writing: 'I want to be in England to look after you . . . I want you to look after me too.' Has he been ill, she wonders, does he need 'a pillow, the pillow that only Peidi can give you?' Tomorrow she will be off work, shopping and packing for her fortnight's holiday in Bournemouth. This is therefore her last chance to talk to Freddy: 'a letter darlint is like food only you have food everyday to keep you alive and I have a letter every how many days?' Then she launches into a discussion of Hichens's *Bella Donna*, followed by a shorter excursion into *The Fruitful Vine*. Since this part of her letter was quoted in court, and in view of the novel's importance for the case as a whole, a brief plot summary is needed to put into context both the bearing of the novel on the lovers' relationship and the uses it was put to in court.

Hichens's novel was published in 1909. Its eponymous protagonist 'Bella Donna' is a disgraced and ageing society belle named Mrs Ruby

Chepstow who, at forty-two, succeeds in marrying a younger scion of wealthy aristocratic descent, the thirty-six-year-old Nigel Armine. Their union, secretly ratified at the Registry Office, is unsuccessfully opposed by Armine's close friend Meyer Isaacson, a highly respected Jewish doctor. The newlyweds depart for Egypt where he farms lands in the Fayyum. On the Mediterranean crossing they meet Mahmoud Baroudi, a Cairo-based buccaneer of 'mixed Greek and Egyptian blood' who dresses well, has mighty shoulders, a deep chest, a neck as 'powerful as a bull's', black and curly hair, thick and rather pouting lips and wide and ardent nostrils. He learns their address on the river Nile and arranges for Mrs Armine to be wooed secretly by having his Egyptian and Nubian servants sing for her at night at the bottom of the Armines' river-fronting gardens. The enchantments of the East, to which the siren-like Bella Donna is susceptible, are unleashed against her in the most cunning way. Before going upriver on his own to attend to business, Armine accompanies his wife on a visit to Baroudi's spectacular yacht, the *Loulia*. The motto of the *Loulia* is a line from the Koran: 'The fate of every man have we bound about his neck.' To Bella Donna its harshness 'rather suggests a prison' and makes her feel uneasy. Momentarily alone in Baroudi's private apartments, she languorously reclines in the strongly scented air on the divan which, soft and yielding, 'held and caressed her body, almost as if it were an affectionate living thing that knew of her present desire'. Soothed and invaded by the drugs in the room, Bella Donna imagines herself in the role of an Eastern woman, supine and surrendering to the desires of a slave-master:

> Slowly she closed her eyes in the Eastern house of Baroudi. Here Baroudi lay as she was lying, and smoked the keef, and ate the Hashish, and dreamed. He would never be the slave of a woman. She felt sure of that. But he might make a woman his slave . . . he might adore a slave with a cruel adoration. She felt cruelty in him, and it attracted her, it lured her, it responded to something in her nature which understood, and respected, cruelty, and which secretly despised gentleness.

Five chapters later, after Nigel's departure upriver, Bella Donna meets Baroudi in the 'garden of oranges'. As she is about to leave, a darweesh enters with a basket of snakes and invites her to feel them:

> She hesitated for a moment, then deliberately pulled off her gloves, put them on the divan, stood up, and plunged her right hand into the bag, at the

same time shutting her eyes. She shut them to enjoy with the utmost keenness a sensation entirely new.

Her hand encountered a dry and writhing life, closed upon it firmly but gently, drew it out and towards her. . . . It twisted itself in her hand, as if trying to escape, but as she held it firmly it presently became quieter, lifted itself . . . slowly she brought it nearer to her nearer, nearer, nearer, till it wavered out from her hand and attained her body.

The only way Bella Donna can see to achieve her ardent desire to be with Baroudi and at the same time maintain her English respectability and wealth is by gradually poisoning Nigel with lead. When Isaacson, who had earlier heard from Armine that he was feeling well and happy, learns of his now rapidly deteriorating condition, he at once departs for the East. Nigel is not readily persuaded by Isaacson that his wife is conspiring against his life. After showing his friend the door Nigel confronts Bella Donna who, in her frantic desire to join Baroudi, angrily admits everything. Then, rejected by her lover and no longer daring to return to the husband, she 'disappeared into the darkness, going blindly towards the distant hills that keep the Arabian desert'.

It is hard to believe now that writing like this was praised in *The Times*, as though it were the equivalent of a Graham Greene novel. It is true that some of the characterisation is intelligently drawn, and the novelist refrains from simplistic moral polarisation and allows scope for motivation. Its racism and anti-semitism accord with prejudices that were rife in the period, and one hardly expects Hichens's novels to reject Kiplingesque sentiments. As a piece of Edwardian middle-brow fiction, *Bella Donna* ranks among the more explicit novels. The local colour derives its authenticity from Hichens's own experience of Egypt. He would recover a similar sense of place in *The Fruitful Vine*, another novel exotically set in the south.

Even from this fragmentary summary of the plot of *Bella Donna*, its appeal to Edith Thompson can be focussed with reasonable certainty: the novel's escapist locations, its illicit sexuality, the age difference between Bella Donna and Armine, the inscrutably passionate and sexually devious Baroudi, the lilting rhythms of the East, the drugged pulse of life in the Delta of the Nile, and of course the poisoning of the husband. Edith read every Hichens novel that she could lay her hands on. Hichens and Locke were her favourite authors. However, *Bella Donna* was not her favourite novel – far from it. In May 1922 she had written to Freddy: 'The book I'm reading, "Bella Donna", is about Egypt – I'd think you would be interested in it – although I don't think you would like the book – at least I hope you wouldn't – I don't.' What interested Edith Thompson in Hichens's novels was their erotic charge and the author's fascination with the sirens of the demi-monde, whether in *Bella Donna*, *The Fruitful Vine*, or in *Felix*. The poison plot in *Bella Donna*, which is artificially foregrounded in her correspondence, is intended to keep up their shared pretence about a deed that neither of them contemplated carrying out. In court, however, the novel, and particularly the letter which refers to *Bella Donna*, will later provide copious fodder for the lovers' prosecution.

On Saturday 15 July the Thompsons and Avis leave for Bournemouth. At about the same time the *Morea* departs for Fremantle from Adelaide. Edith has anticipated this holiday with apprehension, as she will not even be able to withdraw inside her shell by commuting into the City and thus escape the caged feeling of home. She will try to be brave though and 'dance thro. somehow', although she is getting weary of all 'this dancing and pretending'. As a mark of affection for the memory of last year she has left behind her 'peach sports coat' which she wore on the Isle of Wight.

The island and Osborne House were welcoming and exciting. Bournemouth on the other hand proves a 'very stiff starchy place', and the boarding house at which the Thompsons and Avis are lodgers for a fortnight is 'terrible'. Most of the twenty-seven boarders are so staid that the company is as poor as the food – which is sparse. No drinks are allowed indoors and there are signs inside requesting ladies not to smoke in the house. The two sisters quickly decide that the place can do with some livening-up. In her own words:

> We did some mad things – climbed a tree in front of a row of Boarding Houses & had our photos taken up it (Avis & I I mean) everyone in the Bdg. Hses were watching us from the windows & had donkey rides up & down the front: the people stopping in our Boarding Hse could hardly believe (they said) I'd been married as long as I had & I was the age I am: they said I only seemed a child I felt glad they thought this pour vous – altho I really felt very old & miserable & lonely all the time I was away.

The first week of their holiday in this sedate resort passes uneventfully. The weather is dull and cool. The one piece of news is the marriage on Tuesday of Lord Louis Mountbatten to 'England's

Richest Bride', Miss Edwina Ashley. The Prince of Wales officiates as Mountbatten's best man. The papers are full of the wedding.

It may be on this day that Edith writes to Carlton & Prior both to send a postcard and to enquire after Rose Jacobs's and the Dunsfordses' private addresses. Percy at once objects and accuses her of being deceitful, as she appears unable to communicate with Dunsford openly on a postcard seen by her workmates at 168. A 'right royal battle' ensues in the course of which Percy calls her 'impudent' and a lot of other things and that she 'must have a very good tutor' who teaches her cheating and bad temper. The row is over nothing; Edith wants to place bets in London on the races and prefers to do so discreetly through two trusted acquaintances. How misplaced her trust in Rose is, she will learn too late. After this marital confrontation Percy sulks for two days and pays a visit to a phrenologist at Boscombe who tells him that he will live to be quite an old man.

The Thompsons' second week in Bournemouth coincides with Goodwood Week. On Monday Edith sends a wire to Rose to put a pound each way for her on Scamp for the Stewards' Cup on Tuesday. The race is run on a glorious summer day. The winner is Tetrameter, and Edith professes to be fed up with Scamp for letting her down this way. The recovery of summer lures the Thompsons and Avis out for the odd game of tennis on the nearby courts; and on Thursday 27 July the threesome embark on a day-long cruise around the Isle of Wight. As the boat ploughs out of Poole Bay, she must feel thrilled at the thought of revisiting the island, and perhaps catching another glimpse of Shanklin and Osborne House. Today will not hold the same happiness, but it will be a welcome change from the stuffiness of the mainland. The boat eventually docks on the pier in Ventnor, and the passengers disembark. Strolling lightly along the front at Ventnor, the two women complain about the sedateness of Bournemouth and Boscombe, and the fact that a town of 90,000 inhabitants should have only seven licences granted it. One of the locals on the waterfront assures them that 'There's nothing like that about Ventnor – you can walk about naked if you like.' Edith laughingly replies: 'That's the place for us', and then is recommended 'a very nice Boarding Hse right on the front with 2 front lawns very like Osborne Hse last year'. Already she imagines Bywaters and herself here in Ventnor, lodging in this cosy little family pension. Percy wants to take her to Cornwall next summer. She infinitely prefers Ventnor.

After their arrival back in Bournemouth, Edith surreptitiously writes Freddy a note, and posts it. The date she gives reveals where her thoughts lie: she dates it 27.6.21 when she ought to write 27.7.22. She posts it in time for the 8 p.m. collection. The following day, 28 July, is the Thompsons' last day in Bournemouth. At the other end of the world Freddy lies at anchor in Sydney. He is writing to her. It is a short letter and, one surmises, a dismissive one. Fred has a girl here in Sydney. Her presence makes it easier for him to forget about Mrs Thompson.

On Saturday morning, while Percy is packing or in the bathroom, Edith scribbles Bywaters a quick message to remind him and herself of the fact that a year ago they were in Kew. Her comfort is that at least they are now returning to London and the numerous opportunities for escape that the metropolis affords her. As she does not find an unobserved moment to post the card, she slides it into her clothes to send it on Monday from work.

Monday marks the start of Cowes Week. For Edith the week will be a hard one. It is nearly a year since the tensions at 41 Kensington Gardens exploded into an open row between the two men and resulted in Freddy's expulsion from her home. On Tuesday 1 August Edith mourns the 'other' anniversary, the date of the break. This time last year it was a warm summer day, haunted only by the brief memory of a few glorious yesterdays of secret assignations and fervent romantic encounters. Today it is cool outside, and a patter of raindrops against the window panes signals the first of several showers over the City. She sits and broods as the day passes. At night she sleeps fitfully. Images of her lover intrude on her mind's eye, as she tosses in bed next to her husband. In her sleep, dreams and nightmares surge up to disturb her rest. Nearly always these nightly visitations concern her lover who has now all but openly declared his intentions of leaving her:

> One night I dreamed that you had married Avis – because she found out how much was between us (you & I) & threatened to tell everybody unless you married her – another night I dreamed I had been to a theatre with a man I knew – I had told you about him & you came home from sea unexpectedly & when you found me you just threw me over a very deep precipice & I was killed – sometimes Ive dreamed worse things than these & waked up in a fearful fright.

The awesome sense of premonition which these words intimate strikes a numbing chord in anyone reading Mrs Thompson's letters in the inevitably retrospective knowledge of the final scene of the tragedy. Her claim to have 'dreamed worse things than these' sounds an eerily prophetic note. The sensation of falling will be her last on earth.

On Friday 4 August Edith simply *has* to write to Freddy. A year ago was the day of their unforgettable embrace at the corner of Morris Avenue: does he remember it the way she does? As this is her first letter since their return from holiday, she relates to him her various adventures and reminds him of Avis's birthday on 24 September. Could he please try not to forget it this year? She encloses snippets from the 'Russell' case, noting that 'the evidence on enclosed slip struck me as being very similar to evidence I could give'. She enquires after one of the photos that she asked him to destroy last trip and asks whether now everything she says is instantly dismissed. The sole comfort afforded her at the moment is the prospect of his return journey from Sydney on Tuesday, and she concludes:

> However perhaps this coming year will bring us the happiness we both desire more than anything in this world – and if it doesn't? we'll leave this world that we love so much – cling to so desperately.

On Tuesday the countdown from Sydney to London starts. She looks forward to his return, even though 'you say you wont see me – but I shall hope & hope & hope. . . .' At the GPO today she receives a letter from Bombay and a note from Colombo. The letter contains a detailed discussion of *The Fruitful Vine* and was posted on 1 July. Since then he has not sent her anything. She is already writing to Aden to let him have mail that will await him on his return journey. Why then does he not reciprocate in kind? In the meantime she proposes to hold fire with her reply for another week, and it will not be till Friday 18 August when she finally posts him a 1000-word-long discussion of *The Fruitful Vine*.

At 2 p.m. Carlton & Prior break up. Working hours during the summer are flexible and business is slack in the wake of the holiday. Edith and probably Lily, Norman and Avis adjourn to the Waldorf for tea. Before entering the Palm Court proper the other girls excuse themselves for a moment. Edith is briefly left in the vestibule by herself, when a gentleman comes up to her, raises his hat and says, 'Good afternoon, are you Romance?' She stares at him, thinks he must be mad (to make such a gross pass at her), turns away and sits on a couch. He follows her and apologetically says:

I'm sorry if you're not, but I have an appointment here with a lady with whom I've corresponded thro a 'Personal Column'; and she calls herself 'Romance' and she was to wear a black frock and a black lace hat.

Mrs Thompson is indeed wearing the black frock with the roses on it and the lace hat that Freddy likes. But she now ignores him and he backs off. Later, she notices that he shares a table with a girl in a black lace hat, 'so I supposed he was speaking the truth'. Freddy will think otherwise. Unlike her he will not think that it was 'rather funny' to be the object of a pick-up attempt.

It is on Thursday of this week, 10 August, that the murder of Sir Henry Wilson is avenged by the double hanging at Wandsworth of the two IRA men, Reginald Dunn and Joseph O'Sullivan. At 41 Kensington Gardens a truce obtains between husband and wife. On Saturday afternoon Avis Graydon visits for tea. They take it outside in the garden as it is a warm summer day. Somewhat cheekily Avis tell Percy that he has been sighted with a girl:

> My friend Bessie Hughes saw you in Lyons in Bishopsgate the other Friday evening.
>
> *Percy*: Oh did she, its quite possible.
>
> *Avis*: Yes & you were with quite a short fat girl in a brown costume with a white stripe.
>
> *Percy*: Oh yes, I took her in to have something to eat as it was late after working at the office and it was my last night in town for a fortnight.

Both sisters are delighted with this discovery and will go on 'chipping' Percy about the unprepossessing Miss Tucknott. He even assumes, Edith notes, that she might be jealous of his success with other women. In the immediate aftermath of the above exchange she pointedly teases Percy about her not being alone in deceit.

On Tuesday 15 August Edith is again writing to Freddy. This time she tells him that the Turkish Delight which he brought her when he was home on leave last time was stale. Could he remonstrate with the 'old chap' from whom he bought it? Freddy will give her a blistering reply to this ungracious treatment of his gift. She has also read a couple of books and this time she has left no markings in them so that he can for himself, and without being directed, extract from them what is of interest to both of them. She has just acquired W. J. Locke's popular

World War I novel, *The House of Balthazar*, and is starting it about now. She won't get very far at first and then events will overtake her. In the end she will finish it at Holloway. Still in the context of books, Edith notes ruefully that the two which Bywaters ordered for her in a bookshop in St Paul's Churchyard never arrived. The girl at the desk claims that they were not ordered in the first place.

As this dreary and cloudy summer week draws to a close, and since she has had no further mail from her lover, Edith sits down at her desk once again and writes an entire letter about Hichens's *The Fruitful Vine*. Bywaters discussed the novel in his Bombay letter, posted over a month ago. She has longed for more news of him and has waited. Now, in the absence of a further letter, she has decided to pen this piece of literary appreciation. As much as anything, this little essay provides a genuine insight into the workings of Edith Thompson's highly-wrought imagination and her inability to separate herself from the world of fiction. This letter, it must be remembered, was not used in evidence. Yet its relevance to the use of the *Bella Donna* evidence is immediately apparent.

The Fruitful Vine is set in contemporary Rome and adjacent locations. Its narrative focuses on the interlocking lives of three characters in particular: Sir Theodore Cannynge and his younger wife Dolores who, as a wealthy diplomat couple, are retired on 'capital' in Rome, and Cesare Carelli, a thirty-year-old Italian count who for twelve years entertained a tempestuous relationship with the Roman princess Lisetta Mancelli, now aged forty-three. Their relationship has run its course as far as Cesare is concerned. The novel's true protagonist is the 'pervasively feminine and fastidious' Dolores, known affectionately as the 'gazelle'. She is twenty-nine years old, looks like twenty-six, and is beautiful as well as generous in spirit. Above all though, she is profoundly unhappy, because of her seeming inability to bear a child to her husband, now fifty, to whom she has been married for ten years. Theo adores children and increasingly turns to the child-blessed family of his friend Denzil. When the latter dies of cancer, Theo becomes the children's foster-father and looks after the widow. Left alone, Dolores pines away in self-condemning sorrow. Eventually she reawakens to the world of the living and innocently slips into the world of Roman nightlife, where she inevitably meets Cesare, one of its luminaries. Various tribulations and further frustrations ensue. At one point Dolores exclaims in anguish: 'It isn't only that I want to have a child. I *need* to have a child.'

Otherwise she will forfeit Theo's love forever. When Theo leaves for England and a (false) rumour spreads that he might be Mrs Denzil's lover, Dolores consents to joining the 'intensely masculine' Cesare – who by now worships her – on his own in an inn near Rome. They spend all night together and Dolores conceives. But they have been followed to their hide-out by a dishonoured gambler who is also a relative of the princess and who posts her a letter about the adulterous encounter. He shoots himself under the lovers' window to expose them during the police enquiry. Although Cesare and Dolores successfully elude the publicity consequent on the suicide, Princess Mancelli receives the letter and blackmails Dolores into not seeing Cesare again. But Dolores has already decided that she cannot engage in an adulterous relationship of the sort desired by Cesare. When she realises that she is pregnant, she feels the need to be with Theo. She and Theo become lovers again on Sicily. He believes that the baby which is due will be his. Dolores dies in childbirth and her last words to her husband are 'Not for me'. Ultimately she committed the adultery for his sake, even though the instrument of it was the dashing and passionate Cesare. It is then that Theo learns of the adultery from the princess's letter which arrives shortly after the birth. When Cesare comes to claim his child, Theo fights him off, but surrenders the baby to a widowed friend who has lost both her children, Lady Sarah Ides. Only at the very end does Theo realise the depth of the love that was extended to him. It is too late. The baby is gone, the mother is dead:

> As she went out of the room he sank down again on the sofa, and leaned
> forward, with his elbows on his knees and his head in his hands.
>   'Better than I!' he repeated. 'Better than I.'

The Fruitful Vine was Edith Thompson's favourite work of fiction, because of the similarities which she detected between Dolores and herself. It is easy to dismiss it as a slushily sentimental narrative, of which there are hundreds during the period. Nevertheless its attentive portrayal of Dolores as a genteel and sexually aware woman generates an elaborate and legitimate eroticism in the novel. Furthermore, pregnancy and babies inevitably loomed larger in illicit encounters in the early years of the twentieth century than they do now. From her husband's pressing her to have children, to her lover's impregnating her twice, Edith Thompson encountered the consequences of sex at every juncture. Then again, the differences of age in the novel were thrown into relief for her in a way that they might not be to the casual or disinterested reader. Writing to Freddy in July, Edith remarked about an 'age' passage in *The Fruitful Vine*, as it might concern her and Bywaters. The particular passage in question occurs in Chapter 6:

> Such a liaison had been that existing between Princess Mancelli and Cesare Carelli. Yet the Princess was now forty-three and Carelli only just thirty, and when the affair had begun Carelli had been a boy of but eighteen.
>
> In those early days, twelve years before, the Princess had been severely blamed, and, for a short time, had been in danger of losing her social prestige. People said, and thought, it was a shame to break up the life of a boy and impair his freedom. Many mothers were indignant on behalf of their budding daughters; and Cesare's parents were furious, and made efforts to detach their son from a woman they chose to call 'old'. Of course the Prince was an abominable husband. Every one knew that. He was forever in Paris living an 'impossible' life. From the first he had treated his wife atrociously, and after remaining with her for a couple of years had practically deserted her. Nevertheless she had done very wrong in spoiling the boy's life, and in keeping one of the best *partis* in Rome from matrimony.
>
> Why did Rome forgive her? Because she had great force of will, was a *grande dame*, an accomplished *mondaine*, was connected with several of the very greatest families of Italy, and knew how to be determined with discretion. And she genuinely adored Carelli, and never looked at any one else. Rome loves romance.

Commenting in his reply on the princess, Freddy neatly equivocated by saying that he liked her, but that he also felt that Cesare had to leave her. Edith understood his meaning only too well, as her letter makes clear. From it, the extent of her dialogue with Freddy Bywaters and the particular patterns of its mingling of fact and fiction can be gleaned better than any paraphrase would suggest. The letter is quoted in its entirety:

> I was reading the book & I could understand her so well – I should do the same – exactly for the man I love – but you must love him darlint – real & deep & true – because your honour is such a sacred thing – your only covering, that you would only lose it to an 'anybody' for a man you really loved.
>
> You ask if it is sufficient reason that a good woman knows she is wanted, that she sins. Yes I think this right in a measure. A good woman who had no husband or lover – either had never had one or one that had died – would sin with a man whom she knew wanted her & she would willingly give herself – because she felt that she was wanted *so much wanted enough*

148

darlint, but a good woman who had a husband or a lover who really loved him & whom she really loved – would never sin with another man – because she felt that other man wanted her. Have I explained the difference darlingest boy, Ive tried to.

I didnt like Theo myself – but I think he was a good man & would have been a fine man if he had had a child. He was terribly selfish darlint I know, but then every man is selfish in life as well as in fiction, to be selfish is part of their nature. Cesare I loved, I think he was fine – he certainly loved Dolores very very much – but it still didnt make her love him. You say you dont understand Dolores because she wrote when she came back 'All that she told you is true, I sent her to tell you' (Nurse Jennings).

What about Lady Sarah Ides didnt you like her?

About Dolores darlint – I dont agree with you at all about her not loving her husband. You think she loved Cesare – because she gave all – darlingest boy she didnt give herself in the true sense of the word. She loved her husband so much that she would do anything in the wide world – anything in her power – to give him pleasure. She felt for him – as well as for herself – she knew what his pleasure would be if she gave him a child – she also knew more than he did – she knew it was not thro her she didnt have a child – it was thro him – he was the Fruitless Vine & she the Fruitful & because of this she degraded herself in every way for him.

Darlint, if she hadnt loved him, it would have been the easiest thing in the world for her to have said 'It is your fault Theo (that is what she called him isnt it), not mine & he would have probably loved her so much more & she would have been so much happier – instead of which she makes the supreme sacrifice – (darlint it is the supreme sacrifice to give yourself to someone you dont love) for her husband's sake, to make him happy – as well as herself – it was a *big* thing to do darlint, tremendous & it is always the same darlint & will always be the same – *nothing* is too much to do for the man you love – nothing is too much to give – no not even yourself.

I can feel with her & live with her darlint & I did – all the time I certainly think she wronged Cesare more than she did her husband & I think she realised she had & that is why she wrote that.

She wanted Cesare to see how much she had wronged him – how bad she really felt she had been towards him.

Had she loved him – she would never have said or written that – she would have gone anywhere with him – to the ends of the world – she wasnt a woman who was ruled by convention. He, Cesare was just a man who could help her to give her husband what he (& she) wanted most in this world & because Cesare loved her enough to want her & take her as she was – she used him – thats all there is about it darlint.

About the Mancelli darlint, you say you like her in one breath & in another you say you quite understand Cesare wanting to break away from her. These two sentences are absolutely opposite.

I think you said you liked the Mancelli – to please me – I think you thought 'If I say I *dont* like her & could understand Cesare's feelings in trying to get away from her' Peidi will be hurt – she will think of her position & mine in relation to the Mancellis & Cesare's with regard to age, so I will say I like her. Oh I hated her – she was a beast a vampire – Oh I cannot bear her – darlint I should have been much more pleased if you had said you hated her.

I like 'Carissima' better than yours darlint – it sounds so like the 'Great Lover', so much like Cesare as I imagine him.

Just as the callousness of Bella Donna alienated Edith, so it never occurred to her to identify with the 'vampire' Mancelli. She liked Dolores. Bywaters had written 'Forget her romance in connection with you'. But what if she died and left him a baby – he could then 'live in a memory and with a replica'. Increasingly the thought of babies was rising in her mind: the more Freddy withdrew, the more desperate the remedies of healing the rift became.

Summer has returned to London. On Tuesday 22 August Ben Travers's new farce *Dippers* opens at the Criterion Theatre. The fame of the dance numbers, and in particular Binnie Hale's Tango Queen, will contribute substantially to the fortunes of the play, as much as the comic skills of Cyril Maude. The Thompsons, the Laxtons and almost certainly the Aitkens will see *Dippers* on the night of Tuesday 3 October. On Wednesday Edith reads the headline in the *Daily Sketch* that 'Public Opinion saves woman from scaffold'. The Home Secretary reprieved Mrs Elsie Florence Yeldham who with her husband had jointly been sentenced to death for murdering one George Stanley Grimshaw in Epping Forest. The paper refers its readers to the tragic case of Mrs Rhoda Willis and notes that it has been fifteen years since a woman was last hanged in Britain. There is a reassuring quality to the article: the execution of female felons seems to have become a thing of the past.

A long-awaited letter from Fremantle reaches Edith on Thursday 24 August. It is slight, and she grumbles at his formulaic phrases. Particularly reprehensible is his squeezing a letter to her into the last few moments before casting anchor at various ports on the voyage: 'We are getting into so & so tonight', he writes, which to her spells apathy:

Don't you ever feel that you'd like to write a few lines to me & then leave it & write again when you feel like it. Thats how I do darlint, & then when it comes to the last day for posting, I haven't got to sit down & write as a duty.

Among other favourite novels listed at her suggestion, Freddy mentions three novels which he has recently read: Hichens's vaguely supernatural *Mrs Marsden* – a novel about a widowed mother whose son is killed during World War I, and who tries to transcend the confines of matter to communicate with him through spiritualist séances – and Jeffrey Farnol's *Martin Conisby's Revenge* and *The Chronicles of an Imp*. His failure to mention Chambers's *The Common Law* disquiets her, since she admires the book not least for its relevance to their relationship. As for her, she has just re-read W. J. Locke's 'very amusing' novel *Septimus* and is now embarked on Eden Philpotts's *The Secret Woman*, a Hardyesque romance in the style of Stella Gibbons:

> it takes a lot of reading – its very dry & you know the 'Secret Woman'
> practically at the commencement – if you've got any sense.

As if the multiple complications of Edith's love life were not enough, the Thompsons and the Lesters are heading for a showdown over tenancy. The Lesters agreed to move by the end of August, after the Thompsons' original and unsuccessful attempt to evict them over two years ago when they purchased 41 Kensington Gardens. As the deadline approaches without any sign of the Lesters vacating the premises, Percy warns them about their obligation: if by December they should still be in residence, he will take the matter to court. The Thompsons' solicitor has instructed his clients in this matter and assures them that in law the Lesters have absolutely no case: two and a half years is ample time to find another home, although, as Edith realises, not a place as large and comfortable as half The Retreat for a mere 30 shillings a month. In retaliation Mrs Lester withdraws all the voluntary help that she usually gives to Mrs Thompson. During the day, she refuses to take in the deliveries of bread and milk, and tells the window cleaner only to do her side of the house. Most inconvenient of all is her point-blank refusal to take in the laundry or even open the door to Bill when he delivers a parcel for his sister; this means that Edith cannot order her groceries to be sent up to the house. Instead, this Friday evening and for the next two or three weeks she has to rush home after work to do all her shopping and to carry her potatoes herself, or at least to be there when they arrive. How, Edith wonders, can Mrs Lester be so petty after all that she did for Norah and her when they needed help after the father's death? As a result of this added aggravation she and Percy momentarily draw closer to each other. In such domestic affairs as these the two Thompsons invariably pool their resources.

Sunday 27 August: Equipped with a piece of notepaper, Edith is sitting in the bathroom. It is another 27th and therefore a 'birthday'. She always sends him greetings *on* the day, even if she is home, as she is on the Sunday, with Percy. The only place in the house where even her husband dare not follow her provides her with a haven for the few lines needed to voice her longing:

> Fourteen whole months have gone by now, darlint, its so terribly long. Neither you nor I thought we should have to wait all that long time did we? although I said I would wait 5 years – and I will darlint – its only 3 years and ten months now.

The *Morea* is now steadily plying the ocean, bound for England. At every port of call a letter awaits her writer and laundry steward Bywaters. On Tuesday 29 August Edith writes her second Port Said letter, to follow the birthday greetings note. She tells Freddy among others that 'blouses are fashionable again, no more jumpers'. But she is saving her little green one, which he loves, for him to keep.

The end of this week is visited by heavy thunderstorms, and more trouble on Friday 1 September with the Lesters reinforces Edith's conviction that she cannot cope without Ethel Vernon. Even Percy is now relenting about Ethel's staying with them, and before long Ethel will have accepted the offer to join Edith Thompson.

Sunday 3 September: Already the softer rays of the early morning sunlight announce the approach of autumn as unmistakably as the still mists over the waters in Valentine's Park and on the flats of Wanstead. The Thompsons are giving a Sunday dinner party which includes the family from the Crescent and Bessie and Reg, as well as others who are due for afternoon tea. Everyone is in great form. The wife, always an excellent hostess, laughs with her guests. When the husband is momentarily put out by a good-humoured joke at his expense, she steps in with: 'Oh, don't mind him.' Bessie produces her camera and, out in the garden, she takes two remarkable pictures of her hostess on her own and of the two Thompsons together. The first one of these shows a coy and tomboyish Edith in a light silk dress with scalloped edges. Her hair is bobbed now and around her neck she wears a loosely-fitted single strand of pearls. Photographer and subject seem to enjoy a conspiratorial relationship; the uninhibited pose and the welcoming expression in Edith Thompson's face bear witness to her trust in Bessie.

The contrast with the next photo is striking. It has Percy standing behind his wife, who is sitting on the edge of the sofa. Whereas he faces the camera with a look of assertive if not proprietorial defiance, Edith's smile resembles a forced grimace. Her eyes are only vaguely focused, as though she wishes to escape into herself away from the ineluctable imprinted communion of Percy and herself on celluloid. It is as if she were pleading with Bessie and her camera not to give her away. Both Bessie and Lily have spoken to Edith about Freddy Bywaters, and Bessie in particular has intimated a qualified disapproval. Her advice to Edith, that she should avoid Bywaters, or at least not seek him out, has been cold-shouldered: 'It is not *I* who seek out his company, I can take care of myself perfectly well.' Since this incident of failed communication, Bessie has kept her peace. On this warm Sunday nothing is allowed to spoil the fun of the occasion.

On Wednesday 6 September Mrs Bywaters is up in town as is her wont. While shopping for material in the West End she posts a note addressed to 'Miss P. Graydon, c/o Messrs Carlton & Prior, 168 Aldersgate Street, EC1'. It will reach its destination the following morning. Percy is out on this night, and Avis is visiting at No. 41. She tells Edith that her parents are eagerly anticipating the *Morea*'s return home to hear from Freddy about the state of Harold's affair with Doris Grafton and his questionable progress at the Café Elito in Melbourne:

> *Edith*: But I understood he was not coming to England.
>
> *Avis*: Oh that was a lot of rot he was talking. I expect he has thought better of it since we all think we'd like to die at certain times but we all get over it and I suppose he has done the same by now.

Furthermore Avis has heard that the *Morea*'s next voyage is scheduled to take her to China and Japan. This sends a tremor down Edith's spine, as she imagines the trip to the far reaches of the east as taking longer than that to Australia. For once her acute sense of global geography has deserted her. Avis's visit leaves her sister thoughtful and brooding. Can it be possible, she wonders, that her lover is paying court again to her sister, after dropping her fourteen months ago? Is he weary of her demands on him, or is he no longer convinced of her determination to separate from Percy?

On Thursday morning, Edith receives a note posted from the West End. The 'P' for 'E' alarms her, as she immediately apprehends from it that it must have originated with Bywaters. Its message is painfully clear:

September 6th

If you wish to remain the friend of F. Bywaters, be careful. Do not attempt to see him or communicate with him, when he is in England.
Believe this to be a genuine warning from

A Wellwisher

The postmark says 'W1, Sep. 6, 3.15 p.m.' At once Mrs Thompson guesses what has happened: Freddy has invited a mate to take a dictated letter and sign it 'A Wellwisher'. He has dated it 6 September as a pathetic decoy to make it appear that the note had been written in London rather than being sent, as it must have been, from Australia to his mother for her to post on her way up west. Edith feels humiliated by the fact that the much loathed Mrs Bywaters is delegated to send the document of dismissal to her; she is hurt and disillusioned not only by Freddy's cowardice in working through such a transparent subterfuge, but by the elaborateness of what is in any case an uncharacteristic attempt at deceit. But she bridles her anger and hurt and with deliberation she retaliates:

I had rather a shock this morning – I am enclosing you the cause of it – just as I received it. Do you know anything about it? I dont suppose you do darlint, but Im just asking. Im sure if you had reasons for not wanting to see me – you'd tell me and tell me the reasons – you couldnt resort to letters of this description. I dont think it can be from anyone I know – or from any relation of mine, because I am addressed as 'P' you will notice – & no one knows you call me anything but 'Edie'. Also darlint I cant help noticing that it is posted in the *West End on a Wednesday*. Write and tell me what you think about it & if you have no use for the letter – destroy it – because I dont want it.

As long as he cannot bear to confront her with the threat of separation she will be able to handle him.

On Friday Edith completes the letter which returns his note. She tells him of the Lesters' unpleasantness and apologises for boring him with such trifles: 'I just tried to make you live in my life.' At the same time, she informs him of the fact that his watch is ready, and enquires whether or not she ought to send it on to Plymouth along with the books. Could he let her know? The question of the watch is more than a little loaded, and Bywaters will rise to the bait while accusing her of baiting him. He is touched by her solicitous attitude about the watch and her wearing it:

> I have had it put right and often wear it myself at 168 – the strap is so big it comes nearly up to my elbow – also I have had a gold buckle put on it – did you notice it was only R.G. [rolled gold]? I didn't when I bought it – or should have had it altered at the time – however it is done now.

Edith intends to post the letter on Saturday and therefore leaves it at Carlton & Prior. But during the night she is woken by the all too familiar pulling sensation which spreads through her body. Much as her periods usually afflict her, this time is particularly excruciating, and she fails to make it into the office on Monday.

In the lunch hour on Tuesday, Edith is 'speaking' to Freddy again, contrasting this homecoming with the last one. She is now 'just existing with an intense strung up feeling of seeing you and feeling you holding me in your two arms so tightly that it hurts'. She will abide by whatever he decides for them; and already she has regressed, so she intimates, to becoming the 'dutiful wife', whose spirit is 'at last bent to the will of her husband'. What else does he expect? The last note she has from him dates from 28 July, and there are so many unanswered questions in her letters to him. This emotional elixir will work its magic, because Bywaters will react jealously to the prospect of Percy supplanting him in Edith Thompson's realigned wifely duties. The only other item of news – and one which, harmless though it is, will give credence to a preposterous allegation levelled against Edith in due course – is that shortly after Bournemouth she bought herself an expensive fur coat: it cost 27 guineas and, as she had only £13 in saving, she borrowed £15 from the account and is repaying the debt at £1 a week. Also she has treated herself to new lace shoes. She can imagine Freddy making a face at the thought of lace shoes, but hopes that he will sympathise with her. Repeatedly she indicates in her correspondence how much importance they both attach to each other's appearance, and clothes in particular. Freddy expresses vehement likes and dislikes about what she wears, from her garters and camisole to her shoes, hats and small green sweater, not to mention the pearls and beads which he brought her. His energy, drive and vanity contrast with the husband's lethargy.

This last full week before Bywaters's return to Gravesend marks a cold and wet early autumn spell. It is getting dark shortly after 7 p.m., and the sun does not rise till 6.30 a.m. On Saturday 16 September Thompson gives his wife a 'very solemn warning' that Bywaters is due back the following weekend and will call in at No. 231:

> *Edith*: I understood that Freddy Bywaters was not coming back to England any more.
>
> *Percy*: Oh that was all bluff – just an excuse to make it easier to take you out that night.

This time he will not be fooled, and certainly not by rumours circulated by Bywaters to various shared acquaintances and friends that he will not be back in England because of an emotional trauma. Neither the Graydons nor the Thompsons believe this to be the case, and Avis speaks for them all when she dismisses the suggestion as 'a lot of rot'. Yet one particular incident might point in another direction and reveal a residual layer of ingenuousness.

In Sydney the *Morea* rode at anchor for just over a fortnight, from 24 July to 8 August. Even so Freddy missed the ship's departure. This news reached No. 231 through one of Edith's two sailor brothers. Whatever Bywater's excuse was, it was accepted as valid, and his rating remained uniformly V.G. He may have rejoined the vessel in Melbourne, travelling there by train, or he may have been allowed the break by the company for working on board ship during most of his last stay in London. Avis's explanation, 'Oh I suppose he was drunk', is clearly wrong, as this would have resulted in instant suspension. Edith professes to be 'very anxious to know' what has happened. She rightly suspects that the Australian girl – who lives in Sydney – enters the picture, and that she may well have contributed to the cooling of Freddy's ardour. For the time being though, she will hold back; if he is drifting away from her, then the worst strategy to pursue would be to alienate him further by a jealous scene.

The following day, Sunday, Edith Thompson amuses herself 'making jam-chutney & mincemeat with the apples from the garden'. Lily and Norman visit in the afternoon, and Bessie and Reg may also join them for tea. They compliment her on her achievement, and Norman teasingly expresses a desire to borrow her as his cook. Later in the day she finishes *The Firing Line* by R. W. Chambers. She likes its villain, Louis Malcourt, and the book as a whole strikes her as very exciting. Why, she wonders, did Freddy not like it?

No mail reaches Edith on Monday or on Tuesday. Then, on Wednesday 20 September, which is statement day at Carlton & Prior, she receives a long letter from Bywaters. It is here reconstructed point by point, along with her responses to it: He will be in London on Saturday and will proceed straight to Westow Street rather than staying with the Graydons, or lodging on board ship. He has good reason for doing so. How does she feel about that? Is she 'glad or sorry'? He appreciates that she felt responsible for the break between his family and him. Is she pleased about his return to the fold? He admits that he deserved her first letter to Sydney, but fails to mention her second letter sent two days later to make up again. He expresses annoyance at her unguarded comments on the Turkish Delight being stale and has brought her neither Delight nor cigarettes this time. He has been perusing Chambers's *The Firing Line* at about the same time as her, and he asks whether she has read Dumas's classic revenge yarn *The Count of Monte Cristo* – which to him, one imagines, takes on extra dimensions given his familiarity with Marseilles and the gloomy Château d'If perched like Alcatraz on its prison rock in the sound. He asks 'can we be Pals only, Peidi, it will make it easier?' to which she replies with a resounding 'No', because it would be 'impossible physically and mentally' – and she reminds him of an earlier occasion when she offered to remove herself from his life and he pleaded with her not to do so.

In a more conciliatory tone, he enquires about her sleeplessness, of which she has sorely complained. He suggests that she consult a doctor to which she replies that the only doctor who can help her is he: 'I want you for my doctor – my pal – my lover – my everything – just all and the whole world would be changed.' He alludes to missing the ship in Sydney, but remains vague about it. Of Sydney, and possibly to convey a spurious sense of innocence, he remarks: 'I went home to my cousin's every night – quite domesticated.' She is not fooled and replies that it sounds like a sneer and that she does not like it.

In a more stoic vein, Freddy notes that 'Time passes and with it some of the pain – Fate ordained our lot to be hard.' Her immediate response is that *her* pain gets 'less and less bearable' – it hurts 'more and more, every hour really'. In the same breath he warns her that 'other ways only involve the parting of you and I, Peidi, nobody deserves anything more than I do'. The other ways envisaged here are those which involve the two of them in being more than just pals. Above all, he feels, he is 'unnatural' for fearing intimate contacts or relationships with women. This, he tells her, is his shipmates' verdict on him. Edith immediately rallies round and commends him for being 'not an ordinary sensual sort of creature made in the usual mould of men'. He then asks her 'Peidi do you think you could live with a replica – you once said "No"'. She fails to understand the question, forgetting that in a letter of 23 August she assured him that he could 'live in a memory and with a replica', that is a baby and the remembrance of its mother – the word 'replica' for baby is used in *The Fruitful Vine*.

Still replying to one of her letters, Freddy accuses her of snobbery for wishing to patronise the Regent Palace Hotel. He even underlines his remonstration with her. She is stung to the quick. He also maintains that the man who 'mistook' her for Romance must have been a rascal. She agrees, but supposes that she was just the wrong assignation. Finally Freddy tells her how jealous he is of Percy Thompson. Her reply – in a very long letter of Thursday 21 September – will morally damage her case badly in the eyes of judge and jury:

> Yes, darlint you are jealous of *him* – but I want you to be – he has the right by law to all that you have the right to by nature and love – yes darlint be jealous, so much that you will do something desperate.

Retrospectively, and with only the bare facts available, it is not difficult to see how the prosecution could twist such a sentence to make it fit into the wider fabric of a carefully orchestrated plot, devised by the woman to incite the man to murder her husband. In the infinitely more complex and haphazard flow of life, however, Edith's almost joyous invitation to Freddy to be jealous and to act on it is a spontaneous gesture: its lack of deliberateness is attested to by the fact that it refers primarily to a point made by him in his letters. Its note of triumph reveals her pleasure at the thought of having again successfully redirected Bywaters's feelings. Before Wednesday she has had to live with the idea that he will leave her. Now he appears to wish to repossess her. She is ready and only too conscious of how well she has played her hand by being patient and plotting to keep him.

She can do little more than acknowledge his long letter on Wednesday and scribbles a quick reply posted shortly before 5p.m. The real answer follows on Thursday, when she is replying in detail to his letter. For Friday's meeting she planned to

> get off early – rush to Ilford and do the shopping and rush up to meet you –

having had my hair washed in the luncheon hour instead of at night – as I should have said and now all that is no use – so I shant have my hair washed – it must wait until the next Friday – that will mean an extra hour with you – do you mind me having a dirty head for a week darlint – its very very dirty. I've been hanging it out especially for now.

How she hates Australia 'and everything connected with it': it is 109 days since she last saw her lover! As regards the vexed question of the Turkish Delight, well she now feels sorry that she ever fussed about it; shouldn't he soften his line a bit in the knowledge that 'to err is human, to forgive divine'? Also, could he again send his mail to Carlton & Prior as before, because the GPO is just too hard to use? Finally, after dutifully replying to his letter, she confesses to the misdemeanour of holding back his watch in the hope that missing it would make him visit her if all else failed:

> Yes I can make him – I wont send his watch – I'll tell him if he wants it – he's to come to 168 and fetch it.
>   Darlint, was it small? if it was, real big love must make people think of small things, because real, big love made
>   PEIDI

This long letter is not sent, but will be passed to Bywaters by hand on Monday. On Friday morning at 9.28 a.m. she sends him a telegram from the City: 'Can you meet Peidi Broadway 4 pm'. The meeting is intended for Saturday, as the ship is not due in Tilbury till then. To fill in the time Edith buys Avis's birthday present on this day.

It is just past noon when the *Morea* is steering her way through the Thames estuary. The weather is mild and an autumnal light laces the shores of Essex and Kent. The laundry steward doubles on such occasions as a jack of all trades. If everyone chips in, the entire crew will be home more quickly. The ship docks at 2.40 p.m. In the meantime Edith has returned to Ilford after the Saturday shift at Carlton & Prior. At 1 p.m. she prepares dinner for Percy and her father, who is coming up from East Ham. At 3 p.m., and after washing up, she leaves the house for Broadway near the Barking British Rail station, while the two men work in the garden. But Freddy fails to turn up, as the *Morea* is in late. After waiting for a while Edith makes for the Crescent and returns home by 6 p.m. Thompson at once argues with her for being so long, but she manages to shrug it off. Tonight Freddy will sleep in London again, and she won't be able to see him till Monday.

On Sunday Avis Graydon is twenty-six years old. Freddy Bywaters sends her birthday greetings. This year he does not forget. The virginal Avis is after all, Bywaters has discovered, great fun to be with. As much as her sister, Avis awaits the arrival of the sailor boy, and while they all toast her and sing 'Happy Birthday, dear Avis', she misses the voice and the face which ever since 1920 have spelt the future for her.

Monday 25 September 1922: At 10.03 in the morning Edith sends a telegram to Freddy on the *Morea* in Tilbury, where it is received at 10.16 a.m.: 'Must catch 5.49 Fenchurch Reply if can manage'.

It is 4.30 p.m. when Edith at last sees Bywaters standing outside Carlton & Prior. Turning to Lily Vallender she says: 'Fred is outside, would you like to have a cup of coffee with him.' Today of all days she would be kept busy! Lily, who by now knows all about Edith's affair, joins Freddy and takes him across to Fuller's for tea till Edith is free. She is still making polite conversation with Fred about his antipodean voyage, when Edith charges in with her hat and coat on. Their mutual and affectionate embrace is inhibited solely by the restricted space of Fuller's and the tangible presence in the virtually empty premises of gossipy waitresses. Lily Vallender slips out almost unobserved.

By 5.30 the lovers are walking down Aldersgate towards the Royal Exchange and on from there to Fenchurch Street. So far they have stuck to Freddy's stipulation to be 'pals only'. It is nearly 5.45 and they are about to board the 5.49 to Ilford. Still on the platform, Edith hesitates and then suggests they use an occupied carriage. Her reason for doing this, as she will explain to him presently, is to pre-empt any temptation for the two of them to break away from 'pals only'. But as the commuter train pulls out of Fenchurch Street the lovers share a private compartment. After a split-second hesitation by the woman, they kiss passionately. He has again found her personality mesmeric.

Before they part in Ilford at 6.45 p.m., Edith slips Freddy the mammoth letter of Thursday. Exalted, she walks home in the dusk through the Belgrave Road. It's nearly dark as she lets herself into 41 Kensington Gardens. Tonight she may even spare a friendly word for Mrs Lester. After all she has triumphed. In the meantime Bywaters is briskly crossing over from Ilford to Manor Park. He carries Edith's letter and a message from her brother Harold for the family. They are delighted to see him, and no one more so than Avis. They talk of Australia, the sea, and of Harold and Billie.

It is 10.30 p.m. by the time he is on the move again towards East Ham Station, and eventually Victoria and Gipsy Hill. It is still before midnight when, settled in his tiny backroom at 11 Westow Street, he starts a letter to Edith. He has now read hers to him. How quickly everything has changed from the way he planned it. Her letter reminds him of her resilience in the face of a threatened separation, her forbearance and her generosity. He realises how much she needs his love; and perhaps he in turn awakens to the reality of a permanent physical separation from this fascinating woman. He therefore writes her the following letter:

Darling Peidi Mia,
    Tonight was impulse – natural – I couldnt resist – I had to hold you darling little sweetheart of mine – darlint I was afraid – I thought you were going to refuse to kiss me – darlint little girl – I love you so much and the only way I can control myself is by not seeing you and I'm not going to do that. Darlint Peidi Mia – I must have you – I love you darlint – logic and what others call reason do not enter into our lives, and where two halves are concerned. I had no intention darlint of doing that – it just happened thats all – I'm glad now chère – darlint when you suggested the occupied carriage, I didn't want to go in it – did you think that perhaps I did – so that there would have been no opportunity for me, to break the conditions that I had stipulated – darlint I felt quite confident that I would be able to keep my feelings down – I was wrong Peidi. I was reckoning on will power over ordinary forces – but I was fighting what? not ordinary forces – nothing was fighting the whole of me. Peidi you are my magnet – I cannot resist darlint – you draw me to you now and always, I shall never be able to see you and remain impassive. Darlint Peidi Mia Idol mine – I love you – always – always Ma Chère. Last night when I read your questions I didn't know how to answer them – I have now Peidi?
    Darlint I dont think I can talk about other things tonight – I want to hold you so tightly. I'm going to tonight in my sleep. Bon Nuit Ma Petite, cherchez bien pour votre
FREDDY.

On Tuesday evening Freddy again meets Edith, at Fenchurch Street at 5.45 p.m. He has just learned that he has been promoted from laundry steward to storekeeper. The railway carriage to Ilford once again becomes their trysting place. Redeclared lovers now, their passion is fuelled by guilt and the fearful experience of nearly losing each other. When he parts from Edith in Ilford, Bywaters slips her the letter he wrote at midnight. Her reply, another letter by him of Sunday 1 October and one by her of Monday 2 October, are reproduced in full for their importance as the only immediate 'evidence' extant from the last week before the tragedy. Her first letter of Wednesday 27 September is damaged by hot wax from the seal she used – as she scribbled on the back of the envelope:

(On back) – I burnt this sealing it. – PEIDI
[Stamps – Three 1½d.]

well let us accept it then – and bear the hard part as willingly as we enjoy the natural part. Darlint, I didnt think you wanted to go into the other carriage – but I suggested it because I felt there would be less temptation there – not only for you but for me too – do you think it is less pleasure to me, for you to kiss me & hold me, than it is for you to do so? I think its more pleasure to me than it can possibly be to you – at least it always feels so & darlingest, if you had refrained from doing these things (not perhaps last night – but at some time before you went) I am not above compelling you to – darlint I could, couldn't I, just the same as if the position was reversed – you could compel me to – because we have no will power. I felt thats how it would be darlingest lover of mine – I was strong enough in spirit, until I was tempted in the flesh & the result – a mutual tumble from the pedestal of 'Pals only' that we had erected as penance for ourselves. No darlint, it could never be now – I am sure that you see that now dont you? intentions – such as we had – were forced – unnatural – & darlingest we are essentially natural with each other – we always have been, since our first understanding. Why should we choose to be as every other person – when we're not – is every other person such a model that you & I should copy them? Lets be ourselves – always darlingest there can never be any misunderstandings then – it doesnt matter if its harder – you said it was our Fate against each other – we only have will power when we are in accord, not when we are in conflict – tell me if this is how you feel. As I said last night, with you darlint there can never by any pride to stand in the way – it melts in the flame of a great love – I finished with pride Oh a long time ago – do you remember? when I had to come to you in your little room – after washing up. I wonder if you understand how I feel about these things – I do try to explain but some words seem so useless. Please please lover of mine, dont use that word I dont like it – I feel that Im on a pedestal & that I shall always have to strive to remain there & I dont ever want to strive to do anything anything with or for you – thats not being natural & when you use that word – thats just how I feel – not natural – not myself. Would you have me feel like this just so that you could use a term that pleases you & you only? Tell me.

Do you remember me being asked if I had found 'The Great Lover'?

Darlingest lover of mine – I had & I'd found 'The Great Pal' too *the best pal a girl ever had*. One is as much to me as the other, there is no first and second they are equal.

I *am* glad you held me tightly when you went to sleep darlint, I wanted comforting badly – I cried such a lot – no I wasn't unhappy – I look a sight today.

Darlingest – what would have happened had I refused – when you asked me to kiss you? I want to know.

> M. H. R. 27621 from
> PEIDI.

It is worth noting how strongly she reacts to the phrase 'Idol'. The intensity of her passion now demands a physical consummation. It is what they both desire. The place for it is the train. Wednesday is the 27th – and therefore a 'birthday' ('M.H.R.')[1] for both of them – and it signals their first sexual encounter since the early summer. She is just over sixteen days into her menstrual cycle. If they don't make love on 27 September, they will on Thursday night, when they again travel home to Ilford on the 5.49 from Fenchurch Street.

The next five days are crucial. The movements during this period of the couple are documented here as intimately as is possible.

Friday 29 September: At around noon Freddy meets Edith outside Carlton & Prior and whisks her off for lunch. They agree to meet again at Fuller's at tea-time. He arrives there between 3 and 4 p.m. But she cannot get away quite yet. At 3.45 he appears in the porch of Carlton & Prior where Mr Carlton, who is downstairs in the basement, sees him as he looks up. Edith is still busy and motions to him to return to Fuller's. At about 4.15 she hurriedly writes him a note in her office, having previously summoned Rose Jacobs into her presence. The note which she scribbles on a Carlton & Prior order form and misdates (30 September, instead of 29) reads: 'Come *in* for me in ½ an hour – PEIDI.' Passing it to Rose she says: 'Will you take this note over to Fullers. Mr Bywaters will be sitting just inside the door?' Miss Jacobs crosses the road and dutifully hands over the note, an action witnessed by the observant Fuller's waitress Edith Annie Brown. Then, at Edith's prompting, Lily Vallender joins Bywaters at about 4.30 p.m. She tells him that Mrs Thompson will be ready any minute and returns to Carlton & Prior. When she gets back, Edith is 'dressed ready to leave'

[1] 'Many Happy Returns'.

and calls down to Carlton to ask permission to go, which is granted. She rejoins Freddy at once and, after a coffee probably, they
both leave. What happens between five o'clock and their parting in
Ilford is not recorded. Edith is to visit No. 231 tonight, so she will
not be catching the 5.49. As Percy rarely gets to the Crescent before
9 p.m., the lovers have nearly four hours to spend in each other's
company. She has taken Saturday off and tells him so. By the time
she returns to her home in Ilford accompanied by Percy, it is nearly
midnight.

Saturday 30 September: When the Thompsons leave 41 Kensington
Gardens at about 8.15 a.m., Bywaters is already on his way from
Gipsy Hill. After parting from Percy at Liverpool Street, Edith is joined
in the station by her lover. Together they board the nearest Ilford train.
In Ilford they make straight for Wanstead Park which to both of them
is a familiar venue from schooldays and, latterly, from several
assignations here. This one will be different though. By the time they
get there the mists have dispersed and the morning dew is drying in the
pale light of the sun. Crossing over the bridge into the thickets,
perhaps to the north of Perch Pond, the lovers assure themselves of
total privacy. Then Edith, for the first time in her life perhaps, lets go
completely, as Freddy starts to loosen her clothes. She may even take
the initiative, as she archly calls herself his 'little devil' during their
encounter. Whether this refers to her new-found sexual inventiveness
or simply her boldness in teasing him is immaterial. At first he is too
rough, and she attempts to hold him off and encourages him to be
gentle. She has never reached a climax in his arms before. But today
neither will be disappointed. The intensity of her orgasm, when it
happens, surprises them both, and he asks her to explain the sensation
to him.

It is during their love-making that she again raises the matter of the
word 'Idol' and warns him that it might bar her from a natural sexual
encounter with him. In this oblivious embrace the lovers feel that the
park is truly theirs now: 'our Park on Saturday'. It has protected them
from the outside world by its thick growth which is already turning to
a yellow brown. At about 10.15 Edith rises, dresses and alone heads
for the small row of shops on the Belgrave Road, opposite Sackville
Gardens. After getting some groceries from the fruit and vegetable
shop, she walks up to 41 Kensington Gardens, where Mrs Lester meets
her in the house. The two women probably merely exchange nods.
Edith potters about in the kitchen and upstairs in the bedroom. By ten

to eleven she is gone and rejoins Bywaters. For two more hours the lovers enjoy each other, and Edith tells Fred for the first time that this coming Tuesday night, his last night of shore leave, she has agreed to go to the theatre. She cannot possibly get out of it. But Monday's visit to the dreary Thompsons in Seymour Gardens is a different matter, and she promises to do her utmost to make excuses. Parting this time is particularly difficult. They both suspect that they will not be this close again for a long while unless she elopes with him. If she can get Monday night off, perhaps they can prevail on Bessie or Lily to let them have the privacy of a home for their last tryst. If Edith feels exposed, she is also proud, as is he, of her total sexual surrender. Somehow now their relationship has achieved a new level of intimacy and intensity.

Shortly after 1 p.m. Edith is back at No. 41 while her lover is travelling into the City and eventually home where he arrives at four. She starts to prepare dinner for Percy and herself. How wife and husband fare is hard to imagine. Most likely they chat over trivia and the forthcoming dinner at the Birnages. At five the Graydons and Avis meet up outside 74 Argyle Road in Ilford to visit their friends. The Birnages have extended their friendship not only to Mr and Mrs Thompson, but to her entire family. Sidney's soft spot for Edith may have helped in this respect. Throughout the evening Edith Thompson remains self-absorbed, remembering the morning with her lover and longing to be with him.

On Sunday 1 October, at about 7 p.m., the Thompsons leave the house to join friends for the evening. They return at about 10.30. Who the friends are cannot be determined. Perhaps they are Reg and Bessie (neither of whom will give evidence in court, so that their movements remain more of a mystery than those of other characters in this story). While Edith is out with her husband and friends, her lover over in Norwood sits down to write to her. His letter is given here in full. It replies to her two letters of Thursday 21 September from which he quotes the phrases 'the hope of all or the finish of all', and her letter of Wednesday 27 September, in which she begs him not to view her as an 'Idol'. Both her letters were given by hand. Freddy's letter also covers the events from Tuesday 26 September onwards and particularly the Saturday. His clumsy enquiry after Avis at a time like this need not come as a surprise, though it does not necessarily detract from the momentary sincerity of his love for Edith. This letter will be produced in evidence, like Edith's reply:

Peidi Darlint.

Sunday evening, Everybody is out and now I can talk to you. I wonder what you are doing now my own little girl. I hope that Bill has not been the cause of any further unpleasantness darlint. Darlint little girl do you remember saying 'the hope for all'. 'Or the finish of all'. Peidi the finish of all seems terrible even to contemplate. What darlint would it be in practice? Peidi Mia I love you more and more every day – it grows darlint and will keep on growing. Darlint in the park – our Park on Saturday, you were my 'little devil' – I was happy then Peidi – were you? I wasn't thinking of other things – only you darlint – you was my entire world – I love you so much my Peidi – I mustnt ever think of losing you, darlint if I was a poet I could write volumes – but I not – I suppose at the most Ive only spoken about 2 dozen words today I dont try not to speak – but I have no wish to – Im not spoken to much so have no replies to make.

Darlint about the watch – I never really answered your question – I only said I wasnt cross. I cant understand you thinking that the watch would draw me to you – where you yourself wouldnt – is that what you meant darlint or have I misunderstood you. The way you have written looks to me as though you think that I think more of the watch than I do of you darlint – Tell me Peidi Mia that I misunderstood your meaning.

Darlint Peidi Mia – I do remember you coming to me in the little room and I think I understand what it cost you – a lot more then darlint than It could ever now. When I think about that I think how nearly we came to be parted for ever, – if you had not forfeited your pride darlint I dont think there would ever have been yesterday or tomorrow.

My darlint darlint little girl I love you more than I will ever be able to show you. Darlint you are the centre – the world goes on round you, but you ever remain my world – the other part some things are essential – others are on the outskirts and sometimes so far removed from my mind that they seem non existent. Darling Peidi Mia – I answered the question about the word 'Idle' on Saturday – I never mentioned it.

Yes darlint – I remember you being asked if you had found 'The great lover'. It was when you sang 'A Tumble Down Nook'.

What have I found darlint? The darlingest little sweetheart girl in the whole world and 'The Only Pal'. Now darlint pal – Im anxious about Avis – I hope you have found out all there is to know of the other night – I want you to tell me. Supposing she did stay with some fellow and she tells you and asks you not to tell anybody – are you going to tell me Peidi?

Darlint I'm enclosing a slip for you for the books in case I am unable to get them myself – also will you get the 'Tempting of Paul Chester' Alice and Claude Askew. There is 13/– to pay on the others – but darlint I hope to be able to get them myself, also and principally I want to drink Beaune with you.

Good night now darlingest – dearest little sweetheart and big pal.
FREDDY.

Monday 2 October: At 8.15 a.m. Edith and Percy depart for work together. Mrs Lester watches them go. She is now monitoring the couple's movements, since it is this week that Ethel Vernon is scheduled to arrive. Mrs Lester can hardly bear the thought of it, as her sole hold over the Thompsons will then be eroded. She will have to move soon. Edith Thompson arrives at Carlton & Prior by about 9a.m. and immediately rings 11 Westow Street. Mrs Bywaters, who is already downstairs in the shop, answers the phone. An unidentified woman's voice asks for Freddy, who is summoned down from his bedroom to answer it. Fred does not address the voice by name. At about 11 he is getting ready to go to London. He will be meeting Edith outside Aldersgate at 12.30 to take her to lunch. It is cool and cloudy, so he is wearing his blue overcoat and a trilby hat. Before calling on her he will visit the P & O offices briefly, as he often does, to see some of his mates.

In the meantime Carlton & Prior are having a busy morning and the office and sales room needs to be continually manned. Miss Prior takes an early lunch break to interleave with Carlton's and Edith's. Notwithstanding the pressures of the morning, Edith has already written Bywaters half of a longish letter about the Friday and Saturday. As fate would have it, Percy Thompson appears at 168 just as she is about to join Bywaters. She rapidly excuses herself and sends him either away or upstairs to see Lily. She calls for Higgins, their porter. When he gets to her office at the end of the salesroom, she is on her own and is wrapping up a Carlton & Prior order form. The message inside is 'Wait till one he is come. PEIDI'. After placing it into a white envelope, she hands it to him saying, 'Take this and take it to Aldersgate Street station and give it to the gentleman who is wearing a blue overcoat and trilby hat.' Higgins duly delivers the message and recognises Bywaters as the same young man whom he saw in Edith's company outside Carlton & Prior one evening in March. At nearly one o'clock Edith has successfully shaken off Thompson, but now Carlton is off for his lunch and Miss Prior has not yet returned. Again Higgins is dispatched with a message:

Mr Carlton has gone out to lunch now & I must wait until he comes back – Miss P. is not back yet – do you mind waiting there – I am sorry to ask you to wait such a lot but its awkward today – I had a terrible half hour.

PEIDI

It is 2.15 p.m. when she finally meets Freddy outside 168 and they hurry down Aldersgate to have lunch at the Queen Anne's Restaurant in Cheapside. They can only afford an hour, barely enough for her to present him with a new tobacco pouch and for him to pass her the letter which he wrote on Sunday. Freddy enquires again after her movements this evening, and she confesses her failure to get out of dinner at the Thompsons'. What she fears most if she provokes a direct confrontation with Thompson is that he will carry out his threat to descend on her at Carlton & Prior and, in advertising her adultery, will destroy her livelihood and render her wholly dependent on his charity. Perhaps his earlier appearance in the lunch hour still lingers fresh in her memory. Bywaters is sympathetic, but despondent about the fact that she cannot see him on either of his last two evenings on shore. The silent reproach – which she is shortly to acknowledge in her letter to him – is that her protestations of love are belied by her conduct. She will therefore urge him, in writing and within an hour or so of leaving him in Aldersgate, to hurt her in return, by for example taking her sister out, to 'do something tomorrow night will you? something to make you forget. I'll be hurt I know, but I want you to hurt me – I do really . . . [see below]'.

At about 3.15 Edith resumes work, and Freddy enters Fuller's opposite. She at once reads his letter and replies to it by continuing the already started letter with 'I tried so hard. . . .' This is Edith Thompson's last extant letter to Bywaters before the murder. Its importance cannot be overestimated:

> Darlingest lover of mine, thank you, thank you, oh thank you a thousand times for Friday – it was lovely – its always lovely to go out with you.
>
> And then Saturday – yes I did feel happy – I didn't think a teeny bit about anything in this world, except being with you – and all Saturday evening I was thinking about you – I was just with you in a big arm chair in front of a great big fire feeling all the time how much I had won – cos I have darlint, won such a lot – it feels such a great big thing to me sometimes – that I can't breathe.
>
> When you are away and I see girls with men walking along together – perhaps they are acknowledged sweethearts – they look so ordinary then I feel proud – so proud to think and feel that you are my lover and even tho' not acknowledged I can still hold you – just with a tiny 'hope'.
>
> Darlint, we've said we'll always be Pals haven't we, shall we say we'll always be lovers – even tho' secret ones, or is it (this great big love) a thing we can't control – dare we say that – I think I will dare. Yes I will 'I'll

always love you' – if you are dead – if you have left me even if you don't still love me, I always shall you.

Your love to me is new, it is something different, it is my life and if things should go badly with us, I shall always have this past year to look back upon and feel that 'Then I lived' I never did before and I never shall again.

Darlingest lover, what happened last night? I don't know myself I only know how I felt – no not really how I felt but how I could feel – if time and circumstances were different.

It seems like a great welling up of love – of feeling – of inertia, just as if I am wax in your hands – to do with as you will and I feel that if you do as you wish I shall be happy, its physical purely and I can't really describe it – but you will understand darlint wont you? You said you knew it would be like this one day – if it hadn't would you have been disappointed. Darlingest when you are rough, I go dead – try not to be please.

––––––

The book is lovely – it's going to be sad darlint tho', why can't life go on happy always?

I like Clarie – she is so natural so unworldly.

Why ar'nt you an artist and I as she is – I feel when I am reading frightfully jealous of her – its a picture darlint, just how I did once picture that little flat in Chelsea – why can't he go on loving her always – why are men different – I am right when I say that love to a man is a thing apart from his life – but to a woman it is her whole existence.

––––––

I tried so hard to find a way out of tonight darlingest but he was suspicious and still is – I suppose we must make a study of this deceit for some time longer. I hate it. I hate every lie I have to tell to see you – because lies seem such small mean things to attain such an object as ours. We ought to be able to use great big things for great big love like ours. I'd love to be able to say 'I'm going to see my lover tonight'. If I did he would prevent me – there would be scenes and he would come to 168 and interfere and I couldn't bear that – I could be beaten all over at home and still be defiant – but at 168 it's different. It's my living – you wouldn't let me live on him would you and I shouldn't want to – darlint its funds that are our stumbling block – until we have those we can do nothing. Darlingest find me a job abroad. I'll go tomorrow and not say I was going to a soul and not have one little regret. I said I wouldn't think – that I'd try to forget – circumstances – Pal, help me to forget again – I have succeeded up to now – but its thinking of tonight and tomorrow when I can't see you and feel you holding me.

Darlint – do something tomorrow night will you? something to make you forget. I'll be hurt I know, but I want you to hurt me – I do really – the bargain now, seems so one sided – so unfair – but how can I alter it?

———

About the watch – I didn't think you thought more of that – how can I explain what I did feel? I felt that we had parted – you weren't going to see me – I had given you something to remind you of me and I had purposely retained it. If I said 'come for it' you would – but only the once and it would be as a pal, because you would want me so badly at times – that the watch would help you not to feel so badly and if you hadn't got it – the feeling would be so great – it would conquer you against your will.

Darlint do I flatter myself when I think you think more of the watch than of anything else. That wasn't a present – that was something you asked me to give you – when we decided to be *pals* a sort of sealing of the compact. I couldn't afford it then, but immediately I could I did. Do you remember when and where we were when you asked me for it? If you do tell me, if you don't, forget I asked.

How I thought you would feel about the watch, I would feel about something I have.

It isn't mine, but it belongs to us and unless we were differently situated than we are now, I would follow you everywhere – until you gave it to me back.

He's still well – he's going to gaze all day long at you in your temporary home – after Wednesday.

———

Don't forget what we talked in the Tea Room, I'll still risk and try if you will – we only have 3¾ years left darlingest.

    Try & help

    PEIDI.

It is after completing the last sentence of this letter that Edith leaves Carlton & Prior to rejoin Freddy at Fuller's, where she has coffee with him. The waitress sees them sitting together. The lovers again commute home from Fenchurch Street and Freddy leaves her in Ilford, while he strides down the hill towards Shakespeare Crescent. It is about 7 p.m. when he gets there. The Graydons, Avis and Newenham are present and welcome Bywaters. In the course of the evening Freddy asks after some tobacco which Mr Graydon promised to get him, perhaps a special brand produced by the Imperial Tobacco Company. While he is thus engrossed in conversation in the company of the

Graydons, Edith is reluctantly attending the meagre dinner party given by her brother-in-law. To think that instead of this she could be with Freddy! By the time Bywaters leaves the Crescent the Thompsons are already in bed. It is only now, on the District Line home, that Bywaters can relax and read her letter. As a rule the lovers do not read each other's letters when they are together, because they view the letters as an extension of their conversation, of which every precious moment needs to be saved. The immediate bearing that the precise dating and timing of the letter has on the case derives from the uses to which its last two sentences will be put:

> He's still well – he's going to gaze all day long at you in your temporary home – after Wednesday.

> ———

> Don't forget what we talked in the Tea Room, I'll still risk and try if you will – we only have 3¾ years left darlingest.
> Try & help
>   PEIDI

The prosecution will first of all attempt to discredit Edith Thompson with the jury by pretending to misunderstand the meaning of 'he'. This 'he' refers to the bronze 'hear-no-evil' monkey which was given to Freddy as a present and which he handed over to Edith. The 'temporary home' is a sketch of the *Morea* which she is having framed and expects to be able to collect on Wednesday and put on the desk in her office. The thought of 'he' meaning a 'still well' Percy Thompson – as the Crown will hint – is implausible, to say the least.

Secondly, it is important to date correctly the conversation cryptically referred to in the last sentence of Edith's letter. As the letter as a whole was demonstrably written *before* Monday 5 p.m., and the second half of it between 3.15 p.m. and 5 p.m., the 'talk' in the tea room referred to can *only* mean the afternoon of Friday 29 September. The tea room on Friday was Fuller's. Edith thanks Freddy emphatically earlier in this same letter 'for Friday – it was lovely – its always lovely to go out with you', so why should she not refer again to the same Friday and a conversation she and her lover had then about themselves? In court Edith will explain that 'I'll still risk and try' refers to her running away with Bywaters and to 'getting me a post abroad'. They certainly spoke of this on several occasions. An undated note which was written during the week from 25 September to 29 September states despondently: 'Perhaps I shall get my appointment in Bombay this time — I hope so I failed before.' But the interpretation which the prosecution will put on it is that it unmistakably refers to poisoning Percy Thompson; and the Crown will mistakenly assume that the tea room conversation occurred on Monday afternoon, the day before the murder and that it ought therefore to be *causally* linked to the tragedy.

1. Edith, probably on her second birthday
(25 December 1895), from a photograph
given to the press by her parents.

2. A school photo showing Freddy Bywaters as the third boy in the front row.

3. The Kensington Avenue Schools' football eleven in 1915. Bywaters is the first boy from the left sitting between the teacher and the team captain.

4. Bywaters is the third boy from the right in the fourth row from the front. In front of him, first in the third row sits Edith's brother Bill Graydon.

5. Percy Thompson in the uniform of the London Scottish in January 1916.

6. Edith Graydon and Percy Thompson sailing from Ilfracombe to Cardiff in the summer of 1914.

7. Edith Thompson in (probably) 1918.

8. 15 January 1916: Edith Thompson's wedding day, showing (from left to right) Richard Thompson, Avis Graydon, Edith and Percy Thompson.

9. Edith in an affectionate pose with a man, who may be the Thompsons' friend Reg. She is already married so the picture dates from after 1916.

10. Edith in a light summer dress on holiday.

11. The showroom of Carlton & Prior at 168 Aldersgate in 1922, with Miss Prior, Mr Carlton and, on the far right, Rose Jacobs.

12. Edith Thompson in one of the work rooms at Carlton & Prior, perhaps before she rose to be manageress. She is the fourth seated woman on the left, and opposite her, smiling into the camera, is Lily Vellender, the fifth person on the right.

13. Photograph dating from shortly before the meeting between Edith Thompson and Freddy Bywaters. From left to right (back row): Lily and Norman Vellender, Percy Thompson and (probably) Edith's aunt. In the front row are Avis Graydon and Edith Thompson.

14. A contemporary P&O photo of Bywaters's ship *Morea*.

15. An early 1920s view of Kingsway with Holborn Tube Station on the left and the corner of the Holborn Restaurant on the right.

16. The inside of the Holborn Restaurant on Kingsway as it was when Edith Thompson and Freddy Bywaters met there for lunch.

17. The bronze 'hear-no-evil' monkey which Bywaters gave to Edith Thompson as a mascot and which was meant to bring her luck.

18. Edith is in the back row between Percy and Norman Vellender at 66 Albion Grove, Islington. Lily Vellender has her hands on the little boy's shoulders.

19. Freddy, Edith and Percy at Southsea on 11 June 1921 before crossing to the Isle of Wight. This striking photograph was probably taken by Avis Graydon.

20. 25 June 1921, Eastcote, showing (from left to right), in the second row: Miss Prior (6), Rose Jacobs (11); third row: Lily Vellender (3), Edith Thompson (4); back row: Herbert Carlton (3), Percy Thompson (6), Norman Vellender (7).

21. 10 July 1921: (from left to right) Edith and Percy Thompson and Newenham Graydon in the garden of 41 Kensington Gardens, Ilford.

22. 10 July 1921: (from left to right) Freddy Bywaters, Edith and Percy Thompson.

23. 10 July 1921: (from left to right) Freddy Bywaters, Percy and Edith Thompson.

24. 1922, Eastcote: from left to right are Edith Thompson, an unknown woman, Percy Thompson, Lily and Norman Vellender, and another unidentified woman.

25. 24 June 1922, Eastcote: Edith Thompson is first from the left with a sash over her shoulders.

26. 1922, Eastcote: Edith and Percy Thompson are in the second row, third and fourth from the left. Lily Vellender is seventh in the same row, and the man behind her is probably her husband Norman.

27. 1922, Eastcote: Edith is fifth from the left in a three-legged race.

28. 3 September 1922: The last extant photo of Percy and Edith Thompson together in their garden in Ilford a month before the murder.

29. Edith Thompson in her garden on the same date as the 'last' picture of her and Percy of 3 September 1922; or perhaps this picture and the 'last' one date from 17 September since the photographer may have been Lily Vellender who visited the house on that day.

30. The Thompsons' home at 41 Kensington Gardens in Ilford the day after the murder (4 October 1922). Edith's and Percy's drawing-room is partly hidden by the tree in front of it; their bedroom ran above it, and took in the window over the door and the bow-window.

31. Edith Thompson arriving at the Old Bailey on the first day of the trial (6 December 1922), wearing her musquash coat and a hat with a drooping ostrich plume.

32. Edith's father, her sister Avis, her brother Newenham and her mother photographed within a day or two of Edith's death sentence on 11 December 1922.

33. Edith's parents reading telegrams of sympathy and support after her sentence to death. In the inset picture Edith is about twenty.

I have been looking back over my life, & wondering what it has brought me — I once said "Only ashes and dust and bitterness", and today it seems even less than this. —- if there can be any less.

This last ordeal seems to be the ultimate end of that gradual drifting through Life, passing each event, each disappointment, so many of which I have encountered, and met with a smiling face and an aching heart.

34. Edith's longhand, showing an extract from her newly discovered letter of 23 December 1922.

35. The scene of the murder in 1987, looking towards the corner of Kensington Gardens. It shows the scene more or less the way it was in 1922. During the scuffle the two men moved from the right of the picture to the left, and bloodstains start on the pavement halfway down past the first garden wall. The first wooden gate had blood on it, and Percy collapsed and died in front of the furthest wing of the second wooden gate, which in 1922 was part of the wall connecting with the roofed carriageway.

4

The Best Pal

Tuesday 3 October 1922

This is the day that will put Ilford on the map. It is Percy Thompson's last day. The deadly machinery that is set in motion will grind on and will shortly destroy two more people and their families. History will record the events taking place within the next few hours under the name of 'Thompson & Bywaters'.

London is shrouded in a clammy cold on this morning. As Edith and Percy are about to leave the house, Edith turns to Mrs Lester and says: 'We shall be late tonight, as we are going to a theatre.' She is wearing her slate-grey crêpe-de-chine frock, and over it the expensive brown musquash fur coat with its heavy boa collar, light silk stockings and black patent shoes, and a brown velvet hat to match her coat. In her red cloth handbag she is carrying opera glasses, a pair of ladies' brown suède gloves, a pair of gentlemen's chamois gloves and Percy's bowler hat. Her husband is dressed in a smart blue suit, black shoes, and linen shirt and cuff links. He has on him his wallet and a cigarette case of white metal. Although Police Constable Geal is later to refer to 'the sleeve of the coat', it appears from other evidence that on this night Thompson is only wearing his jacket in spite of the increasing chilliness in the air. Before boarding the train in Ilford, Edith buys her copy of the *Daily Sketch* and is presumably amused by its page 2 piece on 'Dancing with the Times!' One suspects that she and Percy share a giggle over the Dean of Durham's advocacy of a return to Victorian dance forms, and that they warmly approve of the reply in the paper which denies that contemporary girls merely flock to dances to flirt.

After all, the Thompsons themselves are tonight attending a 'frivolous' show about precisely the social and human intricacies of professional and amateur dancing in a country house.

Just before 9 a.m. Edith rings Freddy to confirm their lunch arrangement. He expects the call and answers the phone. If he is disappointed to hear that she is still going to the theatre, he does not let on in his mother's hearing. Nor does he bother telling her who called – he never does. Shortly before noon he makes for the station to catch the first train into Victoria. He and Edith meet up at Carlton & Prior's at 12.30 and make for the Queen Anne's Restaurant again. They are more at leisure today. She probably apologises for not being able to wrench herself out of tonight's engagement. Only too aware now of his attraction to her sister, she may suggest again, as she did in yesterday's letter, that he take Avis out.

After lunch she returns to work, while he completes a few errands in the City. They have agreed to meet up briefly at Fuller's after Carlton & Prior close for the day. It is about 4.10 when Bywaters arrives outside Fuller's tea room and waits inside. At 5.10 Edith is at the door of the tea room. He rises to join her, and they slowly walk towards Aldersgate Tube, from where she will take the Metropolitan Line to King's Cross and then change for Piccadilly. Before they separate outside Aldersgate station and while she clings to him for a moment, they promise each other to meet tomorrow at lunch-time – Freddy's last day. She will not be able to see him for tea, because she has arranged to meet Ethel Vernon at Paddington on the 5 p.m. from St Ives, and will have to accompany her back to Ilford. He *must* make lunch tomorrow, and perhaps they can work out something for the evening after all.

At 5.45 p.m. Edith has met Percy and they are on their way to Piccadilly. They have made allowance for rush-hour delays, and therefore get to the Pit entrance of the Criterion slightly ahead of schedule. Here they are expected to meet Edith's Auntie Lily and Uncle Jack from Stamford Hill. At the appointed time Lily and Jack join them and find them 'happy and in their usual spirits'. The performance does not start till 8.40. The intervening time between the meeting of the two families and curtain rise is not satisfactorily accounted for. According to Mr Laxton, 'we all remained in the queue till about 7.45 p.m. when we entered the theatre'. Usually they would have the tickets in advance, and we may assume this to be the case on this night too. The queueing therefore quite possibly relates to entry into the

Criterion Restaurant for an early theatre dinner. It is almost certain that at this point, if not before, the theatre party is joined by Bess and Reg, neither of whom is mentioned during the trial as being present on this crucial last night, or for giving evidence about other events involving the lovers in which they also participated. The sole clue about Bessie's presence on this night comes from the coverage of the evening in *Lloyd's Sunday News* by 'A Lifelong Friend' who could only have been Bessie:

> Incidents of that last West End party come back. I see Edith Thompson as she sat in that restaurant, the centre of the party, its wit and its mainspring. Her eyes sparkle as she breathes in the atmosphere of pleasure and gaiety.
>
> I see her again as she stood outside the foyer of the theatre. I recall an episode that makes incomprehensible to me the murder which was to take place a few hours later.
>
> Another friend who was of our party said to Percy Thompson 'Why haven't you a coat? You will catch your death of cold.' I forget what Thompson answered, but I remember well the laughing remark of his wife:
>
> 'Oh, he's too mean to buy himself an overcoat! I have promised to buy him a dress overcoat: but I won't until he gets a grey one I have asked him to buy.'
>
> A strange jest from a woman with murder in her heart!

It is impossible to dismiss this as fabrication, in spite of the oddity of the court evidence failing to mention that other parties were present. Whatever the reason, the fact is that the Thompsons are their customary selves, as they sit down at about 8.30 p.m. and open their programmes.

The play *The Dippers* is described as a farce in three acts by Ben Travers and features the popular Cyril Maude partnered by Binnie Hale. The song 'Dusky Nipper', sung by Hale and played during the performance, has been specially composed for the occasion by Ivor Novello to words by Travers. As well as giving the cast and details of setting and period, the programme advertises Liberty silk blouses, new petticoats from Debenham & Freebody, Apollinaris Natural Mineral Water, and begs the ladies 'to remove hats, bonnets, or any kind of head dress'.

When the curtain rises, the audience gazes at a country railway station during early evening on a late autumn day. A train is about to pull out for London. An old woman and a small boy just make it. Henry Talboyes, however, an American on 'probation' with his English fiancée, misses it and is about to resign himself to spending the night at the station. At that point the chauffeur of nearby Mellington Hall drives up and, mistaking Talboyes for Dipper, a professional dancer commissioned to perform at Mellingham on this night, invites him to come along. Through a precipitate accumulation of sub-Wildean circumstances, Talboyes comes to be teaming up with the lively Pauline Dippers who has 'mislaid' her husband, played by Jack Raine. In fact they have had a row and he has left her in the lurch, in the full knowledge that if they lose their performing fee of £100, she will end up in prison. Henry only realises at the end of Act I that the part he is expected to deliver is that of a famous dance partner, Hank Dipper. The flavour of the play can be gleaned perhaps best from the following bit of dialogue between Henry and Pauline in Act I:

> *Talboyes*: You see . . . he thought I was Hicks – Hunks – Hanks. Well, directly I got my foot inside the door, old butlers and nephews and people kept dashing up and thinking me Hank. In fact, as I say, you're the only person who doesn't Hank me think – think me Hank.
> *Pauline*: So that all the people downstairs solemnly think that Mr Dipper has arrived.

In due course Dipper does arrive to confront the 'impostor', but not till Mrs Stella Tavistock, Henry's fiancée, has had a chance to confront her seemingly wayward lover – as she happens to be on the premises instead of at her home in the neighbouring countryside.

Before the various plot complications generate the pace which resolves the multiple ambiguities in mad abandon, the ill-matched dance pair have to improvise so as not to disgrace themselves and forfeit the money. Pauline suggests that they offer a totally new dance, the 'Eskimo lumber', something primitive, archaic, and above all stiff – to allow Henry to play his part. The scene and the second act conclude with Pauline explaining the basic dancing steps to Henry and then dancing with him into the ballroom to the tune of 'Dusky Nipper'.

The farce ends happily of course. It needs to be commended for its perfect sense of timing and its mildly risqué qualities, as shown in both Dipper's reputed prowess in designing ladies' hygienic underwear, and in its alertness to the erotic potential of the improvised dance lessons.

In the intimacy of Verity's tiny underground theatre the slickness of Travers's farce leaps into uproarious life. In the interval Percy and Laxton go into the buffet for a quick Bass each. Lily and her niece stay behind in the theatre. Edith is thrilled with the play which explores familiar territory; the comedy of nimble dancing and of teaching heavy-footed men is one which she has lived through at first hand.

It is 10.45 when the party leave the theatre, briefly stopping in the foyer to collect their coats. Then the Thompsons and the Laxtons turn to their right to descend the steps into the bowels of the Circus. Percy and John purchase the tickets, two to Finsbury Park for the Laxtons and two to Liverpool Street for the Thompsons. Edith and Lily wait in the centre of the booking office platform, chatting till the men return with the tickets. Kissing her aunt goodbye and shaking hands with her uncle, Edith motions towards the Finsbury Park lift and says, 'You go that way,' while she and Percy will take the Bakerloo to Oxford Circus and then the Central to Liverpool Street. It is almost eleven when the Thompsons are travelling east on the Central Line. Shortly before it departs, they board the 11.30 from Liverpool Street to Ilford.

In Upper Norwood Mrs Bywaters is already asleep in bed. She is due up in the City tomorrow and is taking it easy tonight. Her son at this very moment is walking towards the railway bridge at Mill Road near the bottom of Ilford Hill. While Edith and Percy were travelling to the theatre, Freddy went to Tower Hill and took the District Line from Mark Lane to East Ham. The journey lasted a mere twenty-one minutes. He arrived at No. 231 at about 6.30 p.m. and probably joined the parents, Newenham and Avis for dinner. Mr Graydon had got Freddy the tobacco which he had requested the previous night and he put it in his new pouch. Both Avis and her mother noticed it, and Mrs Graydon commented:

You have got a new pouch, Freddy. Was it a present?
[He replies 'yes'.] From a girl, I expect?
Freddy: Yes.
Mother: I expect the same girl gave you that as gave you the watch?
Freddy: Yes, the same girl gave it me.
Mother: I know who it is, but I am not going to say. Never mind, we won't argue about it. She is one of the best.
Freddy: There is none better.

Mrs Graydon could not bring herself to acknowledge that her adored daughter was acting improperly. She readily saw how much charm Freddy exuded and sensed that both her girls had fallen for him.

Presumably, she still hoped that it would work out and that Avis would in the end marry young Bywaters. Perhaps she just wanted Freddy to know that she knew – and that she would stick by Edith no matter what she did. This interchange took place, according to Bywaters, just before he left at 11 p.m. For most of the evening Freddy naturally fell in with the rhythms of No. 231. Newnie, Avis and her parents were with him at different times. He was depressed, though, and when he had a moment alone with Avis suggested that they have a drink in the local. She went through to the kitchen dining room and asked her parents' permission. Then she and Bywaters headed for the Avenue Hotel on the Church Road, where Avis ordered a Guinness, while he probably had his favourite Bass.

Also in the course of the evening Avis told Freddy that Edith and Percy were out at the theatre. Her father was present at this point, but Bywaters made no comment, which struck Mr Graydon as odd. As Freddy was about to leave the house, he turned to Avis and said, 'I will be down to take you to the pictures tomorrow evening.' It was 11 p.m. and he walked along the Crescent and into Sibley Grove, before reaching East Ham Station. He would be at the station by 11.15 p.m. Fresh in his mind were Mrs Graydon's words about Edith in connection with the tobacco pouch. His imminent return to sea loomed large, along with a feeling that his relationship with the wife had been indirectly legitimised. Her mother knew of it and seemingly entrusted her daughter to his keeping. According to his own testimony, he told himself:

> I don't want to go home; I feel too miserable. I want to see Mrs Thompson; I want to see if I can help her.

This was almost certainly the last time that he might see her in an evening, as tomorrow she would be wrapped up in the task of meeting Ethel Vernon and then showing her around. He turned away from the station at East Ham and cut down again through the streets of Manor Park, his childhood playgrounds. Whether he grasped the fatefulness of this dark walk through the cold deserted streets, or whether he was deluding himself about the consequences of a direct confrontation with Percy, only he ever knew.

He was carrying a knife purchased at Osborne & Co. of 165–66 Aldersgate Street, just up from Carlton & Prior. No one had ever noticed Bywaters carrying this knife, although he claimed he had owned it with its leather sheath since November 1921, always took it with him abroad and usually kept it in his overcoat pocket. The prosecution poured scorn on this, but failed to prove their case that the knife had been recently acquired from Osborne's. The sales staff would undoubtedly have recognised the young man if he had bought a knife at the shop the week before the murder, the more so since he was hovering about next door. and opposite at Fuller's, virtually every day. It was not uncommon for merchant seamen to be possessed of knives when they were in foreign parts, and particularly in the Far East. Getting a knife under the circumstances was hardly *prima facie* evidence to be used to convict, although his carrying it on this night was a different matter. The dagger itself consisted of a double-edged blade, which measured five and a half inches and protruded from a four-inch long, chequered pattern handle. The weapon caused a stir when it was produced in court, not least among the jury. The police might never have found it, had Bywaters not told them precisely where to look, wholly unaware of the damage its visual impact would inflict on his case.

The 11.30 train from Liverpool Street arrives in Ilford shortly before midnight. On this night the Thompsons use the stairs to the bridge, walk down the balustraded slope and emerge in the York Road entrance. They cross over into Belgrave Road and begin the walk of just under a mile towards Kensington Gardens. It ought to take twenty minutes at most, probably less on a chilly autumn night in deserted suburban streets. There is no conclusive evidence of Bywaters's precise movements at this moment. He certainly arrived at Ilford station before the 11.30 from London. His own two statements on his subsequent movements before the attack are contradictory: 'I waited for Mrs Thompson and her husband', he conceded in his written statement, but later insisted that the word 'waited' was put to him by Inspector Hall. In court, when questioned by his counsel, Bywaters maintained that 'When I got into Belgrave Road I walked for some time, and some distance ahead I saw Mr and Mrs Thompson, their backs turned to me.' What probably happened was that Bywaters waited in York Road to watch the Thompsons emerge. He may originally have wished to have it out with Percy on the spot, but would have been deterred by the appearance before the couple of four other late-night Ilfordians, Mr and Mrs Percy E. Clevely of 62 Mayfair

Avenue, Miss Dora Finch Pittard of 59 Endsleigh Gardens and Mrs Jessie Secretan of 92 Courtland Avenue.

This foursome now make their way towards the Kensington Gardens area, followed at some distance by Edith and Percy Thompson. Behind them, and stalking them at this point, is Freddy Bywaters. He notes that Edith is walking on the inside of the pavement. She is probably holding Thompson's arm. They are discussing the play and a forthcoming dance event which she is urging him to attend with her. The streets of this particular part of Ilford are not well lit. The fifty-candle-power electric standards lights are sparingly spaced out to provide pools of light for the street intersections. Beyond the Northbrook Road the spaces between the avenues – bordered on either side by the abutting back-garden walls of these substantial Edwardian houses – are therefore fairly dark on an overcast night. The huge sycamores and chestnuts which have flourished here since Victorian times further darken stretches of the street. But the night of 3/4 October is clear and crisp. Edith and Percy almost continuously have the foursome in sight, except for a couple of minutes after crossing the Northbrook Road, when the Belgrave Road rises and then gently bends to the right before opening on the avenues in a long straight line (cf. map). At about 12.10 a.m. the party splits at the corner of Mayfair Avenue where the Clevelys live. The two women proceed alone to Courtland Avenue where they stop briefly to say good night. It is then that Mrs Secretan sees a man standing on the left hand side between Courtland Avenue and De Vere Gardens. The man, who is later identified as Joseph Edward James Row, is probably intoxicated, and relieving himself against the wall or being sick. Miss Pittard, who is shortsighted, fails to see him. The two women decide to enlist Clevely's help and ask him to walk them home. He obliges, and they see Mrs Secretan to her door at 92 Courtland Avenue. While their backs are turned on the way down to 92, or outside 92, the Thompsons pass at the top of the Avenue. They also walk past the drunk near Dr Maudsley's garden gate. The time is 12.20 p.m. Pittard and Clevely are still in Courtland, the drunk is in place, Edith and Percy have reached the intersection of Endsleigh Gardens and Belgrave Road.

In the meantime Bywaters has decided – in all likelihood – to cut across to the Drive, possibly through Beal and Mansfield roads, then to descend through, and intercept the Thompsons in, Endsleigh Gardens. The fact that during his first interrogations he will mistakenly assume that he fled through Endsleigh may point to his recollection of running through it at some point during the night, but towards Belgrave rather than away from it. The Thompsons are now crossing Endsleigh Gardens. On their right-hand side is Miss Pittard's corner house, No. 59, and in front of it is a street light. It is probably in this front garden that Bywaters is hiding. The Thompsons have nearly reached the other side when Bywaters rushes out. With his right hand he grabs Edith and roughly pushes her over to the side. She hits the pavement on the unlit corner of Endsleigh and Belgrave and is momentarily dazed. Almost at the same time Bywaters, with his free left hand first and then with both, pushes her husband further up past the house into the dark. The distance from the light in Endsleigh Gardens to this spot measures thirty-seven yards, and it is fifty-four yards from here to the lamp at the south-western corner of Kensington Gardens. By now the two men are fighting, and Bywaters is violently hitting Thompson. He has drawn his dagger and is wielding it in his *right* hand.[1] If the two men are communicating at all, it can only be through muffled sounds. It is highly improbable that they engage in the sort of dialogue that Freddy will contend took place. The fight is a short and bloody one. Frantically Bywaters stabs Thompson again and again, inflicting eight slight cuts on the left side below the ribs, on the front of the chin and on the right side of the lower jaw, as well as a three-and-a-quarter-inch-long cut on the right inner side of the elbow, and three severe stabs in the neck and back of the neck, all of which are situated towards the right. One of these passes upwards and penetrates into the floor of the mouth, another one, which is fatal, severs the carotid artery and leaves a deep cut in the oesophagus. Immediately Thompson's stomach fills with blood, and he is rendered

[1] The prosecution was keen to establish that Bywaters was right-handed, which he never denied. The reason is that the fatal wounds, and particularly the one which severed the carotid artery, could only have been inflicted from the back by a right-hander. A left-hander would have needed to reach round an impossible angle to do so. But Percy was, Bywaters claims, spun round by him, as he instinctively tried to escape from the onslaught and the hurt of the multiple slight wounds. At that moment, and only at the very end of the struggle, his back was turned, when Bywaters struck him. In court Bywaters had been warned about the effect on the jury of a stabbing in the back. He insisted therefore, probably at his counsel's suggestion, that he held the knife in his left hand, while not disputing that he was right-handed. Most importantly of all, the divisional surgeon Dr Percy J. Drought, emphatically stated under oath in court that 'the fatal wound was the last blow that was inflicted'. This point ought to have weighed in Bywaters's favour, as it might be taken to dispose of the charge of a sudden first blow struck from behind against an unsuspecting man.

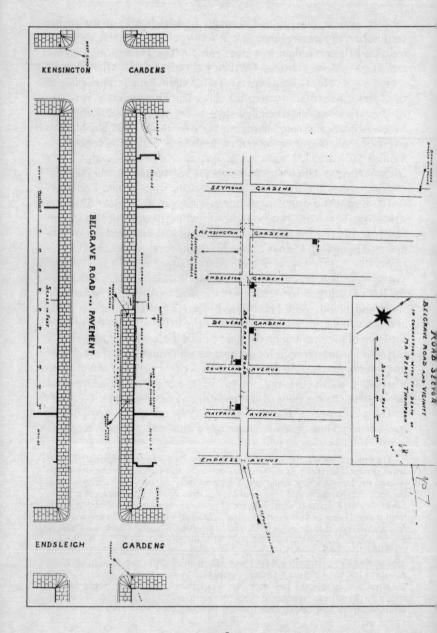

helpless by the blow. During this violent scuffle the two men have moved forty-four feet, from the back wall of 60 Endsleigh Gardens to within half a yard of the carriageway which separates the two gardens. They have been wrestling both on and off the pavement. The entire area is covered in blood, and particularly the wall where Thompson tumbles over and slides down with a pitiful groan. Edith Thompson dimly takes in the scuffle in the badly lit spot. Then, in 'a most piteous manner', she screams: 'Oh don't; oh don't.' These words reach all the way to the bedroom of the sales manager John Webber at 59 De Vere Gardens. They are not heard by Pittard and Clevely down in Courtland, perhaps because they are busy chatting and also because of the sealing effect of the foliage. Webber is already undressed and cannot act immediately. While he is hurriedly dressing, Edith runs up to Percy while Bywaters bolts. Her scream, the first loud noise in the last one or two minutes, may well jolt him. His instinct is to run towards Wanstead Park. He rushes up the Belgrave Road in the direction of Seymour Gardens. In doing so he passes under the pool of light cast by the lamp at 62 Kensington Gardens. At this point Edith clearly recognises the grey trilby hat and the blue overcoat as Bywaters's. She knows already that he is the assailant.

Before his wife reaches him, Thompson, audibly groaning, collapses into a sitting position against the wall. His wife holds him in both her hands and anxiously listens to his breathing. Even as she is bending over him, blood wells from his mouth, over her hands and coat and quickly saturates his clothes at the front. Helpless and panic-sticken, Edith leaps up and rushes across the street. In the middle of the road between Endsleigh and De Vere she runs into Clevely and Miss Pittard. They have turned the corner of Courtland Avenue, got beyond De Vere and decided to cross over towards No. 59 at the corner of Endsleigh Gardens. The woman who, in Clevely's phrase, seemed to surge up to them 'out of the darkness', throws herself at Miss Pittard in a hysterical state and exclaims: 'Oh, my God, help me, my husband is ill, he is bleeding on the pavement.' Miss Pittard holds her up for a moment. She asks for a doctor, and all three of them turn back towards Maudsley's surgery. At precisely this moment Mr Webber steps into Belgrave Road and sees two women and a man charging in his direction and towards Maudsley's house. Edith Thompson is running ahead. She gets to the surgery, rings the bell and once again starts running, this time up the road towards the prostrate body, leaving Pittard and Clevely behind to bring Maudsley along. But Miss

Pittard follows Edith at once after telling the doctor that there is a severe case of sickness just up the road. Edith is already back with the body and strikes a match to look at Percy, when John Webber comes up and enquires whether the man had a fall. Her answer is that she does not know and then, when he offers to be of assistance, she shouts: 'Don't touch him, don't touch him, a lady and a gentleman have gone off for a doctor.'

Within seconds Miss Pittard is back with her and, seeing Thompson lying on the pavement in a pool of blood, asks what happened: 'Oh, don't ask me, I don't know. Somebody flew past, and when I turned to speak to him blood was pouring out of his mouth,' Edith Thompson replies. By now she is wholly incoherent and in a state of hysteria. It is 12.30 a.m. and an interminable five to eight minutes elapse before Maudsley arrives on the scene. He also strikes a match and feels Percy's pulse. He turns to the wife and asks whether her husband was taken ill on the train home from the Criterion Theatre, or on the road. She tells him 'no'. Maudsley is puzzled by the amount of blood still pouring from the man's mouth but, incredibly, misses all the injuries inflicted, in spite of partly undressing Percy's top. He suspects a sudden haemorrhage. The one thing he knows for certain is that the man is dead, and appears to have been so for about ten minutes. He tells the wife this who exclaims: 'Why did you not come sooner and save him?'

The time is now 12.40 a.m. The citizens of Ilford are mostly asleep, as yet happily unconscious of the drama that has burst on the scene of their respectable suburban streets. It is at this moment that the telephone rings at the Ilford police station. Dr Maudsley is on the line and is requesting the ambulance. PCs George Edwin Pearcey and Cyril Geal are directed by Police Sergeant Grimes to leave the station and accompany, or wait for, PC Henry Palmer, who will drive the police ambulance to the scene of the death. The sight that greets the two policemen when on their bikes they arrive at the carriageway gate at 12.50 a.m. consists of five people leaning over the dead man, presumed deceased from a haemorrhage. A yard or so from the body is the wife, supported by two bystanders. She is greatly distressed. The ambulance has now arrived and the policemen lift the body into it to convey it to the Ilford Mortuary. At that moment, at approximately 1.05 a.m., Police Sergeant Walter Mew on patrol appears on the scene. He instructs Geal to accompany Palmer to the mortuary. He and Pearcey then offer to take Mrs Thompson back to No. 41. The two officers are naturally anxious to be as helpful as they possibly can to the widow. She is walking unsupported, and anxiously asks Mew: 'Will he come back?', to which he soothingly replies in the affirmative. Her next agitated statement, almost muttered to herself, will stick in Mew's mind: 'They will blame me for this.' It would be interesting to know whether the stress was on the 'blame' or on the 'me'. The time is 1.15 a.m. when Mew, Pearcey and Edith enter The Retreat and meet Mrs Lester. That something is dreadfully wrong is at once clear to her from the blood spattered all over Edith. She is close to hysteria again, and they take her through to the back morning-room and make her comfortable. Mrs Lester tries to comfort her and at the police's suggestion asks for her parents' address and her brother-in-law's. While the police are gone, Edith moans to Mrs Lester that 'they' would not let her accompany Percy in the ambulance: 'They have taken him away from me; if they would let me go to him, I would make him better.' It occurs to Mrs Lester that Mrs Thompson is frantic and does not realise that Percy is dead. It is nearly 1.45 a.m. when Mew calls at 49 Seymour Gardens to enquire after Richard H. Thompson and to tell him the grim news. He at once hurries across to No. 41. His first impression of his sister-in-law is that she is 'overcome'. He asks her what has happened and Edith replies:

Edith: Percy has been taken away. He had a seizure, coming from the station. He complained of neuritis in his leg and he was rubbing it as he walked along and before I know what had happened he fell against me with a cry 'Oh'. That was the last he ever spoke. I screamed for help and a lady and a gentleman came after some time and assisted me to get a doctor but when he arrived Percy was dead.

In the meantime the ambulance has arrived at the mortuary in St Mary's Church on the High Road, Ilford. The body is taken inside and Geal and Palmer undress it. At once, out of the gashes in the body, the truth stares them in the face. They are dealing with murder, not an accident. The two PCs immediately notify the station and Walter Grimes of the K division of the Metropolitan Police in charge on this night at Ilford informs the divisional inspector. He then waits for his colleague Mew to return. Mew is at the mortuary by now and inspecting the wounds of the deceased. He returns to the police station, and then he and Grimes set out again, cycling through the Mill Road tunnel up Northbrook and back into the Belgrave Road. The time is about 2.40 a.m. They examine more closely what has now become the scene of the crime and search for the murder weapon. They only find large quantities of blood on the pavement for a distance of about forty feet. The two men proceed up the road towards 41 Kensington Gardens. The woman, they know now, is hiding something. She must have seen the assailant, unless she did it herself. But that seems wholly preposterous and Mew, who has already met the widow, probably briefs Grimes to this effect. She undoubtedly is genuinely hysterical, and Mew for a moment wonders whether Percy might have fallen on his own knife during a seizure. But the injuries on the back of the neck rule this out. It has to be murder. When the two officers enter The Retreat once again, it is 3 a.m. Edith is exhausted, terrified and still in shock. Then Mews asks:

Can you account for the cuts on your husband's neck?
Edith: No, we were walking along and my husband said 'Oh', and I said 'Bear up', thinking he had one of his attacks; he then fell on me and walked a little farther; he then fell against the wall and then to the ground.
Mew: Did he have a knife?
Edith: No, I did not see a knife or anything.

Mew then asks her for permission to search her handbag but draws a blank. She explains again how she rushed across the road and into Pittard and Clevely, and that they helped her to get a doctor.

Not satisfied with their progress so far, but convinced that the woman is lying, the officers return to the mortuary, after urging Mrs Thompson to get some rest and cautioning her that they will need to see her again in the morning. Her head feels sore from the fall, and as she drags herself upstairs to her bedroom at about 3.30 a.m., she is desperately fighting off the sensations of utter helplessness which are visited on her in her nightmares. Her most abhorrent visions seem to be crystallising into a formidable reality. Percy is dead. What would she not give now just to recall yesterday, when she professed to loathe his company. Why did Freddy do it? She never meant anything like this to happen. While she sinks back into her empty bed, haunted by fear and sorrow, Freddy Bywaters restlessly tosses in bed in the tawdry villa at 11 Westow Street, the events of the past few hours repeating themselves incessantly in his head. Perhaps he still feels the arresting sensation of ramming the knife into the body in Ilford, and shudders at the memory of Percy's breath on his face, his warm blood sticking to his hands and the dying man's clinging to his coat and hands, as if pleading on the threshold of death. He never saw Edith Thompson after the scuffle started, and his frenzy totally wrenched him from himself. He vaguely registered her scream.

Having attacked Percy, Freddy ran on towards the Park and Seymour Gardens and up to The Drive. It is only then that he realised that he was still carrying the knife. He dropped it down the last drain on the left before the intersection with The Drive. Panting, he carried on up The Drive and down Highlands Gardens for the park, over the enclosure through Wanstead Flats, Leytonstone and then Stratford. Here he commanded a taxi to take him to Aldgate. From Aldgate he crossed to Fenchurch Street where he hailed another cab to Thornton Heath. Then he walked to Upper Norwood. For the two and a half hours which it had taken him from Belgrave Road to the cottage in Westow Street, Freddy Bywaters had been like an alien, dimly remembering once familiar places as he passed through them this night. The taxi that carried him from Stratford to Aldgate on the Romford, Mile End and Whitechapel roads must have seemed like a hearse, as it heaved over the uneven road into the city at night. As he passed Brady Street off the Whitechapel station, he may have looked down into the eastern slumland and thought of the East End murderer of 1888 who had killed near here. Was he like that now, would anyone ever think of him as an assassin? He knew that he had done something awful, and he must have suspected that Percy was fatally injured. But he was not a murderer! That word denoted something so different from himself that he could never accept it. It may be hard to credit, but Bywaters would to the end protest not only Edith Thompson's innocence, but firmly believe in his own.

At 3 a.m. Bywaters let himself into the house with a latchkey. His mother heard him enter and asked, 'Is that you, Mick?' He replied, 'Yes Mum' softly, and went on upstairs. He did not bother to destroy Edith's letters, or to wash his coat which faintly showed brown blood stains. Perhaps he felt safe, or maybe he realised that if the police were going to look for letters they would find them anyway, since quite a few were on board the *Morea*. In any case, he should be off to the Far East shortly and then they could not touch him.

*

Wednesday 4 October 1922: A mean and steady drizzle is falling on Ilford when the first commuters pass to the station through Belgrave Road at the break of dawn. In the row of shops towards the park and up from the blood-stained pavement, rumour at first has it that a dog was run over there last night. But not for long. Gradually the street begins to bustle with unusual activity as policemen and plainclothes officers are seen knocking on doors, kneeling down in front gardens, poking in hedges and drawing figures on the pavement. The news of the murder in the Belgrave Road spreads like wildfire through sleepy Ilford. Any doubts about it are dispelled by the crowd of aggressive young men with identity cards descending like jackals for a carrion dinner on the locals, begging them for photographs: of anything, particularly the area, and of the Thompsons. Did anybody here know them? What is *she* like? How about *him*? And it isn't just the local papers like the *Ilford Recorder* and the *East Ham Echo* either. The big London papers have come to Ilford: the *Daily Mail*, the *Daily Express*, the *Daily Sketch* and even *The Times* will arrive in the course of the afternoon. The eventual headline will be the scoop of the month: 'Murder in quiet Ilford residential road – Wife suspected of Lying by Police! Yard called in!' Within twenty-four hours it will have acquired a riveting new twist and the papers will be able to announce the charging of a young boy and, as they soon dubbed her in some quarters, of the 'Messalina of Ilford', with the murder of the latter's husband.

The press would continue to have a field day with 'Thompson & Bywaters'. As the case unfolded in court, it became clear that the story would more than fulfil its initial promise. Every aspect of it made superb copy: its setting of suburban respectability and intense covert passion, the planning and plotting of the murder, the killing followed by the discovering of the letters and the public humiliation of the woman by hearing her most private language of love read out aloud in two separate law courts in front of her lover, her family, her friends and acquaintances as well as her husband's hostile family. In fact the whole nation were invited to become her audience, when the papers began to print the 'sensational' letters of the Ilford woman. The flavour of the case was enriched immeasurably by the wholesome appearance of the accused: the elegant, intelligent, attractive and well-spoken widow, the smouldering, curly-headed boy, the son of a dead soldier, whose romantic and chivalrous nature would turn him into a tragic and doomed hero overnight. The final act, the lovers' deaths at

Holloway and Pentonville, provided the papers with their tremendous finale, worthy in their view of a Greek tragic ending. They had almost all of them forgotten about the little people who were struggling in this maelstrom. The two exceptions would be Beverley Baxter and, more ambiguously, James Douglas, editors respectively of the *Daily Express* and the *Sunday Express*.

While Ilford is buzzing with excitement, and while anxious parents elect to go and meet their children from school at the corner of Highlands Gardens, Edith, attended by her mother since before dawn, is resting fitfully upstairs at 41 Kensington Gardens. It is nearly 9 a.m. Over in Norwood Freddy Bywaters is getting out of bed. He has slept in his underwear and is not in a communicative mood. He is already rehearsing an alibi in his mind. His mother remarks: 'You were late last night, were you not?' and, when he says 'Yes', she asks: 'Did you go to sleep in the train?' Freddy replies, 'Yes, and went on to Norwood Junction', which is down the line. He does not volunteer any further information and probably withdraws upstairs. His darkish coat does not reveal the bloodstains easily to the naked eye, so he feels reassured on that score. He will just pretend that everything is as usual and will therefore turn up at the Graydons' as promised to take Avis to the cinema. His elder sister Lilian's arrival at 10.20 a.m. may provide a first testing of his composure and of his ability to re-focus his mind away from the horror of last night.

In Ilford at 11 a.m., Francis Hall of Limehouse, a divisional inspector of police, K division, calls at No. 41. Never one to be sentimental and convinced that the woman is lying, Hall introduces himself: 'I am an inspector of police. I understand you were with your husband early this morning in Belgrave Road. I am satisfied he was assaulted.' Edith is still agitated, but according to Hall produces the following answer:

> We were coming along Belgrave Road, and just past the corner of Endsleigh-gardens, when I heard him call out 'Oh-er', and he fell up against me. I put out my arms to save him, and found blood, which I thought was coming from his mouth. I tried to help him out. He staggered for several yards towards Kensington Gardens, and then fell against the wall and slid down; he did not speak to me. I cannot say if I spoke to him. I felt him, and found his clothing wet with blood. He never moved after he fell. We had no quarrel on the way; we were quite happy together. Immediately I saw blood I ran across the road to a doctor's. I appealed to a lady and gentleman who were passing, and the gentleman also went to the

> doctor's. The doctor came, and told me my husband was dead. Just before
> he fell down I was walking on his right hand side, on the inside of the
> pavement, nearest the wall. We were side by side. I did not see anybody
> about at the time. My husband and I were talking about going to a dance.

Hall's record of Edith's statement reflects with reasonable accuracy
what she said. The point needs stressing, as Inspector Hall unscrupulously and with signal ruthlessness will tailor his report to suit his own
interpretation of the events of this day and the next. He will be tripped
up on this at the trial. As he leaves the house he puts it to the widow
and her mother that he might have to invite them shortly to the Ilford
police station, as the death of her husband is now a murder
investigation; the wife ought to be near at hand if she is needed for
information. Half an hour later a taxi hired by the police is conveying
Edith and Mrs Graydon to the station on Ilford Hill, where once she
walked hand in hand with Freddy. The police car probably follows the
same route as the one that she walked with Percy yesterday.

It is noon when Edith crosses the threshold of 41 Kensington
Gardens to leave with the police. She will never see it again. At about
the same time Bywaters and his mother emerge into Westow Street and
start their journey down the hill towards the railway station. He also
will not set eyes on his home again. But he is to enjoy another six hours
of freedom. In the lunch hour on this increasingly dismal wet day, Hall
reports on the telephone to his superior at the Yard. Superintendent
Arthur Neil, usually in charge of the district, is on leave. F. P. Wensley,
one of the Force's most senior and distinguished detectives, handles
the call. Hall explains that the woman is at the station, but that she is
'very much distressed' and has so far failed to come up with a coherent
account of the night's tragedy. Wensley promises to drive to Ilford.

In the meantime the widow and her mother are accommodated in
the matron's room at Ilford Police station. This tiny room faces
south-west and looks out on the station's backyard through barred
windows. In the left-hand corner, down from the sash window, is a gas
stove. The room includes a radiator in the form of a thick heating pipe
running through it, and a couch. There is no lavatory.

The commotion caused at No. 231 by the arrival of a police officer
in the dead of night, bringing the news of Percy's death, is easily
imagined. Retrospectively it seems fitting that, of everyone concerned,
it should be Avis who was to keep the coolest head. It is almost certain
that she accompanied her mother to 41 Kensington Gardens in the

middle of the night of 3/4 October. At some point in these early hours Edith appears to have confided part of the truth to her mother and sister. Certainly the available evidence points that way for two reasons: Avis's movements in the early morning of Wednesday 4 October, and Mrs Graydon's reluctance to talk about Bywaters during the day. In their naïveté the three women must have assumed that, since no one saw Bywaters that night other than Edith, he could not be tied in with the crime, as long as no provable link could be made between them. It is for this reason that at some stage on Wednesday morning, Avis called at Carlton & Prior. The news of her brother-in-law's death had preceded her and had triggered a curious chain of events that was to bear directly on her visit.

When Rose Jacobs heard that Percy Thompson had been murdered, she went to Edith's desk, unlocked it and from it appropriated a small tin box, a 'WHERE IS IT?' book with Bywaters's photo in it, and a letter which she had addressed on Edith's instructions to Miss Fisher. For over a year Rose Jacobs had been privy to the illicit carryings-on between her supervisor and a boy her own age. She may well have resented Miss Graydon's total obliviousness of her presence. Now she would get her own back. It must have struck an ominous note in Rose Jacobs's heart when Avis Graydon suddenly appeared at No. 168, instructing her about the disposal of the items: 'Will you take Miss Graydon's box and "WHERE IS IT?" book home and keep it till I ask for it. You'll find it in the desk.' Rose did take them home, though she subsequently handed almost everything to Sergeant Hancock. The box contained three letters from Bywaters: the Christmas note of December 1921, the letter of Monday 25 September on their abortive attempt at being 'pals only' in Fenchurch Street station, and his reply to her on Sunday night, 1 October. Rose Jacobs thus provided the prosecution with three important letters by Bywaters, two of which they would use successfully to construct a theory of a conspiracy shaping up between the lovers days or even hours before the death of the husband.

On arrival at Ilford Wensley is briefed by Hall, and then he meets Mrs Thompson:

As soon as I had had a word with Hall I saw her. There was no doubt that her distress was genuine. She could scarcely have been called a pretty woman, but she had a distinctly attractive personality. She carried herself well, was dressed tastefully – she still wore the evening gown in which she had gone to the theatre – and spoke with an air of culture. In moments of animation she must have been a woman of considerable fascination. Even seeing her as I did at this original interview, when she was under great stress of mind, she impressed me as being normally a woman above the average in intelligence.[1]

His questioning of her, probing but considerate, elicits details of her married life, her visit to the theatre and their walk back from the station. She co-operates this far, but then becomes vague and confused, and consistently frustrates Wensley's questions. He is puzzled by the seeming randomness of the killing, as the widow fails to think of anyone who might conceivably have reason to desire her husband's death. In the course of the afternoon the Graydons, the father, Newenham and Avis, visit Edith at the police station. As yet she is under no restraint other than being asked not to leave. Had she felt herself to be wholly innocent she might well have insisted on returning to No. 41. But immediate and expert legal advice was not at hand. Even at this juncture a return to her home, given the events of the next twenty-four hours, might well have saved her life. From talking to the Graydons, Wensley senses a certain reluctance on their part fully to co-operate with the enquiry. This puzzles him. His suspicions are aroused when he meets Richard Thompson and asks him: 'What sort of a fellow was your brother?' Thompson is remarkably forthcoming and then, almost casually, drops Bywaters into his conversation with the superintendent, appending the remark that the sailor who lodged at No. 41 was overly familiar with the wife and that he for one could never understand how his brother 'tolerated the situation'. Bywaters, Thompson thinks, has already sailed, as he was due out at about this time. Wensley is impressed by the fact that the other family have given no hint of this other possible participant in the drama, nor have the Graydons let it transpire that their daughter's marriage was less than completely happy. With this new information in hand, he returns to Edith and her mother. He naturally makes no bones about his source of information, which will eventually cause Richard Thompson some heart and headache. Who, Wensley asks of the two women, is Bywaters? The question produces a detailed answer about Freddy's identity and his relationship with the family. Only his whereabouts of the night of 3 October draws some 'fencing' from Mrs Graydon, but eventually she yields and reveals that Freddy stayed with them at No.

[1] F. P. Wensley, *Detective Days* (1931).

231 and that he left at 11 p.m. Wensley's course of action is clear: Bywaters must be considered a suspect. The widow, though not yet seen as having plotted the murder of her husband, is clearly worried and seems to want to shield this man Bywaters. He must be found. It is mid-afternoon. Throughout London the Flying Squad and the local CID offices are put on alert and instructed to keep a watch on 11 Westow Street, the *Morea* in Tilbury, the offices of the P & O in the City, and No. 231 in Shakespeare Crescent, as well as the railway termini at Liverpool Street and at Fenchurch Street. Officers are delegated to watch Paddington Station, where they know Ethel Vernon is due at 5 p.m. She has been wired to go straight to 41 Kensington Gardens where Avis will meet her. The net is closing quickly.

On two or three occasions in the afternoon, in the presence of the matron, Edith complains to her mother about a bump on her head where she fell – although so far she has made no mention of being pushed and hitting her head on the pavement. The mother feels the spot and confirms the existence of a swelling. The matron does likewise, but fails to detect anything out of the ordinary. In court the 'bump' would be ignored.

While her detention continues, Freddy Bywaters spends his lunch hour shopping with his mother for materials. Yesterday he took Edith Thompson for lunch at the Queen Anne Restaurant. Today he is a killer walking the same streets in the same city, and already the police are looking for him. Between 2.30 and 3 p.m. in Paternoster Row, at the corner of Cheapside and just past Nicholson's, he parts from his mother. She has more errands to run and will go on from here to visit friends, while he proposes to stay up in the City and hopes eventually to return home later in the evening. His movements between 3 and 5 p.m. are not accounted for. By five, he has reached Mark Lane Tube station. Before descending the stairs to board the District Line for the journey to East Ham, he buys the *Evening News*. Its headline, 'REPORTED GREEK "REFUSAL" TO LEAVE THRACE', followed by the top billing on the meeting between Venizelos and Lord Curzon, interests him less than the third column on the front page headed 'SHIPPING CLERK MURDERED: Midnight Mystery at Ilford', and which opens with:

Who is responsible for the mysterious death of Percy Thompson (33) . . . It is stated that Mrs Thompson, who is about 27 years of age, has declared that she saw nobody attack her husband. She has shown great distress, and the police have found it difficult to obtain a coherent account of the affair from her . . .

If till now Freddy hoped against hope that he had only injured Thompson, the printed word tells him otherwise. This time the familiar journey east on the Tube assumes the guise of a passage into the unknown. He is weighing up the odds for and against running. In the end it is clear that he has decided to sit it out. Tomorrow, in under eighteen hours' time, he will be sailing down the Thames away from Tilbury and London. Beyond lies the boundless ocean. Darkness is closing in around him, as, in pouring rain, he hastens through Sibley Grove towards No. 231. It is about 6.15 p.m. when he enters the Graydons' house. Newenham and his father are alone. They are visibly distressed. Freddy asks Mr Graydon whether he has seen the *Evening News* to which he replies 'No'. Then, putting it on the kitchen table and pointing out the report on Percy Thompson, Freddy ventures to say, 'This is a terrible thing if it is true,' to which the father responds haplessly, 'I am afraid it is only too true.'

Freddy learns that Edith is at Ilford Police station, attended by Mrs Graydon, while Avis will be over as soon as she has installed Ethel at No. 41. For the next ten minutes and over a cup of tea the three men sit disconsolately in the kitchen/dining room. All this time the house is being watched and Bywaters's presence has been telephoned through to Ilford. The men of CID are ordered to hold fire. Inspector Hall is something of a psychologist and prefers Bywaters – whom he by now strongly suspects – to learn that the woman with whom he appears to be involved is in custody already. For this reason, and to throw Bywaters even more off balance, he instructs Police Sergeant Williams and Detective Sergeant Ernest Foster to run Avis Graydon home from Ilford. At approximately 6.30 p.m., Avis knocks at her parents' door. Her brother opens. With a heavy 'Hullo Newnie', she passes him and is followed in by the two officers.

In the kitchen, on seeing the group, Freddy immediately rises and walks to the fireplace. 'Good evening Freddy,' Avis says, and he replies, 'Good evening Avis.' Foster then asks, 'Is your name Frederick Bywaters?' and, when Freddy says yes, states: 'We are Police Officers and wish you to accompany us to Ilford Police Station to be interviewed in connection with the Ilford murder.' Bywaters remains silent and finishes his tea. Then the two officers, accompanied by Mr

Graydon, Newenham and Freddy Bywaters, drive to Ilford. Avis will prepare dinner. She has already seen her mother and sister whom Mr Graydon and Newenham are now visiting. They are bound to tell Edith that Freddy is also in the station and is helping with enquiries. The police do not object. The reason is that neither suspect can be charged for lack of evidence so far, let alone for a collusive crime. As long as both fear that at any point the other one may crack, there is a fair chance of catching them out by playing them off against each other. In this the police will fail. Rather it is Bywaters's desire to protect the woman which is to provide them, within twenty-four hours, with everything they could have hoped for.

It is nearly 7 p.m. when Bywaters is taken into the presence of Wensley, Hall and a typist. They are sitting in the CID office. He is fully composed and hangs up his overcoat before sitting down. Wensley notices that there are small spots on the sleeves. He sends off for Dr Drought 'to decide whether they were blood or not'. 'What do you want of me?', asks Bywaters indignantly. Looking him over, Wensley takes in his youth. He could be Freddy's father. Perhaps he remembers at this moment his own two sons engulfed by the same catastrophe that had taken away this boy's father. But he is repelled by Bywaters's insolence and firmly reminds him that, if he is as innocent as he claims to be, he need not resent these necessary questions. At that point Drought enters and announces that the stains on the coat sleeves are blood. He simply applied a piece of wet newspaper to them and allowed it to soak up. It came out red. Wensley now bluntly tells Bywaters that his coat will be kept and that he himself will be detained. Freddy replies: 'Why, I know nothing about it.' But the superintendent persists and proceeds to explain that he needs a statement and the material facts. The statement is the result of a question-and-answer session. On several points the two detectives press him hard 'to clear up some obscurity', and Wensley complains that Bywaters appears to resist this. The session lasts about one and a half hours. It is 9 p.m. when Wensley and Hall leave the CID room and ask for Bywaters to be put up in the library for the night. The statement which the two officers are given shortly after reads:

4th October 1922

FREDERICK EDWARD FRANCIS BYWATERS, 11 Westow Street, Upper Norwood, age 20, Laundry Steward, states:—
I have known Mr Percy Thompson for about 4 years, and his wife, Edith,

for about 7 years. Mr Thompson is a shipping clerk; his wife is in a millinery business, and they reside at 41 Kensington Gardens, Ilford. I stayed with them from June 18th 1921, to the 1st August 1921. The first week that I was there, I was there as their guest and the remaining weeks I paid 25/– per week. The cause of my leaving was that Mr Thompson quarrelled with Mrs Thompson and threw her across the room. I thought it a very unmanly thing to do and I interfered. We had a quarrel and he asked me to leave, and I left. I had always been exceedingly good friends with Mrs Thompson. I was also on visiting terms with the mother of Mrs Thompson, a Mrs Graydon, who resides with her husband and family at 231 Shakespeare Crescent, Manor Park. After I left Mrs Thompson I went back to reside with my mother at my present address. On the 7th September 1921 I got a position as writer on board the s.s. 'Morea'. I sailed on the 9th September and returned to England the end of the following month. Shortly after I came back from the voyage I called on Mr and Mrs Thompson at their address Mrs Thompson received me quite friendly, Mr Thompson a little coldly but we parted as friends. The same evening I called on Mrs Graydon and I there again saw Mr and Mrs Thompson, who were visiting her. I have never called upon Mr and Mrs Thompson since that time. I have met them once or twice at Mrs Graydon's since, the last time being in June last. Since that date I have never seen Mr Thompson. I have met Mrs Thompson on several occasions since and always by appointment. They were verbal appointments. On Monday last I met her by appointment at 12.30 p.m. at Aldersgate Street. We went to lunch at the Queen Anne's Restaurant, Cheapside. After lunch she returned to business and I have not seen her since. Mr Thompson was not aware of all our meetings but some of them he was. I have known for a very long time passed that she has led a very unhappy life with him. This is also known to members of Mrs Thompson's family. I have written to her on two occasions. I signed the letters Freddie and I addressed her as 'Dear Edie'. On the evening of Monday 2nd October I called on Mrs Graydon and stayed there till about 10 o'clock. I never mentioned the fact that I had lunched with Mrs Thompson that day and as far as I know Mr Thompson was not aware of it. I left my home yesterday morning about a quarter to twelve. I was dressed in the same clothes that I am now wearing. I went up West and remained there until the evening. I was alone and never met anyone that I knew. I then went to Mrs Graydon's arriving there about 7. I left about 11 o'clock, my impression is that it had gone eleven. Before leaving I remember Mrs Graydon's daughter Avis, saying that Percy (Mr Thompson) had 'phoned her up, and I gathered from the observations she made that he was taking his wife to a theatre that night and that there were other members of the family going. When I left the house I went through Browning Road, into Sibley Grove, to East Ham Railway Station. I booked to Victoria which is my usual custom. I caught a train at 11.30 p.m. and I arrived at Victoria about 12.30 a.m. I then discovered that the last train to Gypsy Hill had gone; it leaves at 12.10 a.m. I had a few pounds in money with me but I decided to walk. I went by way of Vauxhall Road, and Vauxhall Bridge, Kennington, Brixton, turning to the left, into Dulwich, and then on to the Crystal Palace, and from there to my address at Upper Norwood, arriving there about 3 a.m. I never noticed either 'bus or tram going in my direction. On arriving home, I let myself in with a latchkey and went straight to my bedroom. My mother called out to me. She said 'Is that you Mick'. I replied 'Yes', and then went to bed. I got up about 9 a.m. and about 12 I left home with my mother. I left my mother in Paternoster Row about half past two. I stayed in the City till about 5. I then went by train from Mark Lane to East Ham, and from there went on to Mrs Graydon's, arriving there about 6. The first time that I learned that Mr Thompson had been killed was when I bought a newspaper in Mark Lane before I got into the train to go to East Ham. I am never in the habit of carrying a knife. In fact I have never had one. I never met a single person that I knew from the time that I left Mrs Graydon's house until I arrived home. Mrs Thompson has written to me two or three times. I might have received one letter from her at home. The others I have received on board ship. I have destroyed these letters. She used to address me as 'Dear Freddie', and signed herself 'Edie'. I occupy the back bedroom on the top floor at my address, and that is where I keep all my clothing. When I said that I was dressed in precisely the same clothing yesterday, as I am to-day, I meant it to include my under-garments, with the exception of my collar and handkerchief, which are at home.

This statement has been read over to me is voluntary and is true.

(Sgd.) FREDERICK E. F. BYWATERS

While Mrs Graydon and her daughter settle into an uneasy night in the matron's room, Freddy prepares to face the night alone in the library. From its large window he can see the inside courtyard of the building. He does not know that Edith is a mere ten yards away in a room clearly visible from the library. She has been apprised of his presence in the station by her father and brother, and is praying that they will not be connected. These fantasies are about to be shattered. At 11 p.m. Inspector Frank Page, on duty at Westow Street, rings Wensley at New Scotland Yard to relate that Mrs Bywaters has just returned home. He is instructed at once to ask to be allowed to search Freddy's room and at the same time to explain the circumstances of what happened earlier in the evening. Thompson's death, the fact that her son is in custody, and the pressing presence of a police investigator intent on burrowing through his private effects, throw Mrs Bywaters into a panic. She does not dare refuse access to her home to the policeman, who promptly opens Freddy's suitcase and searches through his coat pockets. Within minutes he turns up two long letters from Edith, the one of Thursday 21 September, and her last letter to him dating from Monday 2 October. The first of these contains the damning phrase about jealousy ('he has the right by law to all that you . . .'); the second provides evidence of a long and deep involvement of the two suspects, and, most importantly, it precedes the husband's death by little more than twenty-four hours. Also found in a case are the two notes which Edith sent to Bywaters on Friday 29 September and Monday 2 October, asking him to come or wait for her. Wensley is delighted with this discovery and before midnight the message has been passed on to Ilford and to Hall in particular. He has already made his plans for tomorrow, confident that the waiting and the uncertainty of the two detainees can only be to his advantage as a softening-up. The woman in particular seems brittle. Not long after the events narrated here, Hall will confide his view of Mrs Thompson to A. F. Neil, one of the 'big four' of the Yard:

> Frank Hall told me she did not impress him as a pretty woman by any means. She was of a type, which was all that could be said about her. She had rather nicely-shaped eyebrows and eyelids, which had long, thick lashes. This physical asset accentuated the colour of her eyes, which in certain lights or shades added to her charm. Beyond this she was not a woman a man would turn round and look at a second time.
>
> Her personality was a matter of opinion. His sensible way of describing it was that if a dozen men were intimate with her, three might be influenced, but the other nine would remain impartial.[1]

Hall's 'sensible way' of assessing character did not impress Wensley, who was reputed for his intellectual acuity, not for bludgeoning suspects. The two men would not interact comfortably. It is important to stress that the most controversial incident about to happen between the arrests and the trial occurred in Wensley's momentary absence from the station. He would term it 'one of the most dramatic interludes in the whole case'.

Thursday 5 October: The dismal weather continues unabated. It is mild and wet. At the Ilford Town Hall the coroner has instructed Dr Percy J. Drought to carry out a post mortem on Thompson. It is on this

[1] A. F. Neil, *Forty Years of Man-Hunting* (1932).

day that Bywaters was scheduled to return to the *Morea* for sailing the following morning, while in her office Edith and her monkey would be gazing at the framed sketch of the ship. Instead, within a few yards of each other, they start what is effectively their second day in captivity. The newspapers are all set to go. The police have intimated to their Fleet Street contacts that the case is about to take a dramatic turn.

It is about noon that the detectives advise Mrs Thompson that she will need to make a statement later. Shortly before 3 p.m., she is invited to meet Hall and Wensley in the CID room. Before she enters the office, they have carefully arranged the letters retrieved the previous night from Freddy's home so that she cannot possibly miss them. Hall will feebly attempt to conceal this strategem at the Old Bailey, but will be forced to admit in cross-examination that the 'letters were on the table where we took the statement, and she must have known [that Bywaters was there already as a suspect] on account of the letters'. She knows because her father and brother told her that Freddy was being held. When the policemen notice her eyes wandering over the desk, they impress on her that they are now fully aware of her relationship with Bywaters and motion to the letters asking her to identify them. Then they wonder whether, in view of her being on 'affectionate terms' with her husband, these letters were written with his consent. She admits that they were not. How could they be? Her statement, like Bywaters's, is produced in the form of questions and answers.

5th October, 1922

EDITH JESSIE THOMPSON, 41 Kensington Gardens, Ilford, age 28, married, states:—

My husband's name is Percy Thompson. He is a shipping clerk employed by Messrs O. J. Parker & Co., Peek House, 20 Eastcheap, E.C.

I am employed by Carlton & Prior, Millinery Manufacturers, 168 Aldersgate Street, E.C. as a book-keeper. We have been married 6 years and have no family. We were married in the beginning of the year 1916, in that year my husband joined the London Scottish Regiment, he was discharged as medically unfit a few months later and did no foreign service. I have always been on affectionate terms with my husband. I remember Tuesday 3rd October 1922, we both went to our respective businesses that day, I met my husband by appointment at 1/4 to 6, in Aldersgate Street, that day, we went to the Criterion Theatre, we there met my uncle and aunt, Mr and Mrs J. Laxton, we left the Theatre about 11 p.m. we all four went to the Picadilly Circus Tube, we there separated, my husband and I

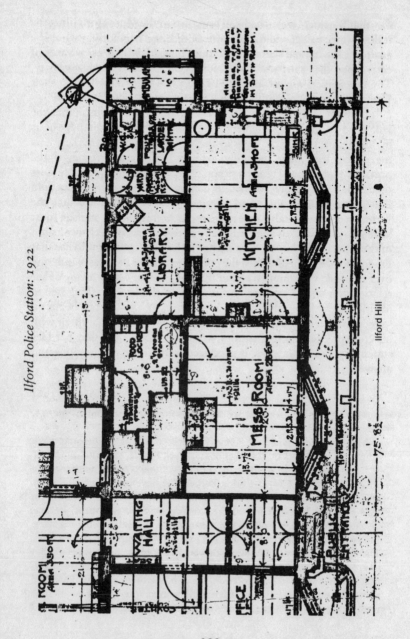

Ilford Police Station: 1922

went to Liverpool Street, and we caught the 11.30 train to Ilford, we arrived at Ilford about 12 o'clock, we then proceeded along York Road, Belgrave Road and when we got between De Vere and Endsleigh Gardens, (we were walking on the right hand side), my husband suddenly went into the roadway I went after him, and he fell up against me, and called out 'oo-er' he was staggering, he was bleeding, and I thought that the blood was coming from his mouth. I cannot remember whether I saw anyone else there or not, I know there was no one there when he staggered up against me. I got hold of my husband with both hands and assisted him to get up against the wall. He stood there for about a minute or two and then slid down on to the footway, he never spoke. I fell on the ground with him. I cannot remember if I shouted out or not. I got up off the ground and ran along to Courtland Avenue, with the intention of calling Dr Maudsley, but on the way I met a lady and gentleman and I said to them something to this effect 'Can I get a Doctor to help me, my husband is ill'. The gentleman said 'I will go for the Doctor'. Dr Maudsley arrived shortly after, although it seemed a long time. A crowd had collected round my husband by this time. The Doctor examined my husband and said that he was dead. An ambulance was sent for and the body was removed. I was accompanied to my home by two Police Officers.

I know Freddie Bywaters, I have known him for several years; we were at school together, at least I wasn't but my two brothers were. He is residing with his widowed mother at 11 Westow St., Norwood. He is a ship's writer and periodically goes away to sea. He has been for a very long time on visiting terms with my family. In June 1921 Bywaters came to reside with my husband and myself at No. 41 Kensington Gardens. He came as a paying guest. I think he paid 25/- or 27/6 per week. He was with us up to the beginning of August 1921. I remember August Bank Holiday 1921. My husband and I quarrelled about something, he struck me. I knocked a chair over. Freddie came in and interfered on my behalf. I left the room and I do not know what transpired between them. As far as my recollection goes, Freddie left on the following Friday, but before he left my husband and he were friends again. We have been in the habit of corresponding with one another. His letters to me and mine to him were couched in affectionate terms. I am not in possession of any letters he writes to me. I have destroyed all as is customary with me with all my correspondence. The letters shown to me by Inspector Hall and addressed to Mr F. Bywaters are some of the letters that I wrote to Freddie, and were written to him without my husband's consent. When he was at home in England, we were in the habit of going out occasionally together without my husband's knowledge.

This statement has been read over to me. It is voluntary and it is true.

(Sgd) EDITH THOMPSON

The taking of the statement lasts approximately one and a half hours.

The time is 4.30 p.m. To understand exactly what happens next one needs to be familiar with the layout of the station at Ilford. Although the matron's room and the cells remain to this day virtually unchanged, the library where Bywaters was held has disappeared as a separate room. Today it is merged into one with the old kitchen. The CID room is harder to identify. But the evidence provided by Wensley, that the CID office 'adjoins the main police station, and passage between them is through a yard which she had to pass on her way back to the matron's room', in conjunction with the architect's plan and particularly his placing of the doors, reveals that CID was located in the mess room which fronts the main road on Ilford Hill. Once it is established that the mess room doubled as the CID office, everything falls into place. The reproduction of the original design helps visualise this scene from Thursday 5 October 1922, 4.30 p.m.

There were two routes of access to the Mess/CID room. Both led through the yard and up either of the two sets of steps. The first one, the more obvious and shorter of the two, led past the food lockers and past the door into the library. But the mess room needed to connect also with the kitchen and the yard passage down the south-west facing steps. Returning this circuitous way to the matron's room would involve passing the library's window on the left. Anyone prominently standing in the window would at once be visible, as the library was lit, and on this wet and overcast 5 October it was virtually dusk at 4.30 p.m. But this very oblique route was not the one that Edith was directed to take on her way to the matron's room. It may, however, have been the way Wensley came into the CID room, for in his recollection of what happened the library window giving on the yard loomed large. Hall, who orchestrated the impending confrontation, curiously could recall no details of it. He merely related that 'we passed the library where Bywaters was detained. She saw him'. He admitted that 'No steps were taken by the police to prevent Mrs Thompson and Bywaters seeing each other.' But both the accused claimed that Bywaters was brought into her presence in the CID office. What really took place is fairly obvious. The police had decided to spring a trap, particularly to throw the woman into disarray. If she realised that he was held and was being taken into the CID room she would suspect the uselessness of trying to shield him. This would be a crucial step forward in the investigation. For although the police might make the charge stick on Bywaters and on her without a confession, it would be much easier to do so if they had implicated each other. The timing was perfect, and the result could not have been better.

As Edith and Hall leave the mess room, the library door swings open and Freddy, accompanied by a police officer, prepares to leave and is moving through the doorway. She instinctively looks to her right as the door opens, and there he is. They are a mere yard apart. The police at once bundle Freddy back into the library and close the door. In shock she exclaims: 'Oh God; oh God, what can I do? Why did he do it; I did not want him to do it.' She is shaken by a fit of hysteria, and as though to herself, she mutters: 'I must tell the truth.' Hall immediately interposes and pretends to caution her: 'Mrs Thompson, you realise what you are saying; what you might say may be used in evidence.' She is numb and looks helplessly about her. Then, still standing outside the library door, Hall tells her an outright lie: 'It is no use your saying he did not do it; he has already told us he has. Go back to the CID room and think about it, and I will come for you in half an hour.' Between 4.30 and 5 p.m. Edith is left to brood in the gloomy room. The impending darkness outside and the continuous patter of rain underline her desolation. Her mother is not at hand to consult, and she does not know whether Hall can be believed. If he strikes her as particularly odious, it may be partly because of the glaring difference between this man and her grandfather, who prided himself on belonging to the finest police force in the world. If Freddy has confessed already – why else would he be here? – there is no point in pretending further that he is not implicated. She knows that he will take the rap, but she will help him to get off. 'They' must believe, understand, and forgive. Her counsel, Sir Henry Curtis-Bennett, will spend hours trying to dissuade her from addressing the world. But he will labour in vain, and she will walk straight into her doom by giving evidence, fully convinced of her innocence and intent on carrying the jury in Bywaters's favour. When Hall enters, Edith informs him of her desire to amend her statement, as follows:

> When we got near Endsleigh Gardens, a man rushed out from the Gardens and knocked me and pushed me away from my husband. I was dazed for a moment. When I recovered I saw my husband scuffling with a man. The man who I know as Freddy Bywaters was running away. He was wearing a blue overcoat and a grey hat. I knew it was him although I did not see his face.

After signing this, she wearily walks back to the matron's room where her mother is waiting. Already she is deprived of privacy, and even close physical contact with the mother will shortly be forbidden. Hall now summons Bywaters into the CID room and asks whether there is anything he wishes to add to his statement. When he hesitates, Hall shows him Edith's confession and plays his trump card: 'I am going to charge you and Mrs Thompson with the wilful murder of Percy Thompson.' Immediately Bywaters replies: 'Why her? Mrs Thompson was not aware of my movements.' According to Bywaters, Hall then promises that Edith and her mother will be allowed to return home, provided he makes a full confession. In his own words recalling the encounter:

> When I saw Mrs Thompson she was so ill I thought she was going to die, and I thought the sooner that I got it down the quicker she would be released and could go home with her mother.

Hall is alone with Bywaters at this point. He has timed it to coincide with Wensley's absence from the station, as his methods would probably not meet with the Yard's approval. It is shortly after 5 p.m. that the following statement is taken from Bywaters, already protesting Edith's innocence:

> I wish to make a voluntary statement. Mrs Edith Thompson was not aware of my movements on Tuesday night 3rd October. I left Manor Park at 11 p.m. and proceeded to Ilford. I waited for Mrs Thompson and her husband. When near Endsleigh Gardens I pushed her to one side, also pushing him further up the street. I said to him 'You have got to separate from your wife'. He said 'No'. I said 'You will have to'. We struggled. I took my knife from my pocket and we fought and he got the worst of it. Mrs Thompson must have been spellbound for I saw nothing of her during the fight. I ran away through Endsleigh Gardens, through Wanstead, Leytonstone, Stratford; got a taxi at Stratford to Aldgate, walked from there to Fenchurch Street, got another taxi to Thornton Heath, then walked to Upper Norwood, arriving home about 3 a.m. The reason I fought with Thompson was because he never acted like a man to his wife. He always seemed several degrees lower than a snake. I loved her and I couldn't go on seeing her leading that life. I did not intend to kill him. I only meant to injure him. I gave him an opportunity of standing up to me as a man but he wouldn't. I have had the knife some time; it was a sheath knife. I threw it down a drain when I was running through Endsleigh Gardens.

It is now 6 p.m., and the police are pleased with their progress. The Ilford murder is all but solved. What remains murky is the extent to which the woman set it up. The letters found at Westow Street can be deemed impressive evidence of collusion, but in themselves they are not enough to implicate her. Also the murder weapon has so far eluded the searchers. Some time that evening, at about 8 p.m., Edith Thompson and Freddy Bywaters are jointly charged with the wilful murder of Percy Thompson. She is petrified and remains silent, while he protests: 'It is wrong, it is wrong.' As of now they are both in remand custody. At 9 p.m. Mrs Graydon hugs her daughter goodbye and leaves for Manor Park, while Edith and Freddy prepare to spend a second night at the station. This time he will sleep in a cell, as will she, their first nights of their remaining ninety-five. Innocent and ignorant of the ways of the law, the Graydon family have to take advice from the police, and then from their solicitor, regarding the daughter's defence. The same is true of young Bywaters, whose family cannot even afford a solicitor. He will have to enlist legal aid.

Friday 6 October is a fairer day. Early showers have subsided by the time the coroner Dr Ambrose opens the inquest on Thompson at the Ilford Town Hall. A jury is empanelled and then proceeds to the mortuary to view the body. The coroner instructs its members to the effect that in this case he only proposes to take evidence of identification. The jury will have to await the police's gathering of evidence and completing of their searches before it can come to a conclusion about the guilt of the two accused, appearing this same morning at Stratford Petty Sessions. Then Mr W. E. Graydon is sworn in and testifies that he saw the body of the deceased in the mortuary and that he is indeed Percy Thompson. At that point the coroner adjourns the inquest till Thursday 19 October. The body of the dead man is transferred from the mortuary to 231 Shakespeare Crescent. It will stay there till Tuesday 10 October, the date set for the funeral.

Crowds have gathered outside the Stratford Police Court, spurred on by the prominence accorded the case in the press. Bywaters arrives first, still wearing his blue suit. He is accompanied by Detective Leonard Williams who has also been delegated to convey Bywaters's and Mrs Thompson's property from the station to the court. When Freddy, who at this point is still unrepresented by a legal adviser, notices these personal effects being prepared for exhibition in court, he unguardedly enquires: 'Have you a knife there?' To the inspector's 'No', he replies:

I told them I ran up Endsleigh Gardens, but coming to think of it after I did it I ran forward along Belgrave Road towards Wanstead Park, turning up a road to the right. I am not sure whether it was Kensington Gardens where they lived or the next road. I then crossed over to the left side of the road and just before I got to the top of [the] Cranbrook Road end I put the knife down a drain; it should be easily found.

It will take the police till Monday to find it. This act of well-meant collaboration will seriously jeopardise Bywaters's standing with the jury, as the dagger will look a formidable sight in the setting of Court 1. Any solicitor would have counselled him to hold his peace.

When finally Bywaters steps into the narrow and elongated oak and cast-iron enclosure of the Stratford Magistrates Court, he is escorted by Detective Ernest Foster who arrested him at No. 231 on Wednesday night. Facing him are three Justices of the Peace, including one woman, and presided over by Mr John Trumble. Shortly after him, Edith Thompson enters the dock supported by a police matron and followed by another police officer. She is separated from Bywaters by Foster. She looks pale, a fact highlighted by her 'shapely eyebrows and long eyelashes', as one contemporary observer remarks. She is dressed almost identically as she was during her night at the theatre, wearing her crêpe-de-chine skirt and over it a long brown jacket. Around her neck she has wrapped the brown fur boa-collar of the coat and on her head is a brown velvet hat. Her hands are in white kid gloves. As she crosses through the court she steals a swift glance at her mother, brother and sister – the father is over in Ilford at the inquest. At first she cannot bear to look up at the court and in panic hides her face in the musquash collar when Trumble starts to read the charge. He stops and asks whether anything is the matter with her. She is induced to drop the collar. Outwardly she appears composed, but her knees are knocking together so badly that she is provided with a chair to sit through the proceedings. A glass of water is offered at her request. Trembling and clutching her garments, she sits listening to the charge and probably wholly unaware of Bywaters's repeated sidelong glances at her. It is Hall's turn now, and he reports his version of the events of 3 and 4 October, up to the point where Bywaters made his first statement. Beyond that he is not prepared to go today. The court is then informed that the two prisoners are remanded till Wednesday 11 October. As they are already leaving the dock Bywaters, through the gaoler, intimates that he wishes to ask a question, and re-enters the dock: 'I want to ask for legal aid.' The clerk replies: 'The police will help you – your friends will be communicated with.' The police van then takes Bywaters to Brixton. Edith is granted a few moments with her mother and then is removed to Holloway Prison.

It is early afternoon when she enters the castellated building north of the Parkhurst Road. Immediately after the huge portals have swallowed her, she is put through the humiliating routine of having her possessions itemised, of changing into coarse prison garments behind a large screen, and of becoming a number. Remand prisoners are subject to the same prison régime as convicted criminals. From now on Edith Thompson, fastidious to the point of vanity, is to share the lives and physical proximity of women of a kind she has never met before. The scented baths of 41 Kensington Gardens have been replaced by the grimy communal tubs at Holloway, few if any of which are even enamelled. The girl who lived on rich lunches at the Holborn, the Waldorf and West End restaurants, whose movements were curtailed solely by an ineffectual husband, is now thrust into a faceless anonymity that will not even allow her the privacy of using the lavatory on her own. Already she feels owned by the prison and its spider-like bureaucracy. They will control everything about her, including her bowel movements. She will be attended by a male doctor – as there is no female physician available yet – and her letters will be monitored, censored and, without her knowledge, repeatedly confiscated.

In the meantime Bywaters has become number 8606 at Brixton. He will shortly write to her, and she will reply. Initially, the governor of neither prison will interfere in their correspondence, rightly assuming that as remand prisoners they are deemed innocent till found guilty. At Brixton Bywaters retains his remarkably insouciant calm, apparently confident that he will only be convicted of manslaughter. The first weekend that the two pass in prison sees the death of Marie Lloyd at the early age of fifty-two. Edith must have seen the only prima donna of music-hall more than once and, like thousands of others, relished her earthy and cheeky comedy.

On Monday 9 October, a cold and miserable day, the police are positioned at last over the top left drain up in Seymour Gardens. By using huge ladles they reach down into the muddy holes. It is in the presence of Hancock and Hall that the dagger is retrieved from the place which Bywaters indicated to detective Williams on Friday. No sheath is found which the police interpret as a significant pointer towards murder rather than manslaughter.

Tuesday 10 October: This day marks the funeral of Percy Thompson. The arrangements are in the hands of Mr James Hawes, undertakers of 45 Station Road, Manor Park. They collect the body from the house in the morning. The coffin which they have prepared for Thompson consists of French polished oak, with brass handles. The inscription, on a brass plate, reads: 'Percy Thompson, died October 4th 1922, aged 32 years.'

Only the Graydons' immediate neighbours know of the time and itinerary of the funeral procession. But many have lowered their blinds out of respect for the dead. The coach and the hearse, covered in floral tributes, arrive outside No. 231 at 11.30 a.m. Mr and Mrs Graydon and Newenham and Billie occupy the coach as it silently heads across the Browning bridge, up Fourth Avenue and over the Romford Road. At the corner of Rabbits Road the cortège is joined by members of the Thompson family, parked in front of the Carnegie library. They were reluctant to join the Graydons in the Crescent – even though the widow's family took the body into their home. As chief mourner Richard Thompson moves to the front of the solemn procession behind the hearse. He shares his coach with two of Percy's colleagues from Messrs O. J. Parker. In another car follow Percy's two sisters. The invalid mother is too sick to attend. At the huge City of London Cemetery where the Graydons, at Edith's prompting, have purchased a private grave, the coffin is taken into the Nonconformist chapel. Some forty mourners apart from the family have congregated by now in the cemetery.

The service is taken by a Congregationalist minister, the Rev Charles Noakes of the Stepney Meeting House. Into the chapel itself only family and close friends of the deceased are admitted. During the burial service Richard Thompson shows signs of great emotional strain, as do his sisters. Towards the end of the ceremony Noakes delivers, as part of his address, the following sermon:

We are met this morning in the presence of tragedy. What we call death is generally painful and affecting under ordinary circumstances, but when it is associated with tragedy it becomes a pathetic nightmare. Doubtless some of you feel just now that there is no star in your sky! you are almost to the point of mental collapse. Oh, the heartache: oh, the soul agony! A useful and honourable life has been cut short by a dark and dastardly deed, which represents human nature at its grossest and worst. But such a dark and dastardly deed is possible because our Creator made us free – free to degrade life and make it ignoble and paltry, and free to make it noble and good. One can but faintly imagine the anguish you are passing through at this moment. You are treading the winepress. You are passing through Gethsemane, and the question arises, 'Has Christianity a message for such a tragic occasion as this?'

The Graydons must be thinking of their daughter and young Bywaters in connection with these words. Every day now their lives are undergoing strange permutations that they can hardly fathom. Standing in this chapel on this day, sharing some of the grief of the family on the other side, a family who are now no longer talking to them, not even to share their common sorrow, they must feel as if propelled by the formidable thrust of events into ever more complex and bewildering responsibilities. What once appeared a tragedy – the death of a loved one – in this extremity is a mere step to overcome. Desperately sorry though they feel for Percy, the mortal danger their daughter stands in is all too evident, and more horrific.

After Noakes has wound up his sermon with the traditional consolations derived from Christian faith, the parties adjourn to the graveside. Percy will be laid to rest here, but not for long. At the head, among a sea of wreaths, sits a cushion of lilies, white chrysanthemums and roses. The tribute reads, 'From Edith'. Next to it is placed a cross from Percy's mother inscribed, 'To my boy. As the light of dawn follows the darkest night, so, after suffering, it pleases our Father to bestow eternal peace – Mother'. On a bunch of lilies are the words, 'My wee token to Uncle Percy. I did love him so – Little Nephew Graham'. Among other tributes are:

'To our brother Percy, in remembrance of happy days', Lily and Ken

'All our woe and sadness, in this world below, belongs not the greatness, we in heaven shall know', from Ethel and Dick

'Your mother and dad' [from the Graydons]

'With deepest sympathy', from Miss Tucknott

'With affectionate remembrance', from Reg and Ruby, Westcliff-on-Sea

'In loving memory', from Bess and Reg

'In loving memory', from Uncle Jack and Aunt Lil

Others, for which no legends are extant, come from 'Uncle Fred, Aunt Edie & Leonard', the Walkinshaws from Highbury; 'Avis, Newnie, Willie & Harold'; 'John and Ethel', probably the Birnages; and 'Mrs and Miss Lester'.

Even as they leave the cemetery the Graydons are anxiously

imagining, and steeling themselves against, the next day's proceedings at the Stratford Petty Sessions.

By seven o'clock on Wednesday morning over 2000 people are mobbing the court rooms. Edith arrives there at 9 a.m. in a taxicab and enters the building. On her solicitor F. A. S. Stern's advice she has changed into mourning and is now wearing the same coat and hat, but a black and white spangled silk skirt and low-cut black jumper. In court Mrs Thompson is allowed to sit. It is 10 a.m. when she takes her place, followed by Bywaters, who has just arrived in the prison van. He is standing up erect, separated from her merely by the presence of a guard. In the well of the court are Wensley and Edith's brothers, mother and sister. Today Edith is far more composed than last time, although her pallor clearly indicates the strain on her. She is sitting mostly with her left leg crossed over her right. As she is listening to the prosecution's case led by Mr William Lewis, she gathers that they have not yet found all her letters to Freddy. He is only referring to their most recent correspondence. Lewis's summing up is thorough and takes up well over an hour. Incredulously the widow attends to his untrue account of their confrontation in the Ilford police station. She becomes agitated and signals her dissent to her solicitor. Stern goes up to her and calms her. He knows the ways of the police and courts, she does not. Lewis's address is succeeded by Drought's forensic evidence, which is followed by Hall quoting Edith's confession and Bywaters's amended version of events. Then Laxton and finally Miss Pittard take the stand in the witness-box. After that the prisoners are remanded in custody till Tuesday.

On her return to Holloway Edith dictates a letter to the branch manager of Barclays Bank at 202, High Street North. The note is typed on her solicitor's official stationery and reads:

Dear Sir

I hereby authorise you to hand to the Bearer, my Mother, all documents and deeds deposited with you for safe custody by either my late husband or myself and I further authorise you to hand over to my Mother the balance of Cash outstanding to our Joint Credit for which I enclose cheque.

   Yours faithfully,
   Signed EDITH THOMPSON

    The Manager,
    Barclays Bank Ltd
    202, High Street North
    East Ham E.6.

Also today, in the laboratories of the Home Office, Dr John Webster of St Mary's Hospital in Paddington is carefully examining Bywaters's overcoat. He establishes that on the left and right sleeve there are a large number of stains of human blood. He also analyses the knife, but fails to conclude categorically that the blood on the blade and handle are of human origin. The case against Bywaters is shaping up, but the prosecution as yet lacks the necessary evidence that would tie the woman in with the killing.

It is in search of further incriminating material that on Thursday 12 October Detective Inspector Alfred Scholes of the Port of London Authority visits SS *Morea* still berthed at Tilbury. From Freddy's cabin Scholes retrieves a locked ditty box and, after a careful search of the cabin, he officially grants the *Morea* permission to sail; she will do so the following day and make for India, without her popular mess steward. The ditty box is handed by Scholes to Sergeant James who in turn passes it to Hall. The police at once drive out to Brixton to wheedle the key out of Bywaters. He surrenders it, and Hall opens the cache. It contains all of her letters as of November 1921, except the ones already found on him and at his home. In his ardent desire to collect all her correspondence, Freddy has virtually signed her death warrant. The police eagerly peruse the extensive correspondence. It matches their wildest hopes. They have now effectively finished compiling their file of material evidence against Mrs Thompson for the Director of Public Prosecutions. Also enclosed in the ditty box is the photograph of Edith Thompson which she sent to Bywaters, and which the police duly appropriate.

On Tuesday 17 October Edith Thompson and Frederick Bywaters appear once more in court. The proceedings consist of calling further witnesses for the prosecution. These include Thompson's brother Richard. Thompson professes to have suspected that his brother and sister-in-law were unhappy together, but Percy 'never complained. I saw Bywaters once, and that was sufficient for me'. At hearing this unexpected jibe – which Thompson will not repeat at the Central Criminal Court – Bywaters laughs out loud. Edith may smile wanly in concert to indicate that she also recognises that they must expect no mercy from that quarter. The court's sympathies are bound to lie with Thompson, for he is repeatedly overcome while giving evidence. Of a naturally timid and vindictive disposition, he anxiously glances up at the young sailor in the dock who stares at him with ironic contempt.

Thursday 19 October: Freddy Bywaters appears at the Ilford Town Hall at the resumed inquest on Percy Thompson. While this sombre and solemn assembly congregates in Ilford, ten miles over to the west a momentous meeting is gathering at the Carlton Club. The Conservatives elect to bring down the Coalition government. Bonar Law's support for the 'putsch' decides the issue. Lloyd George's coalition resigns and the King invites Bonar Law, shortly to be elected leader of the Conservative Party, to form a new government. His Cabinet of sixteen, formed on Monday 23 October, includes Stanley Baldwin whom Edith met fleetingly at Phyllis Court during the Henley Regatta.

Monday also marks the last day of the inquest on Percy Thompson. The weekend, the first blustering and gusty break of true autumn weather, has been taken up by the defence solicitors and particularly by Stern's scanning of Edith Thompson's letters. Stern realises that he *must* prevent these letters being put in evidence at any cost. He succeeds in securing a temporary reprieve for Edith's correspondence at the inquest. The prosecution make Mr Carlton identify sixteen of Mrs Thompson's letters written on violet paper as being in her handwriting. Stern's plea for the letters to be regarded as 'inadmissible evidence' because (a) there is no *prima facie* case against her, and (b) Bywaters has assumed full responsibility, encounters some scepticism from the coroner:

Coroner: I have gone through these letters, and I confess that there is grave suspicion in my mind.

Stern: But you have not heard the explanation.

The coroner, however, yields and tells the jury that whatever the case against the woman may be – particularly in connection with the letters – will be 'thrashed out' at the Old Bailey. Their verdict only relates to the manner of the death and to Bywaters. One hour and a half after the proceedings began, and after consulting for a mere eight minutes, the jury returns a verdict of 'wilful murder' against Bywaters. It makes no mention of Mrs Thompson.

The next two days Thompson and Bywaters are brought up at the Police Court again. If the case is already deemed to contain the makings of a classic spectacle for the mob, Tuesday 24 October at Stratford enshrines it in the popular imagination. This is the day that the now famous letters are first read in court and reach a nationwide audience. Bywaters enters the dock looking genial and nods a friendly acknowledgement to his solicitor. Edith seems much improved and smiles at various acquaintances in the court. Perhaps Stern has been overly sanguine to her about his ability to keep the letters out of the case. When the prosecution suggests that the letters which have come to light since the last session bear on the case and that they are proposing to read them, Stern objects. The presiding magistrate Mr Eliot Howard remarks in response to this:

> She must have known perfectly well who did it, and again and again in the course of that night's detention she told different stories.
>
> *Stern*: She told lies, admittedly, but that does not make her guilty.

Howard, who likes Bywaters and is convinced that the boy was set up by the older woman, rules that there is indeed a *prima facie* case against Mrs Thompson and that the letters can be legitimately submitted. The secrets of Edith Thompson's romantic soul, with all its flaws and none of its beauties, are about to be revealed.

The witnesses today include Carlton, Rose Jacobs, Higgins, and Hancock who will give excerpted readings of the letters, before Lewis resumes after lunch for the Crown. Rose Jacobs's evidence stuns both the prisoners. On the verge of a tearful collapse, Miss Jacobs admits to searching 'Miss Graydon's' desk after the arrest and appropriating the photograph of Bywaters, which she cannot produce because she has burnt it. On hearing this Freddy colours deeply and mumbles a protest. It is about 11 a.m. when Hancock starts on extracts from the letters. He first reads her note of 20 August. The combination in the letters of supremely intimate details and the suggestion of inflicting injury to her husband shatter Edith's resolve to remain brave. Her grand passion suddenly sounds sordid. The further intimation of a cunning set-up to murder the unsuspecting cuckolded husband crushes her spirit and she collapses. Howard orders her removal from the court till the lunch-time adjournment. The morning's proceedings wind up with a long quotation from Exhibit 17, the note of 10 April 1922 describing the bitter taste in the tea and her husband's idle boasting that he was like a cat with nine lives.

On the resumption of the case and having taken up her place again in the dock, Edith at once is exposed to her letters of 21 April and 1 May 1922. In the latter she speaks of her period being slighter than usual and of abortifacient herbs. She refers to the light bulb and a fervent desire to transform their stealthy 'little hour' into twenty-four hours each day. Listening to this language of passion and imaginary crime, the author again collapses. Stern rises and requests permission from the court for her to absent herself during these readings. His presence would be adequate. The clerk curtly informs him that in an indictable offence the prisoner must be in court. The readings continue. Crimson-eared she sits in a trance-like state. A bowl of water has been provided in which she washes her clammy hands. The matron next to her fans her and a bottle of smelling salts are placed on the dock rail in front of her. Her appearance is a poignant one, and observers remark on how elegant she still looks in her new pleated brown skirt and white jumper. She is only sporadically taking the proceedings in, through a mist of voices, faces, scents and outside noises. When Lewis's voice intones the passage describing Thompson's attempt at bludgeoning the wife into submission through a fake heart attack and is thwarted by her calling his bluff, Stern intervenes and urges Lewis not to stop in mid-sentence. Could he continue from ' . . . he got up and stormed – '? At this Bywaters inexplicably laughs loudly, whether because defence counsel caught out Lewis editing his evidence prejudicially, or because the entire scene in the bedroom of No. 41 is so intrinsically farcical and reflects poorly on Percy. Her lover's laughter may jolt the widow out of her trance for a moment, but not for long; and by the time the readings are completed and further evidence has been given regarding Bywaters's overcoat and the finding of the knife, he also is sitting down, weary and looking distressed. He is holding his head and seems dazed. It is late afternoon when the prosecution asks for a further week of remand. Eliot Howard argues that it is cruel to keep the prisoners in gaol for so long: 'We remand the case until tomorrow.'

The three main witnesses summoned on Wednesday 25 October are Mrs Bywaters, Mrs Lester, and Mr Graydon. Somewhat recovered from the harrowing experience of yesterday, Edith smiles faintly as she enters the court and murmurs 'Good morning' to Bywaters in the dock. She keeps her composure throughout Mrs Bywaters's testimony, and when Mrs Lester relates that the Thompsons often had high words between them in their bedroom, 'the faintest suggestion of a smile trembles a second or two on her face'. Edith's father follows Mrs Lester. He briefly tells of her marriage to Thompson and gives her age. When he notes that there are no children of the marriage, Edith breaks into tears and sobs uncontrollably. The father continues, while his daughter, in her fear, shame and pain looks in his direction with mute pleas. Mr Graydon is himself almost overwhelmed as he listens to his weeping daughter a mere ten feet away. The prosecution asks for a further week of remand. Howard grants it, but notes that they are wasting time and that he will not tolerate further stalling because of the distress inflicted on the accused by the drawn-out investigation.

Wintry weather is settling over the capital as Thompson and Bywaters prepare to spend yet another weekend in prison. Through the cell windows they watch the snow fall thickly and gradually shroud the whole of London. Traces of it are still visible on the ground when on Wednesday 1 November, All Saints' Day, the prisoners are driven once again to Stratford. To guard against the invading cold Edith has put on her heavy musquash coat, and is wearing a black velvet tam-o'-shanter from the right side of which projects a spray of feathers which brush repeatedly against the shoulder straps of the prison warden who sits by her in the dock. As she enters the court clutching her coat she is photographed. Once more the prosecution applies for a week's extension of the remand. The Crown is convinced that an exhumation of Thompson's body will conclusively convict the widow, not only or even primarily for aiding and abetting her husband's death, but for procuring it herself by glass and poison.

On Thursday 2 November, under a chilly and bright winter moon, Thompson's body is raised from its resting place and prepared for an autopsy to be carried out independently by Spilsbury and Webster. A heavy police cordon seals off the inside and outside of the cemetery to keep the press away. Spilsbury's and Webster's exhaustive examinations of the tissue of Thompson's heart, stomach, gut, kidneys and liver are recorded in Spilsbury's own report submitted on 1 December 1922.[1] The report concludes:

> I found no indications of poisoning and no changes suggestive of previous attempts at poisoning. I detected no glass in the contents of the intestine.

Spilsbury's resistance to the Solicitor General's imputations regarding the possible inaccuracy of such scientific evidence is well illustrated by the record of his appearance at the Old Bailey. His evidence ought to have allowed the defence successfully to challenge the Crown's case on the basis that its hypotheses about criminal collusion were demonstrably unfounded and rested entirely on the hyperbolised

[1] PRO: Crim 1/206–58186.

rhetoric and incandescent fantasies of the letters. (Mrs Thompson's family was convinced that Spilsbury's report would at once exonerate Edith; and fifty years later her sister again reverted to the exhumation and, erroneously, insisted that it had been let slip by Curtis-Bennett. Unbeknown to her Freddy Bywaters himself had pleaded with the Home Secretary in a letter of 3 January 1923: 'it was said by an officer of the law [that] when the result of the exhumation was known, "The case against Mrs Thompson has failed."')

On Wednesday 8 November Thompson and Bywaters briefly appear in the dock and are remanded for another week; and again on Wednesday 15 November, the day that the country returned a Conservative government under the stewardship of Bonar Law.

It is after the brief session in court that, back in Brixton, Freddy Bywaters sits down and writes to Edith. He has corresponded with her regularly since their arrest. Surprisingly, they continue discussing books and, in a more subdued manner now, their feelings for each other. But today Freddy's letter raises an eyebrow with the usually kindly and indulgent governor of Brixton. Perhaps the letter carelessly alludes to evidence given at Stratford, or he may be hinting cryptically at shared memories, as in the letter of 18 November reproduced here. Whatever the contents of the letter are, the governor decides to seek the advice of the Prison Commissioners at the Home Office in Whitehall. After all, he is a plain-dealing man and readily defers to his superiors, the high-flying and uncomfortably hawkish civil servants. 'This sort of correspondence', he notes in his memo to Whitehall, 'has been going on between this prisoner and his fellow prisoner in Holloway. The letters are not clear.' He encloses Bywaters's most recent letter.

In the meantime, on Friday 17 November, Freddy is writing again. He feels in a great epistolary mood and writes till paper runs out. He is waiting to hear from her. By the following morning he feels uneasy. It appears that she has not written. He does not suspect for a moment that their letters, though censored, might be intercepted. He writes again:

No 8606   Nov: 18th 1922
Name. F Bywaters
Brixton

G.M.M.C.

Today I want to finish the conversation of yesterday. It was rotten – wasn't it – when I was feeling in a mood to talk for a long time I had to desist owing to lack of material. Now P.m. [Peidi mia] comment ca vas –

Why haven't you written to me so that I rcd. letter first post this morning? Answer – A change for me to be in this position? – I'm going to take full advantage of the opportunity. The enclosed cutting – Is the part I have underlined quite correct? If it is – I shall have to use spectacles. Now suppose we have a conversation about the book. My opinion now – yours when you answer. In the first place I don't think I liked it as much as I did 'Atonement'. The best parts I see you noticed. I think Coict made quite an unnecessary sacrifice – though – she was prompted by the highest motives. If she had told Grier she would never had those times of torment – which – you can understand – but I cannot. (It was explained very well by A. & C. Askew – in 'The Shulamite'). Did you like Grier? or Bently?

Funny. – I dreamed last night that you wrote to me & told me that you had been able to finish 'His Daughter'. I would talk about 'Sam's Kid' more, only I have no particular wish to explain my feelings to an audience – you alone yes – it is different.

You understand fully – don't you Pal? You asked me what I do all day – I suppose practically the same as you. Sit on a chair – think or read, eat at specified times & then sleep; One day is over. I look forward to the day at the Court – it breaks the monotony. Do I sound a bit morbid & down – I don't feel over exhilarated: – One of those 'One little hours' would be good now. But this I suppose is only a passing phase – not the longing for 'One little hour' – the other part. I'm going to finish now p.m. Carrissima mia   Goodbye

FREDDY

On Monday 20 November he is writing again. On Tuesday morning J. H. Wall at the Home Office prison division, after conferring with Blackwell, sends a stern rebuke to the governor of Holloway Prison:

21 NOV. 22

Please note that letters written by the woman E. Thompson to the man Bywaters will not be posted. She will not, however, be told of this. If she writes any, they will be sent up to this Office, where they will be retained.

If she has written to him, or if she has received letters from him, why were they not submitted to the Commissioners. None appear to have been sent up.

J. H. WALL

A more detailed missive is posted to Brixton:

This letter [of 16 November] will not be allowed to go – Please leave it with this paper. He should not be told.

No letters from this man to the woman Thompson will be posted. He will not be told of this. He may continue to write to her, but the letters will be forwarded to this Office.

A similar instruction is being sent to Holloway regarding the woman's letters.

The writer then proceeds to wield the cudgel:

What do you mean by 'this sort of correspondence'? No letters to or from the woman Thompson have been submitted by you to the Commisioners. If letters have passed why were they not submitted . . . The letters should not have been allowed to go and you should have asked for instructions before allowing correspondence between two prisoners in the same case, particularly in a such grave case.

The matter does not end here. In their mistaken belief that the two prisoners might either betray their guilty complicity in the letters or in their behaviour at court, the mandarins at the Home Office, acting in concert with the DPP, order a tight watch to be held over the two accused during their last day in court. For a moment it appears as if their hopes of a last minute give-away have been fulfilled. On entry into the dock Mrs Thompson

shouted to the male prisoner (Bywaters), asking if he had received 2 letters she had sent this week. Bywaters replied he had not. He seems to have known they were stopped, as he has not attempted to write since the attached letters of 20 inst.[1]

But since Bywaters would write to Edith the day *after* the committal, on Friday 24 November, it would appear that he retained some hope of getting letters through to her. Again, on Wednesday 29 November, he sends her a telegram addressed to 'Edith Thompson/Remand Hospital/Holloway Prison': 'HAVE YOU RECEIVED LETTER ARE YOU ILL LET ME KNOW From Freddy'. The telegram is not delivered. As the proceedings draw to a close, Edith and young Bywaters must feel traumatised beyond endurance. Their counsel have prepared them for the worst, a committal to the Old Bailey to stand trial for murder. Eliot Howard's words still come as a shock, and particularly to the gathered families. As the prisoners are about to be led out of court, Mrs Graydon rushes forward

[1]According to a report (24 November) by the prison governor of Brixton (*P COM* 8/22/59256).

with a haunting cry of 'My child, my child'. Kindly officials pressed her gently back, but she crept forward, and for one moment clung to her daughter's dress . . . Mrs Graydon sat sobbing bitterly, and was finally let out into the densely-packed street.[1]

With the mother's crying resounding still in her ears, Edith lets herself be guided into the waiting prison van which she boards as if in a trance. Her parents wearily retrace their steps to Manor Park. Already they, the once respectable Graydons, hardly care about the scores of photographers, journalists and intruding spectators who seem to feast off their unhappiness. Their humiliation has been so utterly complete since 24 October when their daughter's letters were first read in court, that now they have done with pride. All they are left with is hope and a terrible fear. The awfulness of what the future might hold only occasionally strikes home, and even then they can barely acknowledge the reality of the gallows. Their lives have been irreproachable, and they have worked hard. Edith has been their brightest and most beautiful child and has never harmed anyone. After all, the autopsy disproved the claim that she tried to poison Percy. So why are the lawyers dragging her through the horrors of more public exposure? The Old Bailey in their minds is associated with crime, vice and the gibbet. Their daughter surely does not belong there, even if she did act like a very foolish girl.

Friday 24 November marks Edith Thompson's first day at Holloway in the certain knowledge that she will face the ordeal of the Old Bailey in thirteen days from now. In the days to come she will sleep poorly and prepare for the day of reckoning. She suspects that she and Freddy are being closely monitored, but still writes to him and her family with astonishing relaxedness. The prison governor and the warders discover in the young woman from Ilford a resilience that they did not anticipate. Her unshakable conviction of her innocence fans her spirited hopefulness: the law is ultimately bound to protect her, not to destroy her. She explains that she has nothing to fear. If the truth can be revealed in its imaginative and emotional entirety, even Freddy, she protests, will be cleared of the charges against him. Once she is allowed to tell their love story, judge and jury will forgive the boy for killing for love. Her solicitor Stern is sceptical. Her leading defence counsel, the recently knighted Henry Curtis-Bennett, is horrified at her briefing him to let her go into the witness-box. He is appalled by her

[1] News of the World, 26 November 1922.

naïveté about the sentimental possibilities of the courtroom, and angered by her refusal to let him answer for the letters. He had, he would state later, 'an answer to every incriminating passage', but she, in her vanity, he thought, hoped to save the boy by her sheer presence and acting ability. She refused to accept that she herself stood in grave danger, and took it for granted that she would be safe.

Bywaters is now transferred to Pentonville, on the day Erskine Childers, whose *The Riddle of the Sands* Freddy read as a young boy, perishes in Dublin's Kilmainham Gaol. During the week and a half before his appearance at the Central Criminal Court, Freddy remains optimistic. The governor of Pentonville, Major Blake, is a humane and well-intentioned man. Young Bywaters will become a great favourite of his.

On Monday 27 November Edith Thompson is persuaded by her solicitor to make a will. She leaves everything to her mother. The short document dictated in her prison cell reads as follows:

THIS IS THE LAST WILL AND TESTAMENT of me JESSIE EDITH THOMPSON lately residing at 41 Kensington Gardens Ilford in the County of Essex but now on remand at His Majesty's Prison at Holloway I HEREBY APPOINT my mother Ethel Jessie Graydon the Wife of William Eustace Graydon of 231 Shakespeare Crescent Manor Park in the County of Essex to be the SOLE EXECUTRIX of this my Will and I GIVE DEVISE and BEQUEATH to the said Ethel Jessie Graydon all my real and personal estate whatsoever and wheresoever situate and over which I shall have any power of testamentary disposition I REVOKE all former Wills by me heretofore made and declare this to be my last Will and Testament IN WITNESS whereof I have hereunto set my hand this 27th day of November One thousand nine hundred and twenty two ——— EDITH JESSIE THOMPSON ——
SIGNED and DECLARED by the abovenamed Testatrix Jessie Edith Thompson as and to be her last Will and Testament in the presence of us both being present at the same time who at her request and in her presence and in the presence of each other have hereunto subscribed our names as witnesses ——— F. A. S. STERN Solicitor 41 The Broadway Stratford ——— J. K. Richards Officer H.M. Prison Holloway ——————

5

The Trial

Wednesday 6 December 1922, 10.30 a.m.

A whispered hush is settling on Court 1 at the Old Bailey. The press are present in force. From the tiny Magistrates Court in Stratford the letters of Edith Thompson have reached out to an audience of millions. Even *The Times* will be giving the case prominent coverage, reproducing the trial verbatim, day by day. The public gallery is packed with well-dressed men and women. They have some of them purchased seats for more than a pound from unemployed labourers and others who queued since 4 a.m. By Monday 11 December, the last day of the trial, seats will be changing hands for over £5, more than an average weekly income. The court is hot, and in the glaring light of the chandeliers it looks like an oak-panelled Oxford or Cambridge lecture hall. Its formidable reputation is almost belied by its unsettling intimacy. That this civilised-looking room should become as much of a life and death arena as a Roman circus is initially hard to credit, were it not for the suspended sword under the lion and unicorn. The distances between judge and accused, dock and jury hardly measure more than thirty feet. Crippen, Casement and Seddon passed through here on their way to death. Under the court are the cells, and barely visible to the spectator is the tiled staircase leading down out of the dock into the bowels of the building which squats on top of what was once Newgate prison, the scene of judgment and of innumerable executions.

Slowly stepping into the dock today is Edith Thompson. She is wearing her heavy musquash coat and, in the words of James

Douglas's eye-witness account, 'a black velvety hat with black quills curving forward from the left side in a scythe-like sweeping droop'. She moves across into the far corner. Bywaters follows her, perfectly groomed. Both have been carefully briefed by their respective counsel for the occasion. Even so the courtroom may appear more frightening to Edith than she imagined. Now all of England will scrutinise her great love affair in the world's most famous court.

The unreality of the place is underlined by the alien look of the bewigged judiciary and the sphinx-like figure of the trial judge, sitting across the well of the court and facing the dock. Mr Justice Shearman, High Church man and stern moralist, presides. A former athlete and the author of a book on football, he is a man of little intellectual distinction. He dislikes courtroom antics and disapproves of female jurors, whom he insists on addressing as 'gentlemen'. The most notable saying of this pillar of the community is that 'The Court is not a theatre.' He is a family man of the old school. To him the ardent and intensely masculine-looking young man opposite will only ever be an 'adulterer', the phrase he is to use again and again about Bywaters, particularly in his summing up. The other members of the judiciary present are men of the world: the recently knighted *bon viveur* and successful barrister Henry Curtis-Bennett, and the urbane Cecil Whiteley, appearing for Mrs Thompson and Bywaters respectively. Also representing Edith Thompson, at the instruction of Stern, are Messrs Walter Frampton and Ivor Snell, and for Bywaters, instructed by Barrington Matthews, Messrs Huntly Jenkins and Myles Elliott. For the Crown, the Director of Public Prosecutions has instructed the newly appointed Solicitor General, Thomas Inskip (a Baldwin protégé) to lead, assisted by the redoubtable Travers Humphreys, reputedly the sharpest legal mind in the country, and Roland Oliver. There are two indictments against the prisoners: the first one is murder and is the one to be tried; the second consists of five counts variously relating to conspiracy to murder, misdemeanour, poison, glass and soliciting murder. The jury consists of eleven men and one woman.

Within the first five minutes of the trial Thompson and Bywaters lose a crucial round, as Shearman refuses the defence application for the two accused to be tried separately. After the prisoners' pleading 'Not Guilty' the jury is empanelled. Even at this late hour Curtis-Bennett still hopes to prevent the letters from being used in evidence. As his client insists on going into the witness-box, he knows that they will be crucial to the Crown's clinching its case, particularly if Inskip can lead Mrs Thompson into contradicting the forensic evidence. Sir Henry therefore formally raises his objection and the jury is asked to retire. Curtis-Bennett points out that in view of the fact that only the first indictment is being tried, Mrs Thompson's letters can only become admissible evidence *if* the prosecution establish that she 'took some active part in the murder'. Some of the letters, counsel argues, date from a long way back and cannot conceivably bear on the manner of Percy Thompson's death on 4 October. Aware of the Crown's likely case against his client, that she will be accused of being a principal in the second degree, Curtis-Bennett writhes skilfully around forensic niceties, aware of the judge's limited intellect. The point is that she may have desired the murder, but had no part in it and was as surprised as any innocent person would have been when it happened. Both judge and Crown demur, and then the judge rules for the Solicitor General on the basis that the letters reveal 'evidence of intention and evidence of motive'. Motive for what? the legal brains in the court must have wondered, since as yet the case against Bywaters had not even started, let alone been proven.

It is gone 11 a.m. when the jurors file back into the court. Inskip opens his address haltingly and sounds subdued. The eyes of the entire court are fixed not on him, but on the accused, and the woman in particular. During the opening words of the Crown the two prisoners, who so far have avoided looking at each other, instinctively examine the jury. Then they relapse into a self-possessed and impassive motionlessness. The Solicitor General's address proceeds hesitantly, with 'apparently' and 'perhaps' and innuendos, as for example when he attempts to impugn Mrs Thompson's integrity because she remained in work as a married woman: 'and, perhaps because there were no children, or for other reasons, she was carrying on her employment'. He notes that she is considerably older than Bywaters and then, a mere ten minutes into his oration, he turns to the letters. He invites the jury to take note of Edith's sending newspaper cuttings referring to 'ground glass', though while winding up concedes magnanimously that 'a post mortem examination showed that there were practically no traces of any poison'. The strategically placed 'practically' is as dishonest and disingenuous as his preliminary conclusion that 'there is the undoubted evidence in the letters upon which you can find that there was a preconcerted meeting between Mrs Thompson and Bywaters *at the place*'. In fact there is not the slightest evidence of this in the letters, but because the jury knows that not all the defendants' correspondence has been submitted as evidence they are led into believing that the place of Percy's death might be mentioned in one of the letters not submitted. (The reason for withholding several of the letters was that they were deemed overly explicit about abortion and sex.)

It is gone noon when the Crown has finished its opening. During the speech Edith has slipped out of her musquash coat and is now sitting in a mourning frock. Her uncle steps into the witness-stand and gives evidence, followed by the Ilford constable who drafted the plan of the area where the crime happened. Miss Pittard is next. When hearing herself quoted on that terrible night and listening to the witnesses describe her agitation and hysteria, Edith bursts into tears.

For the luncheon adjournment shortly after John Webber's evidence, which complements Percy Clevely's and Dora Pittard's, Edith has to be helped downstairs. In the afternoon witnesses for the Crown include Dr Maudsley and Percy J. Drought, as well as some of those dearest to her, like her father, Mr Carlton and Lily Vallender. Also giving evidence are Richard Thompson, Mrs Lilian Bywaters and Mrs Lester, the Thompsons' tenant. This time Edith is more composed during her father's evidence but Mrs Bywaters's and the Ilford divisional surgeon's description of Percy's injuries crack her precarious reserve. Here is how James Douglas saw it:

> There are two terrible moments in her suffering. She looks at that sorrowful mother in the witness-box while she gives evidence about her son. Mrs Bywaters and Mrs Thompson – two tragic women – both linked to the boy sitting there between the warders, both suffering as only women can suffer in such a plight. 'One of the best sons a mother ever had', cries the tragic mother, with a pang of motherly love in her trembling voice. And Mrs Thompson buries her face in her hands while we all shrink from the triangle of misery revealed in the three.
>
> The other dreadful moment is during the evidence of the police surgeon, as the glittering knife is passed to him across the court, and as the blood-stained trousers are taken out of a bag and held up before our eyes. The pale face grows paler, the nostrils quiver, the eyes fill with tears, and her face goes down sobbing into her handkerchief, her slim shoulders quivering.
>
> And this it is that fixes every eye on the pale woman in black who sits all day long in a dreadful solitude. She is so young, so delicately made, so pityfully pale, and yet so tragically wrought that her thoughts are visible as they flit across her face, like a flower fading on its stem, while she listens to her own letters read in dry, colourless legal tones that veil and muffle their passionate import.

And what of the boy? Frederick Bywaters is a handsome youth, with a clear skin, finely carved profile, a trenchant, high forehead, brilliant eyes, and a great wave of thick brown hair brushed back high from his white brow. He is virile and vigorous in his gait, walking with a firm step and swinging arms.

This it is that throbs all day in the court – youth in the toils of destiny. Youth caught in the net of circumstance.[1]

Thursday 7 December: It is bitterly cold when, not long after midnight outside the Central Criminal Court in Newgate Street, the queue for the day's trial on Court 1 begins to form. A 'coloured man' is among those heading it, and there are soon six times as many men as women. Most of them are young and will attempt to tout their seats. A wily street-trader avails himself of the opportunity of making a killing by hiring out campstools. At about 10.30 a.m. Bywaters enters the dock and takes up his seat on the right-hand side, followed shortly after by a weary-looking Mrs Thompson.

The first witness to be called is Edith A. Brown, the manageress of Fuller's at 42 Aldersgate Street. She is succeeded by Amelia A. Lee (one of the waitresses), Rose Jacobs, Charles Higgins, and Mrs Bywaters who has been recalled by Bywaters's counsel to testify to a conversation she had with her wayward son on Mrs Thompson's prospects of a divorce back in August 1921. To Mrs Bywaters's reported parental guidance, that 'there was no law to compel her to live with a man if she was unhappy with him', the judge pompously replies: 'She has obviously not read the House of Lords decision.' Next to take the stand in the witness-box are Frank Page, Alfred Scholes, Percy James, John Hancock and Francis Hall, all of them police officers. Hancock is pummelled by Curtis-Bennett about the precise number of letters found on Bywaters altogether and admits that a mere half are put in evidence. He is also made to agree that of the fifty-odd newspaper cuttings which Edith sent to Bywaters, only a few refer to poisoning. He dutifully reports on finding a bottle of aromatic tincture of opium in the Thompsons' bedroom at 41 Kensington Gardens, and suspects that, as the drawer from which he retrieved it contained none of Thompson's 'collars and ties', but 'only envelopes, notepapers, photographs, and gloves', it is probably hers. Perhaps it is at this point that Edith leans forward over the dock to protest to Stern the identity of the drawer. An observer notices her

[1] 'The Ilford Murder: The Case for and Against a Reprieve', by James Douglas (Daily Express pamphlet, No. 1, 1922).

wedding-ring on her left hand as she grips the rim of the wooden enclosure.

Next into the witness-box is Francis Hall. He has been warned against Curtis-Bennett's no nonsense approach and is therefore rather more nervous than previously at Stratford. He knows that his interrogation of the two prisoners at Ilford might be shown for the fraudulent bullying act it was. He immediately stumbles over the time when he took the woman to the Ilford police station and then reads out the statements made by the two accused, with their corrections. Inskip has already read these the previous day, and although their resurfacing here is legitimate, it clearly is also strategically placed by the Crown to consume time and thereby curtail the scope of the defence's cross-examination of this potentially embarrassing but crucial witness. Of the fact that the Solicitor General is required for other duties of state on Monday, the judge and the defence are fully apprised. Hall's evidence is therefore doubly objectionable, for its calculated evasion of cross-examination and for its deliberate dragging out of the proceedings.

Over half an hour has elapsed when Hall is finally examined by Whiteley who pinpoints the inspector's jealousy of the Scotland Yard Superintendent. He elicits the concession from Hall that he repeatedly interviewed Bywaters on his own and that the statement which has just been read was produced by their questioning him and 'incorporating' his answers into their draft statement, which he signed as if it had been dictated entirely by him. The next admission by Hall is that Wensley was not present when Edith Thompson exclaimed 'why did he do it . . .' on seeing Bywaters, and that 'no steps were taken by the police to prevent Mrs Thompson and Bywaters seeing each other'. Even the judge takes this up and tries to clarify the incident, but without success. Curtis-Bennett invites Hall to correct his error about the time of Mrs Thompson's arrival in the police station and to admit that she at once 'confessed' on seeing Bywaters – which would show a total lack of premeditation on her part and would to some extent redeem her earlier lying. In both instances Hall concurs with the defence's statements. As the inspector leaves the witness box, both the accused feel outraged that, in this of all courts of law, a police officer should have got away with lying under oath.

Finally, for this morning, John Webster and Spilsbury give evidence. Both men are scientists of integrity and widely respected outside the courts and the Home Office. Their findings offer cold comfort for the

Crown. Webster stresses that 'aromatic tincture of opium is quite an ordinary thing', and that until recently it could be 'purchased at any chemist's' without a prescription. Spilsbury categorically remarks: 'I did not find any signs of poisoning, nor did I find any scars in the intestines [and] I found no indication of the presence of glass either in large pieces or in powdered particles.' Since both these statements occur in answer to Inskip's questions, the defence's task seems easy enough. In normal circumstances, one feels, these two admissions alone should have saved Mrs Thompson, notwithstanding the fact that she was being tried as an accessory to Bywaters's killing, as opposed to the five counts of the second indictment. If she took heart from the conclusive scientific evidence regarding her own position, her reprieve was only momentary.

For now, after stating 'That will be the case for the Crown', Inskip has four typed sets of Edith's letters passed to the jury, one lot for each group of three. Then Travers Humphreys begins the reading of them. The time is approximately 12.15 p.m. No sooner have Humphreys's precisely articulated sentences begun to cut through the silence of the courtroom than Edith Thompson slumps forward and, covering her face with both hands, begins to weep, silently but without a break. All eyes in the court bore and burn themselves into her slight, black figure, as passage after passage of her ardent language of love is enunciated by the remorseless voice of the prosecution. She dare not raise her head for fear of seeing her mother and father who share their child's agony and some of her shame. As she is sitting there, and perhaps imagines the endless distance between her feelings when writing these words and Humphreys's dispassionate voice during the readings, she feels utterly destroyed. At 1 p.m. the judge rises and the court officials prepare to adjourn for lunch. Bywaters immediately starts to confer with his solicitor and is seemingly heedless of the woman. The two wardresses, sitting one behind Edith and the other one by her side, try to rouse her. She does not respond. Finally they grasp her firmly by the waist, steady her by the arm and then move her ponderously to the dock steps.

The proceedings resume at 2 p.m. For another forty-five minutes Humphreys reads the letters, intermittently relieved by a junior counsel. Up in the public gallery some of the young men in the audience fail to control their delight at the woman's hyperbolical rhetoric. Repeatedly a ripple of giggles and gleeful laughter emanates from there and subsides only under the stern gaze of the judge. It is out of embarrassment and to save time that the judge, in concert with counsel, decides to cut short the readings and leave what remains to the jury to peruse. After all, he remarks, it is mostly 'gush'. Curtis-Bennett, keen to save his client further hurt and to invalidate the importance of the letters, concurs. It is 3.30 p.m. Edith only barely flinches when Cecil Whiteley announces firmly: 'I will call Bywaters.'

The defence's case has got under way at last. Freddy rises. He is wearing his black jacket, grey trousers and spats. He slowly crosses the dock behind Edith, who is sitting nearest the glass door leading into the court. Preceded by the usher he walks across the well, passes in front of the jury and, brushing against someone, audibly apologises. He then takes his stand in the witness-box. He appears calm and observers notice his striking profile and the way his thick hair brushed back gives him additional height. He clenches his hands and will be tapping the ledge of the witness-box continuously with his right fist during his evidence. His assumed confidence is further belied by his answering in a very low voice – he will be asked repeatedly to speak up. He is sworn in and is handed a thick portfolio of typed and numbered copies of the letters sent him by the woman sitting across the well of the court. He kept them for love and out of pride, and now they will be public property and permanently degraded.

For the next hour and a half Bywaters explains his early acquaint-ance with the Graydons, his remove to Norwood, his voyages, and finally his shared holiday with the Thompsons, the Vallenders and Avis. A mere five minutes into his account the judge interrupts and heavily hints that Bywaters is distorting the evidence. Quick on the uptake, Whiteley invites Bywaters to explain himself further. It is important to dispel from the minds of the jury at once the idea that the boy is a congenital liar. But within minutes Freddy indeed lies, when he denies that he and the woman opposite were lovers in the late summer of 1921. The prosecution will catch him out on this with the letters in question and will suggest that it proves collusion with intent to murder over an extended period. He probably told this lie to exonerate himself and her from the charges of premeditation and of abusing Thompson's hospitality. Even the most sympathetic of jurors would be wary of a situation in which the wife's secret lover takes up residence at the married home.

Listening to Bywaters's edited account of the past year, Edith Thompson must realise that the prosecution will easily puncture it. Only she and Freddy understand that romantic make-believe played a vital role in their relationship. Suicide was a part of this charade. Although Edith toyed with the notion of self-destruction, as her marriage bed was becoming unbearable and the sight of her husband increasingly loathsome to her, she didn't seriously contemplate killing herself. Only once did she really appear to have pondered its implications, when she wrote in November 1921:

> Death seemed horrible last night – when you think about it darlint, it does seem a horrible thing to die, when you have never been happy, really happy, for one little minute.

It is with this passage that Whiteley chooses to open his readings of the letters. By stressing the importance of suicide, real and imaginary, in the relationship, he hopes to divert attention away from poisoning plots and, if he fails to clear Bywaters from the suspicion of murder, he will at least have reduced the element of conspiracy and contributed towards rendering the final act a gesture of despair rather than of premeditated killing. The extracts quoted are in rough chronological order, from November 1921 to September 1922. While he is invited to comment on them by his counsel, Freddy coolly asks for page references and then runs his finger lightly down the page to the passage in question. When he comes to Edith's letter of 1 May referring to 'You said it was enough for an elephant', a wan smile of recognition flickers over his face. A quarter of an hour later, he is invited by Shearman to explain the reference in her letter to 27 August, when his birthday is on 27 June. Furthermore, the judge wishes to know what Mrs Thompson means by writing on 27 August, 'I said I would wait five year.' Bywaters explains that what it specifies is for a certain period of time to elapse before she would commit suicide. Shearman leans forward and half smiling, questions Bywaters incredulously: 'She suggested suicide, and you said "Let's put it off for five years"?' Freddy agrees, while Edith sits in the dock opposite, humiliated and bewildered by the judge's scepticism. But the lovers' ordeal for the day is nearly over. When the court adjourns at 5 p.m. Freddy's examination by his counsel is not complete. Tomorrow will be the big day, when he will be cross-examined and followed into the witness-box by Edith Thompson.

Friday 8 December 1922: Long before dawn on Friday, the queue to the public gallery for Court 1 has grown to look like an ugly oversized snake winding its unwieldy body round the corner of Newgate Street and Old Bailey. The *Evening News* has sent out its reporter for a minor scoop. The first two arrivals, he notes, are two sailors who claim a 'professional interest in the case', as young Bywaters is a seafaring man. They are quickly succeeded by others, some of them unemployed men who will presently be selling their places. This promises to be the trial's most rewarding day, as the woman is forecast to be in the box for at least half the entire session. The first female spectator to arrive reaches the Central Criminal Court at 2 a.m. The sound of her high heels on the night-time pavement carries down Newgate Street. She is young and embarrassed by being the only woman so far, but quickly makes friends, and the two sailors offer her the place at the front. Perhaps it is she who is noticed by the *Daily Sketch*'s man in court in the first row of the gallery, hatless and having removed her cloak and gloves to be comfortable and enjoy the occasion to the full. As more and more onlookers crowd the Newgate street entrance to the gallery, the campstools appear and the conversation gets increasingly animated. Speculations about the case and the verdict abound, coffee and tea are served, messenger boys keep places for patrons, and the spectacle assumes all the atmosphere of a wintry scene outside one of London's innumerable theatres.

10.35 a.m.: Freddy Bywaters takes up his position in the witness-box. During the night he must have rehearsed everything that was said on the preceding day. His counsel will have briefed him on how he performed and also on the strategies the prosecution are likely to employ in today's hearing. Similarly Edith Thompson is briefed by Curtis-Bennett who has made one more effort to dissuade her from giving evidence.

Cecil Whiteley now invites Bywaters to relate the events from his return to London on 23 September to the night of the killing. He still hopes that by telling the truth – and about this bit of the story there is little dispute even in Whiteley's mind – the youth might be able to sway the jury in his favour. The line of defence that Bywaters's counsel would have much preferred, but the one specifically forbidden him by his client, would have been to portray him as the youthful and ultimately gallant victim of a sophisticated older seductress. As it is, he depends on the boy's romantic appeal to rescue him, if anything can. He therefore pointedly asks Bywaters to 'tell us in your own way what your feelings were towards Mrs Thompson'. Freddy replies seemingly unsentimentally, but not without a tremor in his voice, how sorry he felt for her on his way to East Ham Station after leaving the Graydons. At the station, he claims, he could not take it any longer and decided to walk across to Ilford. He now maintains that he eventually saw the two Thompsons ahead of him. His narrative of the assault on Percy itself is accompanied by vivid and, to one observer, 'appallingly realistic', movements. He tries to impress on the court that he acted in self-defence by showing how Thompson reached for a hip-pocket gun – the most recent line of the Bywaters defence – and inadvertently damages his case further. The jury has already been shocked by the sight of the knife and by Percy's bloodstained clothes. To see the assassin himself re-enacting the crime does little to predispose them in his favour. Whiteley makes Bywaters stress the fact that Percy was leaning up against the wall when he ran away, and that he first learned of Thompson's death from the *Evening News*, and had it confirmed by Mr Graydon. Whiteley's final point is to get Bywaters to protest at the way his statements at Ilford were extracted as well as signalling to the court that the police's version of the 'accidental encounter' of the two suspects is a fabrication.

It is nearly 11.30 a.m. when the defence yields its witness to the Crown for cross-examination. So far the youngster has left a mixed impression on the court. Few believe his version of the night, particularly the references to Thompson's gun. It is as a shameless liar that Inskip will portray Bywaters to the jury. He immediately declares his intent by precisely locating the date in June 1921 when the boy first confessed his love to Mrs Thompson. Confronted with the evidence of the letter, Bywaters nevertheless decides to brazen it out, which incenses the judge. Freddy remains cool. Edith now hangs on every word he says, as observers note. Her eyes never leave his face. She seems weary to the point of exhaustion, but does not for a second let go, as though by sympathetic magic she might help him in his ordeal. If her love for him has ever flagged, she now recognises the full extent of his courage, as again and again he struggles to keep her free from the charge against her: 'Never a denial but it was for two, a different reading of a sentence in a letter and it was an explanation for two', wrote one woman spectator, moved by Bywaters's chivalry and stamina.

After establishing the defendant's manifest untrustworthiness, Inskip proceeds to the suggestions of suicide and separation in the letters. He reminds Bywaters of the fact that the easiest way to obtain a separation would have been through confronting Percy with the adultery. As far as suicide goes, when was the idea of it mooted and when was it dropped? Freddy has to explain that he did not always take Edith's threats in the letters seriously. Earlier, to Whiteley, he has used the word 'melodrama' and, convinced that the uneducated boy is ignorant of its meaning, the Solicitor General invites him to define the word. He does so competently and claims that her many references to poison, broken glass and quinine fell into the same category. Furthermore, as Freddy explains, he was fond of chemistry at school, and Edith and her brothers knew of this. He is then confronted by the 'bitter tea' incident, recorded mischievously by Edith: 'He puts great stress on the fact of the tea tasting bitter.' Bywaters emphatically abides by his reading of the letter in terms of this being Mrs Thompson talking about her own tasting rather than the husband. An incredulous Inskip sneers at this. However, Freddy's seemingly implausible suggestion could well be the truth, as has already been argued. When he is finally pushed up against the wall on the issue of quinine and the dose being 'enough for an elephant', Bywaters becomes agitated and passionately asserts that he knew that 'she could not hurt herself with quinine':

Inskip: You were playing with her ideas?
Bywaters: I was pulling her leg.

The sound of this, and particularly its exposing of the young man as a reckless prankster, further detracts from his credibility and hurts, as he knows, the woman opposite whose eyes he senses resting on him. He is asked about the glass particles and replies that he understood that to be 'a lie from her to me'. How can he possibly explain that the 'lie' refers to attempted murder? Of course they 'discussed' an imaginary romantic murder, but to admit that and then to expect the jury to believe that they never meant it, *after it actually happened*, would be an almost impossible task. Pressed further on Edith's query about his study of 'bichloride of mercury' – which Freddy professes to have read as a query about gardening – and the 'light bulb' incident, he bluntly states that she had been 'lying' to him again. He might have preferred, as he will do shortly, to have used the word 'melodrama', but Inskip has already ridiculed it. He now pretends not to have understood Bywaters: 'She had been what?' – 'Lying to me, lying'. Inskip is a barrister of distinctly limited gifts, but he puts Bywaters shrewdly on the spot here. If however he has hoped to trick the youngster into disowning the woman *in extremis*, he has miscalculated. The two of them will keep faith with each other throughout. Nevertheless it is hard to imagine that Edith did not wince at his blunt admission that he knew that she was lying. Presently he is forced to confess that her plea of 'yes darlint be jealous, so much that you will do something desperate' was ineffective because he was *not* jealous, whatever he might have written to the contrary. The Crown asks whether he 'ever thought of marrying her', and Bywaters replies with a single 'No'. She knows he is speaking a truth now that neither of them dared articulate. It hurts even in these awful circumstances.

Gazing at the face of her young lover across the well of the court, Edith notices how the strain is beginning to show in his pallor. His voice remains firm, but he sounds subdued. Inskip now changes tactic and reverts to the afternoon of 3 October, particularly the meeting at Fuller's. Bywaters denies that they plotted a murder, but unwittingly concedes that she mentioned that Percy and she were going to the theatre that night. In his first statement he particularly denied any knowledge of the Thompsons' visit to the theatre prior to his evening stay at the Graydons. He is picked up on this inconsistency at once. It was a white lie, as he will explain later to the defence; he did not wish to involve Mrs Thompson while making his first statement, hence the suggestion that it was only by chance that he learned of the theatre party. But his excuse sounds implausible, as does his sworn evidence in court about acting in self-defence. *Ergo* his police statement is untrustworthy and his evidence in court is equally dishonest. Bywaters bravely maintains that his police statement is misleading, because he was prepared to confess to anything as long as it let *her* go free from the police station. Again he claims that things were put to him by his interrogators. The Crown rounds off the questioning of Bywaters with a graphic rendering of Thompson's fatal struggle with his assailant. Whiteley briefly attempts to clarify the issue of statement and sworn evidence, before resting his case and allowing his client to step down.

The morning session is not over yet. It is just gone noon. Bywaters has taken up his seat in the dock again. Edith Thompson is now called. She pats her hair, adjusts her hat, and quickly wipes her face with a handkerchief. Then, slowly and with deliberation, she crosses the floor of the court, takes the oath and sinks into the chair offered her in the witness-box. Some members of the court scramble to their feet, as she begins her loneliest journey through the glass door and heads for the box. A policeman in the court asks the public gallery to 'Sit down, please . . . Will you please sit down', as the spectators strain forwards to catch a better glimpse of the woman. For a second she closes her eyes and catches her breath. All eyes in the court are bent on her, and she shudders at their gaze. Then she revives, removes her black gloves, and receives from Walter Frampton, her junior counsel, the five-inch-thick pad of her letters. Frampton immediately invites her to relate to the court the course of her life with Thompson and her first encounter with Bywaters. Her voice is low to the point of becoming inaudible, and Shearman several times calls on her to repeat words which he has failed to catch. Irritated, the judge finally asks her to pull her chair forward as far as it goes into the box. Her counsel's procedure will parallel Bywaters's by concentrating on a pre-emptive strategy and confronting the difficult letters head-on. For the letters are the sole evidence against her, a point which cannot be overstressed.

Embarrassed though she is, Mrs Thompson bravely bears up. Her voice may falter and occasionally sound choked, and her right hand repeatedly travels up to her throat and strokes her neck. The famous reference to the 'wrong Porridge' occurs early on, and she replies: 'I really cannot explain.' How can she, a respectable woman, tell this open court full of men that she tried to abort? It would make her look degenerate when, as yet, she naïvely believes that she has nothing to fear, since she is innocent as charged. Her refusal to answer the question does not impress the jury, and the judge at once construes it as a sign of collusion. She concedes that they planned to make Percy 'ill', but without really either of them meaning to carry it into effect. The most salient points of her evidence as elicited by counsel concern the tea tasting bitter, the light bulbs allegedly fed to Thompson, the bottle of aromatic tincture disposed of by Avis Graydon and the relevance to the case of the novel *Bella Donna*. The night of 3 to 4 October Curtis-Bennett reserves to the end, hoping to capitalise on the widow's manifest inability to control her emotions while relating her husband's death. Thanks to the sympathetic prompting of her counsel and the intervening lunch-hour, Mrs Thompson revives and her answers become more confident again. The bitter tea incident is competently re-addressed and gets short shrift – she even manages to indicate that Thompson's mother could undoubtedly bear her out on this, as she is alive still to testify.

When the bottle of aromatic tincture of opium is produced, she coolly refuses to identify it positively as the one that she removed from her husband's medicine cabinet back in April. Her sister Avis will support her on Saturday on this. Repeatedly the evidence reverts to 'divorce' and 'suicide' and Hichens's novel *Bella Donna*. The treatment in court of *Bella Donna* during the trial underlines the extent to which the case against Edith Thompson rested on involuntary as well as deliberate misrepresentations of the available evidence. To indicate the nature of these distortions, it has been necessary to collate the material relating to *Bella Donna* from the remaining three days of the trial.

As soon as her counsel had got Edith Thompson to state that the novel was about Egypt, the trial judge chipped in with:

> I should like to clear this up. Is not the main point of it that the lady killed her husband with slow poisoning?

The Solicitor General immediately rose with 'I was going to deal with it in cross-examination'. The judge had not read the novel, nor did he invite the jury to read it. They must have assumed, as clearly he did at first, that Bella Donna actually succeeded in killing her husband. His comment during the defence's summing up of the novel was 'Are you going to put in the book? If you do, the jury will have to read the whole of it':

> *Curtis-Bennett*: I do not wish to do that. I think your lordship has given a description of the book. I will if necessary put in the book.
>
> *Judge*: Surely not. I don't think that is necessary. I hope not. I hope you will not put it in. You can deal with anything that has been given in evidence about it.

A human life was at stake, but the judge preferred for the jury not to be overburdened with the additional task of reading an entire novel; and the parliamentary schedule of the Solicitor General further required an unseemly, expeditious haste. But Curtis-Bennett ought to have insisted, in view of the judge's earlier intervention and the prosecution's tendentious emphasis on the poison plot in the novel:

> *Solicitor General*: Did she [Bella Donna] arrange a plot to poison her husband by slow doses in order that she might get away to Baroudi?
>
> *Edith Thompson*: I cannot say if she arranged it. There was as plot right at the end of the book.
>
> *Solicitor General*: There is a plot, which is really the plot of the story, to poison her husband, without anybody finding out what she was doing?

Edith Thompson: It is a matter of opinion whether that is absolutely the plot, is it not?

Mrs Thompson was struggling desperately here to disentangle herself from a web of distortion spun from a throwaway remark made in one of her letters. How could she explain in court the complex human interactions that made her pretend to be a would-be assassin? Could she simply step out of herself, with her lover facing her a few yards across the well of the court, and admit that she was playing a part to keep him?

In his cogent address to the jury, Curtis-Bennett advised them to remember Edith's private view of Bella Donna (cited below) as expressed in the letter of 13 July: 'Fortunately we have Mrs Thompson's view of Bella Donna.' Because he sensed that the trial judge was against them, Curtis-Bennett did not wish to antagonise him further by demanding that the novel be submitted to the jury. Since in this case the Crown was allowed the last word, and again pointed the jury to the digitalin passage, the judge might have been expected to set the record straight. He had virtually undertaken to do so by suggesting that evidence about the novel used in court would be enough. But he did not know the novel. When he summarised its relevance in his charge to the jury – and it needs to be quoted in its entirety for its disturbing inadequacy – he noted:

> 'It must be remembered that digitalin is a cumulative poison, and that the same dose harmless if taken once, yet frequently repeated, becomes deadly.' I should not think you should bother much about what is in the book called 'Bella Donna.' The only point about it is, it is the case of a woman – nobody suggested she was like this woman, or the man was like this man. It is the case, admitted on oath by herself, that there is at the end of the book somebody poisoning her husband, or trying to poison her husband. 'It must be remembered that digitalin is a cumulative poison, and that the dose harmless if taken once, yet frequently repeated, becomes deadly.' And there is this remarkable statement – 'The above passage I have just come across in a book I am reading, 'Bella Donna,' by Robert Hichens. Is it any use? . . . I'd like you to read 'Bella Donna' first, you will learn something from it to help us; then you can read the "Fruitful Vine."' No doubt the letter about the 'Fruitful Vine' was something similar; they write chiefly about so-called heroes and heroines, probably wicked people, which no doubt accounts for a great many of these tragedies.

This gross misrepresentation, quite apart from its erroneous assumptions, not the least of which concerns Edith's letter on *The Fruitful Vine*,

wholly ignored the defence's case for a fair hearing on the crucial point
of the novel's legitimacy as evidence. For this is what Edith Thompson
wrote about Bella Donna, in a letter (13 July 1922) only ever intended
for her lover's eyes and therefore speaking from the heart:

> About Bella Donna – no I dont agree with you about her darlint – I hate her
> – hate to think of her – I dont think other people made her what she was –
> that sensual pleasure loving greedy Bella Donna was always there. If she
> had originally been different – a good man like Nigel would have altered
> her darlint – she never knew what it was to be denied anything – she never
> knew 'goodness' as you and I know it – she was never interested in a good
> man – or any man unless he could appease her sensual nature. I don't think
> she could have been happy with nothing – except Baroudi on a desert
> island she liked – no loved and lived for his money or what it could give her
> – the luxury of his yacht the secrecy with which he acted all bought with his
> money – that's what she liked.
>
> Yes she was clever – I admire the cleverness – but she was cunning there
> is a difference darlint, I don't admire that – I certainly don't think she
> would ever have killed Nigel with her hands – she would have been found
> out – she didn't like that did she? being found out – it was that secret
> cunning in Baroudi that she admired so much – the cunning that matched
> her own.
>
> If she had loved Baroudi enough she could have gone to him – but she
> liked the security of being Nigel's wife – for the monetary assets it held.
>
> She doesn't seem a woman to me – she seems abnormal – a monster
> utterly selfish and self living.
>
> Darlint this is where we differ about women.
>
> I usually stand up for them *against* you and in this case its the reverse but
> honestly darlint I dont call her a woman – she is absolutely unnatural in
> every sense.

Bella Donna is here called 'abnormal – a monster utterly selfish and
self-living . . . she is absolutely unnatural in every sense'. Edith
professed to hate Ruby Chepstow for her indecent sensuality and her
cunning, which allowed her coolly to contemplate her husband's
demise. Freddy, it appears, had expressed cautious regard for Bella
Donna's cleverness and had ventured to suggest that she might even
have dared to kill Armine with her hands. He was pandering to his
lover's presumed automatic allegiance to the older woman and her
predicament in relation to a younger husband and lover. Here he
miscalculated. If anything Edith Thompson felt annoyed by the
simple-minded assumptions that her moral sympathy would auto-

matically lie with the temptress. If the judge had even acknowledged the sentiments on Bella Donna quoted above, which had been submitted by the defence and were read out by Curtis-Bennett in Court, it is at least possible that the jury would have deemed there to be a genuine case of doubt with regard to the correspondence. Here at last, in this story of life and fiction, were two irrefutable pieces of mutually illuminating evidence: the novel and the commentary on its moral bearings, both on the page for the world to judge. Instead a grossly excerpted and prejudicial version of a part of the commentary was substituted for the whole.

After her first quizzing on *Bella Donna* on Friday 8 December, Edith Thompson is challenged to explain the five-year period which recurs as a stipulation through the letters like a sinister refrain. Shearman intervenes when she defines it as the time agreed to wait for her to secure a position. He observes: 'The other witness's story was that they wanted to commit suicide, and he said 'Put it off five years', which seems to be the only sensible thing I have heard.' After this damaging and partisan statement which leaves the young widow confounded, the defence redirects her to her last evening out with her husband. Once again she is made to relive the agonising night of 3 October.

She breaks down sobbing, falling forward on her hands when she repeats the doctor's telling her that Percy was 'dead', that she could not therefore take him home. For a long moment the court is silent save for the woman weeping in the witness-box. When she recovers she raises a tear-stained face and explains that she could not believe it. She also calls into further doubt the police's version of the confrontation in Ilford of Bywaters and herself, and maintains that she made her second and true statement *after* Wensley (it was in fact Hall) had informed her of Bywaters's alleged full confession. This takes even the editor of the *Notable British Trials* series by surprise, and he acknowledges that the whole thing seemed odd.

It is about 3 p.m. when the Crown starts its questioning of the witness. Their opening gambit is to invalidate the sympathy that the widow has temporarily elicited from the jury in her bereaved collapse. Surely she is a liar, the Crown implies; did she not do her utmost to mislead the police by a controlled charade? Had she not lied even in her alleged moments of hysteria, as she plunged through the night towards Miss Pittard and Mr Clevely and told them that 'some one flew past'? For over half an hour Inskip bullies her on her lie to the police. He wins this first round by sheer persistence and equivocation. By pretending to be utterly incredulous at some of her replies, he makes the complex seem obvious and the truth so many lies. His task is greatly assisted by the fact that the lovers have lied themselves into several corners unnecessarily. The date of their first kissing is unambiguously established in Edith's letters. But since Bywaters has denied its applicability, she has no choice now but to follow suit. Phrasing his question with judge and jury in mind, Inskip asks:

When did you first begin to address him as your lover?

Edith Thompson: It is just what you mean by 'your lover'.

Inskip: The terms in which a woman does not write to any man except her husband?

Edith Thompson: I cannot remember.

The linchpin of the Crown's strategy for the next two hours is to expose the adulterous couple's deceit over the issue of divorce and suicide, before proving them guilty of a conspiracy to murder and of the killing itself. Why, Inskip asks, did she resort to such secrecy if what she claimed to have wanted to do was to convince Thompson of the need to let her go? Evidence of the clandestine relationship with her lover would surely have produced the ardently desired separation? Edith fights back valiantly, and points out that if her husband was convinced that she and Freddy would get together after a divorce, he would have been that much less likely to let her go.

It is in this context that Edith becomes befuddled by a series of non sequiturs from Inskip. She finds it impossible to disentangle herself from the net woven around one of her statements inviting Bywaters to bring the poison which she would administer to the husband. She explains that she wished to retain the boy's love at any cost, hence this missive. But Shearman intervenes and presses her to explain further how she intended to assist Bywaters in the murder. She refuses to comply with his request, and he warns her about her lack of co-operation. It is immediately after the judge's interruption and under pressure that she implies that Bywaters suggested that she should poison her husband. Her letter of 11 April 1922 headed 'Don't keep this piece' is now cited as further evidence of a conspiracy.[1] Then Inskip points at Bywaters in the dock and says:

[1]The letter is discussed in its context on pp. 104–105.

You are representing that this young man was seriously suggesting that you should poison and kill your husband?
Edith Thompson: I did not suggest it.

Shearman again chips in here and answers the Solicitor General's question for her:

Give him something in his food; you answered my question a little while ago that it was to give him something to make him ill?
Edith Thompson: That is what I surmised, that I should give him something so that when he had a heart attack he would not be able to resist it.

As one contemporary sitting behind the dock with the press noted, 'a sound like a rustle of wind shuddered through the Old Bailey Court' at this astonishing admission. It had been prefaced by 'I surmised' and even if the two accused had ever seriously considered the proposition in question, she knew well that Percy was a shameless hypochondriac, and that he hardly suffered from a dangerous heart condition. In the immediate aftermath of this costly lapse of concentration, Edith is left in even greater distress and recoils when the judge leans her way and, in a manner which illustrates his bias, asks:

One moment, I do not want to be mistaken. Did I take you down rightly as saying, 'I wanted him to think I was willing to take my husband's life'?
Edith Thompson: I wanted him to think I was willing to do what he suggested.
Judge: That is to take your husband's life?
Edith Thompson: Not necessarily.

Edith's final statement of the day, shortly after this, is to concede that she and Bywaters gave each other the impression that what they hoped for was that Thompson should not be able to recover from one of his 'heart attacks' through his having taken something that would make him ill.

During her evidence Freddy Bywaters, who earlier kept his cool with impressive self-control, has appeared agitated and strained by listening hard. His forehead puckers as he concentrates, and he nervously passes his hand through his hair as he witnesses her agony and her blunders. He probably tries to catch her eye as she returns crying and exhausted to the dock. It is to be doubted that she sees anything very much. She has spent four hours in the witness-box.

Saturday 9 December: A very pale Edith Thompson is assisted by a wardress into the witness-box. Her widow's clothes and black hat with its sweeping plumes set off the vulnerability of her face as she moves through this blind white place. She steals a furtive glance at Bywaters, who misses it and is examining his hands. She is again handed the typed pad of her letters and immediately finds herself pressed on further suspicions of poison. Her answers today are even more indistinct than yesterday. The Crown, however, fails to maintain its momentum and therefore turns to Hichens's novel *Bella Donna*. Had Edith been more knowledgeable in the ways of the law and of the witness-box in particular, she might even now have exposed the weaknesses of the Crown's case. Instead she wearily confines herself to repudiating Inskip's preposterous misreadings.

The measure of the Solicitor General's moral limitations is gleaned from his premeditated misreading of the sentence, 'He's still well,' in Edith's last letter to Freddy. 'Is "he" your husband?' Inskip asks. Edith replies, 'No. That refers to a bronze monkey I have.' The implication by Inskip that 'he' refers to a 'still well' Percy Thompson who is failing to submit to any of the poisonous treatments administered by Edith is implausible and downright dishonest.

It takes Inskip less than an hour to complete the cross-examination. Curtis-Bennett rises. He puts the court right on the monkey and other points in the same letter, and finally asks why, over the last summer, she wrote the way she did:

Edith Thompson: I thought he was gradually drifting away from me.

Curtis-Bennett: Did you still love him very much?

The court is hushed by the intimacy of the question, and all eyes bend on her and on him. She sits totally still, closes her eyes, finally nods, and is barely heard to breathe, 'I did.' She looks stunned; her face is shivering; she is biting her lips. A few minutes later she blindly gropes her way back towards the dock. Tears are streaming down her face, and she leans heavily on the nurse in attendance. As soon as she has sunk back into her chair, she buries her head in her hands and, without restraint, sobs loudly.

Through this spasm of unleashed emotion penetrates the name of her sister, and shortly afterwards Avis Graydon's clear voice carries through the impressed silence of the court. Avis stands up firm and exudes elegance and courage. Edith's eyes have come to rest fixedly on the sister who tries to exonerate her to the best of her ability, by refusing to identify the opium tincture bottle and by vigorously denying that Thompson ever complained of Bywaters in the presence of the Graydons. Avis says that this 'is pure imagination on my sister's part'. When she assures Curtis-Bennett that there is no truth in that story at all, she thumps the witness-box with her fist for emphasis. She also confirms her father's account of their last evening with Bywaters whom she calls 'Freddy'. Avis's remarkable performance is followed by poor Mrs Graydon entering the stand. As a mother watching the ordeal of her favourite child, she is on the verge of a nervous collapse. Now, looking across at Edith from the box, she mutely pleads, one imagines, with the powers that be to save her child. She is dressed completely in black, and her hands are clasped in front of her. She tries to remove her gloves, but in vain. Her fingers are too weak to pull them off her clammy palms. In the end she leaves them on. Her evidence lasts a few minutes only, time enough for her to bear out the claim that Edith indeed had a bump on her head when she fell on 3 October.

The witnesses have all been called. Cecil Whiteley rises shortly after Mrs Graydon has relinquished the stand. He is not the most gifted member of the Bar. At times he appears thin-lipped and dispassionate. But on this occasion he will give his utmost in what will be remembered as a short but punchy address to the jury, which with considerable mastery will foreground all the salient points in his client's defence. Facts, he realises, will weigh heavily in favour of the Crown. He therefore will tap the case's fantasy elements and plead Bywaters's love for Mrs Thompson and his youth:

> Judge this young man as you yourselves would be judged. One life has already been sacrificed in this sordid and horrible drama. Is there to be yet another?

He points out that the tragedy of Bywaters's predicament is compounded by the fact that that 'there is sitting next to him in that box one who is charged jointly with him, one who is dearer to him than his own life'. Hence his counsel is not allowed to state anything in his client's defence that could damage the chances of acquittal of the woman. Already Mrs Bywaters and Mrs Graydon are in tears. The thrust of Whiteley's argument is to reduce the charge to one of either justifiable homicide or manslaughter. After all, he notes, Bywaters persuasively maintained that he was not fooled by Mrs Thompson's letters which in any case date back to over four months before the killing. After receiving the last of the letters used by the Crown to prove a homicidal collusion, Bywaters in fact prepared to break off the relationship. His solitary walk to Ilford that night from the Graydons' home was intended to settle the issue of separation and ended in a killing almost by default. He aptly deals with the knife, so competently in fact that the judge and the Crown decide that they will have to address it with special emphasis in their speeches.

Quite properly Whiteley notes with concern that the Crown in this case enjoys the unusual privilege of addressing the jury last. He expresses a fervent desire that this anomalous practice may be changed soon and that the questioning of prisoners in police stations should also be subject to a more satisfactory code of conduct. It is while Whiteley is drawing to his conclusion, and raising the emotional temperature in the court by pleading the boy's youth and foolishness, that for the first time Bywaters's composure cracks. His eyes glisten with tears as he hears his counsel's final words asking the court in his name to believe, and

> by your verdict to proclaim to the whole world that in all this history I am not an assassin I am no murderer.

It is 2.45 p.m. Sir Henry Curtis-Bennett rises to attempt the Herculean task of rescuing the woman from the clutches of the law. He is hugely talented and very theatrical. Shearman loathes his dramatic antics. From the outset it is clear that the judge will try to hamper the defence case at every juncture. A gamble on a point of law by Curtis-Bennett early on immediately gives the judge an opening to put the defence counsel on the spot. He tries to suggest that, on the evidence available, Edith Thompson cannot in law be charged as 'principal in the second degree'. There is no precedent for it. The judge dissents vehemently, and Curtis-Bennett is mildly discomfited. He proceeds however with verve and points out that there is no evidence to indicate that his client knew anything at all about what was going to happen exactly on that night of 3 October. If only the Crown were honest about their case and its direction, they could not possibly mislead jury and court the way they are doing. He remarks that his client inhabits a world of fantasy to such an extent that it renders her an extraordinary person. He compares the case itself to a play or opera, and pleads for the same kind of suspension of belief in the jury that would be extended to fiction. Counsel then refers to the various time-spans mentioned in the letters and adduces them as irrefutable supporting evidence for the lovers' suicide pact. One of his trump cards and one which he repeatedly produces is the prosecution's evidence elicited from its own witness, Spilsbury. The absence of any trace of poison and glass should conclusively point to the woman's innocence, he notes.

How all too easy it is to work a guilty retrospective pattern into events of the past, Curtis-Bennett suggests, or to draw rash conclusions from the mere impressions gained from listening to the putative contents of novels such as *Bella Donna*! Does not the accused describe the woman in it as a monster? Curtis-Bennett is in full swing when Shearman indicates that the time has arrived for the court to adjourn. His parting shot to the jury sends a chill down the spines of defence counsel and of the accused. The judge sternly warns the jury that they are 'trying a vulgar and common crime', they are not, he stresses, 'listening to a play from the stalls of a theatre'. With this—improper—direction still ringing in his ears, Curtis-Bennett spends a few more minutes conferring with his client. Whether he manages to soothe her fears is not known, but he still has at least one and a half hours to go and will put them to good use.

While the lovers spend a very anxious and exhausted Sunday, the members of the jury which is trying them are seeking spiritual guidance at St Paul's. In a secluded part of the cathedral, temporarily out of sight from a posse of journalists who stalk them at the court and at the Manchester in Aldersgate, a mere few yards from where the accused woman used to work, the jury is attending the morning service. After an early lunch nine of them, excluding the woman and two of the men, go for a three-hour ride on a motor coach journey which takes them through Epsom and Richmond.

In the meantime the queue is already forming outside the Central Criminal Court for Monday's session when a verdict is confidently expected.

*

Monday 11 December 1922: Curtis-Bennett briefly recapitulates, thus recovering some of the ground lost by the adjournment on Saturday. He again reminds the jury of the ease with which confusion arises: the monkey, for example, assumed a positively sinister meaning when the Crown pretended to mistake it for Thompson: 'Does that not show the danger of guesswork when people's letters are being looked at?' he asks of the jury. And yet 'letters' provide the sole evidence against Mrs Thompson, and even they do not remotely tie her in with the killing which happened that night in Ilford. The Thompsons took the standard route from the station to their house. This was not a seedy back alley killing, in which the wife lured the unsuspecting husband to his death. He also protests against the sham of the 'meeting' of the accused in the police station and urges the jurors not to let themselves be swayed into finding the accused woman guilty on the basis of the suspected conversations that may or may not have happened in the tea lounge at Fuller's. It is ultimately on a shrewd combination of reason and sentiment that Curtis-Bennett rests his case at 11.30 a.m., after nearly three hours. Intellectually his rhetoric and lucidity have proved formidable. Edith Thompson could hardly have found a stronger champion in court.

The Crown's performance is by contrast lacklustre and only half the length of Sir Henry's Ciceronian oration. Furthermore it so shamelessly distorts the evidence on two points in particular that one must wonder why the judge let it pass. Inskip draws attention again to the fact that there are discrepancies between the lovers' first and second statements to the police and that by implication they are both untrustworthy liars. He pretends not to be concerned over the absence of concrete evidence connecting the accused with Thompson's death and prefers instead to reiterate over and over again the obviousness of his case. It is then that, incredibly, he argues that Spilsbury's forensic evidence *bears out* the prosecution's case: 'it would have been wrong to have left you [the jury] with the impression that an injury must necessarily have been found if glass was used.' What's more, he maintains now that 'I called him as much to assist the defence as the Crown'. Such disingenuousness and particularly the statement that 'the administration of glass, even in large pieces, would' not necessarily cause lesions in the intestines should at once have been exposed. The court's failure to do so severely weighs the odds against the accused. A mere ten minutes later Inskip once again alleges a grossly misleading fact, that the woman in the witness-box admitted that

'Don't forget what we talked in the tea room . . .' meant murder. In fact she specifically repudiated the imputation of the Solicitor General and replied to his question, 'Was that in connection with the same matter, the idea of poisoning your husband?' – 'No, that was not. What we talked of in the tea room was getting me a post abroad'.

In the end it seems that the Crown's case appeared so weak to the judge that he felt it needed a helping hand. Even as Inskip is summing up, Shearman is jotting down notes for his forthcoming address to the jury, including the tell-tale remark: 'great love . . . nonsense: Great and wholesome disgust. You will bear in mind that illicit love may lead to crime, but you must not of course let your disgust carry you too far'. He adds more of the same observations. As Shearman's advice was sought by the Home Secretary before he finally decided against a reprieve, such vengefulness by the trial judge appears doubly immoral and reckless in view of its consequences. It is nearly noon. Shortly after his opening remarks Shearman invites the jury to disregard two specific points from Sir Henry's address: firstly, the allegation about the lack of precedent for Mrs Thompson's being charged without being accused of sharing in the actual act of killing; and secondly, his alleged reference to the Deity.[1] The judge reminds the jurors of their duty and of the fact that the supreme penalty is none of their concern. They will decide only a matter of guilt and innocence. His charge to the jury concerns itself with Bywaters first and is ruthlessly edited to the disadvantage of the accused. He draws the attention of the jurors once again to the knife and highlights the discrepancies between the boy's first and second statements and his sworn evidence. How can any testimony of his be believed? Look at the knife and remember that there were no real signs of a struggle taking place! Even before he reaches the stage of dealing with Mrs Thompson, Shearman intimates that her cry of fear, despair and shock, 'Oh don't, oh don't' was heard by Webber when the salesman finally arrived outside his house from the upstairs bedroom some five minutes after the assault. The truth of course is that the screams were so loud that inside his curtained bedroom Webber heard them and consequently rushed down.

The court adjourns for lunch. Then it is the woman's turn. The judge has already loaded the dice against her by discrediting Webber's evidence as proof of the woman's good faith. He will revert to the

[1] Curtis-Bennett never referred to the Deity in the manner attributed to him by Shearman, but had merely noted that 'Thank God, this is not a Court of morals'. His remark was certainly not intended to frighten the jury, as the judge alleged.

midnight hour of 3 October. Before doing so he needs to comb through and annotate the letters which perpetrated 'this insensate silly affection'. Commenting on the letter concerning *The Fruitful Vine* which was not put in evidence and which he has not read, the judge nevertheless speculates confidently that it is 'something similar' to *Bella Donna*: 'they [these authors] write chiefly about so-called heroes and their heroines, probably wicked people, which no doubt accounts for a great many of these tragedies'. After warming up, Shearman prepares for the kill. Webber's evidence about hearing the woman scream is now conflated with his arrival on the scene of the crime and overhearing the doctor ask the woman whether her husband was taken ill. For the second time round, Shearman makes sure that he calls in doubt altogether Mrs Thompson's screaming. Her hysteria, he hints, is itself open to question. After all, this highly strung woman at this crucial point of crisis proved quite capable of lying to Miss Pittard, the doctor and the police. Is it not possible that her terror was partly put on? Thus the judge is sowing the seeds of suspicion even more in the minds of the jury. The jury, possessed of Bywaters's knife and his overcoat, retires. The time is 3.32 p.m. Outside it is getting dark.

The jury has been out for two hours when a commotion in court signals its return and indicates that it has reached a verdict. The time, shown by the hands of the clock under the public gallery, is 5.43 p.m. The jury files back into court through the narrow doorway. The woman among them enters last. She is very pale. The actual debate has been short. The reading of the letters has taken up most of the time, and it was the alleged moral degeneracy of the correspondence that made the jury find Edith Thompson guilty. In the words of one juror thirty years later: 'it was my duty to read them to the members of the jury . . . "Nauseous" is hardly strong enough to describe their contents . . . The jury performed a painful duty, but Mrs Thompson's letters were her own condemnation.'

The judge enters and focuses his eyes on the dock. The prisoners are still in the cells. The court is thick and heavy with silence. Then at last a blanched Bywaters appears. He moves towards the front of the dock and looks up at the judge unflinchingly. A few moments later Edith Thompson arrives, like Bywaters stumbling to the front of the dock. On each side of her she is supported by a wardress, as she is barely able to stand. Her face is pale and her eyes are glassy. She is clutching the edge of the dock. Her hands are trembling and her wedding-ring on her left hand glitters in the soft electric light of the court. The small finger on her right hand is pressed painfully far back. She doesn't seem to notice. Her mother and father, brother and sister, aunt and uncle as well as Carlton, the Thompsons and others are present in the well of the court. The Graydons' eyes are anxiously fixed on their daughter. In their hearts they are convinced that later she will be walking home with them and the dreadful nightmare of the last three months will be swallowed up by the march of time.

Within seconds the foreman of the jury has shattered their illusions by announcing that both prisoners are guilty. He fails to add any recommendation to mercy. The Clerk of Arraigns asks Bywaters whether there is anything he wishes to say. He flings back his head and slowly, clearly, speaks into the awesome silence:

I say the verdict of the jury is wrong. Edith Thompson is not guilty. I am no murderer. I am not an assassin.

A slight tremor shakes his voice when, for the last time in his life, he speaks her name in her presence. Asked the same question in turn she replies in a thin and faltering voice: 'I am not guilty.' The chaplain now places a little square and black cap on the judge's head. Turning to Bywaters, Shearman peers at the youth over his glasses. Then, staring down at the piece of paper, he mechanically reads out the words of the death sentence. The chaplain breathes a barely audible 'Amen', before the judge bends his eyes towards the woman.

Every eye in court is on her and already dozens of female voices are heard crying for pity of the lost boy. The judge sentences Edith Thompson to death. The Clerk of the Court asks whether she has anything 'to say in stay of execution?' The pale woman in the dock trembles visibly. No sound emanates from her. A whisper ripples through the gallery: if the woman is by any chance with child, seemingly a possibility after the courtroom innuendos about the nature of her affair with the young sailor, then she cannot be made to suffer death – the sentence will automatically be commuted to penal servitude for life.

Already the warders are pulling Bywaters by the sleeves to force him out of the dock. But he resists, his eyes rest dazedly on her, and it is at the precise moment that he agrees to be led downstairs that an agonised scream tears through the air of the courtroom: 'I am not guilty; oh God, I am not guilty.' The woman slumps. Bywaters is taken downstairs. Avis Graydon's eyes fasten on her sister's figure, so close and yet so far. She notices how the wardresses try to wrench free Edith's fingers from the rail of the dock. She is now sobbing hysterically, and they lift her out of the chair and virtually carry her 'weeping and wailing' down the staircase into the cells. Eventually the pitiful sounds fade away.

A stunned court barely takes in the judge's thanking the jury for doing their duty. Another piercing cry was heard as the judge passed sentence. From the middle of the court Edith's mother groaned: 'She is my child – my child. They dare not harm her.' The other mother has spent part of her day in a comatose state, drifting between the inside of Court 1 and the outer hall. She breaks down sobbing when the verdict is delivered. Relatives are seen to crowd around her now and give her what comfort they can. Judge and jury prepare to leave. Bywaters's counsel are still sitting at their tables in disbelief. They must have suspected the likely outcome of the trial, but they still find it hard to accept. One of them is blindly gazing at his propelling pencil.

Outside in Old Bailey the crowds are gathering to see the prisoners emerge. They throng the street in droves, and mounted police push them back to clear the road for traffic. The cars which for the next half hour circulate in Old Bailey are police vehicles which temporarily keep the curious at bay.

Inside the building the ever-faithful Bessie is comforted by one of the many barristers who have been swarming in and out of Court 1 over the past few days to catch a glimpse of the case already famous as 'Thompson & Bywaters'. Bessie vehemently protests her friend's innocence, and he, smiling sadly, says, 'the devil himself knoweth not the heart of man'. Bessie remains unconvinced. The devil might not know the heart of Edith Thompson, but she does. Earlier in the day, fate had seemed to her to step into Newgate Street when, in the courtroom queue, she met a former acquaintance who was barely recognisable because he had become a derelict. He had attended Kensington Avenue School, and he had been in love with Edith Graydon; she had consented to keep a place for him in her heart. He returned from the sea in the winter of 1916 to find that she had gone to · Southend on her honeymoon. Now he was witnessing her suffering and hoping to sell his seat for sustenance.

A few minutes only have elapsed since the prisoners, now under sentence of death, left the court. Whiteley is summoned downstairs. A downcast but resolute Bywaters warmly thanks him for his valiant defence and advice throughout. His mother has joined him for a brief farewell. The Graydons have meanwhile been allowed downstairs to see Edith. They are devastated, but bravely pretend otherwise, as she will need every ounce of strength that they can give her. She is weeping hysterically when they see her. Two policemen as well as Curtis-Bennett are with her in the tiny cell. Suddenly she looks up into those familiar faces and rushes towards them, nearly blinded by tears. She catches hold of her father's coat and hangs on to him. The police immediately disengage them. Pushed back and firmly kept away from either parent, Edith is reaching out her arms to her father and crying: 'Take me home, Dad!' Overwhelmed by grief the Graydons remain speechless. While their daughter's cry still rings in their ears, they are bundled out of the building. Their last impression of Edith is of her arms stretched out. The precise moment would sear itself forever into the memory of her sister. Fifty years later Avis Graydon could not recall this scene without crying.

Her father is so badly shaken that his brother takes him across to the Magpie and Stump for a whisky. The mother, once the dominant figure in the family, clings to her husband like a child. Journalists and photographers still pack the street and, one imagines, the little pub. One of the photographers tries to catch a snap of Avis, but she covers her face with a fur hat which Edith bought her as a present. Unabashed the photographer kneels down to get a shot from underneath, and is nearly stampeded by the terrified young woman. It is 7 p.m. when the Graydons travel home to Shakespeare Crescent. By the time they reach No. 231 their prisoner-daughter has already arrived at Holloway in a taxi. When she gets there at a quarter past six, the governor has left instructions for her to be made comfortable and, if necessary, to spend the night in the prison hospital.

Bywaters is now transferred to Pentonville where he will occupy the same cell as Crippen and Seddon. The governor of Brixton was in court all day, as he would be surrendering his remand prisoner to the authorities at Pentonville in the case of a guilty verdict. He anxiously hoped that the jury would recommend the boy to mercy. He knew that the youth trusted him. Immediately after reaching the cells when they were shaking hands and the governor wished him luck, Bywaters urgently whispered a request to him to relay a last message to Edith Thompson: 'BB and PG', meaning 'be brave' and 'pray God'. The governor assured him that he would do his best. In fact he would write at once to the Prison Commissioners requesting permission to do so on the grounds that 'It was a last request & to him may be of deep sentiment.' The reply reads: 'This cannot be permitted. It is hoped that you did not lead him to think that it could be.' She will not get this message, but there will be others and many will in the end percolate through in spite of the hawks in the Prison Commission.

Tuesday 12 December 1922 Pentonville – 2.30 p.m.: Mrs Lilian Bywaters and her daughter Florrie visit Freddy in prison. He smiles wanly at them, as he takes his seat between two warders at the end of a long table, some ten feet away from them. He has not shaved and is wearing mandatory prison uniform. He is now number 4153. He is very sad. The stoicism which allowed him to bear up throughout his ordeal at the Old Bailey has deserted him. He still manages to hold back his tears, even though his voice repeatedly chokes as he goes through the evidence again with his mother. To her at that moment he looks 'just like a great big boy'. He praises Whiteley and at first refrains from saying anything against Mrs Thompson. Then, suddenly, he remarks: 'I never imagined she would have turned against me as she did in the witness-box', and his voice falters. Even this momentary reaction to her evidence under cross-examination – where she appeared to intimate that his suggestion of poisoning her husband initially shocked her – is quickly dispelled. By tomorrow night he will again have briefed his counsel specifically to safeguard Edith Thompson's interests in the Appeals Court, at whatever cost to himself. This first of twenty-eight remaining daily visits passes, and the tearful family prepare to part. Before she leaves Pentonville Mrs Bywaters reassures her son that she will do everything in her power to get him off. Eight hundred policemen have already declared a willingness to sign the petition for a reprieve, she tells him, and his solicitor is hoping to draft the text of a petition with her help. When Mrs Bywaters asks to kiss Freddy goodbye, permission is refused. It will be granted during the next visit though, and from then on.

As this parent and sibling stumble back into the Caledonian Road, over at Holloway, less than a mile away, Mrs Graydon and Avis visit Edith. She is in the prison hospital and under sedation. The guards accompany the women through the dark corridors of the building. They dimly realise that Edith now lies in a different part of the prison.

Then they reach the narrow hospital cell. Edith is lying propped up in bed trying to read a book from the prison library. At 10 a.m. this morning she has been visited by the governor. She has slept well and told him this: 'I have had the best night I have had for a month, in fact I slept almost all night.' The governor has informed her of the special dietary privileges accorded condemned prisoners. She is keenly interested and has expressed a desire to be allowed to smoke. This is readily granted. After the visit, she settles down for the next few hours waiting for Avis and her mother to come.

She rises to meet them, but is cautioned by the wardress to stay put. They are allowed to sit at the cell door, no closer. The family and the prisoner try hard to keep off the case, and at no point is Bywaters mentioned. The only reference to the trial occurs when a pained and ill-looking Edith remarks:

> It's terrible, mother, to be in here for something I never did and knew nothing about. I cannot believe I have been found guilty.

To this the mother replies that her father will do everything to secure her release. All three of them stake their hopes on the appeal next week. Does she need anything? 'No, there is nothing, I have everything I need.' The moment of parting is imminent. The mother and her two daughters break down completely when it comes.

While the two Graydon women make their solitary way to East Ham, Edith receives a message from the governor: would she be wanting to see a Miss Ida Burton from 778 Barking Road, Plaistow? She may vaguely remember who Ida Burton is, but declines. Miss Burton is informed of this by the governor in his office. She is disappointed, and he explains to her the procedures for seeing condemned prisoners. If he is sympathetic and even solicitous, it is because he is impressed by her urgency and her written reference from a certain Canon Palmer of Ilford. How important Canon Palmer will become in the final stages of this story no one can have anticipated, least of all the governor. In the meantime he patiently attends to Burton's explanation that she and Mrs Thompson were schoolfriends together before the war in Manor Park. Why doesn't she write in then, he suggests, telling Mrs Thompson of this? Perhaps she will then relent. Miss Burton eagerly accepts the invitation. Later this week she will be writing to Mrs Thompson alluding to their schooldays. Edith will agree to see her, and Miss Ida Burton, in the company of Mrs Graydon and Avis, will visit at Holloway on 1 January 1923.

It is dark when mother and daughter enter Shakespeare Crescent arm-in-arm and walk its weary length. The house is almost under siege from reporters eager for a shot of the family. The two women bravely ignore them and enter the dark premises. The mother puts on the kettle for a cup of tea, and then they sit waiting for the father and brother to return from work. The little home which once held such happiness enhances their sense of enclosed loneliness. Every corner is redolent with memories of the luckless child now lying in a London gaol. On the hall table telegrams are piling up already. They have been flooding in since early in the morning. All of them express their deepest sympathy for the suffering family. There is among the Graydons' mail a letter from the editor of the *Daily Sketch*: 'could they let their photographer into the house to take pictures of the parents reading the telegrams? The paper is preparing to launch a massive campaign and petition to rescue the two lovers from the scaffold. The Graydons' limited co-operation would be appreciated'. Reluctantly the family allow the *Daily Sketch* inside. The two photos which feature on the front page of the paper's first edition of the morning of Wednesday 13 December 1922 show the entire family except Bill and Harold in a frozen pose, looking not unlike a late Victorian nuclear clan. The second one portrays the two parents scanning the telegrams of sympathy and condolence. Inset in the picture is the smiling face of young Edith Graydon on holiday in Ilfracombe, contrasting starkly with her mother's anguished and drawn looks, as she pretends to read the pieces of paper in front of her. On the same page adjacent to it the paper shows Mrs Bywaters writing her appeal for Freddy.

The Graydons have not even taken their dinner when the bell rings again and a well-spoken young man gently requests permission to enter. He had earlier left them his card and explained briefly why he wanted to see them. He was a journalist, but one very different from the others. Their first encounter with him would confirm this. His name was Beverley Nichols. For this talented dandy whose natural 1920s haunts coincided with those of the Bright Young People, and who was more at ease with Nellie Melba and the genteel decadence of the Bankheads, Beatons and Cunards, the story of 'Thompson & Bywaters' would form an unsettling landmark. It was his first assignment on the *Weekly Dispatch*. He was fresh down from Cambridge and found himself plunged into Court 1 at the Old Bailey. His horror at the proceedings in court was compounded by his irresistible attraction to the young woman in the dock. She unfailingly reminded him of Diana Cooper. The timbre of her voice and its barely perceptible cockney vowels struck a sympathetic chord in his heart. He witnessed her collapse on Monday and he remembered how years earlier he had burst into uncontrollable tears in a cinema, when it was announced to a jubilant house that Crippen had been sentenced to death. Now here he was about to visit the parents of the tragic woman whose suffering he had witnessed from the press benches at the Central Criminal Court. After leaving his note for them, he strolled through the wet and wintry streets of Manor Park. Perhaps he recalled that these were *her* streets, where she had played and in which she grew up.

When her father lets him in Nichols seems to be almost as upset as the older man, who is crying and shaking his head, as if continuously in despair. Then he says: 'To think that this should happen to people like us . . . !' He leads Nichols into the sitting room. Newenham and the two women greet him quietly. The brother was in tears earlier, and can barely talk. Only Avis retains her calm, as Nichols silently notes with respectful approval. He has come to propose that for a substantial remuneration, the Graydons contribute to his paper the life story of their daughter. He realises that they need the money badly to campaign for Edith's life. He knows how upright they are, and that they would never stoop to 'selling' their daughter's story for money. In the end they are swayed by Nichols's ingenuousness and their desperate need for finance. There will be five instalments by W. E. Graydon, and his writing will be assisted by a ghost writer, probably Nichols himself. In the end only three will materialise, because the father will be unable to carry on, as his daughter's death approaches. But the paper, as part of its tribute to the family, will treat Edith Thompson with sympathy and protest her innocence to the end.

In the meantime and over in Upper Norwood, Lilian Bywaters has completed her first letter of appeal. It is headed 'A Mother's Appeal to the Mothers of the Nation':

> I am appealing to the hearts of all the mothers of the nation to give me their help in getting a reprieve for my boy. You who have dear boys of your own will I am sure understand the terrible agony I am now suffering, and my great anxiety for his life to be spared. His father gave his life for you & yours, don't let them take my boy from me. From a brokenhearted mother.
> LILIAN BYWATERS

On Wednesday 13 December Bywaters is visited by his solicitor to lodge the appeal and, later, by his mother. He reissues specific instructions to his counsel to the effect that nothing must be said in his defence that could possibly harm Edith Thompson. During the mother's visit he compliments her on how improved her looks are since yesterday. He does not mention Edith, but is excited to learn of the *Daily Sketch* petition. Earlier in the morning Mrs Bywaters has read in the paper under the headline 'Save Young Bywaters' that the offices and switchboards of the *Daily Sketch* have been inundated with anxious pleas for Bywaters's life. The paper has printed a remarkable letter by 'One Who Understands' appealing for it to lead the way in a reprieve petition. The *Daily Sketch* has promised that in view of such high and generous public feeling it will proceed at once with the printing of petition forms. They will be available in London, Manchester, Liverpool and other big cities, at the offices of the *Daily Sketch* and in cinemas, kiosks, theatres and at Tube stations. The petition will be advertised by large bills with the words 'Bywaters' reprieve, sign here'. Hearing of this nationwide groundswell in his favour, Freddy colours with delight: 'That's splendid, mum! That is going to make all the difference in the world.'

Also on this day the *Daily Express*, which is well disposed towards the lovers not least because of its editor Beverley Baxter's passionate belief in the abolition of the death penalty, publishes details of Mrs Thompson's estimated worth: 41 Kensington Gardens is valued at £800, half of which is hers as well as half the furniture. Their joint bank account shows a balance of approximately £100, and Thompson's life is insured for £400. The parents in the end would be left with almost nothing from Edith's home and possessions apart from a few personal belongings of their daughter's and some precious photographs and letters.

On Thursday 14 December the *Daily Sketch* launches its petition for the reprieve of Bywaters. It is addressed to the Home Secretary. The text reads:

> We, the undersigned, humbly petition for the commutation of the sentence of death passed on Frederick Edward Francis Bywaters at the Central Criminal Court by the Right Hon. Sir Montague Shearman on December 11, 1922

By 7 a.m. the first Londoner has signed the form in the newspaper's Shoe Lane office, and the trickle a few minutes later has already become a stream. It will be a torrent by night and in the course of the week will assume the proportions of a majestic river. The largest petition ever to be signed in Britain for a convicted prisoner has got under way. In a quick random survey of ordinary Londoners, all of them – chefs, bus drivers, sailors, mannequins, barmaids, soldiers, actresses – quoted verbatim, the paper has failed to elicit a single hostile comment on its mounting the petition. One man reading the paper today and deciding to appeal for the boy's life direct to the Home Office is Eliot Howard, the committing magistrate. Ever since Thursday 24 November he has brooded over the evidence presented in his court. Increasingly he has become convinced that the boy is innocent. His extraordinary resilience at the Old Bailey and his refusal to get off through incriminating the temptress have vindicated the magistrate's sense of Bywaters as a foolish young hothead, unable to resist the blandishments of Mrs Thompson. He points this out in his letter and reminds the Home Office of the boy's previous good character, both at work and at home. His letter is promptly filed.

The massive early response to the petition allows Mrs Bywaters to break good news to Freddy, when she visits him in the company of her daughter Lilian and her sister-in-law Mrs Simmons. She tells him of how she herself has signed the petition at the offices of the *Daily Sketch*, and how people have recognised her and expressed their regard for her and wished her and her boy good luck. He is almost his old self when he tells Mrs Simmons to 'take care of Mum; don't let her worry' as they are leaving. He especially wants his family to thank all those who are signing their names for his life. Among the first to sign are the Graydons. Neatly and on a single petition form, they sign their names, the two parents first, followed by their son and daughter. They desperately want the brave boy to live and know that if his sentence is commuted hers will automatically be also.

Even as the family are signing the petition, the governor of Holloway visits the woman in his charge. He tells her that the date of her execution is fixed for Wednesday 3 January. She takes it calmly and remains collected after he is gone. Her mother will soon be coming, and she will be able to share the news with her. That will make it better.

On Friday 15 December the *Daily Sketch* increases the momentum of its campaign to translate the sentiment which has 'echoed throughout the British Isles' into fact: 'Bywaters must not be hanged', announces its bold headline, and it is followed proudly by a statement that 10,000 letters have arrived in the first post alone and that a double queue has formed at the *Daily Sketch* to sign. At the same time the paper prominently carries a dissenting letter from an outraged Ilfordian, Mr Charles R. Walters of 11 Mortlake Road, Ilford, who is nauseated by all this 'sentimental bosh' and wants to see the lovers hang. The paper's centre-piece, though, is a shrewdly edited biography of Bywaters by his mother, followed by a criminological analysis of the entire case. The mother's article highlights the absence in the family of a father, who gave his life for his country, the importance Freddy attaches to the 'bronze monkey', and his chivalric behaviour to his sisters. By the time Mrs Bywaters visits Freddy again on Friday and Saturday, he has settled more into the prison routine. He now plays draughts and dominoes with the warders, as well as cards and tells them of his voyages. He is allowed to smoke and is given the football results which interest him. But he remains almost obsessively preoccupied with the bronze monkey. He gave the 'hear-no-evil' monkey to Edith Thompson as a keepsake during his absence at sea. He had been warned that the creature would keep him in luck as long as he hung on to it. He now wants it back, convinced that his fate is indissolubly bound up with it. Meeting his mother in the afternoon Freddy sends his gratitude through her to 'the *Daily Sketch* for giving its readers the opportunity to put forth their marvellous effort to save my life'. On the same page the paper records the Home Secretary's reply in the Commons to a question regarding the position of advice sought in capital decisions. It indirectly confirms that the judge's opinion will be taken into account, and notes contiguously that Percy's mother, aged over seventy, 'has lain at death's door' since learning of her son's violent death.

Every day since Tuesday Edith has seen her mother and sister. Now, on Saturday 16 December, her father is at last free to visit, accompanied by Newenham. The cell door is open, and she is up. The two men are requested not to enter, as a heavy deal table is pushed across the doorway and chairs are arranged on either side. Mr Graydon, with a note of enforced jolliness, greets his daughter who slowly walks towards him and her brother with a cheerful 'Hullo, father. How good it is to see you.' Sitting just out of touching range of each other, father and daughter exchange news about mostly ordinary things. He comments on the fact that she is wearing a new dress of grey serge and a small apron of white and blue check. She explains that this uniform is designed specifically for appeal prisoners. Her father remarks on the airy lightness of the room, and she concurs, wondering whether that is why she feels much better and sleeps more soundly now. 'Tell me about mother,' she asks, and Mr Graydon dutifully relates his impressions of the mother and how she is bearing up. It will be her birthday tomorrow and Edith has written her a loving letter to make her feel better. From her father she learns that her mother is coping bravely, but she guesses at the truth as Newenham's eyes fill with tears. Astutely she brings the conversation round to her diet and routine. She is allowed to do some crochet-work, she tells them, and she reads a lot. She is wholly unconstrained as regards the number of letters allowed her, but so far she has felt little need to communicate in writing, apart from the letter to her mother. The prison diet is dreary enough. It consists largely of milk, fish and eggs. The tea is poor, so she drinks milk instead. Her father notices that Bywaters's name has not so far passed her lips, even though she must be thinking of him all the time. Again and again during their conversation her eyes furtively glance up at the barred window. Outside it is a fine wintry day and there was even some sunshine earlier on. Her manifest longing hurts her father who can do so little to help her. Their parting is an emotional occasion, the more so since tomorrow is a Sunday, when no visits are allowed and Mrs Graydon will celebrate her fiftieth birthday. It is the harshest anniversary of her life. Like her daughter at Holloway and every other member in her family, she recalls the sheer insouciant happiness of last year's 17 December.

While Edith breathes a silent prayer and greetings to her mother, Mrs Graydon lies prostrate in her home. She has read and re-read Edith's letter to her: if only the people who decided and will still decide her fate could see writing like this rather than her daughter's unseemly passion in the famous letters! This brave and caring child could never harm a fly, let alone be a killer, the mother reasons. Bessie is visiting No. 231 this Sunday. She has always been part of the family. They took her in during the war when Reg was on active service. Now she will do her utmost to assist Edith and all the Graydons in their ordeal. She writes to Edith in prison and commiserates with her friend about the awfulness of the Monday of the sentencing. How, she enquires, is Edith bearing up and what is the routine at Holloway like? She tells her that on Friday 22 December she and Reg will be off on holiday, but that she will try and see her before going. Has she remembered her mother's birthday? She must be reassured about them; the family are coping, and friends and relative are constantly at hand to help them.

Edith receives Bessie's warm and affectionate letter on Monday 18 December. She replies immediately:

Dear Bessie,

I have just received your letter and I hasten to answer it.

Yes, it was awful last Monday. I can't explain what it felt like. I suppose no one knows unless their position is the same. It would be so much easier to bear if I knew or even felt I deserved that verdict, but I'm hoping for such a lot on Thursday [the day of the appeal]. Everyone seems so hopeful for me. I suppose it is catching.

The time here, on the whole, seems not as long as in remand – so many things are different. I can't tell you because it is against the rules, but it is a fact, and I sleep better here than I did there; really I have very good nights' rest.

There is plenty of time and opportunity to think all day long, so that by the time the night comes my brain is quite worn out and rests quite naturally.

This is something I am really pleased about, because I never – no, I think, not once – had a really good night's sleep. I have asked and obtained permission for you to visit me. Now, as you are going away on Friday, I wonder if you will have time, but if you don't come I shall quite understand, and hope that you will be having a real good rest over the holidays.

I remembered it was mother's birthday yesterday, and wrote to her. I'm glad you went down to see them. I expect they want cheering a little.

You know, dear, it's really about them I worry far more than about myself. It must be painful for them – the publicity alone must be more than they can cope with. You see I am shut away here and know nothing of all that. However, perhaps things will come right even yet.

Ask – to write: only tell him to mind his p's and q's. Now there is nothing else I want to say except to thank you – I can't tell you how much – for all you have done for me and for mother during this time.

It has helped tremendously to know that everybody, friends and relatives, have all stood by me during this time and have believed in me and still do.

I can't say any more, but I'm sure you will understand how I feel, and remember that all I want you to do now is to wish me luck for Thursday.

EDITH

The '–' whom she here invites to write could be anyone in her circle of men friends except Harry Renton, who has already written to her and who will repeatedly visit her in prison.

On this rainy Monday morning Bywaters signs his petition and Edith probably does likewise. Meanwhile the *Daily Sketch* has attracted the prominent support for its petition of an otherwise unrepentant hanger, Edward E. Wallace. Wallace's shrewd letter is one of thousands. The most striking letter to be published in the paper, advocating clemency for the boy, deserves quoting for its indignant humanity:

It is sad to think that so many of our writers and letter-writers cannot originate an argument against Bywaters, but must depend even for their words upon a remark of the judge. He said 'gush'. Those who think it must be fashionable or a sign of super-intelligence to copy the judge, say 'gush'. It is sad, too, to think there are even a few of these left in England. They are the gloomy-minded, the narrow-souled hermits that decry the sun because it sheds light on dark places; poor, disappointed, cynical derelicts in a world that holds no gladness for such as they. They are the kind who never said 'I love you' to a woman or had that sort of 'gush' said to them by a man. Let the rest of England, bright, happy, clean-thinking England, pray for the gloomy minds that are so valiant in their tirades against the gush that spends itself in an effort to save that which may be taken away but never returned – a human life!

Throughout this week the weather in London has been bad. Icy showers and gusty winds make Londoners' lives as miserable as only the British climate can. The day of the appeal approaches.

Thursday 21 December is a bleak day. The august Appeal Courts in the Strand seem to stand up defiantly to the elemental onslaught of gales and hail-showers. Inside three old men are settling down in the court of the Lord Chief Justice to rule on the lives of two very young people. Their only concern should be with points of law, but their comments will betray a gross moral bias.

Bywaters arrives early for the hearings in a taxi-cab, accompanied by three warders. He is dressed in the same blue lounge suit and spotless white shirt and tie that he was wearing at the Old Bailey. For a few minutes he is kept in the cells before the court is ready. Then he enters through the curtained doorway. His mother and Mrs Simmons are sitting on either side of Inspector Hall, by coincidence. Freddy and she exchange a quick smile before he takes up his place in the dock. Inskip is seen sitting behind a pile of law books and a transcript of the trial. Whiteley takes an hour and a half over his appeal before the three judges, Mr Justice Salter, Lord Hewart as Lord Chief Justice, and Mr Justice Darling.

His attack is two-pronged: firstly, to protest against the refusal to allow separate trials and hence the admissibility of the letters which in any case failed as evidence on the indictment for which they were submitted; secondly, Whiteley notes bitterly, Bywaters' defence was severely prejudiced by the fact that the Crown was granted the last address before the summing-up.

It takes the three judges a mere five minutes to agree a verdict, which is to dismiss the appeal on every ground. In the process of so doing, Hewart endorses as 'a true and appropriate description' Shearman's characterising the case as that of a 'common and ordinary charge of a wife and another murdering her husband'. His conclusion is, remarkably, that the case was

> a squalid and rather indecent one of lust and adultery, in which the husband was murdered in a cowardly fashion, partly because he was in the way, and partly because such money as he possessed was desired by them.

Freddy listens to this tirade impassively. He darts a quick glance towards his mother on hearing the verdict, and then responds to the gentle touch on his arm by one of the warders. He has vanished through the curtain door before his mother has fully grasped the implications of the ruling. Inskip has not even been challenged to state or restate the Crown's case.

It is gone noon when Sir Henry Curtis-Bennett rises. He knows that the odds are overwhelmingly stacked against him. For a full three hours he pleads his client's case again. He reminds the court of the inadmissibility of the letters on the first indictment, that they blur fact and fiction, that Spilsbury and Webster conclusively disproved that Thompson had been the victim of a plot to poison him and that furthermore there was not a shred of evidence in the correspondence to point towards a conspiracy to murder Thompson on the night of 3 October. Hewart interrupts and reminds counsel that the woman tried to shield the killer. Curtis-Bennett accepts this, but rightly denies that it in any way proves her connivance before the murder. Repeatedly the three judges chip in, Hewart with bullish seriousness, or, more memorably, Darling with distasteful flippancy. The latter's jokes about the lovers in this matter of life and death and in the presence of Mrs Bywaters and of Mr Graydon attracts some vulgar applause in court, but muted moral opprobrium in the press at large the following day. Eight minutes is all the judges require. Late in the afternoon Edith Thompson's appeal is dismissed on every ground. This is 'a commonplace and unedifying case', Hewart remarks, mindful of Curtis-Bennett's attempt at blowing it up into a great and tragic romance. Mrs Thompson's 'letters are a deplorable correspondence of the most mischievous and venomous kind', and were certainly properly submitted. The guilty affection between the lovers was 'passionate' and 'wicked'. In conclusion, this sordid affair 'exhibits from beginning to end no redeeming feature'. Inskip has still not spoken.

Edith has elected to forfeit her right to be exhibited to the public gaze once more, but all day at Holloway she is hoping, hoping. The news of the progress of the petition has fired her spirit. Already well over half a million people have signed and hundreds of thousands are still putting their names to it up and down the country. Noon comes and goes, and as yet she has no news of what is happening in the Strand.

But a young woman who is shortly afterwards travelling up to Holloway from Edith's familiar haunts over in East Ham catches a glimpse on a billboard: Bywaters's appeal is dismissed, it announces. With a heavy heart Bessie enters the gloomy prison. In the reception hall and in front of a blazing fire her name and address are entered into a ponderous ledger. Then she is escorted across a courtyard, with flagged paths 'bordered with small patches of soot-covered London grass, wherein are set rose bushes. It is the most tragic garden in London'. A short wait in a little vestibule is succeeded by another walk along a narrow, linoleum-covered passage, followed by a staircase and a landing. Eventually she arrives at the hospital.

Bessie is face to face with Edith. She has gathered from Avis and the other Graydons that the family have been allowed to go up and kiss her, in spite of the official instructions to the contrary. 'You are allowed half an hour', the wardress pronounces. Bessie is almost overcome at the sight of the other woman. For so long they have been such close and intimate friends. She is shocked by the unreality of Edith's appearance, in grey, aproned and wearing a white cap. Her mouth droops listlessly and her hands move tremulously in her lap. She looks pale, her eyes appear dark and shadowed from her vigils. Bessie cannot help remembering that this is the same girl with whom she shared everything, all her romantic dreams and their concerns about 'women's things'. Edith was, like herself, such a truly ordinary girl. Why then is her friend sitting there and she over here, divided by a heavy table which demarcates the line between life and death? 'How is mother?' Edith asks. 'Have you seen her and is she coping all right?' Bessie nods, and Edith tells her how she at once assumed that her visitor was her mother when she was informed of a caller. Bessie understands that Edith needs her mother now more than ever. The visitor is also momentarily tongue-tied, because of the hovering presence of the three wardresses. Edith is used to them. They are present even when she uses the lavatory, a ritual whose unsettling intimacy and early awkwardness has curiously bonded the women more closely together, like mother and child.

> Well [Edith says] I suppose you want to know how I am getting on here? I will tell you. Strange as it may seem, I am infinitely more comfortable here than I was when on remand. That was simply horrible. Here, all things considered, I have comfort. Of course, I loathe these clothes.

These last words are accompanied 'with a little dainty gesture of contempt'. The most Bessie can say is 'How do you pass the time here?' to which Edith replies brightly:

> Well, you know, ever since I was sentenced I have been waiting for the appeal which is being heard today. I feel so convinced that it must succeed, that I shall wake from this as from some awful dream, that all will come right yet, as I said in my letter.

Suddenly she asks whether Bessie knows the results of either appeal. Before the wardress can intervene, Bessie has denied any knowledge of the appeals' outcome. She cannot break it to her there and then that her lover has stepped that much closer to the gallows. The wardresses remind the two prisoners that outside news is not allowed to be communicated. To explain further how she passes her day, Edith puts her hand to her throat, which Bessie knows to be an old gesture of hers and one which she repeatedly used during her cross-examination at the Old Bailey. It serves to remind her that where once she wore an amber bead necklace, she now has a simple white string. 'This is the routine', she explains, turning to the wardress: 'I suppose I may tell that?' She nods, and Edith proceeds:

> They are kind to me here in the prison hospital, and I am given breakfast in bed at half-past seven. Then I dress in these and from then on the morning is my own to do what I like in. Sometimes I write, sometimes I read, sometimes I knit mufflers which, I am told, go to the boys of the Borstal Institute.
> Then at midday I have dinner. I am not allowed to have a knife or fork, and it is rather difficult to eat with the wooden spoon they provide; but I suppose that must be put up with!
> After dinner I walk in a yard alone for an hour – that is to say, I see no other prisoners. I do not enjoy that.
> At four I have tea, and at half-past eight I have to go to bed.

Her reading of books sent in by friends and relatives and volumes borrowed from the prison library consists of her favourite authors:

> You know, I have always loved W. J. Locke's romances. Well, I have been reading 'The House of Balthazar'. It is wonderful. But sometimes I feel I

cannot read, for my mind goes back again and again to what is going on outside – I mean the appeal. I can never get away from that for long. But there is one blessing. While I was on remand, and during the trial, I simply couldn't sleep. I think that was why I so nearly collapsed during the trial. But now I sleep every night, and soundly.

How, Bessie wonders, can her friend simply keep the horror of the gallows so wholly at bay? Her courage fires Bessie in turn bravely to ignore and overcome her fears. She decides to spend her remaining moments with Edith Thompson talking of happier childhood memories. They speak of early school adventures and when Bessie reminds Edith of the squashed frog incident on a Sunday long ago she even laughs and remarks: 'Fancy you remembering that.' Together in the death cell at Holloway the two women become two young girls revisiting their childhood in Edwardian England and their adolescence during the Great War.

At 3 p.m. a wardress indicates that the time is up. Edith and Bessie rise and bravely smile goodbye to each other. While the one disappears into the bowels of the grimy gaol, the other is escorted out into the wintry London dusk. Even as she is walking in the grim shadow of Holloway prison to reach the Underground, Bessie is passed by a screaming newspaper boy flashing the latest bill saying that Thompson's appeal has been dismissed. It hits Bessie that at this precise moment her friend Edith Thompson is immured still in hope behind these dreaded walls, when already the law has declared her dead. Now Bessie may never see her again. But she *will* try and freeze these last moments with Edith Thompson in her own and the country's memory, by putting them down on paper in precise detail. Not for money, but to clear this generous woman, as she knows her, from the shame and horror of the fate destined her if no miracle intervenes. *Lloyd's Sunday News* has approached her and she has informed the Graydons of this and consulted them about her course of action. In the end it has been agreed that however repellent they find the newspapers, the money can be pooled to assist with Edith's case, and the columns of the paper can be used to state its urgency to the nation, her sole hope if the appeal fails. The paper has also offered to pay handsomely for any new and therefore 'exclusive' photographs of Edith Thompson and her family. Bessie has provided several of hers, just as Mr Graydon has done for the *Weekly Dispatch*. Edith herself has been briefed on the family's and relatives' use of the press to secure a commutation. She has not objected. She in any case will not see anything of it.

A couple of hours after Bessie's departure, the governor arrives at Edith's cell door and informs her regretfully that the appeal has failed. She looks stunned but remains calm. He tells her that the date of the execution is now fixed for Tuesday 9 January at 9 a.m. 'I understood you to say the date was Jan 3rd,' she remarks quietly. He explains that it has been changed because of the appeal. She thanks him. As Dr Morton walks back to his office, not forgetting the sheer monstrosity of what is happening – he himself cannot quite imagine what hanging a woman would mean – the widow is numbly crying in her cell. The women about her do their utmost to comfort her. They are almost as dumbfounded as she is. Eventually Mrs Thompson comes round and asks for pen and paper. She simply must talk to her parents:

Dearest Mother and Dad –
    Today seems the end of everything. I can't think – I just seem up against a black, thick wall, through which neither my eyes nor my thoughts can penetrate.
    It's not within my powers of realisation that this sentence must stand for something which I have not done, something I did not know of, either previously or at the time. I know you both know this. I know you both have known and believed it all along.
    However, I suppose it is only another landmark in my life – there have been so many when I look back, but somehow they are not landmarks until I look back upon the journey, and then I know that certain events were landmarks.
    I've tried to unravel this tangle of my existence, this existence that we all call life. It is only at these times that we do think about it.
    It has been an existence, that's all, just a 'passing through', meeting trials, and shocks and surprises with a smiling face and an aching heart, and eventually being submerged and facing Death, that thing that there is no escaping – no hope of defeating.
    You both must be feeling as bad and perhaps worse than I do today, and I do so hope that this will not make things harder to bear, but I really felt that I should like to talk to you both for just a little while, after I was told the result.
    Even now I cannot realise all it means: but, dearest mother and dad, you both must bear up – just think that I am trying to do the same, and I am sure that thought will help you.
    EDITH

If the governor is not eager to fight her corner, he nevertheless does his best by her. He has to censor her mail and sends this one up to the

Prison Commissioners for scrutiny. In his covering note he points out that she has written 'a number of letters since she was condemned to death' and that they have all been 'couched in a more or less frivilous [sic] style'. This one at last, he notes, and for the first time, shows that she has begun to realise the meaning of her sentence. Could the Commissioners please consider the paragraph commencing, 'However I suppose' and ending, 'I know that certain events were landmarks'? The letter is harmless enough and could not possibly be objected to. Its submission – unlike the more 'frivolous' ones – suggests that the governor is playing safe by being seen to do his duty by the Prison Commissioners, while simultaneously allowing a fair part of Edith's correspondence to pass without opposition.

There are three more days to go till Christmas. The Graydons have been invited to Highbury by the Walkinshaws to spend the day with them. They have accepted. On Friday 832,104 signatures are delivered by van to the Home Office. Thousands more are pouring in every hour, but the *Daily Sketch* wishes to pre-empt a zealous negative decision by the Home Secretary in the immediate aftermath of the appeals' dismissal. It is probably also banking on the spirit of Christmas coming to the condemned couple's rescue. Hence it seems worth trading the advantage of the magical million figure against a possible and irrevocable decision not to reprieve.

Saturday 23 December 1922: This morning Edith receives a letter from Bessie to share her sense of shock over the appeal. In it she voices her fervent hope and conviction that humanity will prevail and that she, Edith, will not have to suffer the extreme penalty. Wearily the prisoner puts it aside. She will reply later. She has not been out of bed since Thursday night. At 2.30 p.m. her father, mother and sister visit her. She is sitting already in place in an armchair at the table, and is now wearing a blue-grey dressing-gown. It is her first time up in two days and she tries hard to appear cheerful. She enquires after all her friends except Bywaters, and then asks: 'Do you remember last Christmas, Dad?', without sounding wistful or self-pitying. She recalls the 22lb turkey she was given, Percy's good cheer, the chocolates and how the whole family enjoyed themselves. Moreover she expresses a keen appreciation of the lady doctor, Dora Walker, the Assistant Medical Officer at Holloway who is now looking after her. Her parents expect her to be deeply depressed about spending both Christmas and Boxing Day alone, and of course about the outcome of the appeal. The thought of a lonely and cheerless Christmas however hardly seems to impinge on her mind; and she is not bothered by the prospect of a spartan diet throughout these festive days. About the appeal Edith wanly smiles and remarks: 'Wasn't it bad luck?' She nearly chokes on the phrase though and betrays the depth of her emotional upheaval by beginning to weep. Then, turning to Avis, she tells her sister that she has been reading *If Winter Comes* and 'I am very disappointed with it. I have only read a few chapters, but up to the present none of the characters strike me as live men and women.' On this she will change her mind during the next two weeks, after at last finishing Hutchinson's novel; and she will convey her revised sense of it to Bessie in a letter of 3 January, the day she was originally to die.

While talking to her family Edith is seen to be toying nervously with her wedding-ring, and sometimes she leans forward so much that her arms almost touch her father's. She enquires after her house in Kensington Gardens and seems reassured to hear that it is in the hands of the receiver. She is distraught when the time of the visit is up. Not to see them for three days seems an unbearable prospect. In nearby Pentonville young Bywaters also prepares for three days' isolation. Over the summer and after the reconciliation with his mother, Freddy had written to her to tell her that at last they would spend a Christmas together, their first one since he was fifteen years old. Now his mother has written to the Queen and to the Home Secretary separately to appeal for her son's life. In the meantime the petition is still rolling and rumour has it that it will pass the million mark any moment now.

Christmas Eve, Christmas itself and Boxing Day are bleak and wet as heavy gales sweep in from the sea and unleash rain, hail and a chill on the metropolis. 25 December 1922 marks Edith Thompson's twenty-ninth birthday. Her parents well remember that day in Dalston nearly thirty years ago when she was born. For the millionth time they wonder whether this nightmare will suddenly dissipate itself and produce a new awakening; how can the pretty baby who seemed to fulfil all their dreams now be the much-slandered woman lying in Holloway close to death? Mrs Graydon feels the hurt of her daughter's predicament more intimately than anyone else. She gave her life in the first place. Somebody who assisted at Edith's birth was her aunt Edith Walkinshaw who is entertaining the Graydons today, along with the Laxtons and other relatives, like the Graydon children's cousin Leonard, on leave from school. Before lunch Leonard suggests that they all go for a drink. Avis and Newenham trudge along with him to the Barn in Highbury. The others stay behind at 62 Lucerne Road, from where not a sound of Christmas emerges. The grief-struck families are waiting, thinking, praying, hoping.

For the two condemned prisoners, the day serves as a reminder of their total physical apartness both from each other and from the world. Bywaters is fretful and takes an anguished walk round the prison yard in the company of two warders. He spends a little time in the chapel, but remains unmoved by the carol-singing. He prefers to play draughts or sit in his cell chatting to the warders, telling them of his little brother, his sisters and his life at sea. He enjoys his Christmas dinner, which consists of roast beef and plum pudding. He can still joke about only being allowed the use of a fork and spoon, opining that he is not after all likely to take his own life now. Just before Christmas he told his mother:

> I think that they will let me live, though they will not let me out of prison till I am almost an old man. But that will be a great concession.

In Holloway Edith Thompson has declined the invitation to exercise. Since her parents' and sister's visit she has remained in bed. She is calm now on Christmas morning and graciously accepts the muted 'Merry Christmas' and 'Happy Birthday' greetings tendered her by the embarrassed invigilatory staff. She merely nibbles at her Christmas dinner of broth, chicken and fruit. It is shortly thereafter that she flies into a fit of hysteria.

The doctor examines her while she is held down by the wardresses. Again and again she exclaims: 'What a Christmas!' and bursts uncontrollably into tears when she hears the 'neighbouring bells [of Tufnell Park] crash out their merry peal'. Dr Walker injects her with a heavy sedative, and she subsides into sleep. She moans and tosses in her slumber and continues in this manner till evening falls. They wake her from this restless rest to offer her tea. She speaks intermittently to the wardresses, and then only to utter over and over the same cry of 'Why— oh, *why*, am I here?', as though they could possibly give her an explanation. Again they fail to calm her down, and she is drugged afresh. In this state of near-delirium she continues groaning and repeating with monotonous regularity: 'Why did he do it, why?'

On Boxing Day she is calmer. She knows that if the Home Secretary should not reprieve her it will be this morning in a fortnight's time that she and Freddy will die. But that awareness she as yet manages to control. Finally she collects herself enough to write a remarkable letter to Bessie:

Dear Bessie,

I wanted to write to you yesterday and yet I couldn't. I could do nothing but sit and think. Who was it said, 'Some days we sits and thinks, and some we simply sits'? Well, yesterday was a 'sitting and thinking day'.

I got your little letter on Saturday. Yes, the result of the appeal was a great shock – I had such hopes of it – not only hopes for mercy, but hopes for justice; but I realise how very difficult it is to fight prejudice.

If you have facts to fight, and you fail, you seem more reconciled, but when it's only prejudice – oh, it's awful.

You talk about not having to suffer the extreme penalty. Do you know that I don't dread that at all. I feel that would be far easier than banishment – wrongful banishment for life. I feel no apprehension of what might lie ahead after this life.

Yesterday I was twenty-nine; it's not really very old, I suppose, and yet it seems so to me.

I suppose when you're happy age doesn't count; it doesn't seem to matter; it's when you're not that the years seem so frightening.

Yesterday I was thinking about everything that has ever happened, it seems to help in all sorts of ways when I do this. I realise what a mysterious thing life is. We all imagine we can mould our own lives – we seldom can, they are moulded for us – just by the laws and rules and conventions of this world, and if we break any of these, we only have to look forward to a formidable and unattractive wilderness.

I've often thought how good it would be to talk, to pour out everything, it might have pained as well, but it would be pain that comes with sudden relief of intolerable hurt.

However, I'm going to forget all that now. I'm going to hope – because everybody tells me so. I'm going to live in those enormous moments when the whole of life seems bound up in the absolute necessity to win.

Thank you so much for writing to me, and helping to keep me cheerful.

EDITH

Wednesday 27 December brings with it more visits from parents, siblings and other friends and relatives. Everyone pretends to be buoyed up by the progress of the petition and the 'leaked' information in the *Daily Sketch* that the Home Secretary has raised the matter with Cabinet colleagues and the Prime Minister, Bonar Law. The most generous interpretation of this move – authenticated by reports to the same effect elsewhere – is that Bridgeman has experienced genuine moral doubts as to whether to reprieve or to let the law take its course. The cynical view is that Cabinet and Prime

Minister were consulted for reasons of political expediency; the momentum of the petition was such that no politician could simply ignore it.

On Saturday 30 December Edith is visited by her father, her uncle Jack and Avis. To their surprise she advances towards them smiling and humming a tune. She greets them with a warm 'Hullo' and with smiles for everyone. She is now wearing a grey dress and her father notices that her cheeks are flushed from exercise in the yard. It is almost as if she is momentarily rejuvenated. She does not mention the trial at all, nor Bywaters, and merely breathes a single word about the appeal. What she most desires to talk about is 'mater' and how she is bearing up in spite of all the publicity which the case has attracted and is still generating. Reassured on that point, she tells them of the piles of letters which are pouring in from all over England and from abroad. This same morning she received more than thirty of them. This, in conjunction with the prospect of a Cabinet decision on the reprieve, motivates the families anew. Back at home it is decided that a direct approach to the Prime Minister and the Queen must be tried, as well as a separate one to the Cabinet. Avis Graydon and Mrs Graydon who, unlike Edith, are not versed in the epistolary arts, nevertheless write the following two impressive letters:

231 Shakespeare Crescent
Manor Park
London E.12

30–12–22

To the Queens most Excellent Majesty
Most Gracious Sovereign

May it please your Majesty to grant the favour of your Royal influence towards obtaining a reprieve for my unfortunate daughter Mrs Edith Thompson.

As a Mother, you well realise the torment through which I am passing knowing that my daughter is the victim of the most compromising circumstances but yet being absolutely innocent of the awful charge upon which she has been convicted, and I now appeal to you as Mother of the Nation to be pleased to show your gracious mercy towards one who, up to the time of this terrible catastrophe has always been a most dutiful and loving daughter and who has always been the first to help others in the hour of their distress. I hope in your Royal mercy and graciousness you will not fail to hear this cry from the heart of a grief stricken Mother in her hour of need, all of whose three sons served their country in its hour of need.

I have the honour to remain your Majesty's most faithful subject and dutiful servant.

ETHEL J. GRAYDON

Surely her sons' service in their country's uniform ought to appeal to the Queen's maternal and patriotic instincts, Mrs Graydon reasons. Not only is Edith innocent and a mother's daughter, but she is the sister of loyal English soldiers and sailors.

Avis's letter to the Prime Minister is punchier, more spontaneous, visceral and desperate. It remains, like her mother's, a deeply stirring document:

> 231, Shakespeare Crescent
> Manor Park
> E12
> 30/12/22

Sir

Re my sister Mrs Thompson

I beg you kindly to read this letter in the hope that some of the points will enable you to see my sister's character other than presented to the public, by the prosecution.

I can assure you Sir that my sister had no idea that her husband was going to be murdered, as it had been arranged a fortnight before that, I should accompany them to the Theatre, & spend the night with her in Kensington Gdns, & she had no idea until she met her husband in the evening that I was not going to be of the party. Her husband telephoned me late in the afternoon & I told him that I had already made arrangements to go out for mother. How can they pass sentence of *Death* on her?

Dr Spilsbury gave evidence that there was no trace of poison in the deceaseds' body, how then can it be said, she poisoned him. Why was all the evidence of defence put on one side, & only the black side – the foolish letters of an over wrought, unhappy woman – placed before the Jury.

It is untrue that my sister was happy until Bywaters came into her life.

Mrs Lester can prove, & also others with whom she lived before, that she was unhappy; only her great respect & love for her parents, prevented her bringing her troubles home. If she had done anything wrong at any time, she would have told mother at any cost, also my brother in law, would have spoken to my dad.

I should like to say, that Percy Thompson being of a peculiar character had no friends of his own, & naturally very soon disagreed with my sisters friends.

The man is dead, but why should he die blameless. His case was just the same as my sister's which you can see by the letters, not produced.

Mrs Thompson was a hard working woman, of a generous, loving nature & no doubt after Bywaters seeing her unhappiness, she turned to him for sympathy. Her great mistake being – afraid to confide in her family who loved her above everything. Why was it so emphatically said 'She incited Bywaters?' it is obvious her letters are answers to questions, where are Bywaters letters to prove his statement that Mrs Thompson is innocent? Why has no benifit of the doubt been given in this case to the accused!

Can it be my sister is insane! Is this question having the prison doctors attention?

If you had seen my sister at any time, there could not be any doubt in your mind that the verdict is wrong.

I beg you to shew mercy on her, for her parents sake, you are a father therefore understand their feelings.

We are helpless & know she is *Not Guilty*.

May the Great Judge of all guide you in coming to your final decision, to which the family are just clinging, as the last hope.

Committing the above to your kind attention.

I remain in anticipation

    AVIS E. GRAYDON (Miss)

To
The Rt. Hon. Bonar Law Esq. M.P.

The following day, Sunday 31 December, Lily Laxton, who has all along supported Ethel, writes to 'The Gentlemen of the Cabinet':

5 Rostrevor Avenue
Stamford Hill
N.15

31/12/22

To
The Gentlemen of the Cabinet

Dear Sirs

As the Home Secretary has left the decision of the case of Frederick Bywaters & Mrs Thompson to you, I feel I must make a final appeal on their behalf.

My husband & I were the aunt & uncle with whom Mr & Mrs Thompson spent the evening at the theatre, & I assure you Gentlemen, that from Mrs Thompson's manner, conversation, & also arrangements we all made to go to dances, dinners, & other theatres, during the season, it was absolutely impossible for Mrs Thompson to have entered into any arrangement with Bywaters to commit the crime. Moreover, knowing the late Mr Thompson very well, I say the lad's story is true & undoubtedly he acted as he thought in self-defence, Mr Thompson being just the kind of man who would bluff having a weapon.

But Gentlemen, my real plea is on behalf of the parents. By hanging the unhappy couple it is not them who suffer, but the family left behind. I know it is a difficult decision for you to arrive at, & possibly it will make a precedent for the abolition of 'Capital Punishment', but Gentlemen, being a new Government it is possible for you to do this. If burning at the stake was not a deterrent to crime, I am sure the more merciful way of hanging is not. These things or crimes are only committed in a moment of passion & not premeditated. The punishment of years of confinement is bourne by the offenders, but the punishment of hanging, is bourne by the parents and relations. May I therefore ask once again for 'Mercy'.

Yours sincerely

L. LAXTON

(sister to Mrs Thompson's mother)

The last night of the last day of 1922 has arrived. The two lovers in their death cells are pondering their situation. This was to have been the year when everything ought to have worked itself out! They might have eloped, or just gone on holiday together. As Edith reviews 'her' year in numbness and pain, Bywaters keeps up the brave façade of nonchalant stoicism. This morning the warders have communicated to him the results of Saturday's football matches which he has eagerly scrutinised. The final minutes of the old year glide away and bells all over the metropolis start ringing in the New Year 1923. While crowds are jamming the main thoroughfares of London and Trafalgar Square, Edith Thompson lies wide awake, listening intently to the noises of the outside world. Is she really meant to die in this year 1923? Later, when her mother asks her whether she wished herself 'Good luck', she replies: 'Yes, I did; but it doesn't seem to matter now, does it?'

6

When Winter Came

The first day of the New Year is wet and windy. Edith Thompson is visited by her mother, Avis and the former schoolmate Ida Burton. After their first re-acquaintance, Ida Burton says: 'I wish you would let Canon Palmer visit you just as a friend, he won't talk religion, he is very sweet I am sure you would like him.' She explains that the Canon is an Ilfordian and very interested in her welfare. Edith nods assent, and agrees to apply for permission to see him, primarily because her mother and Avis strongly support the idea. For, as much as she has been able to in front of the wardresses, Edith has voiced her indignant objection to the ministrations of the Church of England Senior Chaplain at Holloway, the Reverend S. R. Glanvill Murray. According to her, Murray always presses her for a confession during his visits, notwithstanding her protests about her innocence.

She therefore prefers to dispense with his services altogether now, but would welcome a 'spiritual adviser' sympathetic to her. Canon Palmer appears eminently suitable. At this interview Ida Burton may not tell Edith that Canon Palmer is a Roman Catholic priest. She either knows already, or else finds out through a coded message. The point is that Edith is prepared to lie about this to the governor out of her desperate need to have someone close to her in her final hours who is not a member of the prison service. Above all, as a Catholic priest Canon Palmer will forever be bound by the seal of the confessional not to reveal anything that she might confide in him of whatever gravity. One imagines that what she intends to convey through him is a secret message of love to Bywaters. In the end she will be enabled to exchange a dying message with him through the kind offices of the Bishop of Stepney.

On Tuesday 2 January Edith writes to the governor for permission to be granted for a visit from Canon Palmer 'as a friend'. Morton sees no reason for not complying with her request. In the meantime down the road in Pentonville, Freddy Bywaters once again writes to 'Mrs Edith Thompson, H.M. Prison, Holloway':

2 January 1923

Edie – I want to ask you not to give up hope. I know & you know & some others know also, that you should not be in the position that you find yourself. I'm still hoping that the powers that be, will exercise some common sense & displace their suppositions with facts. I know this must be a terrible strain on you, but Peidi mia, don't lose heart – B.B. I am keeping quite well & I've heard that you are a lot better. I'm glad.

I have seen Florrie today & she told me that she had written to you explaining the misunderstanding. I should dearly like to pull the snub nose of a certain person – Do you know to whom I refer? I've read two books by Baroness Von Sutton 'Pam' & 'What became of Pam' – one of Hichens 'An Imaginative Man' & one of Rolf Wyllards 'There was a Crooked Man'. Since I've been here. If you are able, will you write? I want to say a lot, but cannot, you understand. I can only hope & trust that some time in the future we will be able to talk to one another.

    Goodbye. Peidi mia – B.B. –
    Always,
      FREDDY

This letter is promptly intercepted by the Prison Commission, perhaps because of its intimate character, or more simply because as two convicted felons they are not allowed to correspond. Edith does, however, receive a letter from Florrie Bywaters which she describes as kindly and humane. It is, one surmises, comparable in tone to Florrie's later letter of 6 January which will be confiscated by the Prison Commissioners and thus survives in their files.

Wednesday 3 January: Gale-force winds are forecast, and local showers and even thunder alternate with long spells of sunshine. The sight of the sun cheers Edith up, as does the prospect of her mother's visit later today, because Ethel will bring her daughter a very special present. She sits down and writes Bessie the following long and, under the circumstances, buoyant letter:

January 3rd, 1923

Dear Bessie,

    I know I ought to have written to you yesterday – but I didn't feel I wanted to – that's my only excuse.

Thank you for sending along the book. I haven't [received] it yet, but I soon shall have. When I think I have been longing to get it for three months now and you have had it all the time. I feel so cross that I didn't mention it before. However, I am going to prepare myself to enjoy it to the full, after waiting so long.

Does it seem three whole months since I first came here to you? Some days it seems like three weeks and others like three days. Time is always our enemy, don't you think? It either goes too fast or too slowly always.

I've read lots of books since I've been here; I usually get through one every day – but they, none of them, have been very striking, nothing in them to impress one, or to make you remember them. Of course, I read 'If Winter Comes'. Auntie – sent it in to me. That I enjoyed; it is quite differently written from the usual type of novel, and that fact alone made it interesting, but the plot (which doesn't really appear until quite the end of the book) was even more interesting to me under these circumstances.

Have you read it? You should. Then I read 'A Witness for the Defence', by A. E. W. Mason. I wonder if you have 'The Four Feathers' by him? I should like to have that. Oh! and I read 'His Daughter', a Yankee book by Governour Morris, but there was nothing much in that; at least, nothing much I can discuss in writing.

I could talk to you about it, but I couldn't write. Now I am starting Dickens again. I think I have read all his at least three or four times, but you can always pick up one and feel interested in it at any time.

I remember at school. . . .[1]

Today it is lovely; the sun is shining and everywhere looks bright and cheerful. I begin to feel quite cheerful myself – isn't the sun wonderful, it always raises your spirits. But I don't like it as cold as this. I'll be ever so glad when the summer comes: the heat I love, but I never did like the cold – not out of doors, at any rate. I don't think I should mind inches of snow outside if I was inside in a huge armchair before a great, big fire, with a nice book – yes, and some nuts, I think.

I've still got faith – I'm still hoping. They say 'You can always get what you want if you want it enough, but you can't control the price you have to pay', and I think that's so every time.

I got – letter. Thank him for me; it was very sedate and proper, tell him. I really didn't think he could be like that – I think that is part of him I don't know yet.

Shall I see you again soon – Edith

Freddy Bywaters is also writing a letter, probably the longest of his

[1] See page 6.

life. It is addressed to the Home Secretary and constitutes the boy's petition to reprieve Edith Thompson, as well as a plea for his own life. It is reproduced here in its entirety:

3 January 1923

I am writing to ask you to use your power to avert a great catastrophe and also to rectify a grave injustice. Edith Thompson & I have been found guilty & today stand condemned upon a charge of which we are innocent. In the first instance I wish to speak to you of Edith Thompson. The case for the prosecution was based entirely upon a series of extracts from letters written by her to me. There were, mentioned in these letters, names of some poisons & broken glass. It was suggested that Mrs Thompson had been administering poison & broken glass to her husband. The body was exhumed & no trace of any alien substance was found, but still, Mrs Thompson was committed for trial on the charge of having administered poison to her husband. I am asking you to believe me sir, because what I say is the truth, that Mrs Thompson never had any intention or the slightest inclination to poison her husband or to kill him in any way. The only way to treat those letters is the way in which I read them. She is a hysterical & highly strung woman & when writing letters to me she did not study sentences and phrases before transferring them to paper, but, as different thoughts, no matter what, momentarily flashed through her mind, so they were committed to paper. Sometimes, even I, could not understand her. Now sir, if I had, for one moment, thought or imagined, that there was anything contained in Mrs Thompson's letters to me, that could at any time, harm her, would I not have destroyed them? I was astounded when I heard the sinister translation the prosecution had put to certain phrases, which were written quite innocently. Those letters were the outpourings of a hysterical woman's mind, to relieve the tension & strain caused by the agony she was suffering. If you like sir, merely melodrama. Furthermore I wish to say that she never suggested to me that I should kill her husband. She is not only unjustly condemned but it is wicked & vile to suggest that she incited me to murder. God knows that I speak the truth when I say that there was no plan or agreement between Mrs Thompson & I to murder her husband. I can do no more sir, than ask you to believe me – the truth – & then it is for you to proclaim to the whole world that Edith Thompson is 'Not Guilty' & so remove the stain that is on her name.

It was said by an officer of the law, when the result of the exhumation was known, 'The case against Mrs Thompson has failed'. Why then sir, was she committed for trial? I ask you, I implore you sir, in the name of humanity & justice, to order the release of Edith Jessie Thompson.

I have not much space sir, so will try & be as concise as possible in laying before you my case. I wish to bring to your notice that the evidence against me is only that which has been supplied by myself. I was asked at Ilford if there had been a fight & I said yes. I was not asked for details & I received NO caution. When I saw my solicitor on Oct. 7th I told him exactly what had happened the same as I did to the Judge & Jury at the Old Bailey. When I was at the inquest at Ilford, I was advised by a law officer to get the charge against me reduced. I mentioned that to my solicitor who said it would be best to say nothing until the trial at the Old Bailey. You now know sir, why my explanation was not made known before. Mr Justice Shearman suggested to the Jury, that my knife was in my pocket for one reason only – namely that I had agreed with Mrs Thompson to murder her husband on Oct 3rd. I saw Mrs Thompson at midday on Oct. 3rd & it was then for the first time I learned that she was going to the Criterion Theatre that evening. My knife was in my pocket then & it had been there since 23rd Sept. I was in the habit of always carrying either a knife or a revolver. At the inquest, Dr Drought in his evidence stated that the first blow had been delivered from the front. That is quite true, you have my statement made in the Witness Box at the Old Bailey. If I could speak to you I could explain any point you might wish, more fully, but my space here is limited. I ask you to accept my word sir, or perhaps you can shew me some way in which I can prove to you that I am speaking the truth.

I hope & trust that this will receive your careful & favourable consideration sir, & that you will order another hearing of the case.

  I am, Sir,
    Yours respectfully,
      FREDERICK E. F. BYWATERS

The eagerly awaited hour of the visit at Holloway has arrived, and Mrs Graydon presents Edith with the framed sketch of the *Morea*. It is over three months since she took it to be framed. For a moment all the old excitement lights up in the woman's eyes, as she examines the picture. The monkey was meant to sit opposite it, like herself, and together they would glance at this copy of Freddy's 'home'. But now the *Morea* is a very long way off in the Antipodes, plying the South China Sea while her former laundry steward is waiting to die in a mean spot in a wretched prison. In spite of all this the mother, watching her daughter's delighted handling of the little picture, is momentarily overcome with joy at the knowledge of having brought her this tiny bit of happiness. Her father, she tells Edith, misses her greatly and will be seeing her on Saturday when he will be off work. It may be for this reason that Edith will write him a letter the following day. It is her last extant piece of writing. The version reproduced here is the one that she rewrote at the governor's request:

Dearest Dad. –

Somehow today I feel I'd like to write to you. It seems such a long time since I saw you – and yet it isn't. It's only the same distance from Saturday as it was last week. I wonder why some days seem so long ago and others quite near?

Of course nothing different happens here, every day is the same. The best part of each day (and of course the quickest) is the half an hour's visit I have. It never seems to be longer than ten minutes.

Do you remember the book I told you I wanted? They tell me it is out of print, and I couldn't help thinking that even in little things my luck is entirely absent. You remember I only missed No. 13 because there wasn't one.

I've been reading Dickens's 'Our Mutual Friend', but the print is so frightfully small and indistinct that I can't see anything if the light has to be on, and it is after dark always that I feel I would like to read the most.

Yesterday mother showed me the sketch of the Morea. It looks nice in its frame, don't you think? I was quite pleased about it.

I'm getting quite used to things here now. It's really astonishing what you can do without when it is 'Hobson's choice'.

You'll be coming to see me on Saturday, won't you? On that Saturday of last year, I wonder if you remember what we did?

I do, quite well. We were all at Highbury, and the huge dinner Harold ate I can see now if I close my eyes. And then there were the rattles and trumpets and whistles in the Tube and Avis getting out without her ticket and we throwing it out of the carriage on to the platform when it was too late. Oh, dear! What a lot can happen in a year!

I hope Saturday comes quickly, it's been such a terrible long week. Au revoir until then.

EDITH

Friday 5 January is a mild day. In the corridors of the Home Office in Whitehall it is known that the Home Secretary's decision on the Ilford murderers will be announced any moment now, as he is scheduled to depart for his country estate at Minsterley near Shrewsbury later in the day. There is little doubt in the minds of Wall, Blackwell and others that the politicians will heed their advice, which is to let the law take its course. It is shortly before noon when Blackwell dictates the following letter to the people of Manor Park:

Madam,

With reference to your letter of 30th ultimo, addressed to the Prime

Minister on behalf of your sister, Edith Jessie Thompson, now under sentence of death, I am directed by the Secretary of State to inform you that he has given careful consideration to all the circumstances of the case, and I am to express to you his deep regret that he has failed to discover any grounds which would justify him in advising His Majesty to interfere with the due course of law.

Immediately the decision is known, the Home Office dispatches messengers to the two prisons. The governors are instructed to implement the customary security precautions, including the deployment of additional police. The parental visits are to proceed as normal. The prisoners will be told at the conclusion of the interviews. Simultaneously telegrams are cabled to John Ellis of Rochdale and William Willis of Manchester. The country's chief executioner, Ellis, has already been instructed to be on stand-by in view of the Home Secretary's likely ruling. He at once notifies his two assistants Robert Baxter of Hertford and Thomas Phillips of Bolton. They are to meet in London on Sunday to inspect and prepare the scaffolds. Ellis will hang Mrs Thompson; Willis with Seth Mills and Tom Pierrepoint is to execute Bywaters. While this group prepare to converge on the metropolis, Mrs Graydon and Lily Laxton once more retrace their tired steps to Holloway Prison. They register the increased police presence, but fail to interpret it correctly.

Edith seems in surprisingly high spirits and 'quite bright-eyed', which suggests that she may be drugged. She is sitting in her usual position in the doorway of the cell, separated by the deal table again from her visitors. But this time her visitors are not allowed to sit as close as they used to; their chairs are at a measured distance from the table, and when Lily pulls hers forward she is politely asked to revert to the designated position. Edith thanks her for sending in *If Winter Comes* which she enjoyed, but found more 'ordinary' than she had expected. The magazines which Lily has taken to Holloway have been intercepted and Edith has not seen them. She is sadly amused while relating this and continues:

> This morning the governor sent me back, censored, a letter that I had written home to Manor Park. I had said, or referred to, something that was not allowed. It is the first time I have had such a thing happen, and it is the first time I have had to rewrite anything I have written.

Lily is surprised to hear that this is the 'first time' that such an interference has happened to Edith's correspondence, because the press has implied that letters between the prisoners are being monitored and suppressed. Above all, she has read in the *Daily Mail* that Bywaters has written her a long letter, which may be the confiscated letter of 2 January, or it might have been confused with Bywaters's long letter to the Home Secretary. Has she received it, or does she know anything at all about it? A grave look flits over her face:

> I don't know. He would be sure to ask whether he could write to me. If he was permitted to write and if his letter has left Pentonville, I should receive it in due course; but I have not received it yet.

She has, however, had a letter from Florrie, she tells them, which has cheered her greatly and to which she has replied. More than that, Edith will not say in front of the two wardresses. Instead she cheerfully notes that this morning she has had three letters from relatives and one from a friend, 'all nice cheering letters'. It is her next remark which baffles her visitors who share the prisoner's total innocence of the ways and means of the law: 'I have been weighed as many as three times in one day.' A little wryly she proceeds to explain that she has been consuming two pints of milk a day, because the tea is 'inferior'. While the prison officials are regularly checking her weight and calculating averages for the drop, Edith is concerned about her increase in weight by over a stone since 11 December.

Unsuspecting, she continues to enquire after what is happening 'outside', and when told that the Paris Conference has failed, she replies: 'I am sorry, because it seems as if there must be more trouble.' Lily mentions that the Prince of Wales is rumoured to be set on marrying an aristocratic Scots woman to which Edith replies laughingly: 'What, another one?' She is interested to learn details of the New Year's Honours list and poor Lily can only remember Spilsbury. 'Who else?', her niece asks without further comment, but she is now clearly troubled. She is looking at Lily gravely and intently, as she asks whether she 'has heard any news'. She tells her 'No', and Edith remains silent. The rest of the visit is taken up by more general talk, and by Mrs Graydon filling Edith in on how things are at home. The time for the visit is up and the two women part from the prisoner. As they leave the prison the sisters are still ignorant of Edith's fate. But outside the newspaper-boys are screaming from every street corner that Thompson and Bywaters are to hang on Tuesday. There will be no last-minute reprieve.

Over in Pentonville Florrie Bywaters is reading out to Freddy Edith Thompson's letter to them. Edith has slipped into it a secret love-message which he alone understands. He asks his sister to tell Edith that it is reciprocated. In her letter she offers to return the bronze monkey, but Bywaters prefers her to keep it. He suggests that she arrange for the watch she gave him to be forwarded to his brother Frankie. Above all he is concerned about her welfare and hopes she will bear up. He also wishes her to know that he has written to her.

It is shortly after 3 p.m. when Dr Morton, the governor, calls on Edith Thompson to deliver the news. She remains very calm while he is talking. In the next hour, even as another wintry dusk is settling over London, Edith Thompson is fighting off her intellectual realisation that the cessation of her being is now purely a matter of hours. *Nothing* will now interpose itself between her and the scaffold. What will it be like, hanging there surrounded by men? How much will it hurt? Will she be able to breathe during the last seconds of her life, or will the noose be too tight? She is bewildered and she is very frightened. The women about her are reeling from shock, which exacerbates the prisoner's sense of desolation and utter loss. Where is 'mater' now, or dad to hold her? She sits down at the wardresses' urgings, but she cannot stay still. They try to restrain her gently. It is about 4 p.m.

Trapped, facing certain death, Edith Thompson's relative calm suddenly gives way to hysteria. Madly fighting off the tentacular hands that reach out to drag her back into this cage of cold stone, she is screaming: 'I never did it!' As strange arms and hands pinion her to the bed, she is crying in despair. The governor has been summoned and is rushing towards the cell. He is a doctor, but the spectacle which greets him of the sweat-drenched manic woman would have unsettled many a tougher veteran from the trenches of Flanders. He injects her with $\frac{1}{4}$ grain of morphia. Ten agonising minutes later the woman is 'quite quiet' and subsides into an uneasy sleep. She is medically attended for most of the long sixteen-hour night from Friday to Saturday.

She does not sleep for any length of time. Again and again she wakes in sheer terror, like a little girl rocked into reality by a ghostly presence in her bedroom at night. The strong drug keeps her locked in a stupor, but it fails altogether to remove her awareness of impending doom.

The women who sit with her in shifts urgently talk to her in her waking moments, about anything, in an attempt to keep her mind off the unthinkable and unspeakable topic. She again moans and speaks the name of Bywaters, and 'Why did he do it?' These four nights, from Friday to Tuesday morning, will be remembered as a time of unremitting horror by all the staff at Holloway who were involved in the case of Mrs Thompson. Twenty years later, as Diana Mosley records about her stay at Holloway (*Loved Ones*, 1985), an old wardress who had become attached to Edith Thompson still disliked passing the prison mortuary alone at dusk.

At 231 Shakespeare Crescent in the meantime, Mr and Mrs Graydon are numbly sitting at their kitchen table, supported by Avis, waiting for Newenham to return. He will bring the *Evening News*. Without him the family are unable to cope with the press, who are pleading for a statement. The *Daily Sketch* in particular deserves an interview for its campaign. Over a million people have signed its petition, when previously the highest number of signatories for a reprieve was a mere 150,000. Mr Graydon, like Avis, saw the announcement on the billboards in the City, as he returned home from work. Newenham bought his evening paper in Gracechurch Street and rushed to read it under the light of a streetlamp. Somehow he got home that night. Through the *Daily Chronicle* representative, Newenham and the family released the following statement that evening:

> As a family we consider the decision of the Home Secretary to be inhuman. . . . Our hopes had been buoyed up by the long delay of the authorities in making the announcement with regard to a repeal. The decision has astounded us.
>
> If the sentence is carried out we believe that the public conscience will be shocked. To modern ideas the hanging of a woman is absolutely repugnant.
>
> Our faith in the innocence of Mrs Thompson is as strong as ever it was, and we shall continue to pray that some unforeseen turn may arise to save her life.
>
> We have received no official intimation of the Home Secretary's decision. My father, mother, sister, and I myself all read the news in the evening papers. . . .

Over in Norwood Mrs Bywaters is on the verge of collapse, when she writes the following letter direct to the King, enclosing her husband's letter from the King and the Army Council and certificates of the 1914–15 Star and War medals:

To His Majesty the King

Your Majesty

I do humbly appeal to you to spare the life of my son Fredk. Bywaters, now lying under sentence of death.

I am driven mad with anxiety, so I take this step as the last resource, and implore your Majesty to grant me this request.

Had my poor boy a father to advise him this terrible thing would never have happened, but my husband made the supreme sacrifice in the Great War, leaving me with a family of four young children to support.

I have done my best for them and brought them up respectably.

Freddy, my eldest boy, went out into the world at the age of thirteen and a half years. When only fifteen he joined the Merchant Service (he was not old enough for the Army) and stayed with the P. and O. until Sept. 23 of this year, his character all the time being excellent.

He has always been the best of sons to me, and I am proud of him, but like many other boys of his age he fell under the spell of a woman many years older than himself, who has brought all this terrible suffering on him.

Your Majesty, I implore you to spare his young life. I have given up my husband. For God's sake leave me my boy.

> I am
> Your Majesty's most humble servant.
> (Mrs) LILIAN BYWATERS

Saturday 6 January

Freddy Bywaters has spent a restless night. The news of the petition's failure on Friday upset him, but the kindly governor's sympathetic presence rendered it all so much easier. It almost felt like a sharing of bad news. Throughout the night though, alone in the dark with his thoughts, he again rehearsed the events of the last three months and particularly the trial. His one thought now remains for her: how can they possibly justify hanging her? He has always believed that no one innocent can be found guilty, let alone sentenced to death; and surely the absence of poison and glass from Thompson's body constitutes conclusive proof of Edith's innocence. He has repeatedly explained this to Major Blake, who seems to believe him despite not sharing his conviction about the woman's essentially decent and moral character. Like her, Freddy is now wondering about 'it' and probably discusses it with the warders; two more 'real' nights to go, and then the last one of all. Will death be like sleeping, and why does it happen early in the morning?

Over in the Manor Park where Freddy grew up, the Graydons are poring over the Home Office's letter, horrified by the yawning gap between the official jargon and the stark ineluctable reality which it barely acknowledges. Mrs Bywaters is prostrate. Even now she cannot accept that 'these people' will destroy her son in cold blood. May not the King himself intervene? Across the table from the mother, Florrie is writing a reply to Mrs Thompson's letter of 4 January:

11 Westow St.
Upper Norwood
Jan: 6th 1923

Dear Mrs Thompson

I received your letter this morning and read it out to Mick when I saw him. Oh God what *can* I say to you now? Words are such poor things. Mother is nearly mad today. I wonder if she will pull through?

But I dare say you are anxious to hear what Mick had to say. First of all re: the monkey. He says for you to keep that – but that he would like Frankie (my little brother) to have the watch. So you could perhaps have it sent on. He told me to tell you he understands the message and it is reciprocated. Also he sent his love and says to try and bear up. He has written to you but the letter was first sent to the 'Home Office' – so I doubt whether you will get it now. Of course Mick poor devil – didn't know [about the Home Secretary's decision] when I saw him. Even then he didn't seem much concerned over himself – his one thought was for you. Oh what a great heart he must have. But then you must of course know that as well as I.

I'll be ever so glad if you would drop me a few lines – so that I could let him have any message – will you? I can't say any more now – my heart is too full. With our kind thoughts and wishes.

Sincerely yours,
FLORRIE BYWATERS

In the meantime prisoner 9640/Thompson is sitting up in bed. The deathwatch record that she suffers from a bad headache, caused by the after-effect of the heavy sedation and the shock to her system of the failure of her appeal. Her solicitor has called to see her to speak her whatever comfort he can. She enquires whether in this extremity she may write to Bywaters without the letter being seen by the governor, and is informed that this is not possible. She therefore declines to send him a letter. Already she has decided that Canon Palmer, if anyone, must help her. She sinks back into her bed, only vaguely aware of the time and the mild flickers of sunlight breaking fitfully through her cell windows. At about twelve noon she becomes brighter and takes '2 pieces of bread & butter, cheese, tomato & tea and smokes 2 cigarettes'. Her parents, brother, and sister are visiting early today, she has been told. They are nearly desperate to see her. This time their meeting is one of unutterable pain.

The prisoner looks haggard and tired, notwithstanding the eerie and deceptive shine in her eyes. She dully replies to their questions in monosyllables, but visibly derives some comfort from the knowledge that Canon Palmer is scheduled to see her. He is already on the premises of the prison. Earlier that morning he rang in to Holloway and spoke to the governor. He was granted the necessary permission and Dr Morton suggested that 2 p.m. might be a suitable time, since the relatives did not normally arrive till the appointed time at 2.30. On arrival at 2.10 Canon Palmer calls at the governor's house. He is then led into the prison by Morton himself, who is told that the Graydons have arrived early and are at this moment visiting. The prison governor and the canon therefore adjourn to the former's office for an informal chat, till such time as the prisoner is alone. On what follows the governor's report is remarkably detailed as well as curiously elusive. In view of its documentary importance, it seems right to reproduce it here from the moment that he and Canon Palmer go to his office:

> I therefore spoke to Canon Palmer for some time in my office, no mention was made by him as to what religious denomination he was and I concluded he was C. of E.
>
> Before leaving my office to see Thompson Canon Palmer said: 'I suppose I could see you again after I see Mrs Thompson as I may want to have a talk with you.'
>
> About half an hour after Canon Palmer was brought to my office. He informed me that the prisoner wished to have his ministrations he proceeded to tell me how difficult it would be owing to all his engagements but that he would cancel everything & spend the whole of Monday with her except ½ hour which he would want for 'his office'.
>
> I informed Canon Palmer that it would be necessary for me to speak to the Chaplain on the matter & having had his comments I would then have to present the facts to the Prison Commissioners. I promised to telephone if permission was given or not.
>
> The Chaplain was not at home & I therefore visited the prisoner and asked her if she had any remarks to make to me in connection with Canon Palmer's visit. She replied, Oh yes I want him to attend to me or words to this effect.

I then rang up the Commissioners & spoke to the Secretary Mr Wall, who raised the point what religion Canon Palmer was & informed me that he knew there was a Canon Palmer of Ilford who was a R.C. Priest. Mr Wall instructed me to find out the Chaplain or R.C. Priests' views in the matter as the case might be & if they objected Canon Palmer could not visit.

I first saw the Chaplain he was unable to trace Canon Palmers name in the clergy List as a member of the C. of E. I asked the prisoner if Canon Palmer was a C of E priest to which she replied 'As far as I know he is'.

I consulted the R.C. Priest who informed me that he knew Canon Palmer as a very prominent R C Priest in Ilford. The description of his appearance agreed with that of the priest who visited during the afternoon.

The Chaplain then saw Thompson and asked her did she wish to become a Roman Catholic to which she replied she did not.

In view of the fact that the Chaplain and R.C. Priest both objected to Canon Palmer visiting in any professional capacity I telephoned to him this morning [7, *not* 6th as stated at the heading of the letter] & informed him I could not allow him to see the convict Thompson again. He asked had the woman refused to see him or why would I not admit him, in reply I informed him I could give no reason on the telephone & referred him to the Home Office which he said he would visit to-morrow (Monday). I would like also to state that the matter crossed my mind more than once in talking to Canon Palmer of (what religion is he) and although he used several terms which are very common with R.C. Priests I knew that these terms are also common with High Church Priests of the C. of England. I regret having omitted to state what took place during the visit of Canon Palmer.

I am informed that the great part of the conversation was in a frivolous vein but that Canon Palmer said words to this effect. Miss Burton had something very particular to say but she could not say it with all these people present. He then went on to say would you like me to see you alone to which the prisoner replied, she would. No mention was made of religion or any suggestion as to what religion he belonged to. I beg to state that in one of Miss Burton's letters she used the same words viz I have something very particular to say. As a result of this remark I gave special instructions to the Officers to note carefully anything Miss Burton said but nothing of any importance was reported.

The governor was doing his level best while negotiating what could for him be a potential minefield. He clearly suspected that Canon Palmer was a Roman Catholic priest, but hoped to be allowed to ignore it. After the dreadful scenes the day before and the prisoner's fearful night, he was eager not to deprive her of the comforts provided by this charismatic priest. The fact that her conversation with him was mostly 'in a frivolous vein', presumably at least in part about her love for Bywaters, suggested that she was unlikely to confess to the murder at this stage. But once Wall and Blackwell knew of Canon Palmer's visit, as they must, his hands were tied. He might have tried to lean harder on his two chaplains, but their human failings had proved stronger than their humility. The extent to which the governor's nerve failed him transpires from the slip with the date and the omission from the report of what took place during the Canon's visit itself. By playing it as safe as he could at this stage, Morton exhibited a certain political wisdom, for Canon Palmer was not a man easily dismayed by pompous and invidious officialdom. The repercussions of his visit would stretch well beyond the 6 January.

For Edith Thompson, Canon Palmer's visit proves unexpectedly one of the happiest half-hours that she has had since her incarceration. His failure to secure admission to her on Monday will leave her in a state of bewildered indignation at the thought of such petty cruelty. As the winter day draws to its end, Edith is reminded of the awful pace of time and the ever closer approach of her last hour. Once more she struggles with her fears and once again she fails. She is drugged to sleep, but finds little peace. It is to be doubted that she is alarmed by the noise of carpenters busily hammering away not far from her cell. They are erecting a wooden screen to prevent Mrs Thompson's last journey from being overlooked by the curious from nearby houses. It has been nearly twenty years since the last execution of a woman at Holloway. There has been no need for any such provision in the lifetime of any but a very few serving in Holloway prison in January 1923.

The afternoon at Pentonville is no less traumatic. Freddy is visited by his mother, his two sisters and cousin. They warmly embrace him, a rare privilege but one granted them almost from the beginning of his arrival in Pentonville. He so vehemently protests the woman's innocence that for the first time even his mother and sister are perhaps fully convinced of it. Pale and drawn he says:

> I don't care for myself . . . I lost my temper. He always made her life a hell, and he used to say if she ever left him he would make it worse than ever for her. I didn't know what I was doing. I had no intention of killing him, and I don't remember what happened. I just went blind and killed him

. . . The judge's summing up was just, if you like, but it was cruel. It never gave me a chance. I did it, though, and I can't complain.

. . . I can't believe that they will hang her as a criminal! . . . I swear she is completely innocent. She never knew that I was going to meet them that night. If only we could die together now it wouldn't be so bad, but for her to be hanged as a criminal is too awful. She didn't commit the murder. I did. She never planned it. She never knew about it. She is innocent, innocent, absolutely innocent. I can't believe that they will hang her.

At this he breaks down and starts to cry. His mother's heart nearly bursts as she listens to his sobs. There is so little that she can do now. He recovers and hands her a message to deliver to Mrs Thompson. 'Would you like to see Frankie?' his mother asks, to which Freddy replies: 'No mother, let him think of me as I was. Bring him up to be a man.' Before they depart, he once again reminds them of their pledge to do everything possible for Edith Thompson and remarks bitterly: 'I have not met with justice in this world, but I shall in the next. But I hope I shall die like a gentleman. I have nothing to fear.'

Desperate to comply with Freddy's express wishes regarding his lover, his cousin, young Miss Simmons, boards a taxi to the offices of the *Daily Express*. Its editor Beverley Baxter has openly supported the case for a reprieve of at least the woman. Miss Simmons can only tell Baxter what has just happened at Pentonville, but he interprets the manner in which the boy has admitted his guilt as tantamount to a confession. He assures the young woman that the paper will do everything in its power. He at once rings the Home Office and discovers that Bridgeman is at Minsterley. Stern is contacted next. He agrees to go out to the Welsh border even at this late stage and put Edith Thompson's case to the Home Secretary. There is no public transport available, so the *Daily Express* charters a small aeroplane to Shrewsbury from where Stern and a posse of reporters will proceed to the estate. It is late at night when the car, and in it F. A. S. Stern and the *Daily Express* men, pulls up outside the Home Secretary's estate. He has already retired to bed, but after the initial consternation he agrees to meet them downstairs. Stern apprises the Home Secretary of the new light Bywaters's confession' throws on the case of the woman and, for as long as he can, pleads with the only man in the world who can save Edith Thompson's life now. Bridgeman listens and appears sympathetic. But in the end he regrets that he cannot interfere with the course of the law and that his decision is final. Then for the second time that night he goes to bed, while the party from London listlessly returns home, conscious of the burden of failure.

On this dreary evening an eighty-two-year-old novelist and poet writes a pitiless lyric about the young woman from Manor Park. Since the age of sixteen, when he closely watched the public hanging of Elizabeth Martha Brown at Dorchester for killing her husband in a fit of jealousy, the poet has harboured a keen and undisguisedly erotic interest in the hanging of women. At the time, as he recollects *now*, he noticed: 'what a fine figure she showed against the sky as she hung in the misty rain, and how the tight black silk gown set off her shape as she wheeled half round and back'. Thirty-five years later Hardy would create in *Tess of the D'Urbervilles* one of the most vulnerable and attractive heroines of English fiction whose fate it is to be hanged. Edith Thompson is a real-life Tess for Hardy. He has read her correspondence and has been impressed by her looks. As soon as he hears that she will hang, he sits down and produces the following poem:

On the Portrait of a Woman about to be Hanged

COMELY and capable one of our race,
Posing there in your gown of grace,
    Plain, yet becoming;
        Could subtlest breast
        Ever have guessed
What was behind that innocent face,
    Drumming, drumming!

Would that your Causer, ere knoll your knell
For this riot of passion, might deign to tell
    Why, since It made you
        Sound in the germ,
        It sent a worm
To madden Its handiwork, when It might well
    Not have assayed you.

Not have implanted, to your deep rue,
The Clytaemnestra spirit in you,
    And with purblind vision
        Sowed a tare
        In a field so fair,
And a thing of symmetry, seemly to view,
    Brought to derision!

For all Hardy cares, the woman and her family who at that moment are breathing with the icy grip of death tightening about their hearts might not exist in the flesh at all. T. S. Eliot, the recently published author of *The Waste Land*, also feels a need to participate in the debate about the Ilford murder. He has recently explained that his Rother-mere-funded venture *Criterion* embodies pure Toryism as opposed to 'suburban democracy'. Here is an opportunity now to repay the *Daily Mail* proprietors for past favours by a stern public tribute, encompassing both the Italian Fascists and 'Thompson & Bywaters'. So Eliot writes the following letter which will appear in the *Daily Mail* on Monday 8 January:

> Sir,–
>
> It is so remarkable to find oneself in agreement with the policy of any newspaper on more than one point that I am writing to express my cordial approval of your attitude on nearly every public question of present importance.
>
> Nothing could be more salutary at the present time than the remarkable series of articles which you have been publishing on Fascismo; these alone constitute a public service of the greatest value and would by themselves have impelled me to write to thank you.
>
> On the Ilford murder your attitude has been in striking contrast with the flaccid sentimentality of other papers I have seen, which have been so impudent as to affirm that they represented the great majority of the English people . . .
>
> T. S. Eliot
> Clarence Gate-gardens, N.W.1

Still on Saturday night, at 50 Gordon Square, Eliot's friends the Woolfs are getting ready for a party with Sickert, Roger Fry and other Bloomsbury notables at No. 46. The party will last till the early hours of the morning. Back at No. 50 after 3 a.m., Virginia Woolf vainly tries to sleep:

> People seemed to be walking. Then a woman cried, as if in anguish, in the street, and I thought of Mrs Thompson waiting to be executed. I turned about. Footsteps sounded. A door opened. I heard voices . . . nothing was wrong. The shriek was Mary's.

Woolf had reason to know of Mrs Thompson, as Roger Fry's sister Margery was scheduled to spend some time with the prisoner on Sunday in her capacity as a visiting magistrate. The matter may have been raised at the party from which Margery was conspicuously absent. In January 1923 she was living with Roger at Dalmeny

Avenue, literally next door to Holloway Prison. She called on Edith Thompson to help her pass the hours that carried her closer to Tuesday morning, as well as offering to convey any last messages that the prisoner might have. She met the condemned woman on Sunday 7 January. The experience and its aftermath turned her into a committed abolitionist. Many years later, in giving evidence to the Royal Commission on Capital Punishment in 1950, Margery Fry would testify about this particular execution. Edith struck her 'as a rather foolish girl who had romanticised her sordid little love affair and genuinely thought herself innocent, discounting her own influence on her lover'. Above all, Fry was taken aback by the ordinariness of the woman from Ilford. While she was visiting, another Samaritan appeared in the person of a woman offering to sing negro spirituals to the prisoners, and to Mrs Thompson in particular. The singing, which took place in the chapel, deeply moved Fry who invited the itinerant singer and her husband to accompany her home to have tea with Roger and herself.

On Sunday 7 January Mrs Bywaters is writing a last letter to Edith Thompson from Freddy, on his specific instruction, since he is forbidden to write to her himself. Asked about its content Mrs Bywaters replies: 'It is far too sacred and intimate for me to state its contents.' The Bishop of Stepney is visiting Bywaters today. His mission – perhaps with the tacit collusion of the prison governors, neither of whom mentions the bishop as visiting, presumably because he is deemed to be wholly *bona fide* – is one of Christian charity. But also, and above all, he offers to relay a last message from him to her; and, if he visited her earlier in the day, he would also have taken her message to him. In the end not even the parents of either prisoner will learn the exact substance of these secret messages, the conveying of which is furthermore exempted from the otherwise mandatory presence of prison staff during visits.

Edith's penultimate day on earth has started with the by now customary bad headache, as the morphia wears off. Also, since Friday afternoon her bowels have not moved. During his morning visit therefore, the governor administers a laxative which leads to the desired result. She is only mildly sedated during the rest of the day and again protests her innocence, this time to the smart, well-spoken and kindly elderly lady who speaks to her with such unchallengeable authority. She asks that Fry bear a message of love to Bywaters and refuses even to consider that there was anything improper about this adulterous relationship. As the light fades Edith is getting increasingly restless and panic-struck. To pre-empt a renewed bout of hysteria, Morton injects her with ⅙ grain of morphia which plunges her into a deep sleep, as though she were resting in the precariously reassuring knowledge that this night is yet to be followed by a morning and a day.

Monday 8 January: A mild and grey drizzle is falling over the metropolis. On the glistening pavements and at the mouths of the city's one thousand Tube and railway entrances, paper boys are shouting the news of the latest developments in the 'Thompson & Bywaters' case, particularly the failure of the nocturnal mission to Shropshire. During the governor's morning visit Edith Thompson puts on a brave show. She feels better for her night's rest and is cheered by the news of the impending visit of the Bishop of Stepney. Eager to keep her spirits up, Morton tells her that her family's visit will be three times as long as previous calls. She thanks him, but is baffled and hurt when she learns that Canon Palmer has been refused another visit. She hoped to have him with her at the end: he was so kind, understanding and strong. At this very moment he is in Whitehall, trying hard but in vain to get the Prison Commissioners' decision overturned.

The Bishop of Stepney is announced. He brings the all-important message from Freddy. He will be thinking of her and she will remember him in those dreaded moments before death. Shortly they will be reunited. Before taking his last leave the Bishop asks whether she has anything to confess, to which she replies: 'I am prepared. I have nothing on my soul.' In the time which remains between his departure and the family's visit, Edith, though nearly prostrate, picks up a pen for the last time and begins to write to her mother and father. All that the parents will reveal about its contents was that it did *not* contain a confession. Exhausted, she tries to compose herself for this last and infinitely precious visit. To ensure that the visit passes without 'incident', the governor administers a heavy dose of sedation.

Numb with sorrow, the Graydons embark on this penultimate journey to Holloway. They are repeatedly recognised on public transport and are stalked by the press, although today even the papers keep an almost respectfully low profile. Lily Laxton is anxiously pacing outside the prison gates waiting to intercept the family to be allowed in with them, once more to see her niece. Her brother-in-law tells her that she is welcome to join them, as her name appears on the list of authorised visitors, and since the rules for the day are unchanged. This time Edith is not sitting ready at the table. Two wardresses are just then helping her to rise painfully from her bed, put on her stockings and wrap a dressing gown about her. All pretence of courage and cheer has vanished. The family gaze at the pale and ravaged woman who needs to be supported as she moves slowly towards them. The governor has told them of her general 'cheerfulness' and well being. If only for a fraction of a second he could look at the young woman with the eyes of her mother now. Edith barely murmurs a faint 'hullo'.

There is no need for more. Her appearance speaks and pleads to them with the now muted passion which once beat in those long love letters to Freddy Bywaters. There is a wardress on either side of her and, facing her, are two other attendants keenly watching. This time Lily, Avis, Newenham and the parents are wholly oblivious of the guards and try their utmost to soothe the young woman's fears, which, they sense, lurk just beneath the surface of the temporarily dulled exterior. At first she merely stares at them and replies with nods and 'yes' and 'no'. She then relates to them haltingly the visit by the Bishop of Stepney and complains that Canon Palmer is not allowed to attend to her. But mostly she remains apathetic, and it is only after repeated genialities by her brother that a flicker of light and curiosity returns into her cloudy eyes. Even as Newenham is talking, the governor's messenger delivers the note which Mr Graydon had been passed on his way into the prison. Morton had desired to read it, but lacked time to check it out. He promptly forwarded it to the prisoner's cell, where Newenham reads it out slowly and deliberately:

Graydon, 231, Shakespeare-crescent
     Manor Park, E

> I have sent telegram to the Home Secretary and the
> king for pardon for your daughter. Good news
> coming.

   Bethell, Coldbath-street, Lewisham

The small party crowded into the hospital cell at Holloway at once and naturally assume that Bethell means Lord Bethell, the Member of Parliament for the Romford Division of Essex which used to include Ilford. Such a promise from such a place can only be good news. The tragic scene in the prison is momentarily flooded with the light of hope. Everyone is exhilarated by the news and there is even laughter.

The guards warmly share in the relief prompted by the telegram. Edith alone fails fully to realise the potential importance of this latest development. After their initial flurry of excitement the family become wary again. Their time is nearly up. Mr Graydon is almost overcome as he asks whether they can all embrace and kiss her. This time the guard nods emphatically.

Edith rises to meet her father and then confusedly murmurs that he should take her home. Holding her in his arms, he speaks his last words to her ever. They spell out both his faith in the 'Bethell' message and his knowledge of her sealed fate: 'Well now, don't worry about it, you'll be home with us tomorrow night.' He yields his place to Ethel, followed by Avis, Newenham and Lily who bravely takes her leave with 'See you again tomorrow at half-past two, Edie.' At this the prisoner smiles wanly and, as avidly as her drugged state allows, drinks in the final image of the people she has loved most all her life. After the door has at last closed on them, she remains silent and curiously pensive for a long time. Never again, ever, will she see those faces, hear those voices, look at her adored mother.

It is dark outside. The governor is still waiting for an opportune moment to pass on to the prisoner a very last message from the Home Secretary as well as arranging for her transfer to the death cell proper. Whether she realises the significance of the change-over is impossible to establish. Probably an excuse of some sort is given for moving her thus in the dark, carefully shielded from the ramshackle screen erected over the weekend. Once in the new cell Edith notices that there are two different doors into it. Then Morton reads her the Home Secretary's final communication stating that 'after full consideration of all the representations made to him, he regretted that he found no grounds for departing from his decision'. For a moment she is dazed. Then she starts to scream.

The prostrate family return to Manor Park on public transport. Lily parts from them at Holloway. Back in the Crescent, where Ethel Vernon has been helping the family out for over three months now, Mr Graydon puts his hat and coat on the hallstand. Then they sit down and silently have the tea provided by Ethel. She tells them how the telegram was delivered at ten past eleven in the morning, shortly after they had all gone. Mr Warren called at that moment and immediately opened the telegram in case it contained an important new development. No sooner had he read it than he set off in a taxi to Holloway where he arrived at 12.30 p.m. and waited for the Graydons. But already, even as Ethel is talking, it is clear that the message was a cruel hoax. In a little over twelve hours therefore their daughter and sister will die on the scaffold of Holloway prison as a convicted murderess. The vigil has begun.

A mere couple of yards away to the east of Freddy Bywaters's death cell lies Dr Crippen with Ethel le Neve's letters buried with him. Like Crippen, Casement occupied the cell in which Bywaters is spending his last night. When Casement's cousin Gertrude Bannister visited him here on 27 July 1916, they had cried together, and he had begged her not to let him lie 'in this dreadful place', but to take his body back with her to the old churchyard in Murlough Bay. Forty-eight years later it would finally come to rest in Glasnevin, far from the walls of Pentonville.

While waiting for the afternoon visit he writes a number of last letters, one to a close friend or relative:

> I want you now that you know Edith (Mrs Thompson) always to love and cherish her memory as a brave-hearted, noble, and loyal woman. You can understand what she has suffered. Don't pity her, but love her. We will soon be together, and what was not to be on this sordid planet, the land of cowards and curs, will be in another world.

At 2.30 p.m. Mrs Bywaters begins her visit, accompanied by Freddy's two sisters and Florrie's fiancé, as well as Mrs Simmons and her daughter. No one can blame his mother for comparing him in a moment of tearful collapse to one of the early Christian martyrs. He is so young and yet so old as he faces them all with extraordinary calm, solicitous only for his mother's welfare: 'I'm all right; but you, you mustn't worry. You've done everything possible for me, and now just do everything you can to keep yourself cheerful.' She is weeping, like her companions, and the warders can barely control themselves when they see him display such constancy. Then he anxiously enquires whether his mother has written to Edith Thompson as he asked her to. She has and he is greatly relieved. Again and again he protests her innocence and reiterates his own version of the events of 3 October. He is thinking of tomorrow and of her: 'Why can't I be with her?', he asks his mother.

Poor girl, it must be terrible for her. If only I could be with her at the very end I feel sure it would help her ever so much. – You must never think badly of her, mum. I want you to do this for me – will you promise? Always think of her as your daughter – a very good daughter, and don't believe the evil things you have seen and heard.

The mother promises. The visit passes all too quickly. They speak of his schooldays and early years in Manor Park, and of his father. Then he mentions Frankie and suggests that his mother buy him a copy of *Tom Brown's Schooldays*:

Let him read it all, mum, but don't let him miss that part where the Squire tells Tom not to say or do things he wouldn't like his sisters to know about. I want him to learn that off by heart and never to forget it.

The particular passage in question occurs when the squire sees Tom off and advises him to 'keep a brave and kind heart, and never listen to or say anything you wouldn't have your mother and sister hear, and you'll never feel ashamed to come home, or we to see you'. As the family are about to tear themselves away and kiss him goodbye, he looks intently at his mother and quietly says: 'Give my love to Edie.' He knows that this final message cannot be delivered, but hopes perhaps that it will find its way into the papers, where the Graydons and Avis can read it. He wants them to know how he has kept faith with Edith to the end.

It is 4.30 p.m. by the time a distraught Mrs Bywaters leaves the prison gates, where a taxi-cab is waiting and swiftly carries her off to Hammersmith to stay with relatives. Tomorrow she will leave for the country. Tonight she desires to stay up in London to be physically closer to the boy till it is all over. Now that they are gone, he is alone with the hour of death. The warders around him find it harder than usual to engross him in draughts or football. As the night shift comes on, the men of the day shake hands with Bywaters. Already his steadfastness has become a legend, as his huge mail-bag certifies. The governor is foremost among those who tonight cannot close their eyes to the horror it is their duty to perform the next morning. In four years from now he will confide in his memoirs: 'But whether capital punishment is a preventative or not, I believe it to be morally and inherently wrong.' His account of the night of 8 January 1923 at Pentonville remains a stirring document. Notwithstanding two minor slips, it is remarkably accurate:

Bywaters looked to me such a fine upstanding lad, with bright blue eyes and fair hair – a typical English boy. And his manner was exactly what you would expect, quiet, respectful, and thankful for any little kindness. His eyes showed that he had suffered much more than one usually does at that age. I thought, What a strange thing. This boy, if he had not done that mad action for the sake of a woman, would, I feel certain, have turned out a good citizen. He was not a murderer at heart; it was due to the terrible emotion that possessed him at that time. I liked the boy.

The night before he was to have been hanged, I called him into my room. I could not bear the idea of that boy being all alone with his thoughts, which were enough to drive him mad. He was an only [sic] son; and he must have been thinking of his mother and the woman, the two beings he loved more than anything in the world, whom he was so soon to leave. He must have wondered why his life should be cut short. What had he done? Why had he done this terrible thing?

When he came into my room, he thanked me in a shy way for being so kind to him. I saw he was relieved to have even a short time with me, away from his thoughts. He said, 'I thank you, sir.' He sat down, and I started speaking to him about his travels, and then he told me how beautiful were the colours of the Aurora Borealis, and the wonderful sunsets, and about the strange lands he had visited. He was visualising and telling me of some of these beautiful places, and the many journeys he had made to them, when he seemed to notice my expression, because at that moment I was thinking of the last journey he was to take, at 8 o'clock [sic] the next morning.

I looked at this lad, and I thought, Is it necessary to take his life? He looked up at me and said, 'Do you think they will hurt her? I am always thinking of it, sir. I wish to God I had never done what I did. I must have been mad; but I loved her so much. Please see they do not hurt her. It was my fault; she is innocent. Everyone should have been able to see that. She never did anything – it was me.' I said, 'All right, my boy, we will try in every way to save her as much pain as possible.'

I had been suffering with neuritis in the night, and was rather late in visiting him next morning, but he looked at me with gratitude in his eyes and thanked me. The question that was on his tongue, about Mrs Thompson, he did not ask. But his thoughts were of the woman he loved, and his heart went out to her.

They hanged Mrs Thompson. Her end was terrible. She had been moaning for days, and often the words, 'Why did he do it? Why did he do it?' came from her lips. In the last few days of her life, her hair was going grey, and her sufferings had been so great, that she had had a complete collapse. They carried her to the scaffold, and had to hold her while they fixed the cap round her head; she was moaning all the time. They hanged a practically unconscious woman.[1]

*

[1]Violet Van Der Elst, *On the Gallows* (1937).

While Freddy is talking to the governor in the late hours of Monday night, Edith Thompson is disintegrating at Holloway. In her terror she alternately cherishes the moments of lucidity that remain to her as they are the last ones in her life; and then again she lets herself sink into the morphia-induced stupor, hoping against hope never again to wake from it. Dimly though, she knows that they will wake her to kill her. Morton and Dr Walker carefully monitor her state of mind as she slowly surfaces from the first period of sedation. She fearfully casts her eyes around and asks what the time is. She is offered dinner, but cannot take it. She starts to cry and pleads with them not to put her to death. Then, for the very last time, she rallies all her strength to fight them off and to break out. The governor again injects her with morphia. The antiseptic smell of the injection calms her momentarily, and she motions to the governor and begs him to ensure that her fur coat and the letters she has received be handed over to her mother. He promises to forward her application to the Prison Commissioners and assures her that there will be no problem. She is in such turmoil that the drug fails to work for two hours, as she struggles for consciousness. At 11 p.m. her spirit begins to break and she closes her eyes. At midnight she is asleep. At 3.15 a.m. she is awake and crying out deliriously for 'Freddy'. Again and again his name escapes her lips, as she fights the oppressive pull of unconscious darkness which so shortly she is to inhabit. She calls for her parents, but Bywaters is foremost in her tortured mind. Shortly before 4 a.m. she has again subsided into sleep. At 5.15 a.m. she is wide awake. She is vaguely conscious of a dreadful irony about her use now of the lavatory. The sheer enduring normality of her body's natural rhythms seems almost peculiar at such a time as this. She is calmer now and is given a mug of hot tea which she drinks. She also smokes a cigarette. Morton and Walker have been taking it in turns to look after her, and Walker is present when the nightshift leaves at 6.30 a.m.

The women come away in a state of acute distress, mindful of witnessing what no one ought to have imposed upon them. Edith is sitting up on her couch. She is crying again, like her poor mother over in Manor Park. The two new wardresses attending on her now are talking at her, gently and soothingly. One of them eventually assists her in dressing. She will be wearing her silk slip and underclothes. Over them she will be dressed in the mourning costume that her mother lent her for the trial. Her hair is tied up at the back of her head. As they pull her dress over her, the two women feel how her body is trembling. She is served a piece of buttered toast and an apple, but barely nibbles at them.

Glanvill Murray has entered. She dislikes him. He furtively proceeds to arrange her cell into a *chapelle ardente* with flowers, candles and a crucifix. He is now entirely convinced of her innocence and probably tells her so. He is a kind and intelligent man, and bitterly regrets his earlier obstructing Canon Palmer's ministrations to this cruelly reduced shadow of a young woman. He speaks to her of God's mercy and everlasting light and bliss. She continues crying and asks for a cigarette which is granted.

Outside the sounds of dawn herald the 9 January. The persistent drizzle throughout the night does not deter the crowd from forming at the break of day. It consists predominantly of women, some of them carrying umbrellas, others merely in hats and raincoats facing the forbidding red and grey structure of Holloway. A forlorn middle-aged woman has sandwiched herself into a sign saying 'Murder cannot be abolished by murder' and on the reverse side, 'If these two are hanged Judge & Jury are Murderers also'. The same spectacle is simultaneously enacted over in Pentonville. There the thronging crowd is already congesting the Caledonian Road and mounted police are on duty to clear it should there be a riot.

It is nearly 8 a.m. when prison officers Young and Wood arrive at Holloway from Pentonville. They have been deputed to assist with the hanging of the woman, as the Prison Commission deems this task to be incompatible with the natural inclinations of the fairer sex. Once on the premises and outside the death cell William H. Young decides to take a peep at the famous murderess through the spy hole in the main door. He sees her sitting on the bed, weeping, while a wardress comforts her. His instructions are to use this spy hole shortly before 9 a.m., as it will show him the executioner entering from the door opposite, which is his cue to enter the cell.

At 8.15 a.m. Morton calls on Edith Thompson and injects her with $1/32$ grain of strychnine. She has just finished another cigarette. He also offers her a large measure of brandy. He is only away for a mere fifteen minutes, when the watch tells him that she is still very bad. At 8.40 Morton re-enters the death cell. The being who confronts him is hardly recognisable as her former self. He gives her $1/100$ grain of scopalmine-morphine (Purlight sleep) and $1/6$ grain of morphia. Very shortly after this she becomes dazed and subsides into silence. She is now barely conscious. The hands of the clock point to 8.59 a.m. Ellis and one of his assistants enter hastily with the straps, while Young charges in through the main door. Edith moans and makes as if to say something on seeing Ellis. Then she feels Young's arms round her waist, lifting her up while saying: 'Come on mate – it'll soon be over.' Within seconds Ellis has pinioned her hands behind her back, while the assistant ties her skirt and then her ankles. Young is holding her and feels her breathing, as her head collapses on his shoulder. The chaplain stands by, appalled. He experiences an almost irresistible impulse to act: 'When we were all gathered together it seemed utterly impossible to believe what we were there to do. My God, the impulse to rush in and save her by force was almost too strong for me.' Instead he reads the burial service as the groaning form of the woman, now a mere tied bundle of as yet breathing human flesh, is carried out into the open and into the brick shed. She starts to moan when the cold air and drizzle touch her face. Ellis raises her head to pull the white cap over it. She is still being held up by Young, when he fastens the noose under her chin and left ear. For a fraction of a second the hooded figure on the drop is unsupported and collapses even as the hangman jumps back and kicks the lever. She falls six feet and ten inches. The thud of the trap and the sudden sharp tightening of the rope is followed by an undulatory swaying motion. No fewer than nine men and one woman have crowded into the shed and, except perhaps for the hangmen, Young and Woods, the others are visibly shaken. They are the governor and his deputy Miss Cronin, as well as the chaplain, Shrimpton, the clerk of works, and Dr Walker. Even Ellis appears affected. He does not believe in hanging women, and this particular woman, he suspects, is innocent. Looking down into the yawning gap in their midst at the figure suspended in the pit, Morton derives some comfort from the knowledge that at last it is all over. Dr Walker and he now have to descend into the pit to check the woman's heartbeat. Then she will be winched up for the coroner and the post mortem.

Over in Pentonville Freddy Bywaters has entered eternal sleep. After talking to the governor he retired and tried to rest. But even his great fortitude could not dispel the horror of the morning. So he sat up and once more he and the warders spoke of travels in the Far East, played draughts and discussed Mrs Thompson. He repeated to them what he had been pleading to the world, that he alone ought to die in the morning. He smoked heavily and eventually felt ready to lie down, but not for long. At 6 a.m. he decided that it was useless and dressed in the navy blue suit which he wore at his arrest. He pressed the creases in his trousers as he had always done, and polished his patent leather shoes, all the time chatting with the watch. They recorded that the only outward sign of agitation on the boy was a strained and anxious expression in his eyes. For breakfast he had boiled fish, bread, butter and tea. Then he attended the service in the prison chapel where he received Holy Communion. His next half hour was spent in the yard between the condemned cell, the prison cemetery and the hospital. His open grave was barely screened from his view. He curiously watched the wet dawn of a London January day rise, and dimly took in the chill in the air. He would die like a gentleman and his mates on the *Morea* would read of his courage.

He returned to the condemned cell and attended to the chaplain's words. At 9 a.m. Willis entered, shook hands with him, and pinioned his arms. The governor was present too and accompanied the hurried procession to the drop. Bywaters almost ran towards it. Unlike Edith he took it all in, particularly the white cap which cut out his sight and the noose which tightly fastened under his chin and hurt his breathing. He heard the executioner step aside and felt himself fall the first inches of the seven feet four inch drop.

The night at 231 Shakespeare Crescent consisted mostly of Mr Graydon, his two children and Ethel Vernon attending to Mrs Graydon, who since early evening was in a state of collapse. The grief-struck family rallied round the mother whose wailing and weeping resounded in the house. Mr Bristow from next door came in during the course of the night through the connecting gate at the back of their houses and brought them a bottle of whisky. He had noticed that the house was in almost complete darkness and therefore popped his head through the window: 'you must have a drink', he said. Throughout these dreadful and endless hours the mother prayed in vain to be allowed to be with her little girl. In moments of delirium the family re-experienced a world of childhood and adolescence in the Crescent, when Edith would look after her sister and little brothers. The mother surrendered to momentary spells of unconsciousness, while the father held her hands and wiped her face. At 9 a.m. the family imagined the bell tolling the executions of their *two* loved ones – for their affection for Bywaters had turned into love and respect over the past three months. No newspaper boy entered the Crescent on their side this morning. They had been ordered to keep out so as not to disturb the grief at No. 231.

Ponderously the family set out for the last time to Holloway. They pass through the Caledonian Road and glance at the huge crowd gathered outside Pentonville, where at that very moment Bywaters is still hanging from the gallows. Edith in the meantime has been stripped and washed by the governor and Dr Walker, assisted by a couple of nurses.

When he descended into the pit at 9 a.m., Morton knew what to expect: the beating of the heart for possibly as long as half an hour after the plunge, and the noisome smell of urine and faeces released from the body at the moment of the fracture of the odontoid process. But within hours of Edith Thompson's death, rumours about the manner of it are spreading. By the evening of 9 January one rumour in particular is circulating, namely that 'her insides fell out'. As it happens, she had put on over a stone in the period from 11 December 1922 to 9 January, in conditions of extreme mental stress and sparse eating – lending disturbing support to the hypothesis that she may have been pregnant.

In accordance with the letter of the law, the prisoner will have to hang for another hour. At 10 a.m. she is brought up and taken to the mortuary. Looking at the body of the woman on the slab, Morton notes that her neck is severely bruised from the rope. He at once sends her slip and underwear to be cleaned as her family will be seeing her in it. As regards the dress, it is spoiled and will be burnt. It is this which will cause a few raised eyebrows, as well as considerable frustration to the mother. The woman is washed, and re-dressed in her hastily cleaned underwear. They close her eyes and put her hair in a chaste coif. Then they lower her into the prison's standard elm coffin, where she is framed by the customary white frills. Her neck is covered in white silk. They fold her hands and put a sheaf of white lilies into them. At her feet they lay a bright cross of holly whose red berries are set off by more lilies at her legs. In his post-mortem report Morton fails to fill in any details whatever of the 'Internal Examination', even though the predicated specifications for this take up the bulk of the form. This omission is so striking we may assume he had good reason to be reticent on this point.

The Graydons have arrived. The mother looks very pale and composed. The father is repeatedly overwhelmed by grief, while Avis is comforted by a friend, perhaps Bessie. They are kept waiting for a long time, while the inquest report is drafted, and the coroner completes his preliminaries. Then the body is moved to the front of the building, as far away as possible from the scaffold. The coroner is Dr F. J. Waldo. Twenty years before he presided over the inquest of Annie Walters and Amelia Sach held on the scaffold itself, while their coffins stood across the drop. The woman lying dead by law now was then a mere nine-year-old girl. Waldo takes formal statements from four witnesses, including identification by Mr Graydon as well as Inspector Hall. Turning to the father, Waldo says: 'I do not desire you to see the body if you do not wish, but if you do wish to see it and to give evidence you may do so.' Mr Graydon indicates that he wants to see his child, as do his wife, daughter and her friend.

One by one they bend over her. She looks very still. Avis asks whether she can kiss her sister. Permission is granted, but 'only on her forehead'. So she leans forward and kisses Edith. Her father follows and then, last of all, the mother. Through her tears she looks at the silent face and closed eyes of her child, and is puzzled to know that no sound, no words, no voice, no recognition will ever again pass those lips which she knows so well. With profound emotion her father gives his daughter's husband's name and her age and name. He then asks for her fur coat and wedding-ring. For the last time the bereaved family move inside the prison's walls, then they find themselves outside in Parkhurst Road. Behind them they leave what is dearest to them, their daughter's body. For the rest of her life the mother will try to recover it, but will always be rebuffed. Shortly after the parents' departure the body in the coffin is crudely covered with lime and then sealed. It is lowered to a depth of eight feet in the prison's tiny graveyard. It will stay there for over forty-eight years, till 10.15 p.m. on 31 March 1971.

In Pentonville Freddy Bywaters has been taken down. His mother and her relatives are incapable of giving formal evidence of identification to the coroner, so Francis Hall obliges once more. For him identifying the boy's dead body is part of a job well done. With a certain pride he relishes the fact that he played a prominent part in a famous murder investigation which produced two convictions and two executions. Freddy Bywaters is buried in lot number 38, in the north-eastern corner of the cemetery. Daffodils grow over it today.

This time on Monday he was a living being. Now he is the corpse of a twenty-year-old, wrapped in a sheet of fire.

In the afternoon two men call at the office of the *Daily Express* and ask to see Beverley Baxter. They claim to be two prison officials who officiated at the hanging of Mrs Thompson. If so, they can only be George Wood and William Young, the two warders borrowed from Pentonville. In a report of 1948 commissioned by Lord Waverley (who, as Sir John Anderson, had been Permanent Undersecretary of State at the Home Office at the time of the executions) and in a covering letter to him of 15 April 1948, the then septagenarian Young explicitly denied his participation in the visit to Baxter, because it would render him 'guilty of a Breach of the Secret Act'. Waverley was sceptical about Young's evidence in the report and had it carefully checked against the governor's. The discrepancies remain signalled in the margin.

They clearly show that the former warder was trying to smooth over uncomfortable details of the execution. It is impossible to determine now beyond a doubt *who* went to see Baxter: whether it was the two prison officials who were genuinely shocked and felt compelled to see the paper to plead for women to be exempted from hanging, or wanted to sell their story for money; or whether they conveyed their news to fellow officers who reported it to Baxter. The visit to the *Daily Express* remains an unsolved mystery. However, there was another alleged visit that night,[1] by the governor of Holloway to Thomas Marlowe, the editor of the *Daily Mail*. He apparently went in great distress to persuade the paper to launch a campaign to abolish the hanging of women, because of what had happened that morning.

The fact remains that as a result of these indiscretions the story started, almost as soon as Mrs Thompson had been executed, that her 'insides' had fallen out. It was a rumour of almost certain truth.

The issue is confused further by a curious memo of 24 April 1948 from the Secretary of State to Sir A. Maxwell which notes:

The Lord Chancellor also told me that shortly after this execution Miss Fry told him that one of the horrible things connected with it was that the condemned woman on the morning of her execution had to be sewn into leather knickers because the effect of hanging is to cause the entrails to drop out of the body and that when the woman was told why this had to be done she was very much affected. Is there any truth in this story? Does

[1]Reported by the *Observer*, 18 March 1956.

hanging have this effect & are any similar precautions taken in the case of men?

The reply to this memo correctly maintains that 'no special precautions or special garments were used at the execution of Mrs Thompson'. Margery Fry did not see Edith on the morning of her death, nor does she herself mention this detail in her report on the hanging to the Royal Commission. What probably happened was that Fry heard the rumour of Edith's severe haemorrhage, if not miscarriage, and its horrific impact on all present. She may have been told that leather knickers would have prevented it from splashing out. It seems to be the case that shortly afterwards, special underwear became regulatory for the nine women who were hanged in Britain after Edith Thompson; and it is possible that Margery Fry met some of the others like Susan Newell (executed 10 October 1923) or Louie Calvert (26 June 1926), since as of January 1923 she had vigorously contributed to the crusade against the death sentence.

By 6 p.m. the Graydons are reading in the *Evening News* how their daughter was prostrate all night and asking for Bywaters in moments of lucidity. The parents' agony is alleviated only by the sure knowledge that 'Edie' is now at last and forever at rest. Towards the end of the week Margery Fry revisits the prison, where she meets the governor, Murray the chaplain and Miss Cronin:

> I was greatly impressed by [its] effect upon all of them. I think I have never seen a person look so changed in appearance by mental suffering as the Governor appeared to me to be. Miss Cronin was very greatly troubled by the whole affair. I distinctly remember her saying to me, 'I think if she had been spared she could have become a very good woman'. I was struck by this as Miss Cronin was not at all a sensitive or easily moved person; her avowed preference amongst prisoners was for 'Liverpool toughs'.
>
> Mr Murray was so much shocked by the whole experience that, after retirement, he spent much energy in writing and public speaking in favour of the abolition of the death penalty . . .

Mrs Graydon's fruitless campaign, in the months that followed, to retrieve her daughter's clothes and her body, are documented in the Home Office files. Three letters by the family testify to their lasting sorrow, courage and kindness, and compare all too well with a letter by the Home Office ministers concerned, also reproduced here.

On Sunday 14 January the *Weekly Dispatch* carried the following letter by Mr Graydon:

Sir—

I had hoped that after the execution of my unhappy daughter, I should have been able to retire into obscurity and try, if not to forget, at any rate to be forgotten.

Certain sections of the press, however, are still engaged in publishing intimate details of my daughter's life.

May I, through your columns, protest against this?

Mrs Thompson sinned and she paid the penalty. How great that penalty was only those who knew and loved her can tell. Surely the decent thing is to let the past bury itself, if not out of pity for her, out of consideration for those she left behind.

Wherever I or any member of my family goes we are pointed at, stared at, photographed. My house is besieged all day and every day by anybody who is the victim of morbid curiosity.

During all these terrible weeks we have had no privacy, and now that we desire to go away for a brief period we are haunted always by the thought that we shall be known and followed.

To continue to rake up the past is only to prolong the agony. And when that past is almost entirely fictitious I feel bound to protest.

Nine-tenths of what has been written about my daughter has been completely untrue.

Now that she is dead, cannot these lies cease? Cannot we be left to the privacy which I used to think was the right of all Englishmen to enjoy?

 — I am, Sir, yours faithfully

  W. E. GRAYDON

The following morning, Monday 15 January, the Home Office official Blackwell was redrafting a reply to an anxious letter by T. E. Groves, a Stratford MP, enquiring after the manner of Mrs Thompson's death, in view of the press reports. The original answer had been shown to Anderson, who invited Blackwell to rewrite it. Evidently the two mandarins were eager to ensure that the entire truth about the events of 9 January, in which they played such a leading part, did not come out. So they decided to tamper with the truth, confident that if ever they were challenged on their mendacity they could argue their way out of any corner. Here is the letter:

15 January 1923

Dear Sir

In reply to your letter of the 10th instant, I am desired by the Home Secretary to say that from reports he has received he is satisfied that the execution of Mrs Thompson was carried out in the most humane manner possible. The statement that the prisoner was 'in a state of collapse practically all through the previous night' is without foundation. She slept soundly for several hours. As for the suggestion that she had to be carried to the scaffold, it was thought to be more humane to spare her the necessity of walking from her cell, but she was not unconscious.

Yours faithfully

Unlike Blackwell's, Anderson's conscience would increasingly haunt him. In the wake of the House of Commons debate on the death penalty on 14 April 1948, and again in the arguments in Parliament which followed the serialisation in the *Observer* of Arthur Koestler's book on the death sentence,[1] Anderson (as Lord Waverley) unsuccessfully attempted to gag Beverley Baxter and subsequently Koestler and the *Observer*. Reportedly 'distressed', he once more inspected the file on the woman he had helped to bring to her death, when Lewis Broad's book *The Innocence of Edith Thompson* was launched in the *Sunday Dispatch* of 26 October 1952. It must have brought him little joy. Both books punishingly brought home the guilt of all those involved in the processes of the law of capital crimes.

On 20 January Newenham Graydon wrote the following letter to the governor of Holloway:

> 231 Shakespeare Cres
> Manor Park
> E.12
> 20th January '23

Dr J. H. Morton
    Holloway

Dear Sir

My Mother and Father have asked me to express their thanks to you for your kindness and consideration towards both our family and Mrs Thompson during the time my sister was in your charge.

There were very few visits passed that did not bring from Mrs Thompson some word of thanks due to you, and I only wish it was possible for me to adequately express the feeling of gratitude we have towards you, as well as the whole staff who came into contact with her.

Very sincerely yours.
    Newenham E. Graydon

---

[1] *Reflections on Hanging*, London 1956.

Having done his human best by the prisoner, Morton now intended to impress his superiors and forwarded the brother's generous note to Blackwell with a covering message:

> The attached letter may be useful to the Commissioners in case they should decide to take any action should statements of ill treatment & c. towards the abovenamed whilst in custody here occur in the future.
>
> J. H. Morton

On Thursday 25 January Mrs Graydon wrote to the *Stratford Express* which carried her letter that weekend:

> Would you kindly allow me to use your columns in order to express my thanks to the hundreds of newly found friends in the district covered by the the 'Stratford Express' who have so kindly sent me their sympathy and condolences during the agonising period through which my family and I have just passed. Verily one's true friends are not found until adversity's heavy hand descends upon one's shoulders. It has been the kindness of these unknown friends which has kept my spirits up so far, and my gratitude to them knows no bounds. I thank them all from the bottom of my heart.
>
> Yours sincerely
>
> Ethel J. Graydon
>
> 231 Shakespeare-crescent
>
> Manor Park E.12

The family of Edith Thompson stayed put in the Crescent. Eventually the boys left and married. The little house at 231 Shakespeare Crescent remained home for the parents and for Avis, already resigned to a solitary life. The mother died there in January 1938 at the age of sixty-five. Only then, seventeen years after the tragedy, did Avis and her father move back to Ilford, leaving behind the home in which Edith had grown up and lived out her girlhood. It was for this reason that Mrs Graydon had been unable to leave No. 231, the one place where, in her memories, her daughter lived and continued to breathe untouched. In February 1941, not long after the move to Gants Hill, Avis buried her father. The parents rest side by side in the City of London Cemetery, in the grave bought by Edith and occupied for a few weeks in 1922 by Percy Thompson, who even now lies a mere 100 yards to the north.

Since 1923 Avis had been a devout Catholic and worshipped at St Francis RC church in Stratford. Every year to this day on the 9 January a memorial service is held here to commemorate her sister. After the father's death, and as a new generation of Graydon children were coming up, Avis felt increasingly that their prospects must not be prejudiced by a tragic past. Mindful that the written and printed record remain, she destroyed most of the photographs of her sister in the family's possession, as well as Edith's infinitely precious letters. Edith would live on in her heart, she told herself, and in God's peace. She only kept her sister's fur coat, her watch, an old necklace and a traycloth that she vividly recalled 'Edie' working on as a child. She increasingly became reclusive, but remained interested in the past and the present. She outlived most of the participants in this 1920s tragedy.

She read in the *Ilford Recorder* of Richard Thompson's death in February 1952, and in the summer of 1955 she was deeply pained when another young woman called Ruth Ellis, almost exactly her sister's age, perished on the same scaffold at Holloway. Whether she was aware of renewed interest in Edith's fate during the 1950s cannot be established. In her heart the flame of hope never wavered. Its light would shine till the day that she imagined she would be reunited with the sister who had become a tragic legend.

In 1973 Avis Graydon was traced to her address in Roll Gardens in Gants Hill, and she agreed to discuss Edith Thompson. A sympathetic interviewer whom she came to trust drove her past 41 Kensington Gardens and 231 Shakespeare Crescent.[1] Sitting in a car outside the house in Ilford fifty years on, she gazed at it in silence. She pointed out the Thompsons' bedroom and their front room. Then she remarked that Edith would never have approved of the way the place is made up now. As they passed the spot where Percy fell she expressed sorrow at his terrible death. Throughout this trying journey into the past, she remained composed, true to the dignity that was always hers. Asked whether seeing her sister in her coffin at Holloway was the first time that she 'could actually believe that Edith was dead', she replied:

[1] Mrs Audrey Russell of the Court Welfare Department at the Royal Courts of Justice spent many hours in the company of Avis Graydon and recorded her reflections on Edith Thompson's early life and tragic death. I was fortunate to meet Mrs Russell and am greatly indebted to her unstinting assistance with the research for this book.

Yes, and sometimes I can't believe it now. Do you know, sometimes I think I'll go to that door, and she'll be coming in. I do! I know it's fantasy, but I do sometimes think that . . . I often think to myself one of these Sundays she'll be at the door.

Avis Graydon died at the King George Hospital in Ilford on 6 August 1977. She was eighty-one years old, the same age as her grandmother had been, and is buried at St Patrick's RC cemetery in Leytonstone.

Edith Thompson remains in unconsecrated ground in Brookwood Cemetery. So far her body has not joined her parents, as her mother hoped when she lay dying in the upstairs bedroom at 231 Shakespeare Crescent on the eve of World War II. Had the Home Office or Prison Service cared to inform Avis Graydon of the transfer of the bodies from Holloway in 1971, Edith Thompson would now truly be home with her parents.

Freddy Bywaters has never left Pentonville since the night he entered it on Monday 11 December 1922, after being sentenced to death. The body was not claimed after abolition, and even though (possibly) his younger brother Frank and (certainly) nephews and nieces are alive at the time of writing, it is doubtful that the family will ask for a reinterment.

Postscript

The Rt Hon. Douglas Hurd
The Home Secretary
The Palace of Westminster
London SW1

31 August 1988

Dear Sir

In the course of the afternoon of the recent parliamentary debate
on the death penalty, my publishers, Hamish Hamilton, sent you
a copy of my book, *Criminal Justice: The True Story of Edith
Thompson*. The events related in the book happened over sixty-
five years ago, but the execution of Edith Thompson at Holloway Prison in 1923 remains a tragic blot on this country's tradition of effective and equitable justice. I argue in my book that
Edith Thompson was innocent of the charges brought against
her. In his review of *Criminal Justice* in the *Observer* Mr
Ludovic Kennedy noted that Edith Thompson's innocence was
so well established now as to be hardly a matter of debate any
longer. If so, then the case for a posthumous pardon is considerably strengthened. I realise that clearing Edith Thompson's name
may present some difficulty, because it means reversing a long-
standing judgment, but it would seem to be the right thing to do.

I recognise that a pardon for Mrs Thompson at this late stage
could be interpreted as a mere gesture: it will not return to her

the life that was so tragically and unjustly cut short, nor can it really make amends to her family. Nevertheless, knowing of your own strong sense of justice and fair play, I feel that you may well agree with me that, as a matter of principle, it would be wrong to shun our retrospective responsibilities in this matter. Bearing this in mind, I would heartily beg you to consider whether you cannot see your way clear to restoring true justice to Edith Thompson in whatever symbolic way is possible after all this time.

My case for Edith Thompson's innocence is fully expounded in *Criminal Justice*. I must therefore request your forbearance for drawing attention to some of the more salient points in her defence again.

The case against Mrs Thompson rested almost entirely on a series of fantasy wishfulfilment letters she wrote to Frederick Bywaters. Much of the material in these letters had no basis in reality, but was a sort of 'acting out' in writing of what are not uncommon, albeit rarely expressed, wishes. Some of the early letters were read as expressing a desire for her husband's death and as suggesting that she had tried to procure it through the administration of poisons and particles of glass. But the post mortem produced no evidence that either poison or glass had been consumed. At the most these letters might possibly have been seen as admissible evidence on the second indictment – which consisted of five counts – but this was not the charge that was brought. As I show in my book these letters are open to an innocent interpretation and the most damaging passages all date from several months before Bywaters attacked Thompson.

Mrs Thompson and Bywaters were tried together on the first indictment, that of the murder of Percy Thompson by stabbing in a street in Ilford. That Bywaters killed Thompson has never been disputed. Equally, that Edith Thompson set it up was never proven. Indeed, examination of the known facts and the couple's correspondence does not suggest that she was so involved. Instead, the Crown used a selection of her letters in Court to generate a climate of prejudice against her as an immoral adulteress who seduced and suborned a young man eight years her junior. Despite the fact that there is no evidence of any kind in the letters or otherwise that Edith Thompson knew that her husband would be assaulted that night in that particular place and in that manner, the Solicitor-General stated in his opening address to the jury that 'there is the undoubted evidence in the letters upon which you can find that there was a preconcerted meeting between Mrs Thompson and Bywaters at the place'. As only half of Edith Thompson's correspondence was submitted in Court, the jury may well have been led to believe, by this erroneous claim, that a reference to the place, the time and the manner occurred in one of the letters withheld from them. That the jury was furthermore influenced by the judge's openly expressed disgust concerning the sexual immorality of the correspondence is on record in a letter which a juror wrote to the *Daily Telegraph* thirty years later: 'it was my duty to read them [the letters] to the members of the jury ... "Nauseous" is hardly strong enough to describe their contents ... The jury performed a painful duty, but Mrs Thompson's letters were her own condemnation.'

On what grounds in law rather than on morals could the letters convict Mrs Thompson? Even if they had been used on the *second* indictment, she would have been exonerated by Sir Bernard Spilsbury, who appeared for the Crown and whose post-mortem report on Percy Thompson (*PRO: Crim1/206*) categorically concludes: 'I found no indications of poisoning and no changes suggestive of previous attempts at poisoning. I detected no glass in the contents of the intestine.' In view of this the Solicitor-General's prevarication in Court, that 'a post-mortem examination showed that there were *practically* [my italics] no traces of any poison' must be deemed to fall far short of the accepted high standards of British justice and of fairness to the accused.

Equally unfair to the accused was the prejudicial summing-up by the trial judge. His ignorance of the contents of the novel *Bella Donna* which was used in evidence against Mrs Thompson, his failure to give due weight to her hostile view of the novel's protagonist, whom she described as 'abnormal – a monster utterly selfish and self living', and his loaded misquotations of her evidence in Court, reflect poorly on his grasp of the issues at stake.

Nothing highlights the extent of his prejudice so gravely as his treatment of the important evidence of Mr John Webber about Mrs Thompson's protests during the murder. Webber's evidence in Court (*Notable British Trials: Bywaters and Thompson*, pp.

19–20) is that he heard 'a woman's voice saying "Oh, don't, oh, don't," in a most piteous manner' as he 'was about to retire to bed'. On hearing that, 'he went out into the street'. When the judge first addressed Webber's evidence, he inaccurately claimed that Webber lived at a house 'somewhere opposite, and it was five minutes before he came out, and he heard Mrs Thompson in a piteous tone say "Oh, don't, oh, don't"' (*NBT*, p. 142). Webber in fact lived 50 yards down the road on the same side as the scene of the crime, hardly 'opposite', and he did not hear Mrs Thompson *after* he came out, but before. When the judge re-addressed Webber's evidence (*NBT*, p. 152), he introduced it as 'one other very curious piece of evidence', and told the jury that it may well be unreliable, because Webber was 'some way off' when he heard Mrs Thompson: 'I am not saying it is true; it is for you to say whether it is accurate, or whether it is imaginary, or whether he has made a mistake.' Such reckless impugning of a witness's reliability was particularly damaging, as the jury naturally looked to the judge for guidance. The judge's further intimation to the jury, that Bywaters's running off after the crime and Mrs Thompson's running for a doctor may reflect, as the prosecution alleged, a preconcerted plan about 'how to avoid suspicion' (*NBT*, p. 153), beggars belief in the minds of all fair-minded people.

Under such circumstances, I find it impossible to conclude that Mrs Thompson was given a fair trial. There is no colourable evidence that she helped to plan or knew of this attack and considerable doubt about any active involvement in her husband's death. Moreover, irrelevant moral prejudices coloured the judgment of the Court; rather than for murder she was hanged for adultery. It is, I believe, our bounden duty now at last to clear her name.

René J. A. Weis

Sources

Newspapers

Daily Chronicle, Daily Express, Daily Mail, Daily Mirror, Daily Sketch, Daily Telegraph, East Ham Echo, East London Advertiser, Era, Evening News, Ilford Recorder, Illustrated London News, Isle of Wight Guardian & Shanklin Chronicle, Lloyds Sunday News, News of the World, Observer, Stage, Stratford Express, Sunday Express, Sunday Pictorial, Times, Weekly Dispatch, World's Pictorial News

Public Record Office and Home Office

The two main files in the Public Record Office are the court file, *Crim 1/206* in Chancery Lane, and the police file, *Mepo 3/1582* at Kew. The court file has been open to the general public for some time and contains transcripts of Mrs Thompson's letters, Spilsbury's crucial post mortem report, the lists of exhibits, a police map of the area of the murder, copies of the appeals and their dismissals, and typed depositions from various witnesses.

The police file was opened to the public on 1 January 1986, although the author had been allowed to consult it in December 1985 and before that at New Scotland Yard in September 1984. It is a document of considerable interest and of paramount importance for anyone researching the whereabouts of the originals of Mrs Thompson's letters. As well as transcripts of all Edith Thompson's letters to Bywaters and a number of unsworn testimonies, the file contains several memos regarding the original letters themselves. Mrs Bywaters's repeated requests to have the 'letters written by Mrs

Thompson to my son (which he particularly wished me to have)' are on file, as is a DPP memo of 30 January 1923 instructing the Commissioners of Police to keep Edith Thompson's letters

> in your safe custody at New Scotland Yard. I suggest that Mrs Lilian Bywaters be informed that you are unable to comply with her request with regard to the letters written by Mrs Thompson to her son and that these would be kept in the safe custody of New Scotland Yard, where there is no chance of their 'falling into other hands': and that should Mrs Bywaters press for their return she should be referred to the provisions of the Police Property Act 1897.

The subsequent fate of the letters is indicated by *201/MR/252* (*Minute Sheet 1 & 2*) where a CRO entry of 7 February 1923 acknowledged the receipt of Bywaters's knife from the Home Office and DPP, and noted further that when the letters arrived they would be stored in the same *PPV* [prisoner's property voucher] *12376k*. On 24 May 1923 the letters were received in CRO and recorded as stored.

What the DPP's memo referred to as 'safe custody' in 1923 has turned out to be not so in the 1980s, when the author conducted extensive searches for this material. In two separate letters (21 January and 7 April 1986) the Chief Registrar and Departmental Record Officer of New Scotland Yard conceded that his department had failed to trace *PPV 12376k*, while being unable to confirm that the letters were destroyed. For the time being Edith Thompson's letters must be regarded as missing.

Equally disturbing is the fact that a photograph of Mrs Thompson which Bywaters carried on him when he was arrested, and which the author inspected in 1984, has inexplicably disappeared on the premises of New Scotland Yard when *Mepo 3/1582* was in the temporary custody of the Metropolitan Police. The Chief Registrar's letter on this to the author (24 September 1987) regrets that Scotland Yard's 'strict and disciplined procedure' with archival material broke down on this occasion. This unique photograph – reproduced on the cover of *Criminal Justice* from a copy in the possession of the *Daily Mirror* – must now also be regarded as missing.

The main Home Office files on 'Thompson and Bywaters', *HO 144/2685/438338* (*Parts I & II*) and *P.Com. 8/22/59256* and *8/436/59452* remain subject to extended closure. Among others they contain several letters by Edith Thompson's mother, sister and aunt, as well as several letters addressed to her from Pentonville by Bywaters. After the order of 21 November 1922 to intercept the lovers' letters, both hers and his were posted to the Prison Commissioners' office for censoring and safe-keeping. Bywaters's survive to this day, but hers which were stored in the same place have vanished in the same way as the letters kept in supposedly safe custody at New Scotland Yard. One of several detailed letters to the author from the Home Office Departmental Record Officer on this unintelligible discrimination between the two sets of correspondence acknowledges that the normal procedures in the case of stopped letters would have been to put them with the prisoners' records, which would be retained by the prisons. But as has already been indicated, Bywaters's dagger and Mrs Thompson's letters were centrally kept in a *PPV* at Scotland Yard. One may therefore reasonably conclude that Bywaters's intercepted letters (which did not go to *PPV 12376k*) were segregated from hers, accorded a different status and then filed. Every document which is actually in Edith Thompson's own hand has, it seems, been erased from the records with a disquieting single-mindedness.

Other published material

The most accessible and most useful source of information on 'Thompson and Bywaters' outside the newspapers remains the splendid *Notable British Trials* volume on the case: *Trial of Frederick Bywaters and Edith Thompson*, edited by Filson Young (1923). Also of interest is *The Innocence of Edith Thompson: A Study in Old Bailey Justice*, by Lewis Broad (1952). 'The Echo in the Streets' by Sylvia Margolis (BBC Radio London: 17 June 1973) is a stimulating and atmospheric programme about the Ilford context of the story of Edith Thompson, as is 'Hanged for Adultery' (BBC: 21 July 1973). Most histories of crime and particularly those concerned with miscarriages of justice include discussions of this case. Few of them add much to the information contained in the *Notable British Trials* volume.

I am indebted to the editors of *Hansard* for their reports of the proceedings in the House of Commons on 20 and 21 February 1923, 14 April 1948, and 27 and 29 March 1956; to the Minutes of Evidence taken before the Select Committee on Capital Punishment 1929–30; and to the reports of the Royal Commission on Capital Punishment 1949–53. In *Strange Street* (1935) Beverley Baxter vividly recalls the day of Mrs Thompson's execution. The most authentic tribute to Edith Thompson remains F. Tennyson Jesse's novel *A Pin to See the Peepshow* (1934).

Index

Aitken, Bessie 3, 11, 17, 91, 94, 95,
    100, 102, 104, 120, 150, 152,
    153, 165, 175, 249, 258, 266,
    267, 276
  visits Edith Thompson in Holloway
    262–4
  writes about Edith for newspaper
    264
Aitken, Reg 17, 91, 92, 94, 100, 104,
    120, 150, 152, 165, 175, 258
Aldridge, Myrtle 32, 134
Ambrose, Dr 205
Anderson, Sir John 91, 306, 308
  distress after Edith Thompson's
    execution 309
Armstrong, Herbert Rowse
  charged with suspected poisoning
    101
  hanged, May 1922 122
Ashley, Miss 120
Askew, Claude and Alice
  The Shulamite 96, 112–13, 115
  The Woman Deborah 96
Asquith, H. H. 24

Baldwin, Stanley 136, 212
Bannister, Gertrude 297
Barrington Matthews 222
Baxter, Beverley 189, 255, 306, 309
  final attempt to save Edith Thomp-
    son 290
Baxter, Robert 281

Bethell, Lord 295
  hoax about Thompson reprieve in
    name of 295–6, 297
Birnage, Mrs 30, 31, 74, 93, 102, 109,
    114, 166
Birnage, Sidney J. 30–1, 74, 102, 109,
    114–15, 134, 165
Blackwell, Sir Ernley 91, 123, 217,
    280, 289
  glosses over horror of Edith's execu-
    tion 308–9
  letter rejecting petition for Edith and
    Bywaters 280–1
Blake, Major W. 220, 285
  on Edith Thompson's execution 299
  on Freddy Bywaters 298–9
Bolding, Ada 83, 84
Bolding, Rev. Horace George 83
  suicide by poisoning 84
Bottomley, Horatio 86, 122
Bridgeman, William C. 269, 290
Britain
  Armistice, 1918 29
  'baby farmers' 10n
  Compulsory Service Bill, 1916 24
  hangings 10
  heatwave of 1922 120–3
  influenza epidemics, 1918 and 1919
    29
  relaxed atmosphere of 1920s 41–3
  'surplus women', after First World
    War 42

Brixton Prison 207, 216, 217, 250
Broad, Lewis: *The Innocence of Edith Thompson* 309
Broken Blossoms, film 52
Brown, Edith Annie 163, 225
Burton, Ida 252, 275, 288
Bywaters, Florence May (sister 'Florrie') 5, 97, 130, 283
  kindly letter to Edith Thompson in Holloway 276, 282
  letter to Mrs Thompson, 6 Jan. 1923 286
  visits Freddy in Pentonville 251, 289, 297–8
Bywaters, Frederick Edward Francis (Freddy)
  comments on *The Fruitful Vine* 148–50
  letters from ship to Edith Thompson 66, 67, 69, 73, 75, 86, 90, 109, 111–12, 115–16, 119, 127, 138, 150–1, 157–8, 161, 166–7
  life and death: birth, 1902 5; boisterous boyhood 17–20; friendship with Graydon boys 18, 19; jobs on leaving school 20; early contact with Edith Graydon 20–1; knocked over by bomb from Gotha, 1917 21; life in merchant navy, 1918 21–2, 23; visits Graydons, 1920 33–4, 35; meets Edith Thompson, 1920 34; meets Percy Thompson, 1920 34; beginnings of love affair with Edith 39–41; jumps ship to visit Graydons, 31 Dec. 1920 39; loses and regains job with P & O 40; holidays with Thompsons and Avis Graydon 44–8; first kiss for Edith Thompson 45–6; moves in with Thompsons 48, 50; jealous of Edith's men friends; breaks up with Avis 50; becomes Edith's lover 51, 52; cause of quarrels between Thompsons 53–5, 56; steps between quarrelling husband and wife 55; leaves the Thompsons' house 56–7; meetings with Edith 57, 58; gets job on SS *Morea* 58; meets Edith on

return from voyage 60–1; spends day with Edith 62; confronts Thompson about wife 62–3; sails for Bombay 63; thinks about breaking off liaison with Edith 75, 132; meets Edith, Jan. 1922 79–80; implicated in Edith's abortion 80; meets Bill Graydon in Bombay 86; reunited with Edith, March 1922 122, 124; quarrels with mother over Edith 94, 96–7; gives Graydons doped cigarettes 97–8; sails from Tilbury 97; meetings with Edith, May 1922 122, 124; sails for Australia, June 1922 125; twentieth birthday, June 1922 135; travels home from Australia 152; sends anonymous threatening letter to Edith 154; jealous of Percy Thompson 155; returns from Australia Sept. 1922 159; meetings with Edith 160–72 *passim*; lunches with Edith, 3 Oct. 1922 174; visits the Graydons 177–8; travels towards Thompsons' house 178–9, 180; attacks Thompson with knife in street 181, 183; runs away from dying man 183, 187; disposes of knife 187; returns home 187; plans, next morning 189; implicated by Richard Thompson 192; learns of Percy Thompson's death 193–4; visits the Graydons 194; apprehended by police 194–5; interrogated by police 195; makes statement 195–7; his room searched 197–8; letters from Edith found 198; held at police station 197, 202; sees Edith at police station 202, 203; admits to attacking Thompson 204; court appearances 205, 206, 210–13 *passim*, 216; tells where he has dropped knife 206; asks for legal aid 206; ditty box taken from *Morea* 211; letters from Edith Thompson found 211, 212; letters written in prison to Edith intercepted 216–18; committed for trial at Old Bailey 218; transferred to Pentonville, Nov. 1922 220; Old Bailey trial, *see* Thompson-Bywaters trial; sentenced to death 248; meets mother after sentencing 250; visited by mother and sister in prison 251; appeal against sentence lodged 254–5; attends appeal hearings 260; appeal dismissed 260–1, 262; letter to Edith intercepted, 2 Jan. 1923 276; petitions Home Secretary, 3 Jan. 1923 277–80; receives secret message from Edith 283; hears petition has been dismissed 285; visited by family and cousin 289–90; protests Edith's innocence 289–90; last letters 297; final visit from family 297–8; final night 302; execution 303; formal identification 305; burial at Pentonville 305, 312

love affairs apart from Edith Thompson 41

sailor from age of fifteen 9–10

Bywaters, Frederick Sam (Freddy's father) 5

death, 1919 22

war service 22

Bywaters, Lilian (Freddy's mother) 5, 22, 48, 104, 117, 119, 135, 153, 154, 167, 177, 187, 197–8, 214, 224, 225, 243, 249, 250, 260, 261, 286

actions after Freddy's arrest: visits Freddy in Pentonville 251, 256, 257, 289–90, 297–8; writes 'A Mother's Appeal to the Mothers of the Nation' 254; plea to King for son's life 284–5; writes letter to Edith for Freddy 293

quarrels with Freddy over Edith Thompson 94–5, 96–7

Bywaters, Lilian (Freddy's sister Lily) 5, 189

visits Freddy in Pentonville 256, 289, 297–8

Calvert, Louie 307

Cap Polonia, SS 35

Carlton & Prior, milliners 12, 15, 16, 17, 23, 28, 29, 49, 57, 62, 63, 65, 66, 70, 76, 79, 81, 87, 88, 92, 93, 101, 102, 104, 105, 115, 120–1, 122, 128, 129, 132, 135, 136, 137, 144, 155, 157, 159, 163, 164, 167, 168, 170, 174, 178, 191

Aldersgate premises 31–2

annual outing 49–50, 134

Carlton, Charlie 50

Carlton, Herbert 12, 16, 26, 28, 32, 49, 50, 52, 80, 109, 120, 122, 131, 137, 163, 164, 167, 213, 224

Carpentier, Georges 76, 117–18

Casement, Roger 91, 297

Cavell, Edith 11

Chambers, Graham 128

Chambers, Kenneth 14, 15, 30, 33, 65, 128

Chambers, Lily 30, 33, 65, 128

Chambers, Rev. Charles 14

Chambers, R. W. 117

   The Business of Life 85, 92, 116

   The Common Law 75, 81, 85, 151

   The Firing Line 156–7

Chambers, Victor 15

Chaplin, Charlie 60

Chelsea Flower Show, 1922 121

Childers, Erskine

   dies in Dublin jail 220

   The Riddle of the Sands 220

Clevely, Mrs 179, 180

Clevely, Percy E. 179, 180, 183, 186, 224, 238

Cooper, Lady Diana 81

Co-Optimists, the 87, 116

Cornwell, John T., VC 20, 21

Crippen, Dr 250, 297

Cronin, Miss 302, 307

Curtis-Bennett, Sir Henry 101, 203, 216, 219–20, 250

   defence of Edith Thompson 222, 223, 225, 226, 228, 230, 234, 235, 236, 238, 241, 243–4, 245

   pleads Edith Thompson's appeal 261

Daily Chronicle 284

Daily Express 188, 189, 290

   details Edith Thompson's worth 255

story of prison officers visiting after
    executions 306
Daily Mail 188, 282
    on 'surplus women' after First
        World War 42
Daily Sketch 83, 84, 89, 115, 116, 118,
    173, 188, 230, 269, 284
    campaign on behalf of Edith and
        Freddy 253, 255, 256, 257, 259,
        266
Dane, Clemence: *A Bill of Divorce-
    ment* 41
Darling, Mr Justice 101, 260, 261
De la Mare, Walter: *Memoirs of a
    Midget* 42–3
Derry, Mr 90–1, 136, 137
Dixon, Pat 17, 18
Douglas, James 189
    Ilford Murder, The 225n
    on Edith Thompson at trial 221–2,
        224
    on Freddy Bywaters at trial 225
Drought, Dr Percy J. 181n, 198, 210,
    224, 279
Dumas, Alexandre: *The Count of
    Monte Cristo* 157
Dunn, Reginald 145

East Ham Echo 188
Edward (David), Prince of Wales 42,
    132–3, 142, 282
Egypt, SS: sinks off French coast, 1922
    120
Eliot, T. S.
    on 'sentimentality' over Thompson-
        Bywaters case 292
    The Waste Land 292
Elliott, Myles 222
Ellis, John 23, 301
    alerted about Edith Thompson's
        execution 281
    execution of Edith Thompson
        302
Ellis, Ruth 311
Evening News 193, 194, 229, 231,
    284, 307

Farnol, Jeffrey
    Chronicles of an Imp, The 151
    Martin Conisby's Revenge 151

Foster, Detective Sergeant Ernest 194,
    206
Frampton, Walter 222, 234
Fry, Margery 307
    alleged statement on horrors of
        hanging 306, 307
    crusade against death sentence 307
    on effect of Edith's execution on
        prison officials 307
    visits Edith Thompson in Holloway
        293
Fry, Roger 292, 293

Geal, PC Cyril 173, 184, 185
Gish, Lillian 60
Glanvill Murray, Rev. S. R. 275, 301,
    302, 307
Glorious Adventure, The, film 80
Grafton, Doris 131, 153
Graydon, Avis Ethel (Edith's sister) 2,
    4, 6, 8, 13, 15, 23, 25, 26, 28,
    33–4, 40, 43, 45, 46, 48, 49, 54,
    55, 64, 65, 66, 77, 81, 83, 84, 102,
    106, 107, 108, 110, 120, 123,
    126, 132, 137, 144, 145, 153,
    156, 165, 170, 177, 191, 192,
    193, 195, 234, 249, 250, 254,
    267, 298, 303, 310, 311, 312
    life before Edith's arrest: death of
        lover in First World War 28, 29;
        has crush on Freddy Bywaters 44,
        99–100; jilted by Freddy 50;
        promises to teach Percy Thomp-
        son to dance 70; holiday in Bour-
        nemouth, 1922 141–3; twenty-
        sixth birthday, 1922 160
    life after Edith's arrest: gives evi-
        dence at trial 242; visits Edith in
        Holloway 251–2, 257, 270, 294–
        6; besieged by press 253; petitions
        prime minister about Edith 271–
        2; says farewell to dead sister
        304–5; death, 1977 312
Graydon, Edith Jessie
    amateur theatricals 7, 14–15
    dancing ability 8, 77
    life before marriage: birth 2; educa-
        tion 3, 4, 5–6; childhood 4, 7–8,
        11; early play-acting, 6–7, 8;
        schoolgirl romance 11; early jobs

11–12; settles at Carlton & Prior, 1911 12; meets Percy Thompson 12; courted by Percy Thompson 12–14, 16; trips to Paris for firm, 1913–14 16–17; becomes Percy Thompson's mistress, 1914 17; early meeting with Freddy Bywaters 20–1; doubts about marrying Percy 23–4, 25; marriage, 1916 24–6. *Continued under* Thompson, Edith Jessie

Graydon, Ethel J. (Edith's mother) 1, 2–3, 13, 15, 19, 23, 24, 28, 33, 97, 98, 103, 115, 170, 177, 190, 191, 195, 205, 208, 219, 243, 249, 250, 284, 298, 303, 307
   actions following Edith's arrest: evidence at trial 242; visits Edith in Holloway 251–2, 257, 266–7, 281, 287, 294–6; besieged by press 253; petitions Queen with regard to Edith 270–1; says farewell to dead daughter 304–5; thanks local people for kindness 310; death, 1938 310
   fiftieth birthday, 1922 258
   forty-ninth birthday 72, 73
   illness, 1922 81, 88

Graydon, Harold (Edith's brother 'Towser') 3, 4–5, 13, 18, 23, 28, 33, 108, 127, 131, 153

Graydon, Newenham (Edith's brother 'Newnie') 3, 13, 33, 52, 53, 170, 178, 192, 194, 195, 208, 267, 284, 303
   actions following Edith's arrest: visits Edith in Holloway 257, 258, 287, 294–6; says farewell to dead sister 304–5; thanks Governor of Holloway for kindness 309

Graydon, William (Edith's brother 'Billie') 3, 4, 13, 18, 19, 23, 28, 33, 91, 118, 120, 208
   meets Freddy Bywaters in Bombay, 1922 86

Graydon, William E. (Edith's father) 1, 2–3, 8, 13, 25, 28, 29, 33, 74, 98, 103, 106, 126, 127, 131, 159, 170, 177, 192, 194, 195, 205, 208, 250, 261, 284, 298, 303: gives

evidence in court 214, 215, 224; visits Edith in Holloway 257–8, 266–7, 270, 279, 287, 294–6; writes Edith's life story for newspaper 254; says farewell to dead daughter 304–5; complains about press publicity after Edith's execution 307–8; death, 1941 310

Grimes, Police Sergeant Walter 184, 185, 186

Groves, T. E. 308

Hale, Binnie 150, 175

Hall, Inspector Francis 189, 190, 191, 194, 195, 198, 199, 202, 203, 204, 206, 207, 210, 211, 225, 238, 260, 305
   evidence at Edith's trial 226
   interrogates Edith 189–90

Hancock, John 207, 225

Hardy, Thomas
   'On the Portrait of a Woman about to be Hanged' 291
   Tess of the D'Urbervilles 291

Hari, Mata 11

Haskins, Lewis 15

Henley Regatta, 1922 136

Hewart, Lord 260, 261

Hibbert, George William: death pact with sister-in-law Maud 118

Hichens, Robert
   Bella Donna 109, 116, 119, 121, 138–41, 146, 234–8, 244, 247
   Felix 69–70, 96, 111, 141
   Fruitful Vine, The 109, 111, 116, 119, 138, 140, 141, 144, 146–50, 236, 247
   Garden of Allah, The 43
   Mrs Marsden 151
   Slave, The 89

Higgins, Charles 167, 225

Holloway Prison, Tufnell Park 10, 207, 217, 219, 251, 311
   preparation for Edith Thompson's execution 289

Howard, Eliot 213, 214, 256

Humphreys, Travers 222, 227

Hutchinson, A. S. M.: *If Winter Comes* 42–3, 267, 281

Ilford Police Station 190, 197, 201, 202
Ilford Recorder 188, 311
Inskip, Sir Thomas 222, 261
    prosecutor in Thompson-Bywaters trial 222–3, 226, 227, 231–2, 233, 235, 239, 241, 245–6

Jacobi, Henry 92
    condemned to death, 1922 110
    hanged 122–3
Jacobs, Rose 128, 142, 163, 191, 213, 225
    provides Bywaters's letters for police 191
James, Sergeant Percy 211, 225
Jenkins, Huntly 222

Keane, Doris 51
Kempton, Freda 89
Ketcher, Fanny Florence 4
Koestler, Arthur 309
    Reflections on Hanging 309n

Landru: execution, 1922 86
Lang, Matheson 43
Laxton, John Ambrose Henry 69, 150, 174, 176, 177, 210, 267
    visits Edith Thompson in Holloway 270
Laxton, Lily (Edith's aunt) 2, 67, 69, 150, 174, 176, 177, 267, 296
    petitions Cabinet to save Edith 272–3
    visits Edith in Holloway 281, 294–5
Law, Andrew Bonar 212, 216, 269
Lawrence, D. H.: *Women in Love* 42
Le Neve, Ethel 297
Lee, Amelia A. 225
Lenglen, Suzanne 137
Lester, Mrs Fanny Maria 35, 36, 56, 88, 160, 164, 167, 173, 185, 214, 224, 271
    withdraws voluntary help for Thompsons 151
Lesters, the 48, 50, 53, 55, 57, 62, 70, 88–9, 119, 154
    death of Mr Lester 118
    protected tenants 32, 35–6
    unwilling to leave Thompsons'

home, 1922 151–2
Lewis, Kid 118
Lewis, William 210, 214
Liles, Deborah (Ethel's grandmother) 1, 64
    death and burial 67
Lloyd George, David 212
Lloyd, Marie 207
Lloyd's Sunday News 175, 264
Locke, W. J. 43, 145
    House of Balthazar, The 146, 263
    Red Planet, The 88
    Rough Road, The 88
    Septimus 151
Lockwood, Reg and Ruby 28

Malwa, SS 39
Mannings, the 88
Manor Park, London 3, 8, 9
    Kensington Avenue Schools 4, 5, 6, 17, 18
Marlowe, Thomas 306
Mason, A. E. W.
    Four Feathers, The 277
    Witness for the Defence, A 277
Maude, Cyril 150, 175
Maudsley, Dr 183, 184, 224
Maxwell, Sir A. 306
Maxwell, W. B.: *The Guarded Flame* 66
Melba, Dame Nellie 81
Mew, Police Sergeant Walter 184, 185, 186
Mills, Seth 281
Morea, SS 58, 59, 60, 63, 68, 76, 83, 93, 120, 123, 125, 127, 135, 153, 156, 159, 160, 171, 187, 193, 211, 303
    framed sketch 279
Morton, Dr J. H. 267, 276, 294, 300, 302, 307, 309, 310
    actions as Governor of Holloway Prison: informs Edith Thompson of execution 283; dealings with Canon Palmer 287–9; informs Edith there is no hope of reprieve 296; confirms Edith's death 304
    alleged visit to *Daily Mail* after hanging 306
Mosley, Diana: *Loved Ones* 284

Mountbatten, Lord Louis: marriage to Edwina Ashley, 1922 141–2

Neil, A. F. 198
  Forty Years of Man-Hunting 198n
Nellore, SS 21, 22
Newell, Susan 307
Nichols, Beverley: gets Graydons to write Edith's life story for *Weekly Dispatch* 253–4
Noakes, Rev. Charles: funeral sermon for Percy Thompson 208–9
Notable British Trials 238

Observer 306, 309
Oliver, Roland 222
Orvieto, SS 40, 41, 66
O'Sullivan, Joseph 145

Page, Inspector Frank 197, 225
Palmer, Canon 252, 272, 276, 294, 301
  comforts Edith Thompson in Holloway 287, 288, 289
  problems raised by visit to Edith 287–9
Palmer, PC Henry 184, 185
Patterson, Gerald 137
Pearcey, PC George Edwin 184, 185
Pentonville Prison 220, 250, 251
Phillips, Thomas 281
Philpotts, Eden: *The Secret Woman* 151
Pierrepoint, Henry A. 10
Pierrepoint, Tom 281
Pittard, Dora Finch 180, 181, 183, 184, 186, 210, 224, 238
Plassy, SS 33, 34
Princip, Gavrilo 17
Prior, Ellen 12, 16, 32, 114, 119, 120, 121, 167

Renton, Harry 49, 85, 102, 119
  boyhood romance with Edith Thompson 11
  visits Edith in Holloway 259
Romance, film 51–2
Row, Joseph Edward James 180
Russell, Audrey 311n

Sach, Amelia 10, 305

St Catherine's Point, IOW 46
Salter, Mr Justice 260
Scholes, Detective Inspector Alfred 211, 225
Seamen's Orphanage, Wanstead 133
Secretan, Jessie 180
Service, Robert B.: *Trail of 98* 66, 75
Shanklin, IOW 44
  Chine 45
  entertainment at, 1921 44–5, 46–7
Shearman, Mr Justice (later Sir Montague) 261, 279
  presides at Thompson-Bywaters trial 222, 223, 229, 235, 239, 240, 243, 244
  summing up at trial 246–7
Shrimpton, Mr 302
Simmons, Miss 289, 290, 297
Simmons, Mrs 256, 260, 297
Snell, Ivor 222
Spilsbury, Sir Bernard 108n, 215–16, 226, 227, 244, 271
Stepney, Bishop of 123, 294
  conveys last messages between Edith and Freddy 275, 293, 294
Stepney Elocution Class 12, 13, 14
  amateur theatricals 14–15
Stepney Meeting House 14, 15, 208
Stern, F. A. S. 210, 213, 214, 219, 220, 222, 225, 290
  temporarily keeps Edith's letters out of court 212
Stormont, Charles W. 15
Stratford Express 310
Sun Life Insurance Co. 30, 31
Sunday Dispatch 309
Sunday Express 189
Swann, Emily 10

Thompson-Bywaters trial, Dec. 1922 221–2
  case for defence: Bywaters's evidence 228–9; evidence of suicide pact 229; Bywaters's story of day of killing 230–1; cross-examination of Bywaters 231–3; Edith Thompson's evidence 233–4; defence's attempt to dispose of poison allegations 234–8; Crown's attempt to prove con-

spiracy to murder 238–41;
defence rebuttal of some Crown
points 241; Avis Graydon's evidence 242; Mrs Graydon's evidence 242; defence plea for Bywaters 242–3; defence plea for Edith
Thompson 243–4, 245
case for prosecution: letters held to
indicate conspiracy to murder
223–4; medical evidence 224;
prosecution witnesses 225; police
witness 226; cross-examination
of police witness 226; patholog-
ists' evidence refutes idea of
poisoning 226–7; Edith Thompson's letters to Bywaters read to
court 227–8; Crown's summing
up 245–6
demand for seats 221, 225, 229–30
judge admits introduction of letters
223
judge's summing up 246–7
jury's verdict of guilty for both
defendants 247–8
refusal of separate trials for defendants 222
sentence of death passed by judge
248
Thompson, Edith Jessie
fantasy about poisoning husband
104–5, 107–8
interest in theatre 41, 43
letters to Bywaters 47, 58–9, 60, 66,
68–72 passim, 75–6, 81, 85, 87,
89, 92, 93, 101, 103, 104, 105,
108, 110, 115–18 passim, 121,
124, 125, 128, 130–8 passim,
140, 143, 144, 145–6, 148, 150,
151, 152, 154, 155, 158–9, 168–
70, 171
life and death: married life in
parents' house 27; moves to Westcliff, 1917 28; welcomes brother
Newenham home 28–9; cele-
brates Armistice, 1918 29; moves
to Ilford, 1919 29–30, 31; works
for Carlton & Prior in Aldersgate
31–2; moves to new house in
Ilford, 1920 32–3, 36–7; meets
Freddy Bywaters at parents'
house, 1920 34; meetings with
Freddy over dinners 35; beginnings of love affair with Freddy
39–41; holidays with husband,
sister Avis and Freddy, 1921 43–
8; flirts with Harry Renton 49;
quarrels with Bywaters 49;
becomes Bywaters's mistress 51;
meetings with Bywaters 51–2, 57,
61–2, 63; quarrels with husband
over Bywaters 53–5, 56, 57, 62;
follows Bywaters's ship's progress
60; welcomes Bywaters back from
voyage 60–1; miscarriage, Jan.
1922 62, 63; extra work at Carlton & Prior 65; tells husband she
does not love him 65–6; visits
dying grandmother 67; pregnant
by lover 68–9; attends family
gathering 69; gives way to husband in bed 69; gives abortifacient drug to husband in error 70;
quizzed by friend Mel about
Bywaters 71; refuses husband
conjugal rights 71–2; celebrates
twenty-eighth birthday 73; New
Year's Eve celebrations, 1921 74;
resumes conjugal relations with
husband 75; reunited with Bywaters, Jan. 1922 79–80; back to
work 81; nurses mother through
'flu 81; quarrels with husband
over lover 82–3; prostrated by
period 87; looks after mother 88;
meets brother Bill back from
Bombay 91; reunited with Bywaters, March 1922 92–6; questions
Avis about Bywaters 99–100;
quarrels with husband 100; fears
another pregnancy 101–2, 110;
meets Harry Renton 102; happy
at receiving letter from Freddy
Bywaters 104; events of Easter,
1922 105–9; returns to work 109;
dines with Birnages 109; period
problems, April 1922 109–10;
intrigued by The Shulamite 112–
13; buys mourning clothes for
Miss Prior 114; has lunch and tea
with Sidney Birnage, May 1922

114–15; smashes mirror 115; receives bundle of letters from Freddy 115; identifies with death-pact couple 118; sends parcel to Freddy 119; gives family dinner party 120; meets Freddy on his return home, May 1922 122, 123; plans an abortion 124; quarrels with husband over lover 124–5; arranges GPO address for Freddy's letters 126; further quarrels with husband 126; problems of putting up father for weekend 126–7; collect's Freddy's mail from GPO 128; depressing visit to the Richard Thompsons 128–9; possible abortion, June 1922 129, 131; diagnosed as suffering from anaemia 131; sees return home of Prince of Wales, June 1922 132–3; attends fête for Seamen's Orphanage, Wanstead 133–4; does Miss Prior's job during holiday time 135; problem collecting Freddy's letters 135–6; attends rainy Henley Regatta 136; period problems, July 1922 137; holidays at Bournemouth, July 1922 141, 142; prophetic dream 143–4; avoids 'pick-up' at Waldorf 144–5; enjoyment of Hichens's *The Fruitful Vine* 147–8; writes about *The Fruitful Vine* 148–50; at odds with Mrs Lester 151, 152; gives dinner party 153; unhappy looking in photograph with husband 153; receives threatening note from 'Wellwisher' 152; suspects Freddy of trying to leave her 154; incriminating letter re husband's jealousy 158; meets homecoming Freddy, Sept. 1922 160, 161; declaration of love for Freddy 162–3; meetings with Freddy, autumn 1922 163–72 *passim*, 174; goes to theatre with husband, 3 Oct. 1922 174–7; returns home from theatre 179–81; sees Bywaters knife husband 181, 183; holds dying husband

183; runs for doctor 183; returns to husband 183–4; taken home after husband's death 184–5; conceals Bywaters's part in murder from brother-in-law 185; conceals Bywaters's actions from police 186, 189–90; taken to police station 190; questioned by police 191–2; asked about Bywaters 192–3; night at police station 197; makes statement to police 199–200; sees Bywaters at police station 202–3; amends statement and implicates Bywaters 203; charged, with Bywaters, with husband's murder 205; letters from prison intercepted 207, 217–18; appearances in court 206–7, 210–14 *passim*, 218; incriminating letters 212, 213–14, 219; remanded in custody, Nov. 1922 216; committed to stand trial at Old Bailey 218; makes her will 220; Old Bailey trial, *see* Thompson-Bywaters trial; sentenced to death 248; sad meeting with family after passing of sentence 250; taken to Holloway Prison 250; under sedation in prison hospital 251–2; visited by mother and sister 252; informed of date of execution 256; visited by father and brother Newenham 257–8; replies to letter from Bessie 258–9; receives visit from Bessie 262–4; hears appeal has failed 265; censorship of letters 265–6; visited by family 266–7; twenty-ninth birthday in prison 267; Christmas 1922 in prison 267; letter to Bessie 269; visited by family, late Dec. 1922 270; asks for Canon Palmer to be allowed to visit 275, 276; letter to Bessie, 3 Jan. 1923 276–7; last letter to father 280; visited by mother and aunt 281–2; learns she is to be executed 283, 296; drugged 283; meeting with family 286; visited by Canon Palmer 287, 288, 289; penultimate day

293–4; visited by Bishop of Stepney 294; final letter to mother and father 294; final meeting with family 294–5, 296; fearful last hours 300–2; drugged 301; death on scaffold 299; body prepared for coffin 304; family's farewell 305; burial in Holloway graveyard 305; reburied in Brookwood cemetery, 1971 312
newspaper interest in 188–9
suicide pact with Bywaters 51, 63, 64, 170, 171, 229, 238
view of Hichens's *Bella Donna* 140–1

Thompson, Ethel 31
Thompson, Lily 14, 15
See also Chambers, Lily
Thompson, Margaret ('Maggie') 14, 84
Thompson, Mrs (Percy's mother) 8–9, 13–14, 103, 257
Thompson, Percy 9, 29, 62, 70, 74, 77, 79, 80, 85, 88, 104, 107, 123, 128, 129, 152, 153, 159, 164, 165, 167, 168, 173
amateur theatricals 14–15
life and death: adolescent struggles 9; courts Edith Graydon 12–14, 16, 23–4; becomes Edith's lover, 1914 17; marriage, 1916 25–6; manages to be invalided out of army, 1916 26–7; fear of air raids 27; boasts of army discharge 27–8; moves to Ilford, after First World War 30–3 *passim*; insures life, 1919 30–1; takes part time work for Sun Life 31; liking for Freddy Bywaters 34; gets back Bywaters's job with P & O, 1921 40; holiday with wife, Avis and Freddy 44–8; breakdown of relations with wife 53–7 *passim*, 62, 65–6; meeting with Bywaters 62–3; tries to resume sexual relations with wife 65–6, 68; succeeds in resuming sexual relations with wife 69; jealous of Bywaters 71–2; quarrels with wife over Bywaters, Feb. 1922 82–3; office moves

to Eastcheap, 1922 90; quarrels with wife 100; possession of tincture of opium 107, 108; quarrel with Edith, June 1922 124–5, 126–7; holidays in Bournemouth, July 1922 141–3; relations with Miss Tucknott 145; photographed with wife by Bessie 153; warns wife about seeing Bywaters, Sept. 1922 156; attends theatre with wife, 3 Oct. 1922 174–7; returns home from theatre 177, 179–81; attacked by Bywaters with knife in street 181, 183; injuries and death 183, 184; body taken to mortuary 184, 185; inquest 205–6, 212; funeral 207–9; tributes on wreaths 209; exhumed for autopsy 215; grave 311
singing ability 12–13
Thompson, Richard Halliday 14, 26, 31, 103, 128, 185, 208, 224
death, 1952 311
implicates Bywaters in brother's murder 192, 211
Thurston, E. Temple: *The Wandering Jew* 43
Times, The 140
coverage of Thompson-Bywaters case 221
Travers, Ben: *The Dippers* 150, 175–7
Trumble, John 206
Troup, Sir Edward 91
True, Ronald: reprieved from execution, 1922 90

Vallender, Lily 32, 43, 46, 102, 106, 144, 153, 156, 160, 163, 165, 167, 224
Vallender, Norman 43, 46, 144, 156
Van Der Elst, Violet: *On the Gallows* 299n
Ventnor, IOW 142
Vernon, Ethel 30, 65, 152, 167, 174, 178, 193, 296, 303

Waldo, Dr F. J. 305
Walker, Dr Dora 266, 268, 300, 302, 304

Walkinshaw, Edith (Edith Thompson's aunt) 1, 2, 266, 267
Wall, J. H. 217, 280, 289
Wallace, Edward E. 259
Wallis, Dr Preston 4, 83
  implicated in Bolding suicide 83–4, 89
Wallis, Mrs 83, 84
Walters, Annie 10, 305
Walters, Charles R. 257
Warren, H. McCollin 8, 27, 296
  quarrel with Percy Thompson 28
Waverley, Lord, see Anderson, Sir John
Way Down East, film 60
Webber, John 183, 184, 224, 247
Webster, Dr John 211, 215, 226, 227
Weekly Dispatch 253, 264, 307
Wensley, Detective Inspector F. P. 190, 198, 199, 202, 204, 210, 238
  Detective Days 192n
  instructions for Bywaters to be taken into custody 192–3
  interrogates Bywaters 195
  interrogates Edith Thompson 192
  opinion of Edith Thompson 191–2
West, Bill 17, 18, 19, 23

  on Freddy Bywaters 19
White, Alice, Lady: murdered, 1922 92
White, Sir Edward 92
Whiteley, Cecil 222, 249
  defence of Bywaters 222, 226, 228–33 passim, 242–3
  pleads Bywaters's appeal 260
Williams, Leonard 194, 205, 207
Willie, Lily, see Bywaters, Lilian (Freddy's sister)
Willis, Rhoda 10, 150
Willis, William 281
  alerted about Bywaters's execution 281
  executes Bywaters 303
Wilson, FM Sir Henry 145
  assassinated by IRA, 1922 133
  funeral 135
Wimbledon, 1922 135, 137
Wood, Prison Officer George 301, 302, 306
Woolf, Virginia 292

Yeldham, Elsie Florence: reprieved from execution, 1922 150
Young, Prison Officer William 300, 301, 306